WL

Adva                                    e

# British library cataloguing-in-publication data

A catalogue record for this book is available from the British Library.

Published by:
Kaplan Publishing UK
Unit 2 The Business Centre
Molly Millars Lane
Wokingham
Berkshire
RG41 2QZ

ISBN 978-0-85732-669-0

Printed and bound in the Great Britain.

## Acknowledgements

We are grateful to the Association of Chartered Certified Accountants and the Chartered Institute of Management Accountants for permission to reproduce past examination questions. The answers have been prepared by Kaplan Publishing.

# Contents

**Page**

i Question

# Paper Introduction

# How to Use the Materials

These Kaplan Publishing learning materials have been carefully designed to make your learning experience as easy as possible and to give you the best chances of success in your examinations.

The product range contains a number of features to help you in the study process. They include:

(1)  Detailed study guide and syllabus objectives

(2)  Description of the examination

(3)  Study skills and revision guidance

(4)  Complete text or essential text

(5)  Question practice

The sections on the study guide, the syllabus objectives, the examination and study skills should all be read before you commence your studies. They are designed to familiarise you with the nature and content of the examination and give you tips on how to best to approach your learning.

The **complete text or essential text** comprises the main learning materials and gives guidance as to the importance of topics and where other related resources can be found. Each chapter includes:

- The **learning objectives** contained in each chapter, which have been carefully mapped to the examining body's own syllabus learning objectives or outcomes. You should use these to check you have a clear understanding of all the topics on which you might be assessed in the examination.

- The **chapter diagram** provides a visual reference for the content in the chapter, giving an overview of the topics and how they link together.

- The **content** for each topic area commences with a brief explanation or definition to put the topic into context before covering the topic in detail. You should follow your studying of the content with a review of the illustration/s. These are worked examples which will help you to understand better how to apply the content for the topic.

- **Test your understanding** sections provide an opportunity to assess your understanding of the key topics by applying what you have learned to short questions. Answers can be found at the back of each chapter.

- **Summary diagrams** complete each chapter to show the important links between topics and the overall content of the paper. These diagrams should be used to check that you have covered and understood the core topics before moving on.

- **Question practice** is provided at the back of each text.

## Icon Explanations

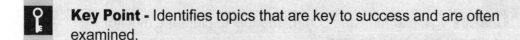 **Definition -** Key definitions that you will need to learn from the core content.

**Key Point -** Identifies topics that are key to success and are often examined.

**Expandable Text -** Expandable text provides you with additional information about a topic area and may help you gain a better understanding of the core content. Essential text users can access this additional content on-line (read it where you need further guidance or skip over when you are happy with the topic).

**Illustration -** Worked examples help you understand the core content better.

**Test Your Understanding -** Exercises for you to complete to ensure that you have understood the topics just learned.

**Tricky topic -** When reviewing these areas care should be taken and all illustrations and test your understanding exercises should be completed to ensure that the topic is understood.

## On-line subscribers

Our on-line resources are designed to increase the flexibility of your learning materials and provide you with immediate feedback on how your studies are progressing. If you are subscribed to our on-line resources you will find:

(1) On-line referenceware: reproduces your Complete or Essential Text on-line, giving you anytime, anywhere access.

(2) On-line testing: provides you with additional on-line objective testing so you can practice what you have learned further.

(3) On-line performance management: immediate access to your on-line testing results. Review your performance by key topics and chart your achievement through the course relative to your peer group.

Ask your local customer services staff if you are not already a subscriber and wish to join.

## Syllabus

### Paper background

The aim of ACCA Paper P5, Advanced performance management, is to apply relevant knowledge and skills and to exercise professional judgement in selecting and applying strategic management accounting techniques in different business contexts, and to contribute to the evaluation of the performance of an organisation and its strategic development.

### Objectives of the syllabus

- Use strategic planning and control models to plan and monitor organisational performance.

- Assess and identify relevant macro-economic, fiscal and market factors and key external influences on organisational performance.

- Identify and evaluate the design features of effective performance management information and monitoring systems.

- Apply appropriate strategic performance measurement techniques in evaluating and improving organisational performance.

- Advise clients and senior management on strategic business performance evaluation and on recognising vulnerability to corporate failure.

- Identify and assess the impact of current developments in management accounting and performance management on measuring, evaluating and improving organisational performance.

### Core areas of the syllabus

- Strategic planning and control.

- External influences on organisational performance.

- Performance measurement systems and design.

- Strategic performance measurement.

- Performance evaluation and corporate failure.

- Current developments and emerging issues in performance management.

### Syllabus objectives

We have reproduced the ACCA's syllabus below, showing where the objectives are explored within this book. Within the chapters, we have broken down the extensive information found in the syllabus into easily digestible and relevant sections, called Content Objectives. These correspond to the objectives at the beginning of each chapter.

| Syllabus learning objective | Chapter reference |
|---|---|

**A STRATEGIC PLANNING AND CONTROL**

**1 Introduction to strategic management accounting**

(a) Explain the role of strategic performance management in strategic planning and control.[2]    1

(b) Discuss the role of corporate planning in clarifying corporate objectives, making strategic decisions and checking progress towards the objectives.[2]    1

(c) Compare planning and control between the strategic and operational levels within a business entity.[2]    1

(d) Assess the use of strategic management accounting in the context of multinational companies.[3]    1

(e) Discuss the scope for potential conflict between strategic business plans and short-term localised decisions.[2]    1

(f) Evaluate how SWOT analysis may assist in the performance management process.[2]    1

(g) Evaluate the methods of benchmarking performance.[3]    1

**2 Performance management and control of the organisation**

(a) Evaluate the strengths and weaknesses of alternative budgeting models and compare such techniques as fixed and flexible, rolling, activity based, zero based and incremental.[3]    3

(b) Assess how budgeting may differ in not-for-profit organisations from profit-seeking organisations.[3]    3

(c) Evaluate the impact to an organisation of a move to 'beyond budgeting'.[3]    3

**3 Changes in business structure and management accounting**

(a) Identify and discuss the particular information needs of organisations adopting a functional, divisional or network form and the implications for performance management.[2]    4

(b) Assess the influence of Business Process Re-engineering on systems development and improvements in organisational performance.[3]    4

(c) Discuss the concept of business integration and the linkage between people, operations, strategy and technology.[2]    4

(d) Analyse the role that performance management systems play in business integration using models such as the value chain and McKinsey's 7s's. [3]    4

(e) Identify and discuss the required changes in management accounting systems as a consequence of empowering staff to manage sectors of a business.[3]    4

## 4 Effect of information technology (IT) on strategic management accounting

(a) Assess the changing accounting needs of modern service orientated businesses compared with the needs of the traditional manufacturing industry.[3]    5

(b) Discuss how IT systems provide the opportunity for instant access to management accounting data throughout the organisation and their potential impact on business performance.[2]    5

(c) Assess how IT systems facilitate the remote input of management accounting data in an acceptable format by non-finance specialists.[2]    5

(d) Explain how information systems provide instant access to previously unavailable data that can be used for benchmarking and control purposes and help improve business performance (for example the use of enterprise resource planning systems and data warehouses).[2]    5

(e) Assess the need for businesses to continually refine and develop their management accounting and information systems if they are to maintain or improve their performance in an increasingly competitive and global market.[3]    5

## 5 Other environmental and ethical issues

(a) Discuss the ways in which stakeholder groups operate and how they effect an organisation and its strategy formulation and implementation (e.g. using Mendelow's matrix).[2]    2

(b) Discuss the ethical issues that may impact on strategy formulation and business performance.[3]    2

(c) Discuss the ways in which stakeholder groups may influence business performance.[2]    2

## B EXTERNAL INFLUENCES ON ORGANISATIONAL PERFORMANCE

## 1 Changing business environment

(a) Assess the continuing effectiveness of traditional management accounting techniques within a rapidly changing business environment.[3]    2

(b) Assess the impact of different risk appetites of stakeholders on performance management.[3]    2

(c) Evaluate how risk and uncertainty play an important role in long term strategic planning and decision-making that relies upon forecast and exogenous variables. [3]    2

(d) Apply different risk analysis techniques in assessing business performance such as maximin, maximax, minimax regret and expected values. [3]    2

**2 Impact of external factors on strategy and performance**

   (a)  Discuss the need to consider the environment in which an       2
organisation is operating when assessing its performance using
models such as PEST and Porter's 5 forces, including areas:[2]

        (i)   political climate

        (ii)  market conditions

        (iii) funding.

   (b)  Assess the impact of governmental regulations and policies on    2
performance measurement techniques used and the performance
levels achieved (for example, in the case of utility services and
former state monopolies).[3]

**C  PERFORMANCE MEASUREMENT SYSTEMS AND DESIGN**

**1  Performance management information systems**

   (a)  Discuss, with reference to performance management, ways in    6
which the information requirements of a management structure are
affected by the features of the structure.[2]

   (b)  Evaluate the compatibility of the objectives of management     5
accounting and management accounting information.[3]

   (c)  Discuss the integration of management accounting information     5
within an overall information system, for example the use of
enterprise resource planning systems.[2]

   (d)  Evaluate whether the management information systems are lean    6
and the value of the information that they provide.[3]

   (e)  Highlight the ways in which contingent (internal and external) factors   6
influence management accounting and its design and use.[3]

   (f)  Evaluate how anticipated human behaviour will influence the design   6
of a management accounting system.[3]

   (g)  Assess the impact of responsibility accounting on information     6
requirements.[3]

**2 Sources of management information**

   (a)  Discuss the principal internal and external sources of management   6
accounting information, their costs and limitations.[2]

   (b)  Demonstrate how the information might be used in planning and     5
controlling activities, e.g. benchmarking against similar activities.[2]

   (c)  Discuss those factors that need to be considered when determining   6
the capacity and development potential of a system.[2]

## 2 Strategic performance measures in private sector

(a) Demonstrate why the primary objective of financial performance should be primarily concerned with the benefits to shareholders.[2]  —  7

(b) Justify the crucial objectives of survival and business growth.[3]  —  7

(c) Discuss the appropriateness of, and apply different measures of performance, including:[3]  —  7, 8

    (i) Return on Capital Employed (ROCE)

    (ii) Return on Investment (ROI)

    (iii) Earnings Per Share (EPS)

    (iv) Earnings Before Interest, Tax and Depreciation Adjustment (EBITDA)

    (v) Residual Income (RI)

    (vi) Net Present value (NPV)

    (vii) Internal Rate of Return and modified internal rate of return (IRF MIRR)

    (viii) Economic Value Added (EVA$^{TM}$).

(d) Discuss why indicators of liquidity and gearing need to considered in conjunction with profitability.[3]  —  7

(e) Compare and contrast short and long run financial performance and the resulting management issues.[3]  —  7

(f) Explore the traditional relationship between profits and share value with the long-term profit expectations of the stock market and recent financial performance of new technology/communications companies.[3]  —  7

(g) Assess the relative financial performance of the organisation compared to appropriate benchmarks.[3]  —  7

## 3 Divisional performance and transfer pricing issues

(a) Describe, compute and evaluate performance measures relevant in a divisionalised organisation structure including ROI, RI and Economic Value Added (EVA).[3]  —  8

(b) Discuss the need for separate measures in respect of managerial and divisional performance.[2]  —  8

(c) Discuss the circumstances in which a transfer pricing policy may be needed and discuss the necessary criteria for its design.[2]  —  8

(d) Demonstrate and evaluate the use of alternative bases for transfer pricing.[3]  —  8

(e) Explain and demonstrate issues that require consideration when setting transfer prices in multinational companies.[2]  —  8

KAPLAN PUBLISHING

## E PERFORMANCE EVALUATION AND CORPORATE FAILURE

### 1 Alternative views of performance measurement and management

(a) Evaluate the 'balanced scorecard' approach as a way in which to improve the range and linkage between performance measures.[3] — 10

(b) Evaluate the 'performance pyramid' as a way in which to link strategy and operations and performance.[3] — 10

(c) Evaluate the work of Fitzgerald and Moon that considers performance measurement in business services using building blocks for dimensions, standards and rewards.[3] — 10

(d) Discuss and apply the Performance Prism.[2] — 10

(e) Discuss and evaluate the application of activity-based management.[3] — 3

(f) Evaluate and apply the value-based management approaches to performance management.[3] — 8

### 2 Strategic performance issues in complex business structures

(a) Evaluate the use and the application of strategic models in assessing the business performance of an entity, such as Ansoff, Boston Consulting Group and Porter.[3] — 8

(b) Discuss the problems encountered in planning, controlling and measuring performance levels, e.g. productivity, profitability, quality and service levels, in complex business structures.[3] — 6, 8

(c) Discuss the impact on performance management of the use of business models involving strategic alliances, joint ventures and complex chain structures.[3] — 6

### 3 Predicting and preventing corporate failure

(a) Assess the potential likelihood for/of corporate failure utilising quantitative and qualitative performance measures and models (such as Z-scores and Argenti).[3] — 10

(b) Assess and critique quantitative and qualitative corporate failure prediction models.[3] — 10

(c) Identify and discuss performance improvement strategies that may be adopted in order to prevent corporate failure.[3] — 10

(d) Discuss how long-term survival necessitates consideration of life-cycle issues.[3] — 10

(e) Identify and discuss operational changes to performance management systems required to implement the performance improvement strategies.[3] — 10

## F CURRENT DEVELOPMENTS AND EMERGING ISSUES IN PERFORMANCE MANAGEMENT

### 1 Current developments in management accounting techniques

(a) Discuss the ways through which management accounting practitioners are made aware of new techniques and how they evaluate them.[3]    2

(b) Discuss, evaluate and apply environmental management accounting using for example lifecycle costing, input/output analysis and activity-based costing. [3]    12

(c) Discuss the use of benchmarking in public sector performance (league tables) and its effects on operational and strategic management and client behaviour.[3]    12

(d) Discuss the issues surrounding the use of targets in public sector organisations.[3]    12

### 2 Current issues and trends in performance management

(a) Assess the changing role of the management accountant in today's business environment as outlined by Burns and Scapens. [3]    2

(b) Discuss contemporary issues in performance management.[2]    12

(c) Discuss how changing organisation's structure, culture and strategy will influence the adoption of new performance measurement methods and techniques.[3]    12

The superscript numbers in square brackets indicate the intellectual depth at which the subject area could be assessed within the examination. Level 1 (knowledge and comprehension) broadly equates with the Knowledge module, Level 2 (application and analysis) with the Skills module and Level 3 (synthesis and evaluation) to the Professional level. However, lower level skills can continue to be assessed as you progress through each module and level.

## The Examination

### Examination format

- The examination will be a three hour paper plus 15 minutes of reading and planning time.

- The examination is in two sections:

|  | Number of marks |
|---|---|
| *Section A* | |
| One compulsory question | 50 |
| *Section B* | |
| A choice of two from three questions each worth 25 marks | 50 |
| | ——— |
| Total | **100** |

- There will be four professional marks available.

- The pass mark is 50%.

- Candidates will receive a present value table and an annuity table.

### Paper-based examination tips

Spend the reading time reading the paper and planning your answers. You are allowed to annotate the question paper, so make use of this – e.g. highlighting key issues in the questions, planning calculations, brainstorming requirements – ensure that you understand the question. A key issue is to decide which questions you wish to attempt from section B – it is worth planning all three in outline before deciding.

**Divide the time** you spend on questions in proportion to the marks on offer. One suggestion **for this examination** is to allocate 1 and $4/5^{ths}$ minutes to each mark available, so a 10-mark requirement should be completed in approximately 18 minutes. A danger in P5 is that you spend too long on the calculation aspects and neglect the written elements, so allocate your time within questions as well as between them.

Stick to the question and **tailor your answer** to what you are asked. Pay particular attention to the verbs in the question.

Spend the last five minutes reading through your answers and making any additions or corrections.

If you **get completely stuck** with a question, leave space in your answer book and **return to it later**.

If you do not understand what a question is asking, state your assumptions. Even if you do not answer in precisely the way the examiner hoped, you should be given some credit, if your assumptions are reasonable.

You should do everything you can to make things easy for the marker. The marker will find it easier to identify the points you have made if your answers are legible.

**Essay questions**: Your essay should have a clear structure. It should contain a brief introduction, a main section and a conclusion. Be concise. It is better to write a little about a lot of different points than a great deal about one or two points.

**Computations**: It is essential to include all your workings in your answers. Many computational questions require the use of a standard format. Be sure you know these formats thoroughly before the exam and use the layouts that you see in the answers given in this book and in model answers.

**Scenario-based questions**: Most questions will contain a hypothetical scenario. To write a good case answer, first identify the area in which there is a problem, outline the main principles/theories you are going to use to answer the question, and then apply the principles/theories to the case. It is vital that you relate your answer to the specific circumstances given.

**Reports, memos and other documents**: some questions ask you to present your answer in the form of a report or a memo or other document. So use the correct format - there could be easy marks to gain here.

### Study skills and revision guidance

This section aims to give guidance on how to study for your ACCA exams and to give ideas on how to improve your existing study techniques.

### Preparing to study

### Set your objectives

Before starting to study decide what you want to achieve - the type of pass you wish to obtain. This will decide the level of commitment and time you need to dedicate to your studies.

**Devise a study plan**

Determine which times of the week you will study.

Split these times into sessions of at least one hour for study of new material. Any shorter periods could be used for revision or practice.

Put the times you plan to study onto a study plan for the weeks from now until the exam and set yourself targets for each period of study - in your sessions make sure you cover the course, course assignments and revision.

If you are studying for more than one paper at a time, try to vary your subjects as this can help you to keep interested and see subjects as part of wider knowledge.

When working through your course, compare your progress with your plan and, if necessary, re-plan your work (perhaps including extra sessions) or, if you are ahead, do some extra revision/practice questions.

**Effective studying**

**Active reading**

You are not expected to learn the text by rote, rather, you must understand what you are reading and be able to use it to pass the exam and develop good practice. A good technique to use is SQ3Rs - Survey, Question, Read, Recall, Review:

(1) **Survey the chapter** - look at the headings and read the introduction, summary and objectives, so as to get an overview of what the chapter deals with.

(2) **Question** - whilst undertaking the survey, ask yourself the questions that you hope the chapter will answer for you.

(3) **Read** through the chapter thoroughly, answering the questions and making sure you can meet the objectives. Attempt the exercises and activities in the text, and work through all the examples.

(4) **Recall** - at the end of each section and at the end of the chapter, try to recall the main ideas of the section/chapter without referring to the text. This is best done after a short break of a couple of minutes after the reading stage.

(5) **Review** - check that your recall notes are correct.

You may also find it helpful to re-read the chapter to try to see the topic(s) it deals with as a whole.

KAPLAN PUBLISHING

## Note-taking

Taking notes is a useful way of learning, but do not simply copy out the text. The notes must:

- be in your own words
- be concise
- cover the key points
- be well-organised
- be modified as you study further chapters in this text or in related ones.

Trying to summarise a chapter without referring to the text can be a useful way of determining which areas you know and which you don't.

### Three ways of taking notes:

**Summarise the key points of a chapter.**

**Make linear notes** - a list of headings, divided up with subheadings listing the key points. If you use linear notes, you can use different colours to highlight key points and keep topic areas together. Use plenty of space to make your notes easy to use.

**Try a diagrammatic form** - the most common of which is a mind-map. To make a mind-map, put the main heading in the centre of the paper and put a circle around it. Then draw short lines radiating from this to the main sub-headings, which again have circles around them. Then continue the process from the sub-headings to sub-sub-headings, advantages, disadvantages, etc.

### Highlighting and underlining

You may find it useful to underline or highlight key points in your study text - but do be selective. You may also wish to make notes in the margins.

### Revision

The best approach to revision is to revise the course as you work through it. Also try to leave four to six weeks before the exam for final revision. Make sure you cover the whole syllabus and pay special attention to those areas where your knowledge is weak. Here are some recommendations:

**Read through the text and your notes again** and condense your notes into key phrases. It may help to put key revision points onto index cards to look at when you have a few minutes to spare.

**Review any assignments** you have completed and look at where you lost marks - put more work into those areas where you were weak.

**Practise exam standard questions** under timed conditions. If you are short of time, list the points that you would cover in your answer and then read the model answer, but do try to complete at least a few questions under exam conditions.

Also practise producing answer plans and comparing them to the model answer.

If you are stuck on a topic find somebody (a tutor) to explain it to you.

**Read good newspapers and professional journals**, especially ACCA's **Student Accountant** - this can give you an advantage in the exam.

Ensure you **know the structure of the exam** - how many questions and of what type you will be expected to answer. During your revision attempt all the different styles of questions you may be asked.

**Further reading**

You can find further reading and technical articles under the student section of ACCA's website.

# Present value table

Present value of 1, i.e. $(1 + r)^{-n}$

Where    r = discount rate

   n = number of periods until payment

| Periods | Discount rate (r) | | | | | | | | | |
|---|---|---|---|---|---|---|---|---|---|---|
| (n) | 1% | 2% | 3% | 4% | 5% | 6% | 7% | 8% | 9% | 10% |
| 1 | 0.990 | 0.980 | 0.971 | 0.962 | 0.952 | 0.943 | 0.935 | 0.926 | 0.917 | 0.909 |
| 2 | 0.980 | 0.961 | 0.943 | 0.925 | 0.907 | 0.890 | 0.873 | 0.857 | 0.842 | 0.826 |
| 3 | 0.971 | 0.942 | 0.915 | 0.889 | 0.864 | 0.840 | 0.816 | 0.794 | 0.772 | 0.751 |
| 4 | 0.961 | 0.924 | 0.888 | 0.855 | 0.823 | 0.792 | 0.763 | 0.735 | 0.708 | 0.683 |
| 5 | 0.951 | 0.906 | 0.863 | 0.822 | 0.784 | 0.747 | 0.713 | 0.681 | 0.650 | 0.621 |
| 6 | 0.942 | 0.888 | 0.837 | 0.790 | 0.746 | 0.705 | 0.666 | 0.630 | 0.596 | 0.564 |
| 7 | 0.933 | 0.871 | 0.813 | 0.760 | 0.711 | 0.665 | 0.623 | 0.583 | 0.547 | 0.513 |
| 8 | 0.923 | 0.853 | 0.789 | 0.731 | 0.677 | 0.627 | 0.582 | 0.540 | 0.502 | 0.467 |
| 9 | 0.914 | 0.837 | 0.766 | 0.703 | 0.645 | 0.592 | 0.544 | 0.500 | 0.460 | 0.424 |
| 10 | 0.905 | 0.820 | 0.744 | 0.676 | 0.614 | 0.558 | 0.508 | 0.463 | 0.422 | 0.386 |
| 11 | 0.896 | 0.804 | 0.722 | 0.650 | 0.585 | 0.527 | 0.475 | 0.429 | 0.388 | 0.350 |
| 12 | 0.887 | 0.788 | 0.701 | 0.625 | 0.557 | 0.497 | 0.444 | 0.397 | 0.356 | 0.319 |
| 13 | 0.879 | 0.773 | 0.681 | 0.601 | 0.530 | 0.469 | 0.415 | 0.368 | 0.326 | 0.290 |
| 14 | 0.870 | 0.758 | 0.661 | 0.577 | 0.505 | 0.442 | 0.388 | 0.340 | 0.299 | 0.263 |
| 15 | 0.861 | 0.743 | 0.642 | 0.555 | 0.481 | 0.417 | 0.362 | 0.315 | 0.275 | 0.239 |

| Periods | Discount rate (r) | | | | | | | | | |
|---|---|---|---|---|---|---|---|---|---|---|
| (n) | 11% | 12% | 13% | 14% | 15% | 16% | 17% | 18% | 19% | 20% |
| 1 | 0.901 | 0.893 | 0.885 | 0.877 | 0.870 | 0.862 | 0.855 | 0.847 | 0.840 | 0.833 |
| 2 | 0.812 | 0.797 | 0.783 | 0.769 | 0.756 | 0.743 | 0.731 | 0.718 | 0.706 | 0.694 |
| 3 | 0.731 | 0.712 | 0.693 | 0.675 | 0.658 | 0.641 | 0.624 | 0.609 | 0.593 | 0.579 |
| 4 | 0.659 | 0.636 | 0.613 | 0.592 | 0.572 | 0.552 | 0.534 | 0.516 | 0.499 | 0.482 |
| 5 | 0.593 | 0.567 | 0.543 | 0.519 | 0.497 | 0.476 | 0.456 | 0.437 | 0.419 | 0.402 |
| 6 | 0.535 | 0.507 | 0.480 | 0.456 | 0.432 | 0.410 | 0.390 | 0.370 | 0.352 | 0.335 |
| 7 | 0.482 | 0.452 | 0.425 | 0.400 | 0.376 | 0.354 | 0.333 | 0.314 | 0.296 | 0.279 |
| 8 | 0.434 | 0.404 | 0.376 | 0.351 | 0.327 | 0.305 | 0.285 | 0.266 | 0.249 | 0.233 |
| 9 | 0.391 | 0.361 | 0.333 | 0.308 | 0.284 | 0.263 | 0.243 | 0.225 | 0.209 | 0.194 |
| 10 | 0.352 | 0.322 | 0.295 | 0.270 | 0.247 | 0.227 | 0.208 | 0.191 | 0.176 | 0.162 |
| 11 | 0.317 | 0.287 | 0.261 | 0.237 | 0.215 | 0.195 | 0.178 | 0.162 | 0.148 | 0.135 |
| 12 | 0.286 | 0.257 | 0.231 | 0.208 | 0.187 | 0.168 | 0.152 | 0.137 | 0.124 | 0.112 |
| 13 | 0.258 | 0.229 | 0.204 | 0.182 | 0.163 | 0.145 | 0.130 | 0.116 | 0.104 | 0.093 |
| 14 | 0.232 | 0.205 | 0.181 | 0.160 | 0.141 | 0.125 | 0.111 | 0.099 | 0.088 | 0.078 |
| 15 | 0.209 | 0.183 | 0.160 | 0.140 | 0.123 | 0.108 | 0.095 | 0.084 | 0.074 | 0.065 |

# Annuity table

Present value of an annuity of 1, i.e. $\dfrac{1-(1+r)^{-n}}{r}$

Where   r = discount rate

n = number of periods

| Periods (n) | Discount rate (r) | | | | | | | | | |
|---|---|---|---|---|---|---|---|---|---|---|
| | 1% | 2% | 3% | 4% | 5% | 6% | 7% | 8% | 9% | 10% |
| 1 | 0.990 | 0.980 | 0.971 | 0.962 | 0.952 | 0.943 | 0.935 | 0.926 | 0.917 | 0.909 |
| 2 | 1.970 | 1.942 | 1.913 | 1.886 | 1.859 | 1.833 | 1.808 | 1.783 | 1.759 | 1.736 |
| 3 | 2.941 | 2.884 | 2.829 | 2.775 | 2.723 | 2.673 | 2.624 | 2.577 | 2.531 | 2.487 |
| 4 | 3.902 | 3.808 | 3.717 | 3.630 | 3.546 | 3.465 | 3.387 | 3.312 | 3.240 | 3.170 |
| 5 | 4.853 | 4.713 | 4.580 | 4.452 | 4.329 | 4.212 | 4.100 | 3.993 | 3.890 | 3.791 |
| 6 | 5.795 | 5.601 | 5.417 | 5.242 | 5.076 | 4.917 | 4.767 | 4.623 | 4.486 | 4.355 |
| 7 | 6.728 | 6.472 | 6.230 | 6.002 | 5.786 | 5.582 | 5.389 | 5.206 | 5.033 | 4.868 |
| 8 | 7.652 | 7.325 | 7.020 | 6.733 | 6.463 | 6.210 | 5.971 | 5.747 | 5.535 | 5.335 |
| 9 | 8.566 | 8.162 | 7.786 | 7.435 | 7.108 | 6.802 | 6.515 | 6.247 | 5.995 | 5.759 |
| 10 | 9.471 | 8.983 | 8.530 | 8.111 | 7.722 | 7.360 | 7.024 | 6.710 | 6.418 | 6.145 |
| 11 | 10.368 | 9.787 | 9.253 | 8.760 | 8.306 | 7.887 | 7.499 | 7.139 | 6.805 | 8.495 |
| 12 | 11.255 | 10.575 | 9.954 | 9.385 | 8.863 | 8.384 | 7.943 | 7.536 | 7.161 | 6.814 |
| 13 | 12.134 | 11.348 | 10.635 | 9.986 | 9.394 | 8.853 | 8.358 | 7.904 | 7.487 | 7.103 |
| 14 | 13.004 | 12.106 | 11.296 | 10.563 | 9.899 | 9.295 | 8.745 | 8.244 | 7.786 | 7.367 |
| 15 | 13.865 | 12.849 | 11.938 | 11.118 | 10.380 | 9.712 | 9.108 | 8.559 | 8.061 | 7.606 |

| Periods (n) | Discount rate (r) | | | | | | | | | |
|---|---|---|---|---|---|---|---|---|---|---|
| | 11% | 12% | 13% | 14% | 15% | 16% | 17% | 18% | 19% | 20% |
| 1 | 0.901 | 0.893 | 0.885 | 0.877 | 0.870 | 0.862 | 0.855 | 0.847 | 0.840 | 0.833 |
| 2 | 1.713 | 1.690 | 1.668 | 1.647 | 1.626 | 1.605 | 1.585 | 1.566 | 1.547 | 1.528 |
| 3 | 2.444 | 2.402 | 2.361 | 2.322 | 2.283 | 2.246 | 2.210 | 2.174 | 2.140 | 2.106 |
| 4 | 3.102 | 3.037 | 2.974 | 2.914 | 2.855 | 2.798 | 2.743 | 2.690 | 2.639 | 2.589 |
| 5 | 3.696 | 3.605 | 3.517 | 3.433 | 3.352 | 3.274 | 3.199 | 3.127 | 3.058 | 2.991 |
| 6 | 4.231 | 4.111 | 3.998 | 3.889 | 3.784 | 3.685 | 3.589 | 3.498 | 3.410 | 3.326 |
| 7 | 4.712 | 4.564 | 4.423 | 4.288 | 4.160 | 4.039 | 3.922 | 3.812 | 3.706 | 3.605 |
| 8 | 5.146 | 4.968 | 4.799 | 4.639 | 4.487 | 4.344 | 4.207 | 4.078 | 3.954 | 3.837 |
| 9 | 5.537 | 5.328 | 5.132 | 4.946 | 4.772 | 4.607 | 4.451 | 4.303 | 4.163 | 4.031 |
| 10 | 5.889 | 5.650 | 5.426 | 5.216 | 5.019 | 4.833 | 4.659 | 4.494 | 4.339 | 4.192 |
| 11 | 6.207 | 5.938 | 5.687 | 5.453 | 5.234 | 5.029 | 4.836 | 4.656 | 4.486 | 4.327 |
| 12 | 6.492 | 6.194 | 5.918 | 5.660 | 5.421 | 5.197 | 4.968 | 4.793 | 4.611 | 4.439 |
| 13 | 6.750 | 6.424 | 6.122 | 5.842 | 5.583 | 5.342 | 5.118 | 4.910 | 4.715 | 4.533 |
| 14 | 6.982 | 6.628 | 6.302 | 6.002 | 5.724 | 5.468 | 5.229 | 5.008 | 4.802 | 4.611 |
| 15 | 7.191 | 6.811 | 6.462 | 6.142 | 5.847 | 5.575 | 5.324 | 5.092 | 4.876 | 4.675 |

# Introduction to strategic management accounting

## Chapter learning objectives

Upon completion of this chapter you will be able to:

- explain the role of strategic performance management in strategic planning and control

- discuss the role of corporate planning in clarifying corporate objectives, making strategic decisions and checking progress towards the objectives

- compare planning and control at the strategic and operational levels within a business entity

- assess the use of strategic management accounting in the context of multinational companies

- discuss the scope for potential conflict between strategic business plans and short-term localised decisions

- evaluate how SWOT analysis may assist in the performance management process

- evaluate the methods of benchmarking performance

- discuss how the purpose, structure and content of a mission statement impacts on business performance

- discuss the ways in which high-level corporate objectives are developed

- identify strategic objectives and discuss how they may be incorporated into the business plan

- discuss how strategic objectives are cascaded down the organisation via the formulation of subsidiary performance objectives

- explain the performance 'planning gap' and evaluate alternative strategies to fill the gap

- apply critical success factor analysis in developing performance metrics from business objectives

- identify and discuss the characteristics of operational performance

- discuss the relative significance of planning against controlling activities at different levels of the performance hierarchy.

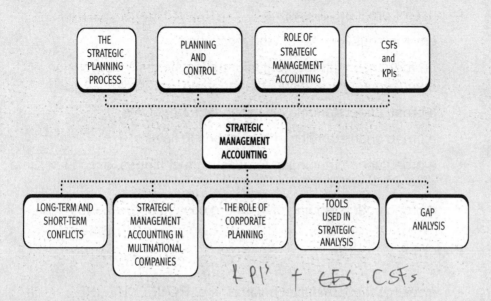

KPI' + CSF .CSFs

# 1 Exam focus

| Exam sitting | Area examined | Question number | Number of marks |
|---|---|---|---|
| June 2012 | Benchmarking | 4 | 17 |
| June 2012 | KPIs | 2(a) | 12 |
| December 2011 | KPIs | 2(a) | 7 |
| December 2010 | CSFs and KPIs | 1 (a)-(c) | 20 |
| December 2010 | KPIs | 4(a) | 4 |
| December 2009 | KPIs | 2(b)(i) | 12 |
| December 2009 | Mission | 5(a) | 11 |
| December 2009 | CSFs and KPIs | 5(b) | 6 |
| December 2008 | Planning gap | 3(a) | 5 |
| June 2008 | Benchmarking | 1(b) | 7 |
| December 2007 | CSFs | 3(b) | 10 |
| Pilot paper | Mission | 2(a)(i) | 5 |

Dec 17    KPIs, CSF + gap    ( ci) (iii) (iv)(v)    36

# 2 Assumed knowledge

June '14    Mission    1 (v)    67

Many of the tools and techniques studied in previous papers are still examinable in P5, including the following:

## Paper F5

- costing methods; specifically activity-based costing but could also touch upon absorption costing, life-cycle costing and target costing

- risk and uncertainty

- budgeting

- financial and non-financial performance measures

- divisional performance measurement

- transfer pricing

- not-for-profit organisations

- environmental management accounting

- performance management information systems, sources of management information, management reports.

- a broad understanding of limiting factor analysis

- a broad understanding of relevant cash flows

- a broad understanding of forecasting techniques, e.g. hi-low, time series, learning curves

- a broad understanding of standard costing and variance analysis

## Paper F9

- investment appraisal techniques, e.g. ROCE, NPV, IRR

- ratio calculations

- the economic environment, e.g. fiscal and monetary policy, regulation

## Paper P3

- the strategic planning process

- environmental analysis, e.g. PEST(EL)

- critical success factors (CSFs) and key performance indicators (KPIs).

## 3 The strategic planning process

The strategic planning process was examined in detail in paper P3. In P5 the focus is more on the performance management aspects of strategic planning and the role of strategic management accounting.

### 3.1 What is strategy?

The core of a company's strategy is about choosing:

- **where** to compete and

- **how** to compete.

It is a means to achieve **sustainable competitive advantage**.

## 3.2 Strategic analysis, choice and implementation (rational model)

This three stage model of strategic planning is a useful framework for seeing the 'bigger picture' of performance management and strategic management accounting issues.

*i identified two aspects to be*
*① conflict vs resolved*
*n vs environment*
*② Facilitate implementation*
*control, objectives*
*SMART*

**Strategic analysis** *+ PESTEL*
- External analysis to identify opportunities and threats *SWOT*
- Internal analysis to identify strengths and weaknesses *agreed on action*
- Stakeholder analysis to identify key objectives and to assess power and interest of different groups  *- mendelow*
- Gap analysis to identify the difference between desired and expected performance. *Variance analysis*

**Strategic choice**
- Strategies are required to 'close the gap'
- Competitive strategy – for each business unit  *– Porters generic strategies*
- Directions for growth – which markets/products should be invested in  *~ Ansoff*
- Whether expansion should be achieved by organic growth, acquisition or some form of joint arrangement. *M n A*

*" played the strength " - Information*

**Strategic implementation**
- Formulation of detailed plans and budgets
- Target setting for KPIs
- Monitoring and control.

## 4 Planning and control

### 4.1 Introduction

*- How set objectives*
*- identify CSF's*
*- choose metrics*
*- implement strategy)*

**Planning** is concerned with: *Objectives / Strategies*

- where an organisation wants to be (usually expressed in terms of its objectives) and

- how it will get there (strategies).

**Control** is concerned with monitoring the achievement of objectives and suggesting corrective action.

### 4.2 The performance hierarchy

The performance hierarchy operates in the following order:

(1)  Mission

(2)  Strategic (corporate) plans and objectives *- senior*

(3)  Tactical plans and objectives *- middle management*

(4)  Operational plans and targets *- staff/employee*

### 4.3 Mission

*not specific* *(handwritten)*

A **mission statement** outlines the broad direction that an organisation will follow and summarises the reasons and values that underlie that organisation.

A mission should be:

- *enduring – long term (handwritten)*
- succinct

- memorable

- a guide for employees to work towards.
- *addressed to stakeholders. (handwritten)*

## Drucker

Drucker concluded that a mission statement should address four fundamental questions.

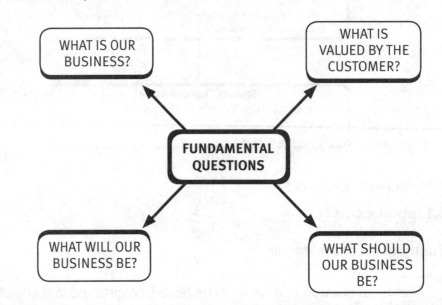

## Mission statement characteristics

Mission statements will have some or all of the following characteristics:

- Usually a brief statement of no more than a page in length.

- Very general statement of entity culture.

- States the aims (or purposes) of the organisation.

- States the business areas in which the organisation intends to operate.

- Open-ended (not stated in quantifiable terms).

- Does not include commercial terms, such as profit.

- Not time-assigned.

- Forms a basis of communication to the people inside the organisation and to people outside the organisation.

- Used to formulate goal statements, objectives and short-term targets.

- Guides the direction of the entity's strategy and as such is part of management information.

## Illustration 1 – Mission

### Ben and Jerry's    18

'Our mission is to make, distribute and sell the finest quality ice cream and euphoric concoctions with a continued commitment to incorporating wholesome, natural elements and promoting business practices that respect the earth and the environment'.

### Microsoft

'To enable people and business throughout the world to realise their full potential'.

### The British Broadcasting Corporation (BBC)

'Inform, educate and entertain'.

### Pepsi

'Beat Coke'.

## Test your understanding 1

### Required:

What are the potential benefits and drawbacks to an organisation of setting a mission statement?

## 4.4 Strategic, tactical and operational plans

To enable an organisation to fulfil its mission, the mission must be translated into strategic, tactical and operational plans.

Each level should be consistent with the one above.

This process will involve moving from general broad aims to more specific objectives and ultimately to detailed targets.

In this chapter we will focus on strategic and operational plans.

**Comparing planning and control between strategic and operational levels**

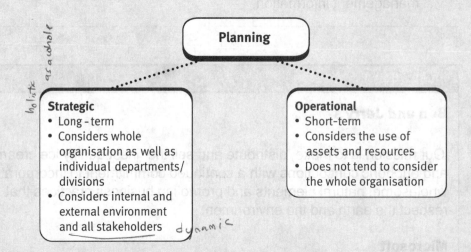

*holistic as a whole*

**Strategic**
- Long-term
- Considers whole organisation as well as individual departments/ divisions
- Considers internal and external environment and all stakeholders   *dynamic*

**Operational**
- Short-term
- Considers the use of assets and resources
- Does not tend to consider the whole organisation

### Illustration 2 – Strategic planning

Strategic planning is usually, but not always, concerned with the long-term. It raises the question of **which business shall we be in**? For example, a company specialising in production and sale of tobacco products may forecast a declining market for these products and may therefore decide to change its objectives to allow a progressive move into the leisure industry, which it considers to be expanding.

### Strategic and operational planning

#### Planning

**Strategic** planning is characterised by the following:

- long-term

- considers the whole organisation as well as individual SBUs

- matches the activities of an organisation to its external environment

- matches the activities of an organisation to its resource capability and specifies future resource requirements

- will be affected by the expectations and values of all stakeholders, not just shareholders

- its complexity distinguishes strategic management from other aspects of management in an organisation. There are several reasons for this including:
  - it involves a high degree of uncertainty
  - it is likely to require an integrated approach to management
  - it may involve major change in the organisation.

Quite apart from strategic planning, the management of an organisation has to undertake a regular series of decisions on matters that are purely **operational** and short-term in character. Such decisions:

- are usually based on a given set of assets and resources
- do not usually involve the scope of an organisation's activities
- rarely involve major change in the organisation
- are unlikely to involve major elements of uncertainty and the techniques used to help make such decisions often seek to minimise the impact of any uncertainty.
- use standard management accounting techniques such as cost-volume-profit analysis, limiting factor analysis and linear programming.

**Control**

**Strategic**
Monitors the implementation of the organisation's strategy to ascertain how well the strategic objectives are being achieved

**Operational** Budgets – make co not overspend
- Concerned with the management of existing assets and resources, given the existing strategic direction
- Will not lead to a change in strategy

**Test your understanding 2**

**Required:**

Is the activity of setting a profit-maximising selling price for a product a strategic or operational decision?

Give reasons for your answer.

## 5 The role of strategic management accounting

*[handwritten: ← Fin.- non. Fin.-]*

*[handwritten: internal    external]*

**Role of management accountant**

### Historically

*[handwritten: External analysis]*

- Role limited to implementation stage, e.g. responsible for operational budgeting and control.
- Focus is on internal factors and financial information.
- *[handwritten:]* Focus on the past

### Today

*[handwritten: Future]*

- Strategic role providing information on financial aspects of strategic planning, e.g. competitors' costs.
- Uses internal and external information. *[handwritten: 3 Branch marking]*
- Monitors performance in financial and non financial terms. *[handwritten: } quality]*

---

### Test your understanding 3

A company selling wooden garden furniture in northern Europe is facing a number of problems:

- demand is seasonal

- it is sometimes difficult to forecast demand as it varies with the weather – more is sold in hot summers than when it is cooler or wetter

- the market is becoming more fashion-conscious with shorter product life cycles

- there is a growth in the use of non-traditional materials such as plastics.

As a result the company finds itself with high inventory levels of some items of furniture which are not selling, and is unable to meet demand for others. A decision is needed on the future strategic direction and possible options which have been identified are to:

- use largely temporary staff to manufacture products on a seasonal basis in response to fluctuations in demand – however it has been identified that this could result in quality problems

- automate production to enable seasonal production with minimum labour-related problems

- concentrate on producing premium products which are smaller volume but high-priced and less dependent on fashion.

> **Required:**
>
> How could strategic management accounting help with the decision making?

## 6 Critical success factors and key performance indicators

### 6.1 What are critical success factors?

*Da 2013 Q1*

**Critical success factors** (CSFs) are the vital areas 'where things must go right' for the business in order for them to achieve their strategic objectives. The achievement of CSFs should allow the organisation to cope better than rivals with any changes in the competitive environment. *+ maximise performance*

*try use own words + give example*

---

**Illustration 3 - CSFs for supermarkets**

CSFs for the supermarket industry may include:

- having the right product mix available in each store
- having the products actually available on the shelves
- pricing the products correctly
- advertising effectively to pull shoppers in.

---

*strength / hard to immitate*

The organisation will need to have in place the **core competencies** that are required to achieve the CSFs, i.e. something that they are able to do that is difficult for competitors to follow.

### 6.2 Sources of CSFs

There are five prime sources of CSFs:

(1) **The structure of the industry** - CSFs will be determined by the characteristics of the industry itself, e.g. in the car industry 'efficient dealer network organisation' will be important where as in the food processing industry 'new product development' will be important.

(2) **Competitive strategy, industry position and geographic location**
- Competitive strategies such as differentiation or cost leadership will impact CSFs.
- Industry position, e.g. a small company's CSFs may be driven by a major competitor's strategy.
- Geographical location will impact factors such as distribution costs and hence CSFs.

(3) **Environmental factors** - factors such as increasing fuel costs can have an impact on the choice of CSFs.

(4) **Temporary factors** - temporary internal factors may drive CSFs, e.g. a supermarket may have been forced to recall certain products due to contamination fears and may therefore generate a short term CSF of ensuring that such contamination does not happen again in the future.

(5) **Functional managerial position** - the function will affect the CSFs, e.g. production managers will be concerned with product quality and cost control. managerial experience

## 6.3 Classifying CSFs

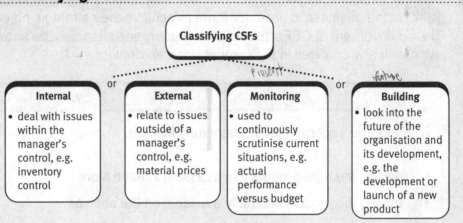

| Internal | External | Monitoring | Building |
|---|---|---|---|
| • deal with issues within the manager's control, e.g. inventory control | • relate to issues outside of a manager's control, e.g. material prices | • used to continuously scrutinise current situations, e.g. actual performance versus budget | • look into the future of the organisation and its development, e.g. the development or launch of a new product |

### Test your understanding 4

The directors of Dream Ice Cream (DI), a successful ice cream producer, with a reputation as a quality supplier, have decided to enter the frozen yogurt market in its country of operation. It has set up a separate operation under the name of Dream Yogurt (DY). The following information is available:

*   DY has recruited a management team but production staff will need to be recruited. There is some concern that there will not be staff available with the required knowledge of food production.

*   DY has agreed to supply yogurts to Jacksons, a chain of supermarkets based in the home country. They have stipulated that delivery must take place within 24 hours of an order being sent.

*   DY hopes to become a major national producer of frozen yogurts.

*   DY produces four varieties of frozen yogurt at present; Mango Tango, Very Berry, Orange Burst and French Vanilla.

**Required:**
Explain five CSFs on which the directors must focus if DY is to achieve success in the marketplace.

**(10 marks)**

## 6.4 What are key performance indicators (KPIs)?

The achievement of CSFs can be measured by establishing **key performance indicators** (KPIs) for each CSF and measuring actual performance against these KPIs. *Dec' 13* *Be specific - includes SMART element*

### Illustration 4 - CSFs and KPIs

A parcel delivery service, such as DHL, may have the following CSFs and KPIs:

| CSF | KPI |
|---|---|
| Speedy collection from customers after their request for a parcel to be delivered. | Collection from customers within 3 hours of receiving the orders, in any part of the country, for orders received before 2.30pm on a working day. |
| Rapid and reliable delivery. | Next day delivery for destinations within the UK or delivery within 2 days for destinations in Europe. |

KPIs are essential to the achievement of strategy since **what gets measured gets done**, i.e. things that are measured get done more often than things that are not measured.

## 6.5 Features of good performance measures
*^ Exam too much focus on finance*

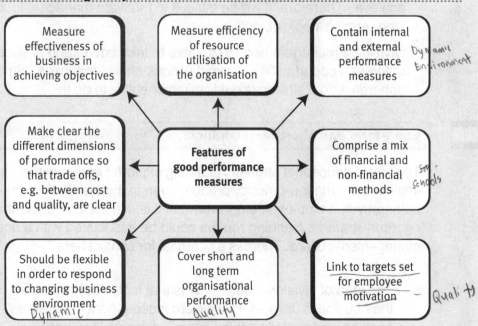

- Measure effectiveness of business in achieving objectives
- Measure efficiency of resource utilisation of the organisation
- Contain internal and external performance measures *Dynamic Environment*
- Make clear the different dimensions of performance so that trade offs, e.g. between cost and quality, are clear
- **Features of good performance measures**
- Comprise a mix of financial and non-financial methods *Soft Schools*
- Should be flexible in order to respond to changing business environment *Dynamic*
- Cover short and long term organisational performance *Quality*
- Link to targets set for employee motivation *Quality*

**Question focus**: Now attempt question 1 part (b) from chapter 13.

*B e*

### Expandable text - CSFs and KPIs

CSFs and KPIs will have a central role in the strategic planning process:

**Strategic analysis**
- Internal analysis to identify the firm's resources and core competences
- External analysis to identify CFSs in markets.

**Strategic choice**
- Select strategies where the firm has (or can acquire) the core competences to meet the CSFs in the markets concerned.

**Strategic implementation**
- Formulation of detailed plans and budgets
- Target setting for KPIs for each CSF
- Monitoring and control – especially of core competences.

## 7 Long-term and short-term conflicts

Strategic planning is a long-term, top-down process. The decisions made can conflict with the short-term localised decisions:

- Divisional managers tend to be rewarded on the short-term results they achieve. Therefore, it will be difficult to motivate managers to achieve long-term strategic objectives.

- Divisional managers need to be able to take advantage of short-term unforseen opportunities or avoid serious short-term crisis. Strict adherence to a strategy could limit their ability to do this.

*Chapter 8*

### Long-term and short-term conflicts

The whole concept of strategic planning explored earlier in this chapter implies a certain top-down approach. Even in the era of divisional autonomy and employee empowerment it is difficult to imagine that a rigorous strategic planning regime could be associated with a bottom-up management culture. There is a potential for conflict here.

- The idea of divisional autonomy is that individual managers operate their business units as if they were independent businesses – seeking and exploiting local opportunities as they arise.

- Managers are rewarded in a manner which reflects the results they achieve.

- The pressures on management are for short-term results and ostensibly strategy is concerned with the long-term. Often it is difficult to motivate managers by setting long-term expectations.

- Long-term plans have to be set out in detail long before the period to which they apply. The rigidity of the long-term plan, particularly in regard to the rationing and scheduling of resources, may place the company in a position where it is unable to react to short-term unforeseen opportunities, or serious short-term crisis.

- Strict adherence to a strategy can limit flair and creativity. Operational managers may need to respond to local situations, avert trouble or improve a situation by quick action outside the strategy. If they then have to defend their actions against criticisms of acting 'outside the plan', irrespective of the resultant benefits, they are likely to become apathetic and indifferent.

- The adoption of corporate strategy requires a tacit acceptance by everyone that the interests of departments, activities and individuals are subordinate to the corporate interests. Department managers are required to consider the contribution to corporate profits or the reduction in corporate costs of any decision. They should not allow their decisions to be limited by short-term departmental parameters.

- It is only natural that local managers should seek personal advancement. A problem of strategic planning is identifying those areas where there may be a clash of interests and loyalties, and in assessing where an individual has allowed vested interests to dominate decisions.

### Test your understanding 5

**Required:** *Goal congruency*

How might an organisation take steps to avoid conflict between strategic business plans and short-term localised decisions?

## 8 Strategic management accounting in multinational companies

A **multinational company** has subsidiaries or operations in a number of countries, e.g. it may acquire raw materials in one country, manufacture the product in a second country, sell its products in the third country and have its head office in its home country.

## Illustration 5 – The development of multinational companies

Typically, a multinational company takes the form of a central corporation with subsidiaries in each of the countries in which it operates. Well-known examples include Ford, Shell, Nestlé, General Motors, Toyota and Microsoft. By the early 1990s, 37,000 multinational companies with annual sales of $5.5 billion controlled about one-third of the world's private sector assets. The advent of these multinationals is associated with the apparent globalisation of the world economy. Various factors have contributed to this development, but one factor is critical. Increases in the scale of technology (in terms of cost, risk and complexity) have rendered even the largest national markets too small to be meaningful economic units on a stand-alone basis. Companies must expand internationally to support the technological development that is needed to remain competitive in many fields.

The modern trend in international business seems to be away from the old multinational corporations and towards networks and alliances. Strategic planning for the latter is another issue altogether.

The strategic process in a multinational company must take account of certain special features which have financial implications. These include:

- process specialisation
- product specialisation
- economic risk
- political sensitivities
- administrative issues.

## Multinational strategic management accounting

**Process specialisation.** There may be a cost advantage in locating certain types of activity in certain countries. For example, a labour intensive operation may be best placed in a low wage area. Many companies (and not just traditional multinationals) have recently relocated customer service desks and telephone call centres to India.

**Product specialisation.** In spite of globalisation and the concept of 'world products', particular countries have characteristic tastes that the multinational must cater to.

**Economic risk.** The economics of a multinational operation may be highly sensitive to issues such as exchange rate fluctuations.

**Political sensitivities.** The multinational company operates across state boundaries and must be acutely aware of associated risk factors.

KAPLAN PUBLISHING

**Administrative issues.** A multinational company will find that even its own internal transactions are vulnerable to exchange rate movements, currency exchange controls and the existence (or absence) of international tax treaties. For example, if a multinational domiciled in country A tries to repatriate profits earned by its subsidiary in country B then it may find that those profits are taxed twice – once in A and again in B.

### Impact of exchange rates

In the 1980s, many car manufacturers (Nissan, Toyota and Peugeot to name but three) built car assembly facilities in the UK to serve the whole of Europe – because the UK was perceived as a low-cost area. The UK's non-adoption of the Euro and the appreciation of the pound in the late 1990s suddenly made the UK a high-cost area. For a time, the viability of several high-profile plants was brought into question.

### Test your understanding 6

**Required:**

A multinational company with subsidiaries in North America and Europe is considering launching its products in South America. As a management accountant supporting senior managers in making strategic decisions, what factors would you need to consider in your assessment of the options facing the company? *How will these factors influence performance measurement / management?*

## 9 The role of corporate planning

### 9.1 Introduction

The term **'corporate planning'** refers to the formal process which facilitates the strategic planning process (described in Section 3).

### Illustration 6 – The role of corporate planning

The description of the role of a corporate planning department of a hospital might be:

- to manage the business planning process through which the objectives of individual clinical departments and support services are agreed

- to compile and publish the annual plan for the hospital

- to monitor performance against the targets set in the business planning process
- to monitor performance compared with other similar organisations
- to undertake specific strategic projects.

### 9.2 The role of corporate planning in clarifying corporate objectives

The first stage of the strategic planning process, strategic analysis, will generate a range of objectives, typically relating to:

- maximisation of shareholder wealth
- maximisation of sales
- growth
- survival
- research and development leadership (innovation)
- quality of service
- contented workforce
- respect for the environment.

These need to be clarified in two respects:

- **conflicts need to be resolved**, e.g. profit versus environmental concerns
- to facilitate implementation and control, objectives need to be translated into **SMART** (specific, measurable, achievable, relevant and time bound) targets.

### Illustration 7 – SMART objectives

A statement such as 'maximise profits' would be of little use in corporate planning terms. The following would be far more helpful:

- achieve a growth in EPS of 5% pa over the coming ten-year period
- obtain a turnover of $10 million within six years
- launch at least two new products per year.

## 9.3 Role of corporate planning in making strategic choices

The viability of a strategic choice should be assessed using three criteria:

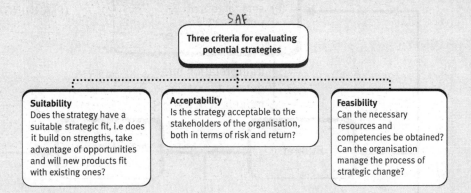

The strategic management accountant will contribute to all aspects of this evaluation, particularly acceptability and feasibility.

| Aspect | Key concern | Examples of typical financial analysis |
|---|---|---|
| Acceptability | Return | • NPV analysis<br>• ROCE |
| Acceptability | Risk | • Sensitivity analysis<br>• Expected values |
| Feasibility | Resources | • Budgeting resource requirements<br>• Cash flow forecasts to identify funding needs |

## 9.4 The role of corporate planning in checking towards the objectives set

It is not enough merely to make plans and implement them.

• The results of the plans have to be compared against stated objectives to assess the firm's performance.

• Action can then be taken to remedy any shortfalls in performance.

Corporate planning is not a once-in-every-ten-years activity, but an on going process which must react quickly to the changing circumstances of the firm and of the environment.

## Diagram of corporate planning activities

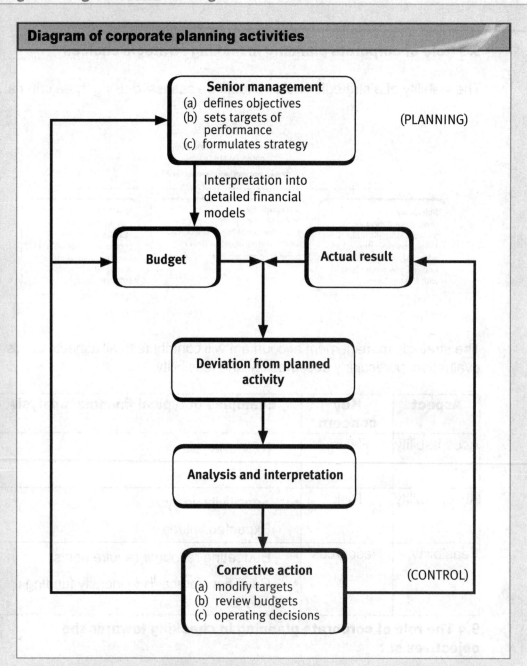

**Senior management**
(a) defines objectives
(b) sets targets of performance
(c) formulates strategy

(PLANNING)

Interpretation into detailed financial models

**Budget**

**Actual result**

**Deviation from planned activity**

**Analysis and interpretation**

**Corrective action**
(a) modify targets
(b) review budgets
(c) operating decisions

(CONTROL)

## Test your understanding 7

**Required:**

Why do you think managers need to understand corporate planning?

## 10 Tools used in strategic analysis

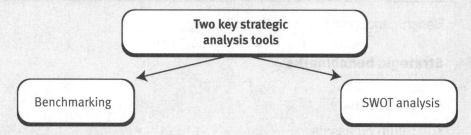

Two key strategic analysis tools

Benchmarking

SWOT analysis

### 10.1 Benchmarking

**Benchmarking** is the process of systematic comparision of a service, practice or process. The yardstick, or benchmark, is based upon the **best in class** and serves to provide a target for action in order to improve the competitive position.

### Types of benchmarking

There are three basic types:

*   **Internal**: this is where another branch or department of the organisation is used as a benchmark.
*   **Competitor**: uses a direct competitor with the same or similar processes as the benchmark. *Problem → obtain info from competitor.*
*   **Process or activity**: focuses on a similar process in another company which is not a direct competitor.

### Illustration 8 – Process benchmarking at Xerox

Among the pioneers in the benchmarking 'movement' were Xerox, Motorola, IBM and AT&T. The best known is the Xerox Corporation.

Some years ago, Xerox confronted its own unsatisfactory performance in **product warehousing and distribution**. It did so by identifying the organisation it considered to be the very best at warehousing and distribution, in the hope that 'best practices' could be adapted from this model. The business judged to provide a model of best practice in this area was L L Bean, a catalogue merchant (i.e. it existed in an unrelated sector). Xerox approached Bean with a request that the two engage in a co-operative benchmarking project. The request was granted and the project yielded major insights in inventory arrangement and order processing, resulting in major gains for Xerox when these insights were adapted to its own operations.

## Strategic, functional and operational benchmarks

Benchmarks could include the following:

### Strategic benchmarks

- market share
- return on assets
- gross profit margin on sales.

### Functional benchmarks

- % deliveries on time
- order costs per order
- order turnaround time
- average stockholding per order.

### Operational benchmarks

These are at a level below functional benchmarks. They yield the reasons for a functional performance gap. An organisation has to understand the benchmarks at the operational level in order to identify the corrective actions needed to close the performance gap.

## The benchmarking process

**Step 1:** Set objectives and decide the areas to benchmark.

**Step 2:** Identify key performance indicators and drivers.

**Step 3:** Select organisations/partners for benchmarking comparison.

**Step 4:** Measure performance of all organisations/partners involved in benchmarking

**Step 5:** Compare performance.

**Step 6:** Specify improvement projects.

**Step 7:** Implement and monitor improvements.

### Illustration 9 - Benchmarking success at Kelloggs

Kelloggs' factories all use the same monitoring techniques, so it is possible to compare performance between sites, although there are always some things that are done differently.

They can interrogate this information to improve performance across every site. As things have improved, Kelloggs have also had to reassess their baseline figures and develop more sophisticated tools to monitor performance to ensure they continue to make progress.

They have seen a 20% increase in productivity in six years using this system.

### Benchmarking evaluation

| Benefits | Drawbacks |
|---|---|
| • Identifies gaps in performance.<br><br>• A method of assessing the relative position of a company or a division.<br><br>• A method for learning and applying best practices.<br><br>• Encourages continuous improvement.<br><br>• A method of learning from the success of others.<br><br>• Minimises complacency and self-satisfaction with your own performance. | • Best practice companies may be unwilling to share data.<br><br>• Lack of commitment by management and staff.  Staff need to be reassured that their status, remuneration and working conditions will not suffer.<br><br>• Identifying best practice is difficult.<br><br>• Costly in terms of time and money.<br><br>• What is best today may not be so tomorrow.<br><br>• Differences, for example in accounting treatment, may make comparisions meaningless.<br><br>• Too much attention is paid to the aspects of performance that are measured as a result of the benchmarking exercise, to the detriment of the organisation's overall performance. |

### Performance comparison with the competition

Comparative analysis can be usefully applied to any value activity which underpins the competitive strategy of an organisation, an industry or a nation.

To find out the level of investment in fixed assets of competitors, the business can use physical observation, information from trade press or trade association announcements, supplier press releases as well as their externally published financial statements, to build a clear picture of the relative scale, capacity, age and cost for each competitor.

The method of operating these assets, in terms of hours and shift patterns, can be established by observation, discussions with suppliers and customers or by asking existing or ex-employees of the particular competitor. If the method of operating can be ascertained it should enable a combination of internal personnel management and industrial engineering managers to work out the likely relative differences in labour costs. The rates of pay and conditions can generally be found with reference to nationally negotiated agreements, local and national press advertising for employees, trade and employment associations and recruitment consultants. When this cost is used alongside an intelligent assessment of how many employees would be needed by the competitor in each area, given their equipment and other resources, a good idea of the labour costs can be obtained.

Another difference which should be noted is the nature of the competitors' costs as well as their relative levels. Where a competitor has a lower level of committed fixed costs, such as lower fixed labour costs due to a larger proportion of temporary workers, it may be able to respond more quickly to a downturn in demand by rapidly laying off the temporary staff. Equally, in a tight labour market and with rising sales, it may have to increase its pay levels to attract new workers.

In some industries, one part of the competitor analysis is surprisingly direct. Each new competitive product is purchased on a regular basis and then systematically taken apart, so that each component can be identified as well as the processes used to put the parts together. The respective areas of the business will then assess the costs associated with each element so that a complete product cost can be found for the competitive product.

A comparison of similar value activities between organisations is useful when the strategic context is taken into consideration. For example, a straight comparison of resource deployment between two competitive organisations may reveal quite different situations in the labour cost as a percentage of the total cost. The conclusions drawn from this, however, depend upon circumstances. If the firms are competing largely on the basis of price, then differentials in these costs could be crucial. In contrast, the additional use of labour by one organisation may be an essential support for the special services provided which differentiate that organisation from its competitors.

One danger of inter-firm analysis is that the company may overlook the fact that the whole industry is performing badly, and is losing out competitively to other countries with better resources or even other industries which can satisfy customers' needs in different ways. Therefore, if an industry comparison is performed it should make some assessment of how the resource utilisation compares with other countries and industries. This can be done by obtaining a measurement of stock turnover or yield from raw materials.

Benchmarking against competitors involves the gathering of a range of information about them. For quoted companies financial information will generally be reasonably easy to obtain, from published accounts and the financial press. Some product information may be obtained by acquiring their products and examining them in detail to ascertain the components used and their construction ('reverse engineering'). Literature will also be available, for example in the form of brochures and trade journals.

However, most non-financial information, concerning areas such as competitors' processes, customer and supplier relationships and customer satisfaction will not be so readily available. To overcome this problem, benchmarking exercises are generally carried out with organisations taken from within the same group of companies (intra-group benchmarking) or from similar but non-competing industries (inter-industry benchmarking).

## 10.2 SWOT analysis

The purpose of **SWOT analysis** is to provide a summarised analysis of the company's present situation in the market place. It can also be used to identify CSFs and KPIs.

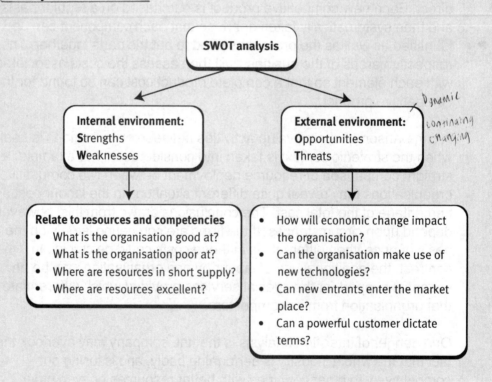

### Using a SWOT anlaysis

Strategies can be developed that:

*   neutralise weaknesses or convert them into strengths.
*   convert threats into opportunities.
*   match strengths with opportunities – a strength is of little use without an opportunity.

### Test your understanding 8

**Required:**

What types of strengths, weaknesses, opportunities and threats would a 'no frills' airline have?

### Test your understanding 9

Envie Co owns a chain of retail clothing stores specialising in ladies' designer fashion and accessories. Jane Smith, the original founder, has been pleasantly surprised by the continuing growth in the fashion industry during the last decade.

The company was established 12 years ago, originally with one store in the capital city. Jane's design skills and entrepreneurial skills have been the driving force behind the expansion. Due to unique designs and good quality control, the business now has ten stores in various cities.

Each store has a shop manger that is completely responsible for managing the staff and stock levels within each store. They produce monthly reports on sales. Some stores are continually late in supplying their monthly figures.

Envie runs several analysis programmes to enable management information to be collated. The information typically provides statistical data on sales trends between categories of items and stores. The analysis and preparation of these reports are conducted in the marketing department. In some cases the information is out of date in terms of trends and variations.

As the business has developed Jane has used the service of a local IT company to implement and develop their systems. She now wants to invest in website development with the view of reaching global markets.

**Required:**

(a) Construct a SWOT analysis with reference to the proposal of website development.

(b) Explain how the use of SWOT analysis may be of assistance to Envie Co.

Dec '13

## 11 Gap analysis

**Gap analysis** is carried out as the final part of strategic analysis. It identifies the difference between the desired and the expected performance.

The example below shows a gap for 'earnings'.

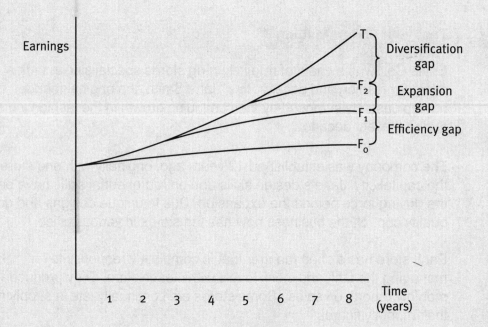

In the diagram showing the gap:

$F_0$ = initial forecast

$F_1$ = forecast adjusted for improvements in **internal efficiency**, e.g. internal cost savings through better use of resources or divestment of a loss-making business unit.

$F_2$ = forecast adjusted for **product-market expansion.** The expansion gap involves the development of a new product **or** market.

T = target. The gap between $F_2$ and the target represents the forecast adjusted for **product-market expansion**. The diversification gap involves the development of new products **and** markets.

Benchmarking and SWOT analysis can both be used to identify the gap and to help the organisation to identify strategies to address the gap.

### Illustration 10 - SWOT analysis and gap identification

SWOT analysis would seek to identify:

- **Threats focusing on weaknesses** - This would have top priority and the company should seek to identify and consider possible solutions. This requires a defensive response of some kind and may well necessitate rapid change.

- **Threats focusing on strengths** - this requires a review of the supposed strength to ensure that it is still as strong as previously thought. Remember, what is good today, may not be so tomorrow.

- **Opportunity focusing on strengths** - this gives the organisation the chance to develop strategic competitive advantage in the marketplace. They should check the research and assesses the strengths again.

- **Opportunity focusing on weakness** - this will require management to make a decision as to whether to change and pursue the opportunity or, alternatively, ignore the prospect and ensure resources are not wasted in this area in future. Usually substantial change will be required if the company is going to pursue the opportunity. The company should check that their internal competencies will allow them to exploit the opportunity.

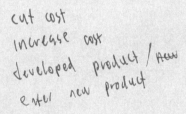

## Chapter summary

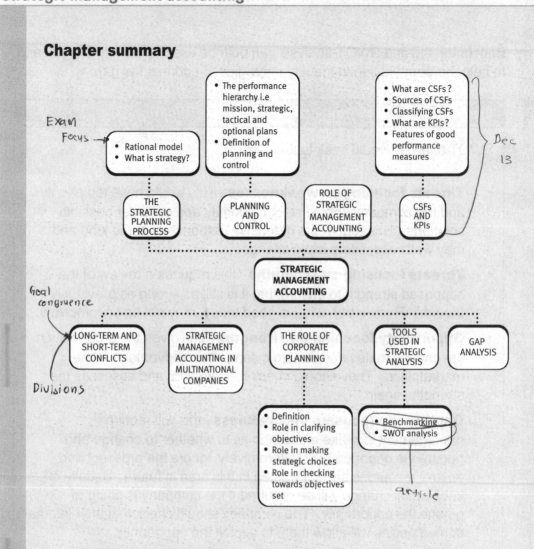

# Test your understanding answers

## Test your understanding 1

| Benefits | Drawbacks |
|---|---|
| • Provides strategic direction thereby assisting in the formation of acceptable strategies.<br><br>• Assists in resolving conflict between stakeholder groups.<br><br>• Provides a framework within which managerial decisions can be made.<br><br>• Assists in communicating key cultural values to employees and other stakeholders.<br><br>• Helps to prevent potential misinterpretations of the organisation's reason for being. | • They may be unclear or vague.<br><br>• They may be unrealistic.<br><br>• There may be inconsistencies between the different elements of the mission statement.<br><br>• They may be inconsistent with management action.<br><br>• They may lack sufficient external focus. |

## Test your understanding 2

This is an **operational** decision. Setting a profit-maximising selling price is an exercise based on forecast demand and marginal costs over a coming period such as a year. It does not involve asking whether a product should be sold at all, whether its design should be modified or how its selling price should be influenced by the position of the product in its life cycle or the product matrix of the business.

### Test your understanding 3

Strategic management accounting may assist the decision making process as follows:

- analysis of the market for different types of product:
    - review of competitors' products
    - likely size and value of different market sectors
    - price comparison of different products
- forecasts of costs of manufacturing new products, comparing different levels of automation/ use of temporary staff
- forecasts of profitability of different products
- investigation of capital costs of different options and investment appraisal of possible options
- analysis of the cost of holding inventory under different options.

### Test your understanding 4

Critical success factors (CSFs) are as follows:

**Product quality** – the fact that production staff may have no previous experience in a food production environment is likely to prove problematic. It is vital that a comprehensive training programme is put in place at the earliest opportunity. DY need to reach and maintain the highest level of quality as soon as possible.

**Supply quality** – the quality and timeliness of delivery into Jacksons supermarkets assumes critical significance. Hence supply chain management must be extremely robust as there is little scope for error.

**Technical quality** – compliance with existing regulators regarding food production including all relevant factory health and safety requirements is vital in order to establish and maintain the reputation of DY as a supplier of quality products. The ability to store products at the correct temperature is critical because yogurts are produced for human consumption and in extreme circumstances could cause fatalities.

**External credibility** – accreditation by relevant trade associations/regulators will be essential if nationwide acceptance of DY as a major producer of frozen yogurts is to be established.

**New produce development** – while DY have produced a range of frozen yogurts it must be recognised that consumer tastes change and that in the face of competition there will always be a need for a continuous focus on new product development.

**Margin** – while DY need to recognise all other CSFs they should always be mindful that the need to obtain desired levels of gross and net margin remain of the utmost importance.

**Note:** only five CSFs were required. Alternative relevant discussion and examples would be appropriate.

### Test your understanding 5

Possible steps include:

- involving local managers in strategy formulation

- agreeing strategies with business units within certain boundaries

- ensuring performance management reflects a combination of short- and long-term issues

- permitting flexibility within the strategic planning process to allow for changes due to local circumstances

- a combination of strategic planning and freewheeling opportunism (no strategic plans). For example, strategic planning may be used for activities such as identifying the organisation's resource capability and its resources. Freewheeling opportunism may be used to exploit an organisation's competences, e.g. the skills of particular individuals or groups.

## Test your understanding 6

Possible factors could include:

### Process

The company needs to determine where best to locate activities related to the new market, e.g. whether to manufacture products in South America as well as selling there. This will require a comparison of the total product costs with manufacture in different locations, including factors such as:

- labour costs

- materials – costs of purchasing in different areas, costs of sourcing elsewhere and transporting to manufacturing site

- distribution – costs under different scenarios including setting up own sales force, using existing distributors

- costs of after-sales support.

### Product

In addition to changes in manufacturing costs due to the location of manufacture there may be additional costs if products need to be tailored for the South American market. These need to be estimated.

### Exchange rates

The company needs to assess the impact of exchange rate fluctuations on the value of income earned in South America. There is a need to consider how this risk will be managed, e.g. by hedging.

### Political risk

The company needs to be aware of the possibility of an unexpected politically motivated event in S.America affecting the outcome of the investment, e.g. the government may decide to raise taxation.

### Administrative issues

The financial impact of a number of other factors needs to be incorporated into the evaluation of the options such as the impact on internal transactions of exchange rate movements, currency exchange controls and tax regimes. There will, e.g. be implications for any transfer pricing system. Exchange rate fluctuations also need to be taken into account in developing performance measures for business unit managers in overseas locations to ensure that they are not being penalised for changes in income which are out of their control.

## Test your understanding 7

- An understanding of corporate planning is essential for all management because lower-level objectives are inexorably linked to higher-level strategies. An appreciation of these strategies and how they are formulated can be an effective guide to action.

- Moreover, whatever the level at which a manager operates within an organisation, he or she can have some influence over that organisation's corporate strategy.

## Test your understanding 8

| Strengths: | Weaknesses: |
|---|---|
| • Airports used are better than those used by competitors<br>• Management skills<br>• Lower costs than established airlines<br>• Ease of booking flights<br>• Recognised logo<br>• IT facilities<br>• Good employee relations. | • Airports used are worse than those used by the big carriers<br>• Punctuality<br>• Cash flows<br>• No established safety record<br>• Poorer than average customer service. |
| **Opportunities:** | **Threats:** |
| • Strong business demand for cheap air fares<br>• Strong leisure demand for cheap air fares<br>• Full exploitation of the Internet<br>• Many secondary airports underused. | • Higher airport charges<br>• Stringent security checks<br>• Entry of subsidiaries of big carriers. |

### Test your understanding 9

(a)

**Strengths:**
Successful company
Steady increase in market share
Experience in the market
Founder's entrepreneurial skills
Good designs
Good quality control
Keen to exploit to technology
Strong IT

**Weakness:**
Management of information is often out of date
No in-house IT expertise
No web experience
Not sure if the new system will generate new sales
Lack of control over store managers
Out of date reporting from some stores
Over reliance on IT provider

**Opportunities:**
E-trading can provide a new sales channel and revenue stream
Identification and recording of customer details to enhance customer relationships
Extension of customer base
Global market potential
Cut costs in many areas
Create a vision of a modern company
Develop product range further
Look at employing an IT specialist

**Threats:**
Customer resistance to on-line shopping
Loss of unique identity; may become just another website trader
Resistance within the company
Effects on existing personnel and working conditions
Costs of developing the website may outweigh the benefits
Security issues
Loss of competitive edge

**Note:** marks would be awarded for other relevant points.

(b) The use of SWOT analysis will focus management attention on current strengths and weaknesses of the organisation which will be of assistance in formulating the business strategy. It will also enable management to monitor trends and developments in the changing business environment. Each trend or development may be classified as an opportunity or a threat that will provide a stimulus for an appropriate management response.

Management can make an assessment of the feasibility of required actions in order that the company may capitalise upon opportunities whilst considering how best to negate or minimise the effect of any threats.

EXAM

*20/02/2014 | 25/02/2014*

# Environmental influences

*Ethical — very limited*

## Chapter learning objectives

Upon completion of this chapter you will be able to:

- discuss the ways in which stakeholder groups operate and how they effect an organisation and its strategy formulation and implementation (e.g. using Mendelow's matrix)

- discuss the *limited* ethical issues that may impact on strategy formulation and business performance

- discuss the ways in which stakeholder groups may influence business performance

- assess the continuing effectiveness of traditional management accounting techniques within a rapidly changing business environment

- assess the impact of different risk appetites of stakeholders on performance management

- evaluate how risk and uncertainty play an important role in long term strategic planning and decision-making that relies upon forecasts and exogenous variables

- apply different risk analysis techniques in assessing business performance such as maximax, maximin, minimax regret and expected values

- discuss the need to consider the environment in which an organisation is operating when assessing its performance using models such as PEST *Dec'13* and Porter's 5 forces, including areas:
  - political climate        *June'A*
  - market conditions
  - funding       *Financial regulator*
- assess the impact of government regulations and policies on performance measurement techniques used and the performance levels achieved (for example, in the case of utility services and former state monopolies)

*"the examiner likes to use specific writers"*

- discuss social and ethical obligations that should be considered in the pursuit of corporate performance objectives

- discuss the ways through which management accounting practitioners are made aware of new techniques and how they evaluate them

- assess the changing role of the management accountant in today's business environment as outlined by <u>Burns and Scapens.</u>

June '12
Dec

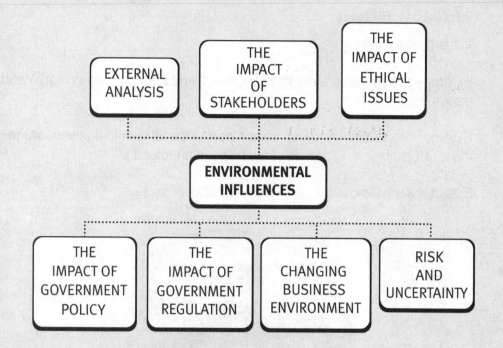

## 1 Exam focus

| Exam sitting | Area examined | Question number | Number of marks |
|---|---|---|---|
| December 2011 | Risk | 1 | 35 |
| June 2011 | Stakeholders | 2(c) | 6 |
| December 2010 | PEST(EL) | 4(a) | 4 |
| June 2010 | Expected values | 2(b)(i)(ii) | 12 |
| December 2009 | Economic, financial and social considerations | 4(b) | 14 |
| June 2009 | Maximax, maximin and minimax regret | 2(d) | 7 |
| December 2008 | Ethical issues/CSR | 3(c) | 5 |
| December 2008 | How government can aid business performance | 3(d) | 5 |
| June 2008 | Strategic and economic factors | 3(a) | 14 |
| December 2007 | Porter's 5 forces | 5(a) | 10 |
| Pilot paper | Ethics | 1(d) | 3 |
| Pilot paper | Risk | 3(b) | 10 |

**Student Accountant articles**: visit the ACCA website, www.accaglobal.com, to review the following articles on the topics in this chapter:

The risks of uncertainty (article 1) - April 2009

The risks of uncertainty (article 2) - October 2009

Business strategy and performance models - April 2006

## 2 External analysis

### 2.1 Introduction

External analysis was first met in paper F1 and then studied in more detail in paper P3.

External analysis forms an important part of the 'strategic analysis' stage of the strategic planning process (reviewed in chapter 1).

External analysis can be performed at different levels:

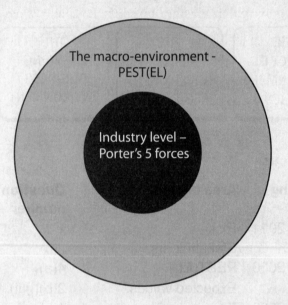

### 2.2 PEST(EL) analysis

The PEST(EL) model looks at the macro-environment, using the following headings:

| Heading | Examples |
|---------|----------|
| **P**olitical factors | • Taxation policy<br>• Government stability<br>• Foreign trade regulations |
| **E**conomic factors | • Interest rates<br>• Inflation<br>• Unemployment<br>• Business cycles |

| Social factors | • Population demographics _western europe aging population_ |
| | • Social mobility |
| | • Income distribution |
| | • Lifestyle changes _- people looking to work ot_ |
| | • Attitudes to work and leisure |
| | • Levels of education and consumerism |
| **Technological factors** | • Speed of technological transfer _obcelentes_ |
| | • Rates of obsolescence |
| **E**cological/environmental factors | • How to produce goods with minimal environmental damage _EMA - Environmental management Accounting chapter 12_ |
| **L**egal factors | • Taxation |
| | • Employment law |
| | • Monopoly legislation |
| | • Environment protection legislation |

The key issue in P5 is to appreciate that, as well as being used for strategic analysis, this model can be used to identify key performance management issues. For example:

- to identify CSFs and KPIs

- targets may need revising if market conditions change.

## PEST(EL) analysis

Environmental legislation may have been identified as being particularly important to a chemicals producer, in which case it should set up a series of targets to measure compliance. For example:

- level of fines

- number of environmental prosecutions

- number of environmental enforcement actions

- number of 'notifiable' incidents (local legislation will define what is 'notifiable' and what is not)

- percentage of employees working within an ISO 14001 compliant Environmental Management System

- the firm's rating in independent benchmarking such as the 'Business in the Environment' Index.

### 2.3 Porter's five forces model

**Porter's five forces** analysis applies to industry sectors. All businesses in a particular industry are likely to be subject to similar pressures that determine how attractive the sector is.  Industry attractiveness depends on five factors or forces:

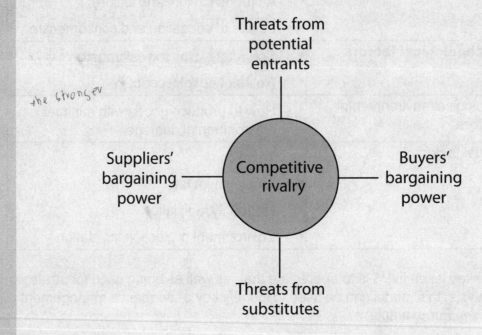

*the stronger*

As with PEST(EL) analysis above, Porter's five forces model can be used to identify key performance management issues as well as being used for strategic analysis.  If they are able to, businesses should:

*   avoid business sectors which are unattractive because of the five forces

*   try to mitigate the effects of the five forces. For example, supplier power is lessened if a long-term contract is negotiated or competition is reduced by taking over a rival.

## Porter's five forces

- **Competitive rivalry**: There will be a tough environment if there are many competitors but a much easier one if there is a monopoly.

- **Buyer's bargaining power**: A few, large customers can exert powerful bargaining power. Many, small customers find it harder to apply pressure.

- **Supplier's bargaining power**: A monopoly supplier of a vital component can apply great pressure. Any one of many suppliers of an ordinary component cannot.

- **Threat from potential entrants**: The key issue here is to assess barriers to entry. For example, high capital costs, know-how and regulation of all present barriers to entry which will help to reduce competition.

- **Threat from substitutes**: The level of the threat is determined by relative price/performance. *differentiation . coke + pepsi*

## Illustration 1 – Porter's five forces

A **Porter's** five forces analysis may have concluded that there is currently a low threat of new entrants due to the incumbent firm having economies of scale that create an effective barrier to entry. The firm concerned would be wise to monitor its cost per unit compared to those of potential new entrants to see if the threat increases.

## Test your understanding 1

### PEST(EL) and Porter's five forces model *Dec 2013*

*use to assess CSFs + KPIs*

In the United Kingdom, railways are facing major challenges. Customers are complaining about poor services. The government is reluctant to spend vast amounts of public money on developing the decaying infrastructure. The inflated costs of commuting by car, such as fuel and congestion charges, are increasing the number of people wanting to use the railways.

### Required:

Construct an outline PEST(EL) analysis and briefly apply Porter's five forces model to the railways in the UK.

**Question focus**: Now attempt question 2 from chapter 13.

### 3 The impact of stakeholders

### 3.1 Introduction

A **stakeholder** of an organisation is anyone affected by the organisation.

The mission and objectives of an organisation need to be developed with the needs of the stakeholders in mind.

| Illustration 2 - Strategic planning and stakeholder needs |
| --- |
| When planning, management has to take into account stakeholder requirements, power and ambition. For example, there is no point devising changes to production methodologies if: <br><br> • employees will not be prepared to adapt to them <br> • customers do not like the quality of what is offered <br> • suppliers cannot supply parts at the required frequency. |

### 3.2 Stakeholder mapping

Managers can make use of **Mendelow**'s matrix to help manage stakeholders' conflicting demands.

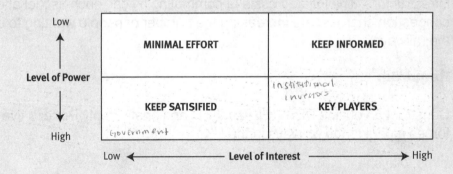

### Expandable text - Mendelow's matrix

- **Key players**: These stakeholders are the major drivers of change and could stop management plans if not satisfied. Their participation in the planning process is vital.

- **Keep satisfied**: These stakeholders have high power and need to be reassured of the outcome of the strategy well in advance to stop them from gaining interest.

- **Keep informed**: These stakeholders are interested in the strategy but lack power. Managers must justify their plans to these stakeholders. Otherwise they will gain power by joining forces with other stakeholders.

- **Minimal effort**: These stakeholders lack interest and power and are more likely than others to accept what they are told and follow instructions.

## 3.3 Stakeholders influence on business performance

Stakeholders can influence business performance in a number of ways. For example:

- **control of strategic resources** - e.g. workers may go on strike and so withold their labour.

- **possession of knowledge or skills** - e.g. by the partners in a joint venture.

### Illustration 3 – Stakeholders influence

British Airways plc has regular labour relations problems with cabin attendants and check-in staff. These employees would be classed as 'key players' in **Mendelow**'s matrix. The airline cannot operate without check-in staff, and particularly without legal minimum numbers of cabin attendants. So, these employees have great power and have shown over many years that they are happy to exercise that power.

### Test your understanding 2

Chatman Theatre is a charitable trust with the objective of making multicultural films and stage productions available to a regional audience. The organisation is not for profit. The aim to bring diversity of films, plays and dance that would otherwise be inaccessible to a regional audience.

The theatre needs to have strict budget focus, since a charity can become bankrupt. In order to achieve the required income, relationships must be built with a range of stakeholders.

**Required:**

Identify a few key stakeholders and ideas that would assist in building relationships.

### 3.4 Stakeholder conflict

Stakeholders' requirements and aspirations often conflict:

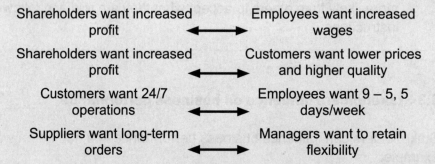

| | |
|---|---|
| Shareholders want increased profit | Employees want increased wages |
| Shareholders want increased profit | Customers want lower prices and higher quality |
| Customers want 24/7 operations | Employees want 9 – 5, 5 days/week |
| Suppliers want long-term orders | Managers want to retain flexibility |

### Resolving conflicting objectives (Cyert and March)

Management can seek to manage conflicting objectives through the following.

- Prioritisation *mendelow's*
- Negotiation and 'satisficing'  *keep both party on board*
- Sequential attention
- Side payments *build community centre at affected areas*
- Exercise of power

### Resolving conflicting (Cyert and March)

**Prioritisation** – this could follow from Mendelow's matrix above.

**Negotiation and 'satisficing'** – finding the minimum acceptable outcome for each group to achieve a compromise.

**Sequential attention** – each period a different stakeholder group is focused upon, e.g. the workers' canteen could be updated this year with the implication that employees should not expect any improvements in working conditions for the next few years.

> **Side payments** – this can often involve benefiting a group without giving them what they actually want, e.g. the local community may be concerned with cuts in jobs and increased pollution but the firm seeks to placate them by building new sports facilities and sponsoring a local fete.
>
> **Exercise of power** - when a deadlock is resolved by a senior figure forcing through a decision simply based on the power they possess.

**Test your understanding 3**

The trustees of a museum are faced with the following conflicting objectives:

- to educate the public
- to preserve antiquities for study and research.

**Required:**

Give two examples of policies that would be affected by the prioritisation of these objectives.

*PG- analysing + make actions*

## 4 The impact of ethical issues

### 4.1 Ethics    *moral compass    EMA :*

- Ethics is a set of moral principles that guide behaviour, based on what is 'felt' to be right.
- Comprises principles and standards that govern business behaviour.
- Actions can be judged to be right or wrong, ethical or unethical by individuals inside or outside the organisation.

For example, is it ethical to:

- experiment on animals?
- drill for oil?
- build roads through the countryside?
- allow smoking in public areas?
- pay senior executives large increases in salary?
- train students to pass exams?

Apart from any moral duty to be ethical, the prime purpose of a business is to maximise shareholder wealth and the chance of this happening is increased by the adoption of ethical behaviour.

## Test your understanding 4

**Required:**

How can the adoption of ethical behaviour by an organisation help to assist to maximise shareholder wealth?

## Illustration 4 - Nestle and Ethics

Nestle was criticised in the past for taking advantage of the poor and uneducated populations in developing countries in order to increase their own profits.

The company gave gifts and incentives to local health officials, as encouragement in promoting their baby milk formula and therefore discouraging breast feeding.  Nestle employees were heard telling midwives that 'all western women use formula to feed their babies, so that they grow up big and strong'.

Nestle didn't educate mothers about sterilising bottles  and therefore mothers mixed the formula with dirty water at the cost of many babies' health.  The free samples provided to mothers in hospitals and clinics soon dried up and mothers then had to pay almost western prices for the baby milk formula, a price that most families could not afford.

### 4.2 Corporate social responsibility

**Corporate social responsibility (CSR)** refers to the idea that a company should be sensitive to the needs of all stakeholders in its business operations and not just shareholders.  As such, ethics is just one dimension of corporate social responsibility.

By aligning the company's core values with the values of society, the company can improve its reputation and ensure it has a long term future.

## Benefits of a CSR strategy

- Differentiation - the firm's CSR strategy can act as a method of differentiation.

- High calibre staff will be attracted and retained due to the firm's CSR policies.

- Brand strengthening - due to the firm's honest approach.

- Lower costs - can be achieved in a number of ways, e.g. due to the use of less packaging or energy.

- The identification of new market opportunities and of changing social expectations.

- An overall increase in profitability as a result of the above - project NPVs will increase due to increased sales, lower costs, an extended project life and a lower level of risk.

### Test your understanding 5

**Required:**

Many commentators believe that CSR is a morally correct pursuit, but there are powerful arguments against it. Identify and discuss these arguments.

## CSR and metrics

- Remember, things that get measured get done more often than things that are not measured.

- Therefore, the company should measure the result of any CSR programme.

### Test your understanding 6

RFG has set up manufacturing plants in many developing countries, some of which have much lower legislation standards regarding health and safety than RFG's target markets. To improve its global reputation, the firm wishes to improve its performance for health and safety.

**Required:**

Suggest some metrics for measuring health and safety.

## 5 The impact of government policy

### 5.1 Introduction

Government policies will influence the performance levels achieved by an organisation and the performance measurement techniques chosen.

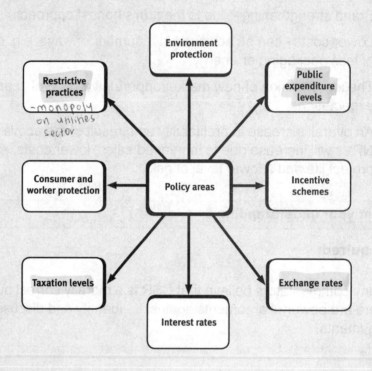

### Test your understanding 7

**Required:**

Evaluate the circumstances in which a government can act as an aid to business performance.

### Illustration 5 - The role of government policy

The capital engaged in some business operations is a direct function of relations with government. The following is an extreme example of this.

The UK Independent Television regional franchises were 'auctioned' in the early 1990s. The system is that a public body owns the transmitter network but franchises the right to broadcast programmes (and advertising) from regional centres every 10 years. Organisations interested in obtaining a franchise were required to submit sealed bids prior to certain dates. Those bids stated (among other things) the amount that the applicant was prepared to pay for the franchise.

Some of the franchises were keenly contested – particularly some of the more attractive ones in London and the south east. Several well-resourced consortia offered substantial nine-figure sums for the London franchises.

One organisation, Central Television, was preparing a bid for the Birmingham franchise. Through discreet enquiries it found that no other bids were going to be made for the franchise. So, it submitted a bid for £2,000 – which the government had to accept. A rich franchise, worth millions, was thereby acquired without any significant capital outlay.

The performance of Central Television on the basis of ROCE would have been phenomenal – but this had nothing to do with commercial success or efficiency. It was just an accident of the way that the industry is regulated.

## Porter's view

### The influence of government on an industry

**Porter** identifies seven ways in which a government can affect the structure of an industry.

- **Capacity expansion**. The government can take actions to encourage firms or an industry as a whole to increase or cut capacity. Examples include capital allowances to encourage investment in equipment; regional incentives to encourage firms to locate new capacity in a particular area, and incentives to attract investment from overseas firms. The government is also (directly or indirectly) a supplier of infrastructure such as roads and railways, and this may influence expansion in a particular area.

- **Demand**. The government is a major customer of business in all areas of life and can influence demand by buying more or less. It can also influence demand by legislative measures. The tax system for cars is a good example: a change in the tax relief available for different engine sizes has a direct effect on the car manufacturers' product and the relative numbers of each type produced. Regulations and controls in an industry will affect the growth and profits of the industry, for example minimum product quality standards.

- **Divestment and exit**. A firm may wish to sell off a business to a foreign competitor or close it down, but the government might prevent this action because it is not in the public interest (there could be examples in health, defence, transport, education, agriculture and so on).

- **Emerging industries may be controlled by the government**. For instance governments may control numbers of licences to create networks for next generation mobile phones.

  *Gov. ↓ monopoly (private)*

- **Entry barriers**. Government policy may restrict investment or competition or make it harder by use of quotas and tariffs for overseas firms. This kind of protectionism is generally frowned upon by the World Trade Organisation, but there may be political and economic circumstances in which it becomes necessary.

- **Competition policy**. Governments might devise policies which are deliberately intended to keep an industry fragmented, preventing one or two producers from having too much market share.

- **New product adoption**. Governments regulate the adoption of new products (e.g. new drugs) in some industries. They may go so far as to ban the use of a new product if it is not considered safe (a new form of transport, say). Policies may influence the rate of adoption of new products, e.g. the UK government 'switch off' of the analogue television networks by 2012, effectively forcing users to buy digital cable or satellite services.

## Legislation and regulation

Strategic planners cannot plan intelligently without a good working knowledge of the laws and regulations that affect their own companies and the businesses they operate in.

- There is an almost endless list of laws, or categories of legislation, that affect business enterprises in domestic, national or international dimensions. The main categories are listed below:

  – local by-laws (for example planning permission, construction of roads, licences)

  – labour legislation (such as safety at work, employee protection, redundancy payments)

  – trade union legislation

  – consumer protection legislation

  – company legislation

  – taxation legislation

  – anti-trust (monopolies) legislation and rulings

  – trade legislation (e.g. countries restricted for export)

  – business legislation (e.g. contract and agency law)

  – social legislation such as welfare benefits.

- At a more general level, laws are passed that enable government to levy taxes which will have an impact both on demand and the organisation's profits.

- There are special regulatory regimes for particular industries or sectors, such as nuclear energy, transport, broadcasting or food.

- Legislation is becoming more complex, particularly for those companies that trade internationally where the interface, indeed probable conflict, between domestic laws, the host country's laws, and probably also the laws of the trading block of nations the host country belongs to, provides an extremely complicated legal scenario.

## Government and the public sector

In public sector organisations the government is the major stakeholder. This can have a number of particular impacts:

- the motivation to meet customer needs may be reduced

- the consequences of failure to provide an appropriate level of service for the organisation and the individual are reduced

- being dependent on government policy also means that objectives may change rapidly as policy changes and this political dimension reduces the scope of management options and increases the time for decisions to be taken

- when the public sector companies are privatised they may still remain subject to elaborate regulatory regimes. The performance of the operations involved is monitored and measured using various indicators, with the possibility of fines for poor performance or price restrictions imposed by regulators.

## Planning for political change

The problem facing strategic planners is how to plan for changes in the political environment. It is necessary to consider what type of political change could affect the enterprise rather than trying to estimate all the political changes that might occur, by:

- examining changes in social behaviour and values, economic activity, and problems arising from the physical infrastructure or environment which can be related to the trend of political actions

- monitoring indicators of possible or intended future government actions and policy. These indicators are obtained from:

  - annual conferences of political parties

  - public utterances of party leaders and seniors

  - international events

  - directives from international trading groups

  - political commentators and analysts

  - international summit meetings

  - staged legislation

  - efforts of public pressure groups (particularly with regard to local government policy)

  - political manifestos.

### Test your understanding 8

**Required:**

Give some examples of areas of government policy that are likely to affect a multinational electronics company and how the impact will be felt?

## 5.2 The impact of fiscal policy and monetary policy

Fiscal and monetary policies are the tools used by governments to control their economies.

### Fiscal policy

- Looks at the balance between government income (taxation + borrowing) and expenditure.

### Monetary policy

- Is the process by which the government and central bank controls the supply, availability and cost of money.

KAPLAN PUBLISHING

| Fiscal policy | Monetary policy |
|---|---|
| Government adjusts:<br><br>• taxation<br>• public borrowing<br>• public spending. | Government adjusts:<br><br>• money supply<br>• interest rates<br>• exchange rates<br>• availability of credit. |

## Fiscal and monetary policy - more detail

### Fiscal policy

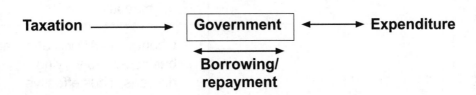

• To stimulate the economy, the government can spend more money. However, if the extra expenditure is met by raising taxes, the public will have less to spend and economic growth will be small. To really get things moving, the government needs to borrow and spend.

• The economy can also be stimulated by cutting tax and allowing individuals to spend more. If government expenditure is cut to match the tax cuts, there will be little stimulation, so government borrowing is needed to keep government spending high.

• Too much economic stimulation is likely to cause inflation as consumers compete for resources and services.

### Monetary policy

Changes in monetary policy will influence the following factors.

• The availability and cost of finance. These in turn affect the level of investment and expenditure by firms.

• The level of consumer demand e.g. low interest rates will stimulate the economy as it is cheaper to borrow and savings do not earn a lot of interest. Similarly, the easy availability of credit also encourages borrowing and spending).

• The level of inflation.

• The level of exchange rates.

## Impact of macroeconomics

In order for macroeconomic policy to work, its instruments must have an impact on economic activity. This means that it must affect the business sector. It does so in two broad forms.

| **Macroeconomic policy will influence the level of aggregate demand (AD) and thus activity in the economy as a whole.**<br><br>(AD is the total demand for goods and services in the economy.) | • The level of AD is central to the determination of the level of unemployment and the rate of inflation.<br>• If AD is too low, unemployment might result; if AD is too high, inflation induced by excess demand might result. |
| --- | --- |
| | • Changes in AD will affect all businesses to varying degrees. Thus effective business planning requires that businesses can:<br>– predict the likely thrust of macroeconomic policy in the short- to medium-term<br>– predict the consequences for sales growth of the overall stance of macroeconomic policy and any likely changes in it.<br>• The more stable government policy is, the easier it is for businesses to plan, especially in terms of investment, employment and future output capacity. |
| **Macroeconomic policy may influence the costs of the business sector.** | • Macroeconomic policy may involve changes in **exchange rates**. This can have the effect of raising the domestic price of imported goods. Most businesses use some imported goods in the production process; hence this leads to a rise in production costs. |

KAPLAN PUBLISHING

- **Fiscal policy** involves the use of **taxation:** changes in tax rates or the structure of taxation will affect businesses. For example, a change in the employer's national insurance contribution will have a direct effect on labour costs for all businesses. Changes in indirect taxes (for example, a rise in sales tax or excise duties) will either have to be absorbed or the business will have to attempt to pass on the tax to its customers.

- **Monetary policy** involves changes in **interest rates**; these changes will directly affect firms in two ways:

  - costs of servicing debts will change especially for highly geared firms

  - the viability of investment will be affected since all models of investment appraisal include the rate of interest as one, if not the main, variable.

### Test your understanding 9

**Required:**

A carpet retailer imports carpets and sells them domestically. The domestic currency does not have a fixed exchange rate with any other currency. What are the likely effects on this business of a rise in domestic interest rates?

**Test your understanding 10**

Suppose the two main political parties in a hypothetical country have the following priorities:

| | Party A<br>(currently in government) | Party B<br>(the opposition) |
|---|---|---|
| Priorities | • Low unemployment | • Low inflation |
| Policy choices | • Fiscal policy<br><br>• Increase government spending to boost demand to create jobs<br><br>• High government intervention in business | • Monetary policy<br><br>• Increase interest rates to reduce inflation<br><br>• Low taxes<br><br>• Low levels of intervention |

Recent polls suggest that Party B could win the next election.

**Required:**

Comment on the implications of this for a major construction company based in the country concerned.

## 6 The impact of government regulation

### 6.1 Introduction

financial regulator ~ Bank

**Regulation** is any form of government interference and is required to ensure that the needs of stakeholders can be met and that businesses act in the public interest.

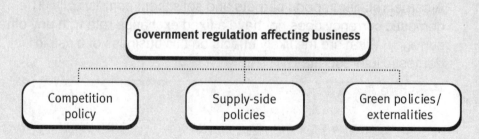

## 6.2 Competition policy

### Monopolies

Most governments consider the disadvantages of monopolies to outweigh the advantages.

| **Disadvantages** to the economy as a whole | Possible **advantages** |
|---|---|
| • Supernormal profits<br>• Economic inefficiency<br>• Monopolies may be able to engage in price discrimination<br>• Disincentive to innovate<br>• Pricing practices | • Large firms may secure economies of scale reducing production costs<br>• The special case of natural monopolies<br>• Research and development (R&D) using profits |

### Disadvantages/advantages of monopolies

**Disadvantages to the economy as a whole:**

- **Supernormal profits:** the lack of competition allows monopolists to charge high prices at the expense of customers.

- **Economic inefficiency:** output is produced at a higher cost than necessary. For example, there may be no incentive to reduce costs by improving technology used.

- **Monopolies may be able to engage in price discrimination:** charging different prices to different customers for the same good or service, e.g. peak and off-peak pricing. This may act against the interests of customers.

- **Disincentive to innovate:** the absence of competition may reduce the incentive to develop new products or new production processes.

- **Pricing practices:** monopolies may adopt pricing practices to make it uneconomic for new firms to enter the industry, thus reducing competition in the long run.

**Possible Advantages:**

- **Large firms may secure economies of scale:** it is possible that there are significant economies of scale, reducing production costs, but that these require large firms and hence the number of firms in an industry is restricted.

- **The special case of natural monopolies:** this is the case where the economies of scale in the provision of some basic infrastructure are so great that only one producer is feasible. This may be the case in the public utilities of energy and water.

- **Research and development (R&D):** it may be that monopoly profits are both the reward for, and the source of finance for, technological and organisational innovation. Thus some static welfare losses have to be accepted in order to ensure a dynamic and innovative business sector.

**Possible government responses to monopolies**:

- The **control of monopolies**, e.g. the UK Competition Act prohibits anti-competitive agreements (such as illegal cartels) and prohibits the abuse of a dominant position.

- **Public regulation.** Many governments tried to increase the efficiency and performance of state-owned monopolies by privatisation, e.g. UK utilities were privatised in the 1980s. Privatisation needs to be controlled through the activities of an industry regulator.

- **Self regulation**, e.g. of the accounting and legal professions.

- **Public provision** through nationalisation, e.g. nationalisation of a number of large UK banks in 2008/09.

### Privatisation

The regulator has to balance the following issues:

- protecting customer interests

- ensuring sufficient investment in infrastructure

- controlling quality (e.g. in the case of water utilities, water quality and the treatment of sewerage)

- ensuring shareholders and other investors achieve a reasonable return

- ensuring that the firm has, or can raise, the necessary funds for investment.

These are usually controlled by:

- setting a limit on price increases

- agreeing investment targets

- putting in place a detailed framework of KPIs that the firm must achieve to retain its licence and to avoid fines.

## Test your understanding 11

**Required:**

Discuss whether and how a regulated water utilities company can improve its ROCE.

### 6.3 Supply-side policies

- Supply-side economists take the view that **the supply of suitable, cost-effective and adequate materials, services and labour is vital to an economy.**

- If these resources are made available, then they will be used to produce goods and services.

- The amounts paid to suppliers and employees will create the extra income necessary to buy the extra outputs.

- For example improving education would increase the supply of educated workers in the workforce.

### Supply side policies examples

Supply-side policies are therefore largely anti-regulation and anti-government interference. For example, supply-side economists would claim that:

- wage regulation prevents the labour market from achieving full employment

- government grants encourage weak businesses

- employment legislation limits risk taking and can lead to over-manning of industries

- high taxes act as a disincentive to work and enterprise and lead ultimately to lower output, employment and wealth.

### 6.4 Green policies/externalities

A **negative externality** is the cost of production experienced by society but not by producers or consumers themselves, for example:

- production, e.g. river pollution from manufacturing

- consumption, e.g. car emissions causing air pollution.

As a result, the government may impose green policies, e.g. an increase in tax on fuel.

## 7 The changing business environment

### 7.1 The relevance of traditional management accounting techniques

**Burns and Scapens** recognised that there have been changes in the environment in which management accountants work, e.g. due to greater globalisation and increased use of IT.

*real time information*

*Budget*

The changes have had a number of implications for the roles and skills of the management accountant:

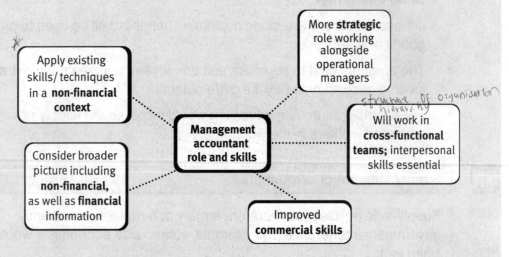

- Apply existing skills/techniques in a **non-financial context**
- More **strategic** role working alongside operational managers
- **Management accountant role and skills**
- Will work in **cross-functional teams;** interpersonal skills essential
- Consider broader picture including **non-financial,** as well as **financial** information
- Improved **commercial skills**

*structure of organisation hierarchy*

### 7.2 Sources of information

There are a number of sources of information for the management accountant who wants to learn about new techniques. For example:

- articles published in professional journals and the press
- studies published in specialised journals
- information provided by professional bodies
- networking and exchanging ideas
- seminars
- tv, radio, books and the Internet.

## Role of a management accountant

A scan of current job advertisements for management accountants would show that they are frequently being asked to:

- inform strategic decisions and formulate business strategies
- lead the organisation's business risk management
- ensure the efficient use of financial and other resources
- advise on ways of improving business performance
- liaise with other managers to put the finance view in context
- train functional and business managers in budget management
- identify the implications of product and service changes
- work in cross-functional teams involved in strategic planning or new product development.

## 8 Risk and uncertainty

### 8.1 Introduction ~~~~ pre pilot paper question ~~~~~~~~~~~~~~~~~~~~~~~~~~

The changing business environment has made it increasingly important for a business to consider risk and uncertainty.

**Risk** is the variability of possible returns. There are a number of possible outcomes and the probability of each outcome is known.

**Uncertainty** also means that there are a number of possible outcomes. However, the probability of each outcome is not known.

All business face risk/uncertainty. Risk management is the process of understanding and managing the risks that an organisation is inevitably subject to.

uncontrollable costs → Head office cost = chapter 8

**Exogenous variables** are variables that do not originate from within the organisation itself and are not controllable by management, e.g. government policy. Their existence means that strategic planning will always be subject to some risk and uncertainty.

rewards system

## The impact of exogenous variables

A hospital has developed a new surgical technique as a more expensive alternative to existing treatments. It is considering whether to begin to provide the treatment to all its patients, which would mean building a new facility. In order to inform the decision, the hospital is considering the likely effect of a number of variables.

- The likelihood that another alternative cheaper treatment, either a surgical technique or a drug regime, will be discovered.

- The likelihood that other hospitals will begin to offer similar services which will limit demand.

- Government policy – changes in the way that treatment is funded and therefore whether the costs of the treatment will be paid for.

## 8.2 Dealing with risk/uncertainty

A number of tools can be used to incorporate the impact of risk/uncertainty.

| Tool | Explanation |
|---|---|
| Scenario planning | Looks at a number of different but plausible future situations. For example, Shell was the only major oil company to have prepared for the shock of the 1970s oil crisis through scenario planning and was able to respond faster than its competitors. |
| Computer simulations | A modelling technique which shows the effect of more than one variable changing at a time and gives management a view of the likely range and level of outcomes so that a more informed decision can be taken. |
| Sensitivity analysis | Takes each uncertain factor in turn, and calculates the change that would be necessary in that factor before the original decision is reversed. |
| Expected values (EVs) | Shows the weighted average of all possible outcomes. |
| Maximax, maximin and minimax regret | These are three different tools for incorporating risk/uncertainty. The attitude of management towards risk will determine which of the three tools is used. |

EVs and maximin, maximax and minimax regret will be explored in more detail below.

### 8.3 Expected values (EVs)

The formula for expected values is: **EV = ∑px**

where: x = the value of the possible outcome

p = the probability of the possible outcome.

| Illustration 6 - Simple EV calculation |
| --- |

Returns from a new restaurant depend on whether a company decides to open in the same area. The following estimates are made:

| Competitor opens up | Probability (p) | Project NPV (x) | px |
| --- | --- | --- | --- |
| Yes | 0.30 | ($10,000) | ($3,000) |
| No | 0.70 | $20,000 | $14,000 |
| | | | **$11,000** |

The EV = ∑px = $11,000. Since the expected value shows the long run average outcome of a decision which is repeated time and time again, it is a useful decision rule for a risk neutral decision maker. This is because a **risk neutral decision maker** neither seeks or avoids risk; he is happy to accept the average outcome.

### Pay-off (profit) tables

A pay-off (profit) table is useful for calculating EVs when there is a range of possible outcomes and a variety of possible responses.

| Illustration 7 - Simple pay-off (profit) table |
| --- |

Geoffrey Ramsbottom runs a kitchen that provides food for various canteens throughout a large organisation. A particular salad generates a profit of $2. Daily demand is as follows:

| Demand | Probability | |
| --- | --- | --- |
| 40 salads | 0.10 | 4 |
| 50 salads | 0.20 | 10 |
| 60 salads | 0.40 | 24 |
| 70 salads | 0.30 | 21 |
| | 1.00 | |

**Required:**

The kitchen must prepare the salad in batches of 10. Its staff have asked you to help them decide how many salads it should supply per day.

**Answer:**

There are a range of possible outcomes (levels of demand) and a variety of possible responses (number of salads to supply) and therefore it is useful to construct a payoff table:

| Daily demand | Prob (p) | Daily supply profit/(loss) outcome (x) | | | |
|---|---|---|---|---|---|
| | | 40 salads | 50 salads | 60 salads | 70 salads |
| 40 salads | 0.10 | $80 (w1) | $0 | ($80) | ($160) |
| 50 salads | 0.20 | $80 | $100 | $20 | ($60) |
| 60 salads | 0.40 | $80 | $100 | $120 | $40 |
| 70 salads | 0.30 | $80 | $100 | $120 | $140 |
| | | ——— | ——— | ——— | ——— |
| | EV = | $80 | $90 | $80 | $30 (w2) |
| | | ——— | ——— | ——— | ——— |

**Workings:**

(W1) Profit is calculated as follows = 40 salads × $2 = **$80**

(W2) EV is calculated as follows = (0.10 × –$160) + (0.20 × –$60) + (0.40 × $40) + (0.30 × $140) = **$30**

**Conclusion:**

Therefore, based on EVs, daily supply should be **50 salads** since this yields the highest expected value of $90.

In the illustration above, there was only one variable outcome, i.e. the level of demand. However, in some situations there may be more than one variable outcome, e.g. demand and inflation. In this case, a **two way data table** should be prepared before the EV is calculated.

### Test your understanding 12

*Homework*

Confused Company is seeking to establish the likely profit to be generated from the forthcoming year. This is very much dependent upon the anticipated demand, and the impact of inflation upon the fixed costs of the business.

Probabilities have been estimated for both demand and inflation as shown below.

| Demand | Probability | Inflation | Probability |
|--------|-------------|-----------|-------------|
| Strong | 0.20 | None | 0.30 |
| Normal | 0.50 | 2% | 0.50 |
| Weak | 0.30 | 4% | 0.20 |

A **two way data table** has been prepared which estimates the changes in net profit (in $) for a range of changes in demand and inflation:

| | | Inflation | | | | |
|--------|--------|--------|--------|--------|--------|--------|
| | | None | 1% | 2% | 3% | 4% |
| **Demand** | Strong | 95,000 | 85,000 | 75,000 | 65,000 | 55,000 |
| | Normal | 60,000 | 50,000 | 40,000 | 30,000 | 20,000 |
| | Weak | 25,000 | 15,000 | 5,000 | (5,000) | (15,000) |

### Required:

Prepare a summary that shows:

- the range of possible net profit and loss outcomes
- the combined probability of each outcome
- the expected value of the profit for the year.

Management will be awarded a bonus if profit exceeds $50,000. What are the chances of this occurring?

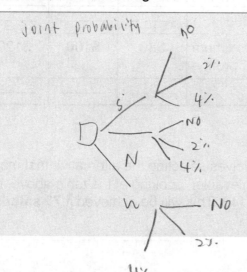

## 8.4 Maximax, maximin and minimax regret

The **maximax rule** involves selecting the alternative that maximises the maximum pay-off achievable.

The **maximin rule** involves selecting the alternative that maximises the minimum pay-off achievable.

The **minimax regret** strategy is the one that minimises the maximum regret, i.e. the opportunity loss through having made the wrong decision.

### Illustration 8 - Geoffrey Ramsbottom

**Required:**

Using the information from illustration 7 decide how many salads should be supplied per day using:

(a)  the maximax rule

(b)  the maximin rule

(c)  the minimax regret rule.

**Answer:**

(a)  **Maximax**

| | | Daily supply profit/(loss) outcome (x) | | | |
|---|---|---|---|---|---|
| **Daily demand** | **Prob (p)** | **40 salads** | **50 salads** | **60 salads** | **70 salads** |
| 40 salads | 0.10 | $80 | $0 | ($80) | ($160) |
| 50 salads | 0.20 | $80 | $100 | $20 | ($60) |
| 60 salads | 0.40 | $80 | $100 | $120 | $40 |
| 70 salads | 0.30 | $80 | $100 | $120 | $140 |
| | | ——— | ——— | ——— | ——— |
| | Maximum profit = | $80 | $100 | $120 | **$140** |
| | | ——— | ——— | ——— | ——— |

The maximax rule involves selecting the alternative that maximises the maximum pay-off achievable.  Looking at the table above, the maximum profit achievable is $140. This will be achieved if **70 salads** are supplied.

## (b) Maximin

| Daily demand | Prob (p) | Daily supply profit/(loss) outcome (x) | | | |
|---|---|---|---|---|---|
| | | 40 salads | 50 salads | 60 salads | 70 salads |
| 40 salads | 0.10 | $80 | $0 | ($80) | ($160) |
| 50 salads | 0.20 | $80 | $100 | $20 | ($60) |
| 60 salads | 0.40 | $80 | $100 | $120 | $40 |
| 70 salads | 0.30 | $80 | $100 | $120 | $140 |
| | | ____ | ____ | ____ | ____ |
| | Minimum profit = | **$80** | $0 | ($80) | ($160) |
| | | ____ | ____ | ____ | ____ |

The minimax rule involves selecting the alternative that maximises the minimum pay-off achievable. Looking at the table above, the maximum of the minimum profits is $80. This will be achieved if **40 salads** are supplied.

## (c) Minimax regret

The minimax regret strategy is the one that minimises the maximum regret (opportunity cost). A regret table should be used:

| Daily demand | Daily supply regret (opportunity cost) | | | |
|---|---|---|---|---|
| | 40 salads | 50 salads | 60 salads | 70 salads |
| 40 salads | Right decision | $80 (w1) | $160 (w1) | $240 (w1) |
| 50 salads | $20 | Right decision | $80 | $160 |
| 60 salads | $40 | $20 | Right decision | $80 |
| 70 salads | $60 | $40 | $20 | Right decision |
| | ____ | ____ | ____ | ____ |
| Maximum regret = | **$60** | $80 | $160 | $240 |
| | ____ | ____ | ____ | ____ |

Therefore, to minimise the maximum regret, **40 salads** should be supplied.

**W1**: If daily demand is 40 salads, it would be the right decision for the business to supply 40 salads since the profit of supplying 40 salads is the highest, i.e. $80.

- If the business decided instead to supply 50 salads, the regret (opportunity cost) would be the $80 it could have made supplying 40 salads minus the $0 it did make supplying the 50 salads = $80.

- If the business decided instead to supply 60 salads, the regret (opportunity cost) would be the $80 it could have made supplying 40 salads minus the $80 loss it did make supplying the 60 salads = $160.

- If the business decided instead to supply 70 salads, the regret (opportunity cost) would be the $80 it could have made supplying 40 salads minus the $160 loss it did make supplying the 70 salads = $240.

**Risk seekers** are optimists and will aim to maximise the possible returns from the different scenarios. The **maximax** method would be appropriate in this situation.

**Risk averse** decision makers are pessimists and will aim to maximise the minimum possible returns from the different scenarios. The **maximin** method would be appropriate in this situation.

### Test your understanding 13

Stow Health Centre specialises in the provision of exercise and dietary advice to clients. The service is provided on a residential basis and clients stay for whatever number of days suits their needs.

Budgeted estimates for the year ending 30 June 20X9 are as follows:

- The maximum capacity of the centre is 50 clients per day for 350 days in the year.

- Clients will be invoiced at a fee per day. The budgeted occupancy level will vary with the client fee level per day and is estimated at different percentages of maximum capacity as follows:

| Client fee per day | Occupancy level | Occupancy as percentage of maximum capacity |
|---|---|---|
| $180 | High | 90% |
| $200 | Most likely | 75% |
| $220 | Low | 60% |

- Variable costs are also estimated at one of three levels per client day. The high, medium and low levels per client day are $95, $85 and $70 respectively.

The range of cost levels reflects only the possible effect of the purchase prices of goods and services.

**Required:**

(a) Prepare a summary which shows the budgeted contribution earned by Stow Health Centre for the year ended 30 June 20X9 for each of nine possible outcomes.

(b) State the client fee strategy for the year to 30 June 20X9 which will result from the use of each of the following decision rules:

–   maximax

–   maximin

–   minimax regret.

Your answer should explain the basis of operation of each rule. Use the information from your answer to (a) as relevant and show any additional working calculations as necessary.

## 8.5 Risk appetite of stakeholders  ~~risk alignment~~

Stakeholders will have different appetites for risk. For example:

- **Shareholders** - investing in shares is often viewed as risky since there is no guaranteed return. However, shareholders can choose their investments and can spread their risk by holding a portfolio of investments.

- **Employees and managers** - they should act in the best interests of the shareholders but this does not always happen since they may be:

    - **risk averse**: employees and managers may be reluctant to take risks, e.g. to invest in a new project, if an unsuccessful outcome would impact their performance evaluation or the survival of the company (and hence their job). Therefore, even though risk taking may be in the best interests of the company and its shareholders they tend to exercise caution and are unwilling to take risks.

    - **risk seeking**: employees and managers may be encouraged to take risks by the promise of huge rewards or bonuses.

### e.g  Illustration 9 - Risk appetite of employees

In 2008, the governor of the bank of England, Mervyn King, criticised City banks who rewarded staff with huge sums for taking risks and concluded that the credit crisis was caused by bankers betting on high-risk complex financial products.

# Chapter summary

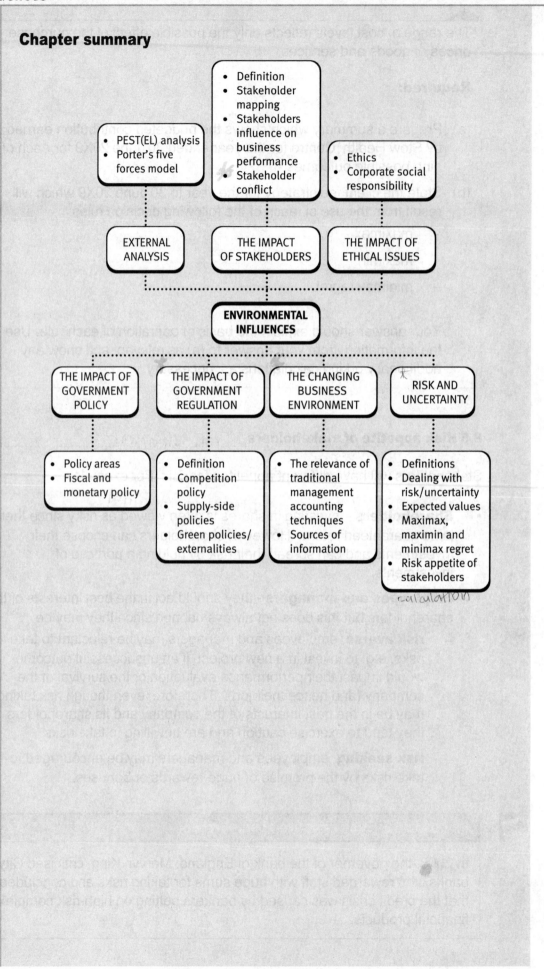

## Test your understanding answers

### Test your understanding 1

#### PEST(EL) Analysis for UK railways

**Political**

The balance of public - private involvement in the running costs and capital investment for rail development is a major issue

**Economic**

The growth of commuter travel on the rail system means it is working at close to full capacity. This trend is likely to continue with the rising costs of fuel, making car travel expensive.

There is a need for investment in infrastructure in areas such as longer platforms and new signal systems. Financing this investment may be difficult.

**Social**

Increasing concerns about reliability, particularly in rural areas.

Concerns about the effect that railway construction and travel has on the environment.

Safety issues on trains and at railway stations.

**Technological**

The development of new train technologies such as the tilting train.

Also following the trends set by air travel by introducing ways to improve the customer experience. For example, offering Internet access and on-train entertainment.

**Environmental**

Environmental impact of major infrastructure developments is a key issue.

**Legal**

The legal framework for the regulation and power of the railways is a major issue for operators.

### Conclusion

Overall, the switch to rail travel is seen to have a positive environmental impact, reducing the congestion and pollution associated with car based travel.

### Porter's five forces model - UK railways

### Competitive rivalry

In certain areas rail operators may be directly competing over the same routes.

### Threats from substitutes

There are other forms of transport available such as travel by road (e.g. cars and buses) and travel by air.

### Buyers' bargaining power

Severe competition over price with low-cost airlines on longer city routes.

Online price comparisons make it easy for customers to select lowest cost option.

### Threat from potential entrants

New companies may enter the market when rail franchises become available for re-tender. For example, Virgin entered the UK market some years ago.

### Suppliers' bargaining power

With an increasing number of discrete rail and train operators, the allocation of capacity becomes an issue. This is similar to landing slots at airports.

## Test your understanding 2

### Loyal customers

Chatman Theatre, which is a charity, can use of a database to profile their interests and wants. A tailored communication can then be sent.

Given the need to contain costs, this might be by getting customers to sign up to e-list to get up-to-date news and information on future performances.

They could set up a website with booking facilities and send confirmation by email rather than post.

Develop a friend of the theatre group, giving discounts to regular loyal customers.

### First time customers

The website could be linked to other relevant websites, such as local attractions and tourist boards, to attract new customers.

The theatre could produce an information pack to attract new mailing list subscribers. These could be made available in local churches and shops.

### Local arts groups

A partnership agreement could be established with arts groups, to co-sponsor events of special interest to given groups of customers.

### Local organisations

Try to obtain commercial sponsorship from local companies. Acknowledgement could be given in the monthly programme mailings and preferential facilities offered for corporate hospitality.

### Media

Personal invitations could be issued to opening nights, to interview the performers and give an overview of the show.

**Note:** The above is just a selection of potential relationships with stakeholders.

## Test your understanding 3

- **Whether or not the museum should charge an entry fee** – this would discourage some people from going to the museum (compromising the first objective) but would provide extra cash for funding research.

- **Which artefacts should be displayed** – education would require a wide range of exhibits with the most prestigious on display. An emphasis on preservation would prevent the most significant items from being displayed for fear of damage.

## Test your understanding 4

- Ethical behaviour is likely to be favoured by:
    - customers: resulting in higher sales volumes and/or prices.

    - employees: resulting in the attraction/retention of the best employees and increased employee productivity.

    - business collaborators: resulting in increased opportunities for profitable projects.

- Ethical behaviour reduces risk and gives access to cheaper funds which in turn increase project NPVs.

- Unethical behaviour will, at some point be discovered resulting in a damage to reputation and potential legal charges.

## Test your understanding 5

- The purpose of a business is to make profits. Profit is a good thing in its own right as it supports stable employment, innovation, allows higher taxes to be paid and makes economies richer. Companies have no need to feel guilty about making profits and buying off some of that guilt by embarking on good works.

- The prime stakeholders are the shareholders and directors should always attempt to maximise shareholder wealth. If directors embark on a CSR programme, have shareholders given permission? It is, after all, shareholders' money that is being used.

- CSR allows directors to feel generous and righteous – but with someone else's money. Better, perhaps, that directors and shareholders make private donations out of their remuneration and dividends.

- What is the democratic basis which companies use to choose between CSR projects? Simply choosing a project because the chief executive likes it does not mean the money is being well spent – the project could be already well-funded.

## Test your understanding 6

Suitable metrics could include:

- number of fatalities

- number of permanently disabling injuries

- number of enforcement actions

- accident frequency rate (AFR) e.g. the number of reportable accidents per 100,000 hours worked

- lost time incident frequency rate (LTIFR)

- sickness absence rate

- health and safety training rate (days/employee)

- percentage of employees working within an ISO 18001 compliant Health and Safety Management System.

**Test your understanding 7**

Governments can act as an aid to business performance in the following ways:

- A government can increase aggregate demand for goods and services by increased government spending and/or by reducing taxation so that firms (and individuals) have more income available to spend.

- Government policy may encourage firms to locate in particular areas. This is particularly the case where there is high unemployment in such areas.

- Government policy via the use of quotas and import tariffs might make it more difficult for overseas firms to compete in domestic markets.

- A government can regulate monopolies in particular with regard to the prices they charge and the quality of their goods and services.

- Government policy can regulate the activities of those firms which do not act in the best interests of the environment.

## Test your understanding 8

Areas could include:

### Interest rates

Changes in the interest rates for consumer debt may affect demand for luxury goods which may include high-value electronic products.

The company's cost of debt may change, affecting the cost of developing new facilities.

### Exchange rates

Changes in interest rates may change the value of profits earned in different countries or the price to consumers of imported goods.

### Taxation levels

The level of personal taxation will affect the demand for products. Changes in the company tax regime will affect the returns to shareholders.

### Incentive schemes

The availability of incentive schemes may make expanding into certain countries more attractive.

### Worker protection

Legislation in this area may have an impact on the requirements for facilities and their costs.

### Restrictive practices

These may affect the company's ability to export to certain countries.

### Environment protection

The company may need to develop new products which are more economical to run or which use materials which are less harmful to the environment when thrown away.

## Test your understanding 9

(1) Customers' mortgages and loans will become more expensive, giving less net disposable income for major purchases, such as new carpets.

(2) Customers will be less ready to borrow to finance carpet purchase.

(3) The cost of capital will rise so the retailer will be less prepared to undertake major projects.

(4) The domestic currency will strengthen, reducing the cost of imports.

## Test your understanding 10

- Higher interest rates will increase the cost of borrowing and the gearing risk of the firm, making it less likely that long-term earnings targets will be met.

- A fall in government spending could see a downturn in orders, particularly if the firm currently is engaged in government contracts (e.g. building roads, hospitals). Future plans may have to be revised to reflect this and alternative strategies sought. Analysis of sales mix between public and private sector contracts will become more important.

- Potentially lower levels of taxation could increase profitability.

- Lower inflation will reduce business uncertainty, making planning easier. Plans may have to be revised to reflect lower inflation.

- Higher unemployment in the economy could allow the firm to reduce planned pay increases.

**Test your understanding 11**

Depending on the degree of regulation in the country concerned the firm could find it difficult to improve performance due to the following:

- It may be difficult to win new customers as the firm already has a regional monopoly.

- Price rises will probably be capped by the regulator.

- Minimum spending plans will be agreed with the regulator. These could be delayed to boost short-term ROCE.

- The formula for calculating ROCE will probably be set by the regulator (e.g. calculation of depreciation, definition of capital employed, adjustments for inflation).

- Quality targets make it difficult to cut corners to reduce operating costs.

These emphasise the importance of negotiating a 'good deal' with the regulator when spending plans are agreed.

The company should also look to developing non-core activities (though these may also be regulated).

- Water sports facilities, such as sailing.

- Whether land could be developed, e.g. building apartments.

## Test your understanding 12

| Possible demand | Possible inflation | Net profit \$ = x | Combined prob = p | px (\$) | Bonus prob (profit > \$50,000) |
|---|---|---|---|---|---|
| Strong (prob = 0.20) | None (prob 0.30) | 95,000 | 0.20 × 0.30 = 0.06 | 5,700 | 0.06 |
| | 2% (prob = 0.50) | 75,000 | 0.20 × 0.50 = 0.10 | 7,500 | 0.10 |
| | 4% (prob = 0.20) | 55,000 | 0.20 × 0.20 = 0.04 | 2,200 | 0.04 |
| Normal (prob = 0.50) | None (prob 0.30) | 60,000 | 0.50 × 0.30 = 0.15 | 9,000 | 0.15 |
| | 2% (prob = 0.50) | 40,000 | 0.50 × 0.050 = 0.25 | 10,000 | – |
| | 4% (prob = 0.20) | 20,000 | 0.50 × 0.20 = 0.10 | 2,000 | – |
| Weak (prob = 0.30) | None (prob 0.30) | 25,000 | 0.30 × 0.30 = 0.09 | 2,250 | – |
| | 2% (prob = 0.50) | 5,000 | 0.30 × 0.50 = 0.15 | 750 | – |
| | 4% (prob = 0.20) | (15,000) | 0.30 × 0.20 = 0.06 | (900) | – |
| | | | | | |
| | | | EV = $\sum$px | **38,500** | **0.35** |
| | | | | | |

KAPLAN PUBLISHING

### Test your understanding 13

(a) **Summary of budgeted contribution**

|  | Occupancy level and fee | | |
|---|---|---|---|
| **Variable cost** | **High 90% (fee $180)** | **Most likely 75% (fee $200)** | **Low 60% (fee $220)** |
| $95 | $1,338,750 | $1,378,125 | $1,312,500 |
| $85 | $1,496,250 | $1,509,375 | $1,417,500 |
| $70 | $1,732,500 | $1,706,250 | $1,575,000 |
|  | ——— | ——— | ——— |
| Max contn = | **$1,732,500** | $1,706,250 | $1,575,000 |
| Min contn = | $1,338,750 | **$1,378,125** | $1,312,500 |

**W1:** Number of clients = 50 per day × 350 days × 90% = 15,750 per year.

Contribution = ($180 × 15,750 clients) – ($95 × 15,750) = $1,338,750.

(b) **Maximax**

The client fee should be **$180** since this maximises the maximum return at $1,732,500.

**Maximin**

The client fee should be **$200** since this maximises the minimum return at $1,378,125.

## Minimax regret

A regret table should be produced:

| Variable cost | Occupancy level and fee | | |
| :---: | :---: | :---: | :---: |
| | High 90% (fee $180) | Most likely 75% (fee $200) | Low 60% (fee $220) |
| $95 | $39,375 (w2) | Right decision | $65,625 |
| $85 | $13,125 | Right decision | $91,875 |
| $70 | Right decision | $26,250 | $157,500 |
| | —— | —— | —— |
| Max regret = | $39,375 | **$26,250** | $157,500 |
| | —— | —— | —— |

The client fee should be **$200** since this minimises the maximum regret at $26,250.

**W2**: Regret (opportunity cost) = $1,378,125 – $1,338,750 = $39,375.

# 3

*Exam topic*
*Evaluation*      *How to control*

*Shell*

*let bygone be bygone*

# Approaches to budgets

## Chapter learning objectives

Upon completion of this chapter you will be able to:

- evaluate the strengths and weaknesses of alternative budgeting models and compare such techniques as fixed and flexible, rolling, activity based, zero based and incremental   *3 Es*

- assess how budgeting may differ in not-for-profit organisations from profit-seeking organisations   *chapter 9*

- *evaluate the impact to an organisation of a move to 'beyond budgeting'*   *article*

- discuss and evaluate the application of activity-based management.

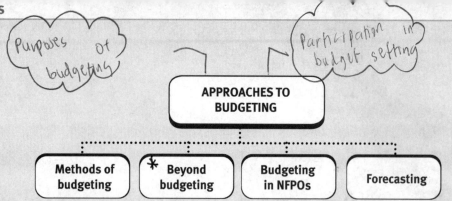

Purposes of budgeting

Participation in budget setting

APPROACHES TO BUDGETING

| Methods of budgeting | * Beyond budgeting | Budgeting in NFPOs | Forecasting |

## 1 Exam focus

| Exam sitting | Area examined | Question number | Number of marks |
|---|---|---|---|
| December 2010 | ABC vs absorption costing | 2(a) | 15 |
| December 2010 | Beyond budgeting | 2(b) | 10 |
| June 2010 | ABC and ABM | 4 | 20 |
| June 2010 | Calculation of budgeted net profit/(loss) | 2(a) | 7 |
| December 2009 | Preparation of budgeted and actual income statement | 1(i) | 10 |
| December 2009 | Beyond budgeting | 2(a) | 14 |
| December 2008 | ABC and ABM | 5(a)(c) | 14 |
| June 2008 | Problems with budgeting | 2 | 24 |
| December 2007 | Forecasting | 3(a) | 5 |
| December 2007 | ABC | 4(b)(c) | 15 |
| Pilot paper | Actual vs budget comparison | 1(a) | 14 |
| Pilot paper | Uses of budgeting | 5 | 8 |
| Pilot paper | Advantages of ABB | 5 | 6 |
| Pilot paper | Reasons for beyond budgeting | 5 | 6 |

**Student Accountant articles**: visit the ACCA website, www.accaglobal.com, to review the following article on the topic in this chapter:

Beyond budgeting - March 2005

## 2 Introduction

*limitation- outdated*

A **budget** is a quantitative plan prepared for a specific time period. It is normally expressed in financial terms and prepared for one year.

Budgeting serves a number of purposes:

- Planning *- budget compels planning*
- Control *- senior management*
- Communication
- Co-ordination *- between departments "= goal congruence"*
- Evaluation *- responsibility + accountability*
- Motivation *- sales staff*
- Authorisation *- senior management*
- Delegation *- responsibility*

*abc + absorption budgeting*
*standard costing + variances*
*forecasting*

### Purposes of budgeting

Budgeting serves a number of purposes:

#### Planning

A budgeting process forces the business to look into the future. This is essential for survival since it stops management from relying on ad hoc or poorly co-ordinated planning.

#### Control

Actual results are compared against the budget and action is taken as appropriate.

#### Communication

The budget is a formal communication channel that allows junior and senior staff to converse.

#### Co-ordination

The budget allows co-ordination of all parts of the business towards a common corporate goal.

### Evaluation

Responsibility accounting divides the organisation into budget centres, each of which has a manager who is responsible for its performance. The budget may be used to evaluate the actions of a manager within the business in terms of costs and revenues over which they have control.

### Motivation

The budget may be used as a target for managers to aim for. Rewards should be given for operating within or under budgeted levels of expenditure. This acts as a motivator for managers.

### Authorisation

The budget acts as a formal method of authorisation for a manager for expenditure, hiring staff and the pursuit of plans contained within the budget.

### Delegation

Managers may be involved in setting the budget. Extra responsibility may motivate managers. Management involvement may also result in more realistic targets.

*\* Evaluation*

## 3 Methods of budgeting

Different approaches to budgeting have been studied in paper F5. Section 3 of this chapter is thus primarily a recap of 'deemed' knowledge.

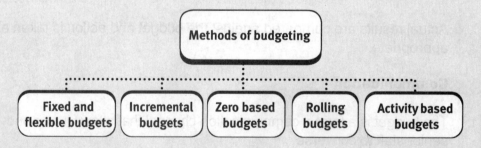

### 3.1 Fixed and flexible budgeting

**A fixed budget** is a budget prepared at a single level of activity.

**A flexible budget** is a budget prepared with the cost behaviour of all cost elements known and classified as either fixed or variable. The budget may be prepared at a number of activity levels and can be 'flexed' or changed to the actual level of activity for budgetary control purposes.

*IR 100, 200*

## Test your understanding 1

A company has the following budgeted and actual information for a department.

*operational gearing*
*fixed cost → variable cost*

|  | Budget | Actual |
|---|---|---|
| Level of activity (units of output) | 1,000 | 1,200 |
| Cost ($) | 20,000 | 23,000 |

*10*  *24*  *1300*

**Required:**

(a) Assuming all costs are variable, has the company done better or worse than expected?   *Better*

(b) If $10,000 of the budgeted costs are fixed costs, the remainder being variable, has the company performed better or worse than expected?   *worse   10.83*

| Advantages | Disadvantages |
|---|---|
| Should enable better performance evaluation as comparing like with like. | • May be perceived by some as 'moving the goal posts' resulting in demotivation – especially if bonuses are lost despite beating the original budget.<br>• Difficulties splitting costs into fixed and variable elements.<br>• In the long run it could be argued that all costs are variable. |

## Test your understanding 2

Redfern hospital is a government funded hospital in the country of Newland. Relevant cost data for the year ended 31 December 20X0 are as follows:

(1) Salary costs per staff member were payable as follows:

|  | Budget ($) | Actual ($) |
|---|---|---|
| Doctors *(60)* | 100,000 | 105,000 ↑ 5000 |
| Nurses *(150)* | 37,000 | 34,500 ↓ 2500 |

Budgeted and actual staff were 60 doctors and 150 nurses.

(2) Budgeted costs for the year based on 20,000 patients per annum were as follows:

| | $ | Variable cost (%) | Fixed cost (%) |
|---|---|---|---|
| Other staff costs | 1,440,000 | 100 | - |
| Catering | 200,000 | 70 | 30 |
| Cleaning | 80,000 | 35 | 65 52 |
| Other operating costs | 1,200,000 | 30 | 70 840 |
| Depreciation | 80,000 | - | 100 |

Variable costs vary according to the number of patients.

(3) The actual number of patients for the year was 23,750. Actual costs (excluding the cost of doctors and nurses) incurred during the year were as follows:

| | | $ |
|---|---|---|
| Other staff costs | 1710 | 1,500,000 |
| Catering | 226 250 | 187,500 |
| Cleaning | | 142,000 |
| Other operating costs | | 1,050,000 |
| Depreciation | | 80,000 |

**Required:**

Prepare a statement which shows the actual and budgeted costs for Redfern hospital in respect of the year ended 31 December 20X0 on a comparable basis.

## 3.2 Incremental budgets

*inefficient use of resources*

An **incremental budget** starts with the previous period's budget or actual results, and adds (or subtracts) an incremental amount to cover inflation and other known changes.

### Suitability

- It is suitable for stable businesses, where costs are not expected to change significantly.

- There should be good cost control.

- There should be limited discretionary costs.

| Advantages | Disadvantages |
|---|---|
| • Quickest and easiest method.<br>• Assuming that the historic figures are acceptable, only the increment needs to be justified.<br>• Avoids 'reinventing the wheel'. | • Builds in previous problems and inefficiencies.<br>• Uneconomic activities may be continued. |

-IT, pharmaceutical => dynamic environment

## Incremental approach to budgets

AW produces two products, A and C. In the last year (20X4) it produced 640 units of A and 350 units of C incurring costs of $672,000. Analysis of the costs has shown that 75% of the total costs are variable. 60% of these variable costs vary in line with the number of A produced and the remainder with the number of C.

The budget for the year 20X5 is now being prepared using an incremental budgeting approach. The following additional information is available for 20X5:

- All costs will be 4% higher than the average paid in 20X4.
- Efficiency levels will remain unchanged.
- Expected output of A is 750 units and of C is 340 units.

**Required:**

What is the budgeted total variable cost of product C (to the nearest $100) for the full year 20X5?

**Solution:**

**20X4 costs:**

| | | |
|---|---|---|
| Total variable costs | = 75% x $672,000 | = $504,000 |
| Proportion relating to product C | = 40% x $504,000 | = $201,600 |
| Cost per unit of product C | = $201,600/350 | = $576 |

**20X5 budget costs:**

| | | |
|---|---|---|
| Inflated cost per unit of C | = 1.04 x $576 | = $599.04 |
| Total variable cost for product C | = 340 x $599.04 | = $203,674 |

i.e. $203,700 to nearest $100.

## Test your understanding 3

The NW Entertainments Company (NWEC) is a privately owned organisation which operates an amusement park in a rural area within the North West region of a country which has a good climate all year round. The amusement park comprises a large fairground with high-quality rides and numerous attractions designed to appeal to people of all ages.

The park is open for 365 days in the year.

Each day spent by a guest at the park is classed as a 'Visitor Day'. During the year ended 30 November 20X3 a total of 2,090,400 visitor days were paid for and were made up as follows:

| Visitor category | % of total visitor days |
|---|---|
| Adults | 40 |
| 14–18 years of age and Senior Citizens | 20 |
| Under 14 years of age | 40 |

Two types of admission pass are available for purchase, these are:

The 'One-day Visitor's pass' and the 'Two-day Visitor's pass', which entitles the holder of the pass to admission to the amusement park on any two days within the year commencing 1 December.

The pricing structure was as follows:

(i)   The cost of a One-day pass for an adult was $40. Visitors aged 14–18 years and Senior Citizens receive a 25% discount against the cost of adult passes. Visitors aged below 14 years receive a 50% discount against the cost of adult passes.

(ii)  The purchase of a Two-day Visitor's pass gave the purchaser a 25% saving against the cost of two One-day Visitor's passes.

(iii) 25% of the total visitor days were paid for by the purchase of One-day passes. The remainder were paid for by the purchase of Two-day passes.

Total operating costs of the park during the year amounted to $37,600,000.

NWEC receives income from traders who provide catering and other facilities to visitors to the amusement park. There are 30 such traders from whom payments are received. The amount of the payment made by each trader is dependent upon the size of the premises that they occupy in the amusement park as shown in the following summary:

KAPLAN PUBLISHING

| Size of premises | No of Annual Traders | Payment per Trader |
|---|---|---|
| | | $ |
| Large | 8 | 54,000 |
| Medium | 12 | 36,000 |
| Small | 10 | 18,000 |

The income from each trader is received under 3 year contracts which became effective on 1 December 20X3. The income is fixed for the duration of each contract.

All operating costs of the park incurred during the year ending 30 November 20X4 are expected to increase by 4%. This has led to a decision by management to increase the selling price of all categories of admission passes by 4% with effect from 1 December 20X3. Management expect the number of visitor days, visitor mix and the mix of admission passes purchased to be the same as in the previous year.

NWEC also own a 400 bedroom hotel with leisure facilities, which is located 20 kilometres from the amusement park.

During the year ended 30 November 20X3, the charge per room on an all-inclusive basis was $100 per room, per night. The total operating costs of the hotel amounted to $7,950,000. Average occupancy during the year was 240 rooms per night. The hotel is open for 365 days in the year.

It is anticipated that the operating costs of the hotel will increase by 4% in the year ending 30 November 20X4. Management have decided to increase the charge per room, per night by 4% with effect from 1 December 20X3 and expect average occupancy will remain at the same level during the year ending 30 November 20X4.

The revenue of the hotel is independent of the number of visitors to the amusement park.

**Required:**

Prepare a statement showing the budgeted net profit or loss for the year to 30 November 20X4.

*not bother with previous budget ( new every year)*

## 3.3 Zero based budgets → *Efficient resource use*
*useful for public sector*

**Zero based budgeting** (ZBB) is a method of budgeting that requires each cost element to be specifically justified, as though the activities to which the budget relates were being undertaken for the first time. Without approval, the budget allowance is zero.

*every spend has to be justified*

### Suitability

- Fast moving businesses/industries
- Discretionary costs such as research and development (R&D).
- Public sector organisations such as local authorities.   council

### ZBB process

There are four distinct stages in the implementation of ZBB:

(1) Managers should <u>specify for their responsibility centre</u>s those activities that can be individually evaluated.

(2) Each of the individual activities is then described in a decision package. The decision package should <u>state the costs and revenues expected from the given activity</u>. It should be drawn up in such a way that the package can be evaluated and ranked against other packages.

(3) Each decision package is <u>evaluated and ranked usually using cost/benefit analysis</u>.

(4) The resources are then <u>allocated to the various packages</u>.

> ### ZBB
>
> A decision package was defined by Peter Pyhrr (who first formulated the ZBB approach at Texas Instruments) as:
>
> 'A document that identifies and describes a specific activity in such a manner that senior management can:
>
> A   evaluate it and rank it against other activities competing for limited resources and
>
> B   decide whether to approve or disapprove it.'
>
> A decision package is a document that does the following:
>
> - Analyses the cost of the activity. (Costs may be built up from a zero base, but costing information can be obtained from historical records or last year's budget.)
> - States the purpose of the activity.
> - Identifies alternative methods of achieving the same purpose.
> - Assesses the consequence of not doing the activity at all, or performing the activity at a different level.
> - Establishes measures of performance for the activity.

Pyhrr identifies two types of package:

I    Mutually-exclusive packages. These contain different methods of obtaining the same objective.

II   Incremental packages. These divide the activity into a number of different levels of activity. The base package describes the minimum effort and cost that is needed to carry out the activity. The other packages describe the incremental costs and benefits when added to the base.

## ZBB exercise

A company is conducting a ZBB exercise, and a decision package is being prepared for its materials-handling operations.

- The manager responsible has identified a base package for the minimum resources needed to perform the materials-handling function. This is to have a team of five workers and a supervisor, operating without any labour-saving machinery. The estimated annual cost of wages and salaries, with overtime, would be $375,000.

- In addition to the base package, the manager has identified an incremental package. The company could lease two forklift trucks at a cost of $20,000 each year. This would provide a better system because materials could be stacked higher and moved more quickly. Health and safety risks for the workers would be reduced, and there would be savings of $5,000 each year in overtime payments.

- Another incremental package has been prepared, in which the company introduces new computer software to plan materials-handling schedules. The cost of buying and implementing the system would be $60,000, but the benefits are expected to be improvements in efficiency that reduce production downtime and result in savings of $10,000 each year in overtime payments.

The base package would be considered essential, and so given a high priority. The two incremental packages should be evaluated and ranked. Here, the forklift trucks option might be ranked more highly than the computer software.

In the budget that is eventually decided by senior management, the forklift truck package might be approved, but the computer software package rejected on the grounds that there are other demands for resources with a higher priority.

**Test your understanding 4**

For a number of years, the research division of Z has produced its annual budget (for new and continuing projects) using incremental budgeting techniques. The company is now under new management and the annual budget for 20X4 is to be prepared using ZBB techniques.

**Required:**

Explain how Z could operate a ZBB system for its research projects.

| Advantages | Disadvantages |
|---|---|
| • Inefficient or obsolete operations can be identified and discontinued. | • The time involved and the cost of preparing the budget are much greater than for less elaborate budgeting methods. *takes months* |
| • ZBB leads to increased staff involvement at all levels. This should lead to better communication and motivation. | • It may emphasise short-term benefits to the detriment of long-term benefits. |
| • It responds to changes in the business environment. *short term thinking* | • The budgeting process may become too rigid and the company may not be able to react to unforeseen opportunities or threats. |
| • Knowledge and understanding of the cost-behaviour patterns of the organisation will be enhanced. | • There is a need for management skills that may not be present in the organisation. |
| • Resources should be allocated efficiently and economically. | • Managers may feel demotivated due to the large amount of time spent on the budgeting process. |
| | • It is difficult to compare and rank completely different types of activity. |
| | • The rankings of packages may be subjective where the benefits are of a qualitative nature. |

**Question focus**: Now attempt question 4 from chapter 13.

### 3.4 Rolling budgets *tighter*

A **rolling budget** is one that is kept continuously up to date by adding another accounting period (e.g. month or quarter) when the earliest accounting period has expired.

**Suitability**

*   Accurate forecasts cannot be made.
*   For any area of business that needs tight control.

| Advantages | Disadvantages |
| --- | --- |
| • ✓ The budgeting process should be more accurate. | • More costly and time consuming. |
| • ✓ Much better information upon which to appraise the performance of management. | • An increase in budgeting work may lead to less control of the actual results. |
| • The budget will be much more 'relevant' by the end of the traditional budgeting period. | • There is a danger that the budget may become the last budget 'plus or minus a bit'. |
| • It forces management to take the budgeting process more seriously. | • The budget may be demotivating because the targets are changing regularly. |

1. 40
2. 85
4. 31
569

**Test your understanding 5**

A company uses rolling budgeting and has a sales budget as follows:

| | Quarter 1 $ | Quarter 2 $ | Quarter 3 $ | Quarter 4 $ | Total |
| --- | --- | --- | --- | --- | --- |
| Sales | 125,750 | 132,038 | 138,640 | 145,572 | 542,000 |

*123,450*

Actual sales for Quarter 1 were $123,450. The adverse variance is fully explained by competition being more intense than expected and growth being lower than anticipated. The budget committee has proposed that the revised assumption for sales growth should be 3% per quarter for Quarters 2, 3 and 4.

**Required:**

Update the budget figures for Quarters 2-4 as appropriate.

*Dec 13   Q3 (a)   P3*

*GARANG*

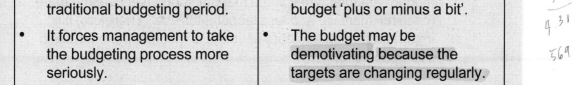

### 3.5 Activity-based budgeting (ABB)

Before we look at activity-based budgeting, it is useful to review the activity based models in general.

*what drive our costs.*

### 3.5.1 Activity-based costing (ABC)
*Direct*
*Indirect \**
*cost driver*

*IT, Pharma, dynamic*

**Aim**: the aim of ABC is to calculate the full production cost per unit. It is an alternative to absorption costing in a modern business environment.

| Reasons for the development of ABC |
| --- |

- Absorption costing is based on the principle that production overheads are driven by the level of production. This was true in the past when businesses tended to produce only one product or a few simple and similar products. However, a higher level of competition has resulted in the **diversity** and **complexity** of the products increasing. As a result, there are a number of different factors that drive overheads, not simply the level of production.

- Production overheads are a **larger proportion** of total costs in modern manufacturing since manufacturing has become more machine intensive and less labour intensive. Therefore, it is important that an accurate estimate is made of the production overhead per unit.

### Steps in ABC

**Step 1**: Group production overheads into activities (cost pools), according to how they are driven.

**Step 2**: Identify cost drivers for each activity, i.e. what causes the activity costs to be incurred.

*cost driver rate*

**Step 3**: Calculate an overhead absorption rate (OAR) for each activity.

**Step 4:** Absorb the activity costs into the product.

**Step 5**: Calculate the full production cost and/or the profit or loss.

The test your understanding below recaps the calculation of the full production cost per unit using traditional absorption costing and using ABC. Ensure you understand the calculation and that you can comment on the reasons for the differences between the full production cost per unit under the two costing methods.

Exam

## Test your understanding 6

Trimake makes three main products, using broadly the same production methods and equipment for each. A conventional absorption costing system is used at present, although an activity based costing (ABC) system is being considered. Details of the three products for a typical period are:

|  | Hours per unit | | Materials per unit | Volumes |
|---|---|---|---|---|
|  | Labour | Machinery | $ | Units |
| Product X | ½ | 1 ½ | 20 | 750 |
| Product Y | 1 ½ | 1 | 12 | 1,250 |
| Product Z | 1 | 3 | 25 | 7,000 |

Direct labour costs $6 per hour and production overheads are absorbed on a machine hour basis. The rate for the period is $28 per machine hour (i.e. the OAR) and a total of 23,375 machine hours were worked.

Traditional **absorption costing** would give a full production cost per unit as follows:

|  | X ($) | Y ($) | Z ($) |
|---|---|---|---|
| Materials | 20 | 12 | 25 |
| Labour | 3 | 9 | 6 |
|  | — | — | — |
| Total direct cost | 23 | 21 | 31 |
| Production overhead @$28 per hour | 42 | 28 | 84 |
|  | — | — | — |
| Total | 64 | 49 | 115 |

large porhon of overall cosry - hrigger ABC

Further analysis shows the total production overhead of $654,500 is not entirely driven by machine hours and can be divided as follows:

|  |  | % |
|---|---|---|
| Costs relating to set-ups | 229075 | 35 |
| Costs relating to machinery | 130,900 | 20 |
| Costs relating to materials handling | 98175 | 15 |
| Costs relating to inspection | 196,350 | 30 |
|  |  | — |
| Total production overhead |  | 100 |

cost pools

individual project = Decision packages = 2BB

Gill & McMillan

The following total activity volumes are associated with the product line for the period as a whole:

| | Number of set-ups | Number of movements of materials | Number of inspections |
|---|---|---|---|
| Product X | 75 | 12 | 150 |
| Product Y | 115 | 21 | 180 |
| Product Z | 480 | 87 | 670 |
| Total | 670 | 120 | 1,000 |

**Required:**

Calculate the cost per unit for each product using ABC principles.

## Advantages and disadvantages of ABC

| Advantages | Disadvantages |
|---|---|
| • Provides a more accurate cost per unit leading to better pricing, decision making and performance management. | • Limited benefit if overheads are primarily volume related or a small proportion of total costs. |
| • It provides a better insight into what drives overhead costs resulting in better control of costs. | • It is impossible to allocate all overheads to specific activities. |
| • It recognises that overhead costs are not all related to production and sales volumes. services | • The choice of activities and cost drivers might be inappropriate. |
| • It can be applied to all overhead costs, not just production overheads. | • The benefits might not justify the costs since a large amount of data must be collected. |
| • It can be used just as easily in service costing as product costing. | |

cost benefit

cost benefit analysis
CBA analysis

### 3.5.2 Activity based management (ABM)

**Activity based management** (ABM) is the use of ABC information for management purposes to improve operational and strategic decisions.

**Uses**

By identifying the underlying drivers of activities, ABM provides an understanding of the resource implications of various courses of action and therefore ensures that unfeasible courses of action are not taken.

*Strip costs but Product not compromis°*

```
              Two types of ABM
```

**Operational ABM**
- Uses ABC information to improve efficiency
- Activities which add value to a product are indentified and improved
- Activities that don't add value to the product can be reduced to cut costs without reducing product value

*still has Inspection Cost (eg)*

**Strategic ABM**
- Uses ABC information to to decide which products to develop and which activities to use
- Uses ABC information to identify which customers are the most profitable and focuses more on them

*customer Profitability index*

ABM can help middle managers to make decisions that benefit the whole organisation, not just their activities' bottom line.

---

**Use of ABM**

Companies use ABM to

- **Re-price products and optimise new product design**.
  Managers can more accurately analyse product profitability by combining activity-based cost data with price information. This can result in the re-pricing or elimination of unprofitable products. This information is also used to accurately estimate new product costs. By understanding cost drivers managers can design new products more efficiently.

- **Reduce costs**. ABC identifies the components of overhead costs and the drivers of cost variability. Managers can reduce costs by decreasing the cost of an activity or the number of activities per unit.

*P - 1.49*
*P - 3.99*
*P - 7.60*

*R - 2.82*
*R - 6.00*
*R - 20.66*
*R - 3.00*

- **Influence strategic and operational planning**. Implications for action from an ABM study include target costing, performance measurement for continuous improvement, and resource allocation based on projected demand by product, customer, and facility. ABM can also assist a company in considering a new business opportunity or venture.

### Test your understanding 7

**Required:**

Briefly discuss the potential risks associated with ABM. ˣ

### Illustration 1 - The application of ABM at DHL

In the 1990s, DHL saw its margins decreasing and used ABM to reverse this trend.

- Falling margins were mainly due to changes in product, destination and customer mixes.

- DHL concluded that they did not have sufficient visibility of margins to enable better pricing policies (and had different policies in different countries) so implemented ABC.

- A greater understanding of margins allowed DHL to design and implement a new pricing structure that was adopted worldwide.

*June 2013*

### 3.5.3 Activity-based budgeting (ABB)

Now that we understand the concepts of ABC and ABM, we can review the final approach to budgeting, ABB.

\*Activity-based budgeting** (ABB) uses the principles of ABC to estimate the firm's future demand for resources and hence can help the firm to acquire these resources more efficiently.

*predictive nature*

*Discussions*

## Illustration 2 – Steps in ABB

The operating divisions of Z have in the past always used a traditional (absorption costing) approach to analysing costs into their fixed and variable components. A single measure of activity was used which, for simplicity, was the number of units produced. The new management does not accept that such a simplistic approach is appropriate for budgeting in the modern environment and has requested that the managers adopt an activity-based approach to their budgets in the future.

**Required**

Explain how ABB would be implemented by the operating divisions of Z.

**Solution**

**Step 1**: Estimate the production and sales volumes of individual products or customers.

**Step 2**: Estimate the demand for organisational activities.

**Step 3**: Determine the resources that are required to perform organisational activities.

**Step 4**: Estimate for each resource the quantity that must be supplied to meet the demand.

**Step 5**: Take action to adjust the capacity of resources to match the projected supply.

| Advantages | Disadvantages |
|---|---|
| • ＊ ABB draws attention to the costs of 'overhead activities' which can be a <u>large proportion of total operating costs</u>. | • A considerable amount of time and effort might be needed to establish an ABB system. (identifying the key activities and their cost drivers). |
| • It recognises that it is activities that drive costs. If we can control the causes (drivers) of costs, then costs should be better managed and understood. | • ABB might not be appropriate for the organisation and its activities and <u>cost structures</u>. |

*Fixed ?*

*no point using ABB*

*operational gearing*
↓
*measures fixed & variable costs*

*if fixed difficult to lower =*
*cost based, so other alternative*
*↑ sales + revenue*

| | |
|---|---|
| • It provides information for the control of activity costs, by assuming that they are variable, at least in the longer-term. | • It may be difficult to identify clear individual responsibilities for activities. |
| • ABB can provide useful information for a total quality management (TQM) environment, by relating the cost of an activity to the level of service provided. | • It could be argued that in the short-term many overhead costs are not controllable and do not vary directly with changes in the volume of activity for the cost driver. The only cost variances to report would be fixed overhead expenditure variances for each activity. |

## ABB

A company has prepared an activity-based budget for its stores department. The budgeted costs are:

| | Cost driver | Budgeted cost |
|---|---|---|
| Receiving goods | Number of deliveries | $80 per delivery |
| Issuing goods from store | Number of stores' requisitions | $40 per requisition |
| Ordering | Number of orders | $25 per order |
| Counting stock | Number of stock counts | $1,000 per count |
| Keeping records | – | $24,000 each year |
| Supervision | – | $30,000 each year |

| Activity | | Actual cost $ |
|---|---|---|
| Receiving goods | 45 orders delivered | 3,450 |
| Issuing goods | 100 requisitions | 4,400 |
| Ordering | 36 orders | 960 |
| Counting | 2 stock counts | 1,750 |
| Record keeping | | 1,900 |
| Supervision | | 2,700 |
| | | ——— |
| | | 15,160 |
| | | ——— |

**Required:**

Prepare a variance report for the month.

**Solution:**

| Activity | | Expected cost | Actual cost | Variance |
|---|---|---|---|---|
| | | $ | $ | $ |
| Receiving goods | 45 orders delivered | 3,600 | 3,450 | 150 F |
| Issuing goods | 100 requisitions | 4,000 | 4,400 | 400 A |
| Ordering | 36 orders | 900 | 960 | 60 A |
| Counting | 2 stock counts | 2,000 | 1,750 | 250 F |
| Record keeping | | 2,000 | 1,900 | 100 F |
| Supervision | | 2,500 | 2,700 | 200 A |
| | | 15,000 | 15,160 | 160 A |

**Question focus**: Now attempt question 5 from chapter 13. This question examines ABB and benchmarking (which was covered in chapter 1).

article

# 4 Beyond budgeting    IT, Pharma

## 4.1 Criticisms of traditional budgeting

Traditional budgets based on fixed annual periods:

- encourage rigid planning and a lack of flexibility. This may not be appropriate in a fast moving business environment.

- are time consuming

- encourage managers and employees to meet only the lowest target rather than attempting to beat the target set (this is inconsistent with a TQM approach)

- encourage managers and employees to achieve the budget even if this results in undesirable action

- encourage managers and employees to spend what is in the budget, even if it is not necessary, to guard against next year's budget

- reinforce the barriers between departments rather than encourage knowledge sharing

- are seen as a mechanism for top-down control by senior management but organisations should be empowering individuals on the front-line

- ignore key drivers of shareholder value by focusing on short term financial performance

- produced inadequate variance reports leaving the 'how' and 'what' unanswered.

### 4.2 What is beyond budgeting?

**Beyond budgeting** is a leadership philosophy that relates to an alternative approach to budgeting which should be used instead of traditional annual budgeting.

### Characteristics

* Rolling budgets, produced on a quarterly or monthly basis, are suggested as the main alternative to annual budgeting. These are flexible, do not rely on obsolete figures and should result in more timely allocation of resources.

* The rolling forecasts will embrace KPIs based on the balanced scorecard (balanced scorecards will be discussed in chapter 10) which is linked to organisation strategy. Managers' performance measures will be based on this.

* The budget may also incorporate benchmarking linking managers' targets to external benchmarks and not past performance.

* Focus efforts on managing future results and not explaining past performance.

* Devolves authority and allows operational managers to react to the environment.

* Encourage a culture of innovation.

* Information systems are credited to produce fast and open communication throughout the organisation.

**Traditional versus beyond budgeting**

Below is a summary of the main differences between the traditional and the new beyond budgeting model as outlined by Jeremy Hope:

|  | Traditional Budgeting Management Model | Beyond Budgeting Management Model |
|---|---|---|
| Targets & rewards | Incremental targets<br>Fixed incentives | Stretch goals<br>Relative targets & rewards |
| Planning & controls | Fixed annual plans<br>Variance controls | Continuous planning<br>KPI's & rolling forecasts |
| Resource & coordination | Pre-allocated resources<br>Central co-ordination | Resources on demand<br>Dynamic coordination |
| Organisational culture | Central control<br>Focus on managing numbers | Local control of goals/plans<br>Focus on value creation |

### Suitability

- Industries where there is rapid change in the business environment. Flexible targets will be responsive to change.

- Organisations using management methods such as TQM. Continuous improvement will be key.

- Organisations undergoing radical change, e.g. using business process re-engineering. Budgets may be hard to achieve in such circumstances.

**Question focus**: Now attempt question 1 part (a) from chapter 13.

## Beyond budgeting in the public and private sector

### Beyond budgeting in the private sector

This entails devolved managerial responsibility where power and responsibility go hand in hand.

- The focus moves from beating other managers to beating the competition.

- It motivates people giving them challenges, responsibilities and clear guidelines.

- Rewards are team based.

- Performance responsibilities are given to operational management who are closer to the action.

- It empowers managers to remove resource constraints

- Creation of open information systems throughout the organisation.

### Beyond budgeting in the public sector

The greater flexibility that lies at the heart of beyond budgeting may prevent successful application of the model in the public sector.

Beyond budgeting would require a mindset which not only moves away from control but also requires a reduction in internal politics which has been at the heart of the public sector for many years.

The managers within the public sector may have the desire for flexibility but are likely to remain constrained by the inability of their organisation to change.

advantages beyond budgeting → notes
new text

## 5 Budgeting in not-for-profit organisations

### 5.1 Introduction

**Not-for-profit organisations**, NFPOs, include organisations of many different forms, for example schools and universities, social clubs, sports clubs, sports governing bodies, hospitals, museum/library/arts organisations, government organisations/local authorities and charities.

### 5.2 Things to consider when preparing a budget in a NFPO

- **No profit motive** - but these organisations still need to control costs.

- **Non-quantifiable benefits** - many of the benefits arising from expenditure by these bodies are non-quantifiable (certainly not in monetary terms, e.g. social welfare). So how can measurable budgets be prepared which meet the organisation's objectives?

- **No revenue generated** - often revenue is not generated and there is a fixed budget for spending within which they have to keep. 'Value for money' is often quoted as an objective here but it does not get round the problem of measuring 'value'.

- **Multiple stakeholders** - give rise to multiple objectives so there is a need to prioritise/compromise (e.g. hospital – patients, staff, government, taxpayers, local community, society at large, contractors, management, donors/contributors, etc.).

- **Objectives** - may be difficult to define, may change as a result of the political process and may be achievable in different ways.

| Objectives |
| --- |
| A further consideration is that the distinction between objectives and ways of achieving these is often misunderstood. For example, one public objective is 'to contain crime within reasonable limits'. One means of achieving that objective is to have police officers patrolling the streets on foot. In fact, police foot patrols are a very inefficient method of containing crime. The use of video surveillance cameras and police response units using fast cars is much more cost effective. |

### 5.3 Public sector budgets

- Budgets tend to concentrate on planning for one year ahead.

- Incremental budgeting is traditionally used.

- Other budgeting approaches such as ZBB and planned programme budgeting systems (PPBS) have been used.

## PPBS

- PPBS breaks work down into programmes designed towards achieving various objectives.

- Several departments may contribute towards a single programme.

- Budget targets may spread over more than one year.

- The means used to achieve programmes should be efficient and cost-effective.

### Efficiency

Efficiency revolves around making the maximum possible use of a given set of resources. That is, it involves a straight comparison of output and input.

Many UK local authorities in the 1970s were judged to be making an inefficient use of the resources available to them. They undertook most of their activities (e.g. council house maintenance, road repairs, maintenance of parks and gardens, etc.) using large numbers of direct council employees. It was often found that the use of obsolete equipment and inefficient working practices (strict job demarcation was widespread) resulted in the operation involving excessive costs.

Financial management initiatives in the 1980s required local authorities to put many of their activities 'out to tender'. Private contractors may submit bids in order to undertake programmes of work for the local authorities. If the councils retain a direct works department, then that department has to bid in competition with private contractors for most available work.

The advent of executive agencies in national government is another example of this approach. Government has devolved some of its functions to agencies (e.g. the DVLA at Swansea) which are run on semi-commercial lines. The performance of these agencies is monitored using target performance indicators (e.g. the average time it takes to issue a new driving licence or the average time it takes to respond to a police enquiry concerning a vehicle).

## 6 Forecasting

### 6.1 Introduction

You may be asked to prepare a forecast in the exam. A number of forecasting methods were reviewed in paper F5 including:

- the hi-low method
- regression analysis
- time series analysis
- the learning curve model.

The learning curve model will be recapped below.

### 6.2 The learning curve effect

As workers become more familiar with the production of a new product, the average labour time (and average labour cost) per unit will decline.

**Wright's Law** states that as output doubles, the average time per unit falls to a fixed percentage (referred to as the learning rate) of the previous average time.

The learning curve effect can be calculated using the following formula:

$$y = ax^b$$

where:

y = the average time (or average cost) per unit/batch

a = time (or cost) for the first unit/batch

x = output in units/batches

b = log r/log 2 (r = rate of learning, expressed as a decimal).

The formula can be used to forecast the cost of labour but would normally be examined as part of a bigger forecasting question such as the one below.

### The learning curve and the steady state

The learning effect will only apply for a certain range of production. Once the steady state is reached the direct labour hours will not reduce any further.

## Test your understanding 8

BFG is investigating the financial viability of a new product, the S-pro. The S-pro is a short-life product for which a market has been identified at an agreed design specification. The product will only have a life of 12 months.

The following estimated information is available in respect of the S-pro.:

(1)  Sales should be 120,000 in the year in batches of 100 units. An average selling price of $1,050 per batch of 100 units is expected.

(2)  An 80% learning curve will apply for the first 700 batches after which a steady state production time will apply, with the labour time per batch after the first 700 batches being equal to the time of the 700th batch. The labour cost of the first batch was measured at $2,500. This was for 500 hours at $5 per hour.

(3)  Variable overhead is estimated at $2 per labour hour.

(4)  Direct material will be $500 per batch for the S-pro for the first 200 batches produced. The second 200 batches will cost 90% of the cost per batch of the first 200 batches. All batches from then on will cost 90% of the batch cost for each of the second 200 batches.

(5)  S-pro will require additional space to be rented. These directly attributable fixed costs will be $15,000 per month.

A target net cash flow of $130,000 is required in order for the project to be acceptable.

Note: At the learning curve rate of 80% the learning factor (b) is equal to $-0.3219$.

## Required:

Prepare detailed calculations to show whether S-pro will provide the target net cash flow.

## Limitations of the learning curve model

The learning curve model on applies if:

- **there are no breaks in production**: a break in production may result in the learning effect being lost.

- **the product is new**: the introduction of a new product makes it more probable that there will be a learning effect.

- **the product is complex**: the more complex the product, the more probable that the learning effect will be significant and the longer it will take for the learning effect to reach the steady state.

- **the process is repetitive**: if the process is not repetitive, a learning effect will not be enjoyed.

- **the process is labour intensive**: the learning effect will not apply if machines limit the speed of labour.

**Question focus**: Now attempt question 3 from chapter 13.

# Chapter summary

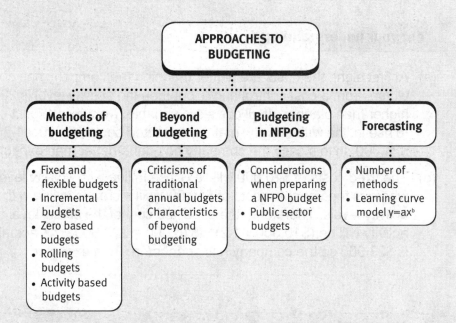

## Test your understanding answers

### Test your understanding 1

(a) At first sight, the costs are higher meaning the company has done worse, from a cost control angle, but then the activity level is 20% higher than planned. If all costs are variable, we would expect costs to rise in line with activity, making expected costs 20,000 x 1.2 = $24,000. In this case the company has done better than expected.

(b) The fixed costs of $10,000 will NOT rise in line with activity levels whereas the variable costs of $10,000 will increase in line with activity levels. Therefore, the expected cost of the actual level of activity will be ($10,000 x 1.2) + $10,000 = $22,000. The actual cost is $23,000 so the company has spent more than expected.

### Test your understanding 2

**(W1)** Actual patient numbers were 18.75% above budget, i.e. ((23,750 – 20,000) ÷ 20,000) × 100 = 18.75%. Therefore, budgeted variable costs should be increased by 18.75%.

**Cost statements for the year ended 31 December 20X0**

|  | Budget ($) | Actual ($) |
|---|---|---|
| Doctors | 60 × $100,000 = 6,000,000 | 60 × $105,000 = 6,300,000 |
| Nurses | 150 × $37,000 = 5,550,000 | 150 × $34,500 = 5,175,000 |
| Other staff costs | 1.1875 (W1) × 1,440,000 = 1,710,000 | 1,500,000 |
| Catering | (1.1875 (W1) × $200,000 × 70%) + ($200,000 × 30%) = 226,250 | 187,500 |
| Cleaning | (1.1875 (W1) × $80,000 × 35%) + ($80,000 × 65%) = 85,250 | 142,000 |
| Other operating costs | (1.1875 (W1) × $1,200,000 × 30%) + ($1,200,000 × 70%) = 1,267,500 | 1,050,000 |
| Depreciation | 80,000 | 80,000 |
| **Total costs** | **14,919,000** | **14,434,500** |

## Test your understanding 3

### NWEC Budgeted Profit and Loss Statement for year to 30 November 20X4

| | $ | $ |
|---|---|---|
| Amusement Park – admission receipts: | | |
| One-day pass: | | |
| Adults: | 8,696,064 | |
| 14–18 years, senior citizens | 3,261,024 | |
| Under 14 years | 4,348,032 | |
| Two-day pass: | | |
| Adults: | 19,566,144 | |
| 14–18 years, senior citizens | 7,337,304 | |
| Under 14 years | 9,783,072 | |
| | | 52,991,640 |
| Other revenue Income from traders | | 1,044,000 |
| Total revenue – park | | 54,035,640 |
| Operating costs | | 39,104,000 |
| Budgeted profit of park | | 14,931,640 |
| Hotel income | 9,110,400 | |
| Hotel operating costs | 8,268,000 | |
| Budgeted profit of hotel | | 842,400 |
| | | 15,774,040 |

**Workings:**

| | |
|---|---|
| No. of Visitor days for year to 30 November 20X4 | = 2,090,400 |
| One-day passes = 2,090,400 x 25% | = 522,600 |
| Two-day passes (2,090,400 x 75%)/2 | = 783,900 |

Admission fees applicable from 1 December 20X3. (increased by 4% per annum).

|  | One-day pass ($) | Two-day pass ($) |
|---|---|---|
| Adults | 41.60 (40*1.04) | 62.40 (41.60*2 less 25%) |
| 14–18 years; senior citizens | 31.20 (30*1.04) | 46.80 (31.20*2 less 25%) |
| Under 14's | 20.80 (20*1.04) | 31.20 (20.80*2 less 25%) |

| Split | One-day pass revenue | | | Two-day pass revenue | | |
|---|---|---|---|---|---|---|
| 40% | 209,040 | $41.60 | $8,696,064 | 313,560 | $62.40 | $19,566,144 |
| 20% | 104,520 | $31.20 | $3,261,024 | 156,780 | $46.80 | $ 7,337,304 |
| 40% | 209,040 | $20.80 | $4,348,032 | 313,560 | $31.20 | $ 9,783,072 |
| | 522,600 | | | 783,900 | | |

## Test your understanding 4

The managers/researchers responsible for each project should decide which projects they wish to undertake in the forthcoming period. These projects will be a mixture of continued projects and new projects.

For the projects which have already been started and which the managers want to continue in the next period, we should ignore any cash flows already incurred (they are sunk costs), and we should look only at future costs and benefits. Similarly, for the new projects we should only look at the future costs and benefits.

Different ways of achieving the same research goals should also be investigated and the projects should go ahead only if the benefit exceeds the cost.

Once all the potential projects have been evaluated, if there are insufficient funds to undertake all the worthwhile projects, then the funds should be allocated to the best projects on the basis of a cost-benefit analysis.

ZBB is usually of a highly-subjective nature. (The costs are often reasonably certain, but usually a lot of uncertainty is attached to the estimated benefits.) This will be even more true of a research division where the researchers may have their own pet projects which they are unable to view in an objective light.

KAPLAN PUBLISHING

## Test your understanding 5

The revised budget should incorporate 3% growth starting from the actual sales figure of Q1.

| | Quarter 2 $ | Quarter 3 $ | Quarter 4 $ |
|---|---|---|---|
| Sales | 127,154 | 130,969 | 134,898 |

### Workings

- Q2: Budget = $123,450 x 103%
- Q3: Budget = $127,154 x 103%
- Q4: Budget = $130,969 x 103%

## Test your understanding 6

### (W1) Overheads

| Type of overhead | % | Total overhead $ |
|---|---|---|
| Set-ups | 35 | 229,075 |
| Machining | 30 | 130,900 |
| Material's handling | 15 | 98,175 |
| Inspection | 30 | 196,350 |
| | 100 | 654,500 |

| Step 1: Group production overhead into activities | Step 2: Identify cost drivers for each activity |
|---|---|
| Set-ups | Number of set-ups |
| Machining | Number of machine hours |
| Material's handling | Number of movements of materials |
| Inspection | Number of inspections |

## Step 3: Calculate an OAR for each activity

| Activity cost (W1) | Cost driver | OAR = activity cost ÷ cost driver |
|---|---|---|
| Set-ups = $229,075 | 670 set ups | $341.90 per set up |
| Machining = $130,900 | 23,375 machine hours | $5.60 per machine hour |
| Materials handling = $98,175 | 120 material movements | $818.13 per movement of material |
| Inspection = $196,350 | 1,000 inspections | $196.35 per inspection |

## Step 4: Absorb activity costs into products

| | Product X ($) | Product Y ($) | Product Z ($) | Total ($) |
|---|---|---|---|---|
| Set-ups @ $341.90 per set-up | 25,642.50 | 39,318.50 | 164,112.00 | 229,073 |
| Machining @ $5.60 per machine hour | 6,300 | 7,000 | 117,600 | 130,900 |
| Materials handling @ $818.13 per movement of material | 9,817.56 | 17,180.73 | 71,177.31 | 98,175.60 |
| Inspection @ $196.35 per inspection | 29,452.50 | 35,343.00 | 131,554.50 | 196,350 |
| Total production overhead | 71,212.56 | 98,842.23 | 484,443.81 | 654,498.60 |
| Production overhead per unit | **94.95** | **79.07** | **69.21** | |

## Step 5: Calculate the full production cost per unit

| | Product X ($) | Product Y ($) | Product Z ($) |
|---|---|---|---|
| Direct costs (from question) | 23.00 | 21.00 | 31.00 |
| Production overhead (step 4) | 94.95 | 79.07 | 69.21 |
| Full production cost under ABC | **117.95** | **100.07** | **100.21** |
| Full production cost under absorption costing | **64** | **49** | **115** |

ABC has resulted in a significant change in the full production cost per unit. The cost of products X and Y have approximately doubled where as the cost of product Z has decreased by approximately 13%.

**Test your understanding 7**

Some activities will have an implicit value which is not necessarily reflected in the financial value of the product. For example:

- A pleasant workplace can help attract/retain the best staff. A risk of operational ABM is that this activity is eliminated.

- A low value customer may open up new leads in the market. A risk of strategic ABM is that this customer is eliminated.

**Test your understanding 8**

**BFG net cash flow calculation**

| | |
|---|---:|
| Sales units | 120,000 |
| | $ |
| Sales revenue | 1,260,000 |
| **Costs:** | |
| Direct material (W1) | 514,000 |
| Direct labour (W2) | 315,423 |
| Variable overhead (W3) | 126,169 |
| Rent | 180,000 |
| | ———— |
| Net cash flow | 124,408 |
| Target cash flow | 130,000 |

The target cash flow will not be achieved.

**Workings:**

**(W1) Direct material**

| Batches | $ |
|---|---:|
| First 200 @ $500 | 100,000 |
| Second 200 @ $450 | 90,000 |
| Remaining 800 @ $405 | 324,000 |
| | ———— |
| Total | 514,000 |

## (W2) Direct labour

$v = ax^b$

where; a = 2,500 and b = -0.3219

Total cost for first 700 batches (x = 700);

| | |
|---|---:|
| $700 \times 2.500 \times 700^{-0.3219}$ | = \$212,423 |
| Total cost for first 699 batches (x = 699); | |
| $699 \times 2.500 \times 699^{-0.3219}$ | = \$212,217 |
| Cost of 700th batch (\$212,423 - \$212,217) | = \$206 |
| Total cost of final 500 batches; | |
| \$206 x 500 | = \$103,000 |
| Total labour cost (\$212,423 + \$103,000) | = \$315,423 |

## (W3) Variable overhead

Variable overhead is \$2 per labour hour, or 40% of the direct labour cost.

# Changes in business structure and management accounting

## Chapter learning objectives

Upon completion of this chapter you will be able to:

- identify and discuss the particular information needs of _amazon (e-commerce)_ organisations adopting a functional, divisional or network form and the implications for performance management

- assess the influence of business process re-engineering (BPR) _1990's_ on systems development and improvements in organisational performance

- discuss the concept of business integration and the linkages between people, operations, strategy and technology

- analyse the role that performance management systems play in business integration using models such as the value chain and McKinsey's 7S's

- identify and discuss the required changes in management accounting systems as a consequence of empowering staff to manage sectors of a business.

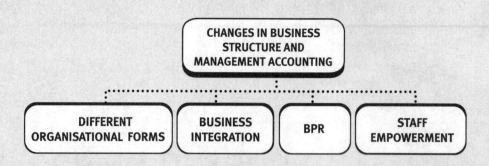

## 1 Organisational forms

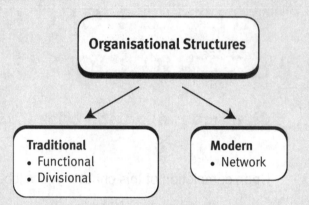

### 1.1 Introduction

Different types of organisational structure were studied in papers F1 and P3.

In P5 you could be asked to:

- discuss the information needs of organisations adopting a particular structure

- discuss the implications of a particular structure for performance management.

### 1.2 Functional structure

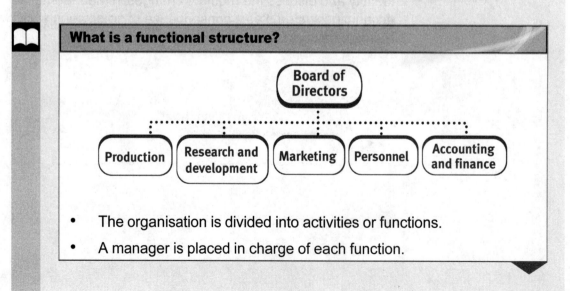

**What is a functional structure?**

- The organisation is divided into activities or functions.
- A manager is placed in charge of each function.

> • A narrow band of senior management co-ordinates the functions and retains the authority to make most of the decisions, i.e. decision making tends to be centralised.

## Information needs of a functional structure

The centralised structure results in:

- Data being passed from the functional level to the upper level.
- Data is then aggregated and analysed at the upper level for planning and control purposes.
- Feedback is then given at functional level.

### Test your understanding 1

**Required:**

Discuss ONE potential advantage and ONE disadvantage of a functional structure for performance management.

*chapter 8*

### 1.3 Divisional structure    *autonomy / independence*

### What is a divisional structure?

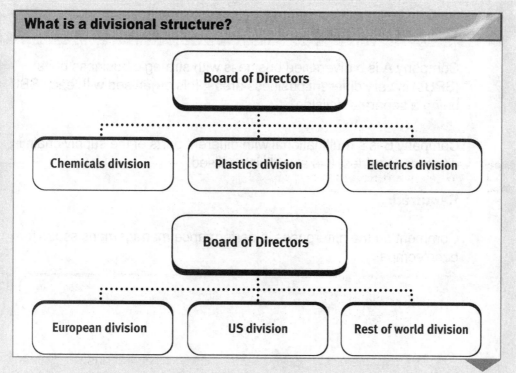

- A divisional organisation is divided along product or geographical lines.

- Divisional structures tend to be decentralised, i.e. the divisional managers have the authority to make most of the decisions.

## Information needs of a divisional structure

The decentralised structure results in:

- Information being required lower down the hierarchy.

- For example, information will be required by the divisions for budgeting purposes.

### Test your understanding 2

**Required:**

Discuss the potential advantages and disadvantages of a divisional structure for performance management.

*Note*: Divisional performance appraisal will be reviewed in detail in chapter 8.

### Test your understanding 3

Company A is a diversified business with strategic business units (SBUs) in very different business areas. It is organised with each SBU being a separate division.

Company B is a multinational with different parts of the supply chain in different countries. It is also divisionalised.

**Required:**

Comment on the differences in performance management issues for each company.

## 1.4 Network (virtual) structures

*[handwritten: Modern era  Callisto  June 2012]*

*[handwritten: no office]*

A **network (virtual) organisation** uses computer and telecommunications technologies to extend its capabilities by working routinely with employees or contractors located throughout the country or world. Using email, faxes, instant messages and videoconferencing, it implies a high degree of working away from the office as well as using remote facilities.

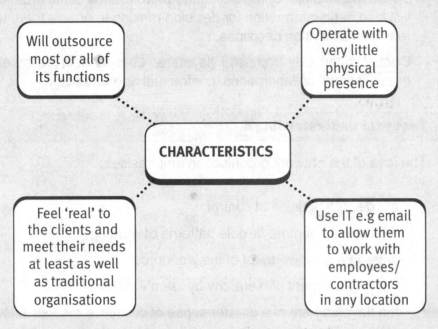

Will outsource most or all of its functions

Operate with very little physical presence

**CHARACTERISTICS**

Feel 'real' to the clients and meet their needs at least as well as traditional organisations

Use IT e.g email to allow them to work with employees/ contractors in any location

**e.g**

## Illustration 1 – Network structures

**Amazon.com** *(e-commerce)*

Many internet companies are examples of networks – Amazon being perhaps one of the best known on-line retailers.

- Amazon operates its website but relies on external book publishers, book warehouses, couriers and credit card companies to deliver the rest of the customer experience.

- These partners are also expected to provide Amazon with information on, for example, stock availability, delivery times, promotional material, etc.

- The customer feels that they are dealing with one organisation, not many.

### Information needs of a network structure

With network structures targeted information is needed to make decisions:

- Each party needs to have feedback as to how it is performing in relation to others.

- Those responsible for regulating the performance of the organisation will also need information for decision making to enable them to take resource allocation decisions.

- Control is normally exercised via shared goals and, in the case of inter-organisational collaborations, contractual agreements.

    SLAs

### Test your understanding 4

The idea of the network organisation emphasises:

- the decentralisation of control

- the creation of more flexible patterns of working

- a greater empowerment of the workforce

- the displacement of hierarchy by team working

- the development of a greater sense of collective responsibility

- the creation of more collaborative relationships among co-workers.

**Required:**

Comment on the importance of information to such an organisation.

## 2 Business integration

### 2.1 What is business integration?

**Business integration** means that all aspects of the business must be aligned to secure the most efficient use of the organisation's resources so that it can achieve its objectives effectively.

## Hammer and Davenport

Modern writers such as **Hammer** and **Davenport** argue that many organisations have departments and functions that try to maximise their own performance and efficiency at the expense of the whole.

*autonomous*

*no goal congruence*

*not achieving goal congruence*

Their proposed solution is twofold:

(1) Processes need to be viewed as complete entities that stretch from initial order to final delivery of a product.

(2) IT needs to be used to integrate these activities.

*ERP - SAP, ORACLE*

Four aspects in particular need to be linked.

- people
- operations
- strategy
- technology.

## Test your understanding 5

**Required:**

*centralised*

XYZ has a conventional functional structure. Assess how many different people in the organisation may have to deal with customers, and the problems this creates.

There are two frameworks for understanding integrated processes and the linkages within them:

- Porter's value chain model.
- McKinsey's 7S model

## 2.2 Porter's value chain

The value chain is the linked set of value-creating activities from the acquisition of raw materials to the delivery of the final product to the customer.

- Margin, i.e. profit will be achieved if the customer is willing to pay more for the product/service than the sum of the costs of all the activities in the value chain.

- Value chain analysis aims to maximise margin by understanding how the value chain activities are performed and how they interact with each other.

- There are five primary activities and four support activities.

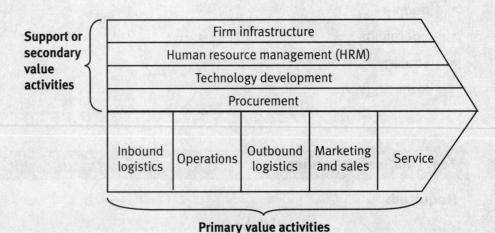

**Support or secondary value activities**

| Firm infrastructure |
| Human resource management (HRM) |
| Technology development |
| Procurement |

| Inbound logistics | Operations | Outbound logistics | Marketing and sales | Service |

**Primary value activities**

### Illustration 2 - Value chain activities

| Primary activity | Description | Example |
|---|---|---|
| **Inbound logistics** | Receiving, storing and handling raw material inputs | A just-in-time stock system could give a cost advantage (see chapter 11) |
| **Operations** | Transformation of raw materials into finished goods and services | Using skilled craftsmen could give a quality advantage |
| **Outbound logistics** | Storing, distributing and delivering finished goods to customers | Outsourcing activities could give a cost advantage |
| **Marketing and sales** | Market research and the marketing mix (product, price, place, promotion) | Sponsorship of a sports celebrity could enhance the image of a product |

| **After sales service** | All activities that occur after the point of sale, such as installation, training and repair | A flexible approach to customer returns could enhance a quality image |
|---|---|---|
| **Firm infrastructure** | How the firm is organised | Centralised buying could result in cost savings due to bulk discounts |
| **Technology development** | How the firm uses technology | Modern computer-controlled machinery gives greater flexibility to tailor products to meet customer specifications |
| **Human resource management** | How people contribute to competitive advantage | Employing expert buyers could enable a supermarket to purchase better wine than their competitors |
| **Procurement** | Purchasing, but not just limited to materials | Buying a building out of town could give a cost advantage over High Street competitors |

## Illustration 3 - Value chain

Value chain analysis helps managers to decide how individual activities might be changed to reduce costs of operation or to improve the value of the organisation's offerings. Such changes will increase margin.

For example, a clothes manufacturer may spend large amounts on:

- buying good quality raw materials (inbound logistics)
- hand-finishing garments (operations)
- building a successful brand image (marketing)
- running its own fleet of delivery trucks in order to deliver finished clothes quickly to customers (outbound logistics).

All of these should add value to the product, allowing the company to charge a premium for its clothes.

Another clothes manufacturer may:

- reduce the cost of its raw materials by buying in cheaper supplies from abroad (inbound logistics)

- making all its clothes using machinery that runs 24 hours a day (operations)

- delaying distribution until delivery trucks can be filled with garments for a particular location (outbound logistics).

All of these should enable the company to gain economies of scale and to sell clothes at a cheaper price than its rivals.

## Evaluation of the value chain

### Advantages of the value chain model

- Particularly useful for focusing on how each activity in the process adds to the firm's overall competitive advantage.

- Emphasises critical success factors (CSFs) within each activity and overall.

- Examines both primary activities (e.g. production) and support activities, such as HRM, which may otherwise be dismissed as overheads.

- Highlights linkages between activities.

### Disadvantages of the value chain model

- It is more suited to a manufacturing environment and can be hard to apply to a service provider.

- It is intended as a quantitative analysis tool but this can be time consuming since it often requires recalibrating the system to allocate costs to individual activities.

### Test your understanding 6

Many European clothing manufacturers, even those aiming at the top end of the market, outsource production to countries with lower wage costs such as Sri Lanka and China.

**Required:**

Comment on whether you feel this is an example of poor integration (or poor linkage in Porter's terminology).

### Uses in performance management

- As well as being part of strategic analysis to identify strengths or weaknesses, the value chain can be used for ongoing performance management as targets can be set and monitored for the different activities.

- This enables the performance of the overall process to be assessed and managed.

**Question focus**: Now attempt question 6 from chapter 13.

### 2.3 McKinsey's 7s model   *always   work   together*

The **McKinsey 7S model** describes an organisation as consisting of seven interrelated internal elements.

A change in one element will have repercussions on the others. All seven elements must be aligned to ensure organisational success, e.g:

- to determine how best to implement a strategy
- to improve organisational performance
- to examine the effects of future changes within a company
- to align departments or processes during a merger or acquisition.

*working towards*
*same Goal*

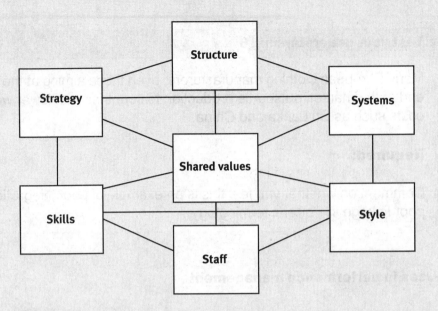

### McKinsey's 7S model

There are three **hard** elements of business behaviour

- Strategy - what will the company do?
- Structure - how should it be organised?
- Systems - what procedures need to be in place (few or many)?

Hard elements are easier to define or identify and management can directly influence them.

There are four **soft** elements

- Staff - what staff will we require?
- Style - what management style will work best?
- Shared values - what culture (attitudes) will be most suitable?
- Skills - what skills will our staff/company need?

Soft elements are more difficult to describe, less tangible and are more influenced by culture.

## 3 Business Process Re-engineering (BPR)

### 3.1 What is BPR?

BPR is the **fundamental rethinking and radical redesign of business processes** to achieve dramatic improvements in critical, contemporary measures of performance, such as cost, quality, service and speed. Improved customer satisfaction is often the primary aim.

## Illustration 4 - IBM and BPR

Prior to re-engineering, it took IBM Credit between one and two weeks to issue credit, often losing customers during this period.

- On investigation it was found that performing the actual work only took 90 minutes. The rest of the time (more than seven days!) was spent passing the form from one department to the next.
- The solution was to replace specialists (e.g. credit checkers) with generalists – one person (a deal 'structurer') processes the entire application from beginning to end.
- Post re-engineering, the process took only minutes or hours.

## Test your understanding 7

A business process is a series of activities that are linked together in order to achieve given objectives. For example, materials handling might be classed as a business process in which the separate activities are scheduling production, storing materials, processing purchase orders, inspecting materials and paying suppliers.

**Required:**

Suggest ways in which materials handling might be re-engineered.

## Features of a re-engineered process

The following are common features of re-engineered processes:

- several jobs are combined into one
- workers make real decisions
- work is performed where it makes most sense
- checks and controls are reduced
- reconciliation processes are reduced
- a case manager provides a point of contact.

### 3.2 The influence of BPR on organisational performance

- Despite some success stories, e.g. at IBM and Ford, BPR became unpopular in the late 1990s due to some widely discussed failures.

- Numerous organisations have attempted to redesign their business processes but have failed to enjoy the enormous improvements in organisational performance that were promised.

- The key to realising these improvements in performance seems to be continuous learning. As problems emerge, they must be identified, analysed and communicated in order to improve the future success rate of BPR.

*Continous looped*

## Advantages and disadvantages of BPR

### Advantages of BPR

- BPR revolves around customer needs and helps to give an appropriate focus to the business.

- BPR provides cost advantages that assist the organisation's competitive position.

- BPR encourages a long-term strategic view of operational processes by asking radical questions about how things are done and how processes could be improved.

- BPR helps overcome the short-sighted approaches that sometimes emerge from excessive concentration on functional boundaries. By focusing on entire processes the exercise can streamline activities throughout the organisation.

- BPR can help to reduce organisational complexity by eliminating unnecessary activities.

### Criticisms of BPR

- BPR was sometimes seen (incorrectly) as a means of making small improvements in existing practices. In reality, it should be a more radical approach that questions whether existing practices make any sense in their present form.

- BPR was often perceived (incorrectly) as a single, once-for-all cost-cutting exercise. In reality, it is not primarily concerned with cost cutting (though cost reductions often result), and should be regarded as on-going rather than once-for-all. This misconception often creates hostility in the minds of staff who see the exercise as a threat to their security.

- BPR requires a far-reaching and long-term commitment by management and staff. Securing this is not an easy task, and many organisations have rejected the whole idea as not worth the effort.

KAPLAN PUBLISHING

- In many cases business processes were not redesigned but merely automated.

- In some cases the efficiency of one department was improved at the expense of the overall process. To make BPR work requires a focus on integrated processes (as discussed above) that often involves obliterating existing processes and creating new ones.

- Some companies became so focused on improving internal processes that they failed to keep up with competitors' activities in the market.

Most companies are now more likely to talk about 'business process redesign' instead.

### 3.3 The influence of BPR on systems development

BPR results in more automation and greater use of IT/IS to integrate processes.

Some of the key technologies that allow fundamental shifts in business operations to occur are:

- shared database access from any location

- expert systems (a database system providing expert knowledge and advice) to devolve expertise

- powerful communication networks for remote offices

- wireless communication for on-the-spot decision making

- tracking technology for warehouses and delivery systems

- Internet services to re-engineer channels of distribution.

**Question focus**: Now attempt question 7 from chapter 13.

## 4 Staff empowerment    *Beyond budgeting*

### 4.1 Introduction

**Empowerment** is the delegation of certain aspects of business decisions to those lower down in the hierarchy.

For example, customer service staff may have the discretion to issue on-the-spot refunds or discounts.

## 4.2 Changes to management accounting systems as a result of staff empowerment

Characteristics of the information needs of an empowered organisation.

- There may have to be a budget for each empowered team of members of staff.
- Transparency and immediacy.
- Common definitions to allow comparison across the organisation.
- Mixture of financial and non-financial information.   operations
- Relevant to each empowered team of members of staff.

Generic

If staff are empowered to manage sectors of a business then typically there will need to be a number of changes in the management accounting system.

- these individuals or teams will need targeted information to make decisions
- individuals and teams will need feedback on their performance.

# Chapter summary

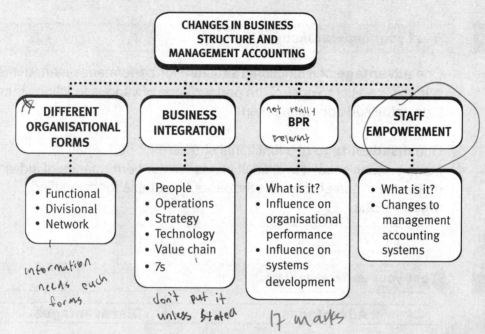

**CHANGES IN BUSINESS STRUCTURE AND MANAGEMENT ACCOUNTING**

*✗* **DIFFERENT ORGANISATIONAL FORMS**
- Functional
- Divisional
- Network

*information needs each forms*

**BUSINESS INTEGRATION**
- People
- Operations
- Strategy
- Technology
- Value chain
- 7s

*don't put it unless stated*

*not really relevant* **BPR**
- What is it?
- Influence on organisational performance
- Influence on systems development

*17 marks*

**STAFF EMPOWERMENT**
- What is it?
- Changes to management accounting systems

## Test your understanding answers

### Test your understanding 1

One **advantage** of a functional structure for performance management is that it is easier to control the performance of various functions due to the centralised approach taken.

One **disadvantage** of a functional structure for performance management is that it is difficult to assess the performance of individual products or markets and it is therefore unsuitable for diversified organisations.

### Test your understanding 2

| Advantages | Disadvantages |
|---|---|
| • Easier to assess the performance of individual products or markets. | • Potential loss of goal congruence. |
| • There is clear responsibility for the performance of each division. | • Difficult to allocate head office costs. |
| • Performance management systems can be tailored to meet divisional needs. | • Difficult to set a transfer price to fairly reflect the performance of the divisions. |

### Test your understanding 3

Company A

- Given that business units are in unrelated markets, there is likely to be more devolved management, with the use of divisional performance measures and reliance on the measurement systems, particularly financial reporting, for control.

Company B

- There is a need for a high level of interaction between business units, so senior management control is more important, whether in terms of standardisation or detailed operational targets.

- The performance measurement system may aid communication between managers and provide a common language.

**Test your understanding 4**

Information is key to a successful network organisation:

- this is mainly through the systems that facilitate co-ordination and communication, decision making and the sharing of knowledge, skills and resources

- information systems can reduce the number of levels in an organisation by providing managers with information to manage and control larger numbers of workers spread over greater distances and by giving lower-level employees more decision-making authority

- it is no longer necessary for these employees to work standard hours every day, nor work in an office or even the same country as their manager

- with the emergence of global networks, team members can collaborate closely even from distant locations

- information technology permits tight co-ordination of geographically dispersed workers across time zones and cultures

- different companies can join together to provide goods and services.

**Test your understanding 5**

(1) Sales staff to make the original sale.

(2) Delivery staff to arrange delivery.

(3) Accounts staff chasing up payment if invoices are overdue.

(4) Customer service staff if there is a problem with the product.

Possible problems include:

- delivery staff may be unaware of any special delivery requirements agreed by the sales staff

- accounts staff may be unaware of any special discounts offered

- aggressive credit controllers could damage sales negotiations for potential new sales

- credit controllers might not be aware of special terms offered to the client to win their business

- customers may resent having to re-explain their circumstances to each point of contact

- customer service may be unaware of the key factors in why the client bought the product and hence not prioritise buying.

Customer service could be improved by having one customer-facing point of contact.

### Test your understanding 6

Firms following a cost leadership strategy have found that outsourcing to China, say, has cut costs considerably, even after taking into account distribution costs.

Differentiators have, on the whole, found that they have saved costs without compromising quality. Thus the apparent conflict between low cost production and high quality branding has not been a problem. Furthermore the perceived quality of Chinese garments is rising with some manufacturers claiming that quality is higher than in older European factories.

**Note:** Commercial awareness – given that many firms do it, be wary of criticising the approach too heavily! They must have their reasons.

### Test your understanding 7

In the case of materials handling, the activity of processing purchase orders might be re-engineered by:

- integrating the production planning system with that of the supplier (an exercise in supply chain management (or SCM)) and thus sending purchase orders direct to the supplier without any intermediate administrative activity

- joint quality control procedures might be agreed thus avoiding the need to check incoming materials. In this manner, the cost of material procurement, receiving, holding and handling is reduced.

# 5

# The impact of information technology *on services*

*sec B 2013 / Q3*

## Chapter learning objectives

Upon completion of this chapter you will be able to:

- assess the changing accounting needs of modern service orientated businesses compared with the needs of traditional manufacturing industry

- discuss how IT systems provide the opportunity *real-time information* for instant access to management accounting data throughout the organisation and their potential impact on business performance

- assess how IT systems facilitate the remote input of management accounting data in an acceptable format by non-finance specialists → *audience*

- explain how information systems provide instant access to previously unavailable data that can be used for benchmarking and control purposes and help improve performance (for example, through the use of enterprise resource planning systems and data warehouses)

- assess the need for businesses to continually refine and develop their management accounting and information systems if they are to maintain or improve their performance in an increasingly competitive and global market  *Dynamic*

- evaluate the compatibility of the objectives of management accounting and management accounting information

- discuss the integration of management accounting information within an overall information system, for example the use of enterprise resource planning systems  *SAP*

- *(information makes sense of data)*
- demonstrate how the information might be used in planning and controlling activities, e.g. benchmarking against similar activities

- discuss how IT developments, e.g. unified corporate databases, RFIDs and network technology may influence management accounting systems.

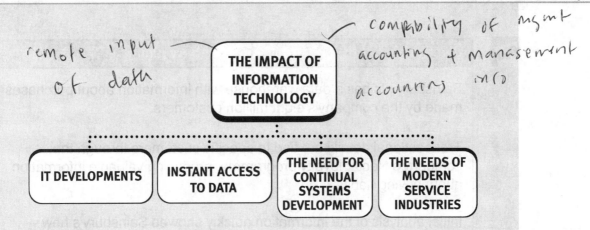

*remote input of data*

*compability of mgmt accounting + management accounting info*

THE IMPACT OF INFORMATION TECHNOLOGY

| IT DEVELOPMENTS | INSTANT ACCESS TO DATA | THE NEED FOR CONTINUAL SYSTEMS DEVELOPMENT | THE NEEDS OF MODERN SERVICE INDUSTRIES |

## 1 Exam focus

*Dec 2013 - 25 marks*

| Exam sitting | Area examined | Question number | Number of marks |
|---|---|---|---|
| December 2011 | Control and development of IS | 3 | 20 |
| June 2010 | IT systems and ABC | 4(a)(ii) | 4 |
| June 2010 | Characteristics of services | 3(iii) | 8 |
| December 2009 | Measurement of service quality | 5(c) | 3 |
| December 2008 | Service quality | 2(c)(d) | 10 |
| Pilot paper | Service quality | 1(e) | 6 |

## 2 Introduction

This chapter discusses the influence of information technology (IT) on strategic management accounting.

There has been a wealth of recent IT developments. These include:

- **Data warehouses**: a data warehouse is a:
  - database: data is combined from multiple and varied sources (internal and external) into one comprehensive, secure and easily manipulated data store. A unified corporate database allows all users to access the same information.
  - data extraction tool: data can be extracted from the database to meet the individual user's needs.
  - a decision support system: data mining is used to analyse the data and unearth unknown patterns or correlations in data.

    *customer lists.*

### Illustration 1 - Influence of IT on Sainsbury plc

Sainsbury plc has a data warehouse with information about purchases made by the company's eight million customers.

Transactional details are tied to specific customers through the company's Nectar loyalty programme, producing valuable information about buying habits.

Initial analysis of the information quickly showed Sainsbury's how ineffective its traditional mass-mailing approaches were – where large numbers of coupons were widely distributed in an attempt to get customers through its doors. Rather than buying more, many customers would cherry-pick the specials and go to its competitors for other items. This meant many advertising campaigns were running at a loss.

Since those initial findings, a concerted focus on timely data analysis and relevant marketing has helped Sainsbury to design far more effective direct marketing campaigns based on customers' actual purchasing habits.

In one campaign designed to increase the value of customers' shopping baskets, Sainsbury's analysed purchases and identified the product category from which each customer purchased most frequently. A coupon for that category would then be sent, along with five other coupons for areas in which it was hoping to boost sales – to encourage customers to buy other types of products. The response rate was 26%, a tremendous amount in retail.

- **Data mining** - this is the analysis of data contained within a data warehouse to unearth relationships between them.

### Illustration 2 - Data mining relationships

Data mining results may include: linkages

- **Associations** - when one event can be correlated to another, e.g. beer purchasers buy peanuts a certain percentage of the time.

- **Sequences** - one event leading to another event, e.g. a rug purchase followed by a purchase of matching curtains.

- **Classifications** - profiles of customers who make purchases can be set up.

- **Networks** - most organisations connect their computers together in local area networks (LANs), enabling them to share data (e.g. via email) and to share devices such as printers. Wide area networks (WANs) are used to connect LANs together, so that computer users in one location can communicate with computer users in another location. Improvements in broadband speed and security have eased communication across sites and from home.

- **Intranet** - this is a private network contained within an organisation. It allows company information and computing resources to be shared among employees.

- **Extranet** - this is a private, secure extension of an Intranet. It allows the organisation to share information with suppliers, customers and other business partners.

- **Internet** - a global system of interconnected networks carrying a vast array of information and resources.

- * **Enterprise resource planning system (ERPS)** - this is a way of *drill down system* integrating the data from all operations within the organisation, e.g. operations, sales and marketing, human resources and purchasing, into one single system.//It ensures that everyone is working off the same system/and includes decision support features to assist management with decision making. Software companies like SAP and Oracle have specialised in the provision of ERP systems across many different industries.

  *more into in new book*

  *- helps identify + plan resources needed to fulfill customers order*

- * **Radio frequency identification (RFID)** - organisations use small radio receivers to tag items and hence to keep track of their assets. It can be used for a variety of purposes, for example:

  - to track inventory in retail stores

  - to tag livestock after the BSE crisis in the United Kingdom in 2002

  - to track the location of doctors in a hospital.

---

### RFID

Many clothing retailers began the phased rollout of item-level radio frequency identification (RFID) tags in 2007 following extensive testing of the technology. Stock accuracy has improved and stores and customers have commented on the more consistent availability of sizes in the pilot departments.

*competitive advantages*

The tags allow staff to carry out stocktaking 20 times faster than bar code scanners by passing an RFID reader over goods. At the end of each day, stock on the shop floor will be scanned and the data collected will be compared with information in a central database containing each store's stock profile, to determine what products need to be replaced. This has led to improved sales through greater product availability.

---

## Test your understanding 1

**Required:**

Explain how the introduction of an ERPS could impact on the role of management accountants.

## Illustration 3 - The internet and management information

An Internet site that allows customers to place orders on-line can provide the following useful management accounting information:

| Data | Use |
| --- | --- |
| Customer details | For delivery purposes; also to build up a record of customer interests and purchases. |
| Product details accessed and products bought | For delivery purposes; also to build up patterns such as products that are often bought together. |
| Value of products bought | Sales accounting and customer profiling. |
| Product details accessed but product not bought | Other items that the customer might be interested in. Why were they not bought? Has a rival got better prices? |
| Date of purchase | Seasonal variations; tie in with special offers and advertising campaigns. |
| Time of purchase | Some web-sites might be particularly busy at certain times of the day. Why that pattern? Avoid busy times when carrying out web-site maintenance. |
| Delivery method chosen | Most Internet sellers give a choice of delivery costs and times. Analysis of this information could help the company to increase its profits. |

## Test your understanding 2

**Required:**

Discuss the impact of recent IT developments on management accounting and on business performance.

## Accounting information

**Required:**

Evaluate the compatibility of the objectives of management accounting and management accounting information.

**Answer:**

**Management accounting information** may be used to:

- **assess the performance** of the business as a whole or of individual divisions or products
- **value inventories**
- **make future plans** _– strategy_ – the provision of management accounting information may assist in making future business plans
- **control the business** – for example, through variance reporting
- **make decisions** - for example, through the provision of summary information (which can be used to make strategic decisions) or through the provision of more detailed information (which can be used to make tactical and operational decisions). _value added_

**Management accounting** involves the provision and analysis of _Buss· support_ detailed information to help managers to run the business today and in the future, i.e. they provide the management accounting information which is used in the ways detailed above. However, for this information to be useful the management accountant must ensure that it is:

- **relevant** - to the needs of the user
- **accurate and complete** - to inspire confidence in the user
- **timely** - in the right place at the right time    _report : quantitative (figures) qualitative_
- **appropriately communicated** - using a suitable format and communication medium
- **cost < benefit**. _cost benefit analysis_

It is important that the management accountant is **available** to answer any questions that arise as a result of the provision of the management accounting information. They also need to be **flexible** in order to respond to the changing needs of the organisation.

_competive economic environment_

## Conclusion

In summary, the objectives of management accounting should be compatible with management accounting information.

## 3 Instant access to data

### 3.1 Introduction

- The information systems discussed in section 2 provide instant access to previously unavailable data. The impact on a business is as follows:
    - real time transaction processing
    - real time billing
    - real time performance monitoring.

    This information can be used by managers for benchmarking and control purposes (see below) and will allow targets and strategies to be updated on a regular basis.

- The new systems also facilitate the remote input of management accounting data in an acceptable format by non-finance specialists.

### 3.2 IT systems and benchmarking

Instant access to data allows managers continuous access to:

- internal data so that they can see patterns trends and changes quickly
- external data so that they can revise benchmarks quickly.

Together these ensure that decision makers have the most up-to-date information about relative performance and can act accordingly:

(1) Organisational performance compared with the performance of 'best in class' organisations.

(2) Gaps in performance identified.

(3) Methods of improving performance identified.

(4) New methods implemented.

(5) Benefits monitored and necessary control action taken.

**IT systems and benchmarking: Pricechallenger.com**

This site claims the following:

'Pricechallenger.com is a web-enabled solution that allows companies to benchmark, control and then substantially reduce costs.'

The data at the heart of the system is drawn from the results of thousands of real negotiations and genuine purchases – not published price lists from supplier catalogues.

KAPLAN PUBLISHING

Reports provide each member with straight forward benchmarks which allow them to:

- assess their own suppliers

- measure the effectiveness of their buying team

- discover where and how to find better prices – the result being savings often between 10% and 20%.

The system searches out individual savings across hundreds of product and service lines, and presents them to the buyer who gains great efficiencies by focusing on the categories with the greatest savings potential. What is more, the savings are on-going and sustainable. Through live market benchmarking there is no need to repeatedly issue tenders. Now members access benchmarking tools to sustain their buying position within the market.

## 3.3 IT systems and budgetary control

A **budgetary control system** compares actual financial performance to budgeted financial performance.

The elements of the control system are:

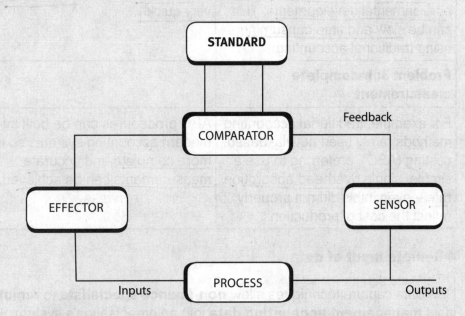

*Budget*
*v*
*variance*
*analysis*

- **standard**: the budget

- **sensor**: the method of recording the actual output

- **feedback**: the actual results for the period, collected by the sensor

- **comparator**: the comparison between actual and budget (e.g. variance analysis)

- **effector**: the manager of the department, in consultation with others, takes action to minimise future adverse variances and to exploit opportunities resulting from favourable variances.

Improvements in IT systems have resulted in a more robust system of budgetary control:

| Problems caused by traditional accounting systems | How a modern accounting system can address the problem |
|---|---|
| **Problem 1: Delays** | |
| For example, sales have to be recorded manually by accounting staff, analysed, posted, compared to budget, variances calculated and action effected. Typically, there could be weeks of delay before knowing whether actual results were in line with those planned. | Sales are recorded and processed in real time by non-accounting staff. Results and comparisons are continually available, certainly by the end of each day. Amended orders to suppliers can be placed quickly. There is a much closer alignment between customers' requirements and goods available. |
| **Problem 2: Environmental impact** | |
| From time to time, budgets need to be adjusted to stay in line with environmental developments. This can be slow and time consuming using traditional accounting. | Budgets and financial models set up on spreadsheets can be changed very quickly. |
| **Problem 3: Incomplete measurement** | |
| For example, traditional accounting methods rarely used activity based costing (ABC), preferring to use a simple, single overhead absorption rate – even if this did not properly reflect the cost of production. | ABC procedures can be built into modern accounting systems so that more complete and accurate measurements can be achieved. |

## 4 Remote input of data

New data capture techniques allow **non-finance specialists** to **remotely** input **management accounting data** into an organisation's system. For example:

- Mobile sales staff can record orders using laptops or hand held computers.

- Shop floor sales staff use multi-purpose barcode scanners to collect information about what products are being bought, at what time and by which customers.

## Test your understanding 3

**Required:**

How would equipping a mobile sales force with laptops capable of communicating accounting information to and from head office help to improve a company's profitability?

## 5 The need for continual systems development

Information and accounting systems need to be developed continually otherwise they will become out of date either because of advances in technology or because of environmental changes.

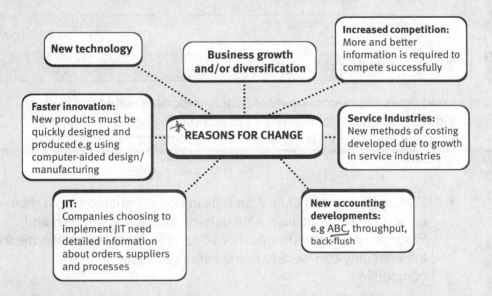

## Test your understanding 4

Blueberry is a quoted hotel resort chain based in Europe. It is considering the use of an activity-based management approach and has identified five activity areas (cost pools) and cost drivers.

The company has recently invested in a 'state of the art' IT system which has the capability to collate all of the data necessary for budgeting in each of the activity areas.

**Required:**

Explain the problems that Blueberry might experience in the successful implementation of an activity-based costing system using its recently acquired 'state of the art' IT system.

## Illustration 4 – The need for continual systems development

New technology, such as radio frequency identification (RFID) technology allows individual items of inventory (like individual tins of beans) to be uniquely identified and tagged.

Marks and Spencer became an early adopter of RFID in autumn 2002, using tags embedded into standard trays which transported fresh food from suppliers to depots. Their aim was to achieve high stock accuracy throughout the supply chain in a very efficient and cost-effective manner.

There are now 4.5 million trays in the Marks and Spencer's supply chain, used by 100 food suppliers. This makes 90% of its food supply RFID-compliant. The data collected is used to confirm deliveries and automate procurement four times more quickly than previous barcode scanning methods, with 100% accuracy.

## Test your understanding 5

Lead times are becoming increasingly important within the clothing industry. An interesting example of a company going against the conventional wisdom is Zara International, part of the Inditex group (Spain).

- Zara produces half of its garments in-house, whereas most retailers outsource all production. Although manufacturing in Spain and Portugal has a cost premium of 10 to 15%, local production means the company can react to market changes faster than the competition.

- Instead of predicting months before a season starts what women will want to wear, Zara observes what is selling and what is not and continuously adjusts what it produces on that basis. This known as a 'design-on-demand' operating model.

- Rather than focusing on economies of scale, Zara manufactures and distributes products in small batches.

- Instead of using outside partners, Zara manages all design, warehousing, distribution, and logistics functions itself.

- The result is that Zara can design, produce, and deliver a new garment to its 600-plus stores worldwide in a mere 15 days.

By comparison a typical shirt manufacturer may take 30 days just to source fabric and then a further ten days to make the shirt. For some firms overall lead time could be between three and eight months from conception to shelf.

### Required:

Comment on the importance of IT systems to Zara's competitive strategy.

## The use of Intranets to enhance performance

HI is a large importer of cleaning products; HI has its head office situated in the centre of the capital city. This head office supports its area branches; a branch consists of an area office and a warehouse. The branches are spread geographically throughout the country; a total of seven area branches are supported.

Currently each HI area office and warehouse supports and supplies its own dealers with the required products. When stocks become low they place a Required Stock Form (RSF) with head office. On receipt of the RSF, head office despatch the goods from their central warehouse to the appropriate area office. When the central warehouse becomes low on any particular item(s) HI will raise purchase orders and send them to one of their many international suppliers.

Typically, each area office has its own stock recording system, running on locally networked personal computer systems (PCs). RSFs are e-mailed to head office.

### Required:

How would the introduction of an Intranet enhance performance within HI?

### Solution:

Goal congruence

An Intranet could provide an excellent opportunity for HI to link all the areas in a number of ways: i.e. allowing access to a central database would be a substantial improvement on the current system, where updates are faxed or e-mailed to head office. This may possibly lead to the development of an integrated database system.

An automatic stock replenishment system could be introduced for the branches, replacing RSFs. If some branches were short of specific items and other branches had ample stocks, then movement between branches may be possible. Currently head office may order goods from suppliers when the organisation has sufficient stocks internally.

Dissemination of best practice throughout the organisation can be encouraged and savings in terms of printing and distributing paper based manuals, catalogues and handbooks. All the current internal documentation can easily be maintained and distributed.

The Intranet would enable the establishment of versatile and standard methods of communication throughout the company.

The Intranet could encourage group or shared development, currently several area offices have their own IT systems working independently on very similar projects.

An Intranet could also enable automatic transfer of information and data i.e. the quarterly figures could be circulated. Monthly returns of business volumes could be calculated on an as required basis.

Information can be provided to all in a user-friendly format.

## 6 The needs of modern service industries

### 6.1 Introduction

Traditional manufacturing companies have been replaced by modern service industries, e.g. insurance, management consultancy and professional services.

The differences between the products of manufacturing companies and those of service businesses:

- can create problems in measuring and controlling performance and
- this, in turn, affects the information needs of service organisations.

### 6.2 Characteristics of services

*8 marks - 2012*

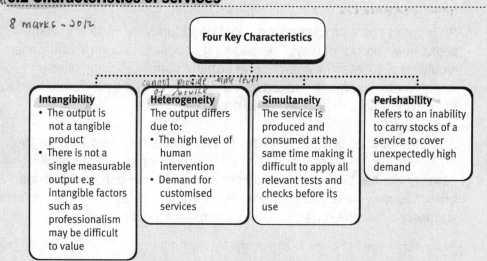

## 6.3 Measuring service quality ~cp chapter 11

Service providers do not have a physical product so base competitive advantage on less tangible customer benefits such as:

- soundness of advice given
- attitude of staff
- ambience of premises
- speed of service
- flexibility/responsiveness
- consistent quality.

### Test your understanding 6

**Required:**

State the performance measures that may be used to in order to assess the surgical quality provided by a hospital indicating how each measure may be addressed.

Ratio
- feedback from patient
- time taken to finish surgery
- complexity of surgery.
- hygiene and cleanliness
- responsiveness of staff

## Chapter summary

*Benefits*

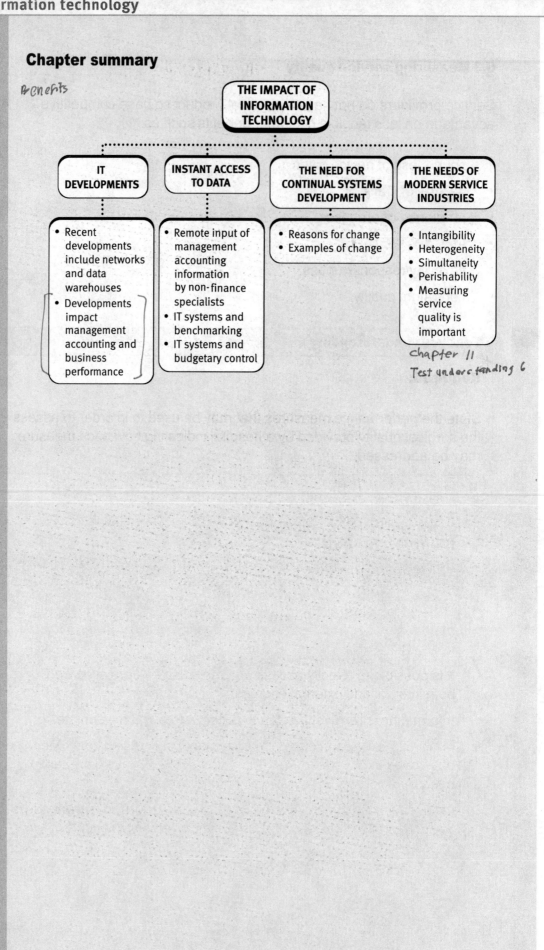

THE IMPACT OF INFORMATION TECHNOLOGY

**IT DEVELOPMENTS**

- Recent developments include networks and data warehouses
- Developments impact management accounting and business performance

**INSTANT ACCESS TO DATA**

- Remote input of management accounting information by non-finance specialists
- IT systems and benchmarking
- IT systems and budgetary control

**THE NEED FOR CONTINUAL SYSTEMS DEVELOPMENT**

- Reasons for change
- Examples of change

**THE NEEDS OF MODERN SERVICE INDUSTRIES**

- Intangibility
- Heterogeneity
- Simultaneity
- Perishability
- Measuring service quality is important

*Chapter 11*
*Test understanding 6*

## Test your understanding answers

### Test your understanding 1

The introduction of ERPS has the potential to have a significant impact on the work of management accountants.

- The use of ERPS causes a substantial reduction in the gathering and processing of routine information by management accountants.

- Instead of relying on management accountants to provide them with information, managers are able to access the system to obtain the information they require directly via a suitable electronic access medium.

- ERPS perform routine tasks that not so long ago were seen as an essential part of the daily routines of management accountants, for example perpetual inventory valuation. Therefore, if management accountants are not to be diminished then it is of necessity that management accountants should seek to expand their roles within their organisations.

- Management accountants may be involved in interpreting the information generated from the ERPS and to provide business support for all levels of management within an organisation.

### Test your understanding 2

- IT developments, such as networks and databases, provide the opportunity for instant access to management accounting information.

- It is possible to directly access and manipulate information from both internal and external sources.

- Information is relatively cheap to collect, store and manipulate.

- Many of the modern forms of management accounting have been developed in conjunction with IT systems, e.g. it may be difficult to run a meaningful ABC system without IT support.

- Data mining techniques can be used to uncover previously unknown patterns and correlations and hence improve performance.

**Test your understanding 3**

The principal accounting information that will be provided by the sales force to head office will be about new sales orders. This information can be used for instant initiation of despatch/manufacture and ordering components.

The information can also be used to produce sales analyses and comparisons to budgets. If sales of certain components are lower than expected, quick decisions can be made about lowering their prices.

The principal accounting information be provided to the sales force from head office is likely to be the latest selling prices, stock availability and customer related information, such as current balances.

**Test your understanding 4**

- A large amount of data will need to be collected initially on each activity. Therefore, the cost of buying, implementing and maintaining a system of activity-based costing will be high.

- Incorrect identification of cost pools and cost drivers would result in inaccurate information being produced by the ABC system and hence incorrect decisions by managers.

**Test your understanding 5**

IT systems are critical to Zara's short lead times.

Zara needs comprehensive information in the following areas:

- which garments are selling, at what price points and in what quantities – key information will relate to both Zara stores and those of competitors

- detailed product specifications for these garments to enable design of new products

- compatibility between reporting and design software systems

- supply chain management

- order and delivery systems.

KAPLAN PUBLISHING

## Test your understanding 6

- The percentage of satisfied patients which could be measured by using the number of customer complaints or via a patient survey.

- The time spent waiting for non-emergency operations which could be measured by reference to the time elapsed from the date when an operation was deemed necessary until it was actually performed.

- The number of successful operations as a percentage of total operations performed which could be measured by the number of remedial operations undertaken.

- The percentage of total operations performed in accordance with agreed schedules which could be measured by reference to agreed operation schedules.

  *– health authority*

- The standards of cleanliness and hygiene maintained which could be measured by observation or by the number of cases of hospital bugs such as MRSA.

- The staff to patient ratio which could be measured by reference to personnel and patient records.

- The responsiveness of staff to requests of patients which could be measured via a patient survey.

structure
layout
referencing

# 6

# Performance measurement systems and design and behavioural aspects

## Chapter learning objectives

Upon completion of this chapter you will be able to:

- discuss, with reference to performance management, ways in which the information requirements of a management structure are affected by the features of the structure

- evaluate whether the management information systems are lean and the value of the information that they provide

- highlight the ways in which contingent (internal and external) factors influence management accounting and its design and use

- evaluate how anticipated human behaviour will influence the design of a management accounting system

- assess the impact of responsibility accounting on information requirements

- discuss the principal internal and external sources of management accounting information, their costs and limitations

- discuss those factors that need to be considered when determining the capacity and development potential of a system

- demonstrate how the type of business entity will influence the recording and processing methods

- discuss the difficulties associated with recording and processing data of a qualitative nature

- evaluate the output reports of an information system in the light of:
  - (i) best practice in presentation
  - (ii) the objectives of the report/organisation
  - (iii) the needs of the readers of the reports
  - (iv) avoiding the problem of information overload
- explain how the effective recruitment, management and motivation of people is necessary for enabling strategic and operational success
- discuss the judgemental and developmental role of assessment and appraisal and their role in improving business performance
- advise on the relationship of performance management to performance measurement (performance rating) and determine the implications of performance measurement to the quality initiatives and process redesign
- explore the meaning and scope of reward systems
- discuss and evaluate different methods of reward practices
- explore the principles and difficulty of aligning reward practices with strategy
- advice on the relationship of reward management to quality initiatives, process re-design and harnessing e-business opportunities
- assess the potential beneficial and adverse consequences of linking reward schemes to performance measurement, for example, how it can affect the risk appetite of employees
- discuss the accountability issues that might arise from performance measurement systems
- evaluate the ways in which performance measurement systems may send the wrong signals and result in undesirable business consequences
- demonstrate how management style needs to be considered when designing and effective performance measurement system
- discuss the problems encountered in planning, controlling and measuring performance levels, e.g. productivity, profitability, quality and service levels, in complex business structures
- discuss the impact on performance management of the use of business models involving strategic alliances, joint ventures and complex supply chain structures.

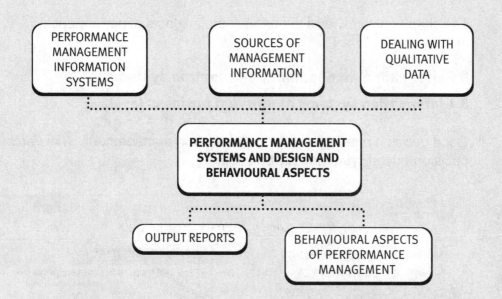

## 1 Exam focus

| Exam sitting | Area examined | Question number | Number of marks |
|---|---|---|---|
| June 2012 | Complex business structures | 5 | 17 |
| December 2011 | Performance appraisal system, Hopwood | 4(b) and (c) | 12 |
| June 2011 | EIS | 1(c) | 5 |
| December 2010 | Impact of KPIs on system design | 1(d) | 9 |
| December 2009 | Acceptance of a performance measurement system | 1(iii) | 6 |
| June 2009 | Agency and expectancy theory | 3(a) | 12 |

**Student Accountant article**: visit the ACCA website, www.accaglobal.com, to review the following article on the topics in this chapter:

Management control - a pre-requisite for survival - October 2004

## 2 Introduction

This chapter focuses on a number of important topics with regards to performance measurement systems. These include:

- the points to consider when designing a system
- the different types of system
- the sources of information
- the control and quality of management report information.

The chapter also reviews the behavioural aspects of performance management.

## 3 Performance management information systems

### 3.1 Information systems at different business levels

Good decision making is at the heart of good management. A hierarchy of decision-based systems may be used:

*senior management*

**Strategic planning**

**Executive information system**
(EIS): gives senior executives access to internal and external information. Information is provided in a summarised form with the option to 'drill down' to a greater level of activity

**Management control**

**Decision support system**
DSS: an aid to making decisions. The system predicts the consequences of a number of possible scenarios and the manager then uses their judgement to make the final decision

**Operational control**

**Transaction processing system**
TPS: a system for processing routine business transactions, often in large volumes, e.g sales and purchase information

*external*

- **Expert systems:** hold specialist knowledge, e.g. on law and taxation, and allow non-experts to interrogate them for information, advice and recommended decisions. Can be used at all levels of management.

- **Management information systems (MIS):** *useful - middle* provide information to all levels of management to enable them to make timely and effective decisions for planning and controlling the activities for which they are responsible. Middle managers will find these systems particularly useful. *internal* *SBU*

---

### Management information systems (MIS)

- A MIS will collate information from individual transactions recorded in the accounting system to allow middle managers to control the business.

- Customer purchases are summarised into reports to provide information about the customers and products providing the most revenue.

- The level of repeat business can be viewed giving an indication of customer satisfaction.

- Management accounts can be produced by the system showing margins for individual products and customers. This will assist in setting individual/ team rewards.

## Test your understanding 1

CB publishing is considering the impact of a new system based on an integrated, single database which would support a management information system (MIS) and an executive information system (EIS). A network update would allow real time input of data.

*access revenue, Gap analysis, variance*

**Required:**

Evaluate the potential impact of the introduction of the new system.

*lean management info system*

*✱ IMPORTANT*

## 3.2 The influence of structure on information requirements

| Characteristics of organisation structure | Information system |
|---|---|
| Large, complex structure. | A sophisticated system will be beneficial and cost effective. |
| High level of interaction between business units. | System should aid communication between managers. |
| Responsibility centres in place, i.e. the business is split into parts which are the responsibility of a single manager. The area of responsibility may be a cost centre, profit centre or investment centre (see chapter 8).  *Divisions* | Management accounting systems should be designed to reflect the responsibility structure in place and ensure that costs and revenues can be traced to those responsible. Managers of responsibility centres will require: <br><br>• the correct information <br><br>• in the correct form <br><br>• at the correct intervals. |

## Responsibility centres

**Responsibility accounting** is a system of accounting based upon the identification of individual parts of a business which are the responsibility of a single manager.

Budgetary control and responsibility accounting are inseparable.

• An organisation chart must be drawn up in order to implement a budgetary control system satisfactorily. It may even be necessary to revise the existing organisation structure before designing the system.

*lean management info system*
*no wastage / excess*

- The aim is to ensure that each manager has a well-defined area of responsibility and the authority to make decisions within that area, and that no parts of the organisation remain as 'grey' areas where it is uncertain who is responsible for them.

- This area of responsibility may be simply a cost centre, or it may be a profit centre (implying that the manager has control over sales revenues as well as costs) or an investment centre (implying that the manager is empowered to take decisions about capital investment for his department). Appropriate performance measures for such structures are discussed in later chapters .

- Once senior management have set up such a structure, with the degree of delegation implied, some form of responsibility accounting system is needed.

- Each centre will have its own budget, and the manager will receive control information relevant to that budget centre.

- Costs (and possibly revenue, assets and liabilities) must be traced to the person primarily responsible for taking the related decisions, and identified with the appropriate department.

- Some accountants would go as far as to advocate charging departments with costs that arise strictly as a result of decisions made by the management of those departments.

Management accounting systems should be designed to reflect the responsibility structure in place and ensure that costs and revenues can be traced to those responsible.

### Controllability  *chapter 8*

The principal of controllability is very important in responsibility accounting. Whilst controllability refers mainly to costs, it is important to remember that its principles can also apply to revenues and investments.

- Controllability can depend on the time scale being considered.
    - Over a long enough time-span, most costs are controllable by someone in the organisation.
    - In the short-term some costs, such as rent, are uncontrollable even by senior managers, and certainly uncontrollable by managers lower down the organisational hierarchy.

- There may be no clear-cut distinction between controllable and non-controllable costs for a given manager, who may also be exercising control jointly with another manager.

- The aim under a responsibility accounting system will be to assign and report on the cost to the person having primary responsibility. The most effective control is thereby achieved, since immediate action can be taken.

- Some authorities would favour the alternative idea that reports should include all costs caused by a department, whether controllable or uncontrollable by the departmental manager. The idea here is that, even if he has no direct control, he might influence the manager who does have control.

## Test your understanding 2

**Required:** ① Budgeting - which areas need more/less
② maintain sustainability (strategic direction)
③
Explain why, as businesses become larger and more diverse, <u>strict</u> <u>financial controls</u> are more likely to be used by top management.

## Test your understanding 3

A production manager will have control over the usage of raw materials but not over price, as buying is done by a separate department.

Responsibility accounting would suggest that the price and usage variances are separated and, under the first approach, the production manager would be told only about the usage variance, a separate report being made to the purchasing manager about the price variance.

**Required:**

Give an alternative argument as to why the production manager should also be told about the price variance.

## Complex business structures

Complex business structures include:

- joint ventures
- strategic alliances
- multinationals
- virtual organisations
- supply chains
- divisionalised structures

The high level of interaction and inter-dependence between partners makes performance management and measurement difficult.

## Test your understanding 4

**Required:**

Discuss the difficulty of performance management and measurement in a virtual organisation which has a number of outsourcing arrangements in place.

## Problems associated with complex structures

| Business Structure | Problems in planning, controlling and measuring performance |
|---|---|
| **Joint venture** - a separate business entity whose shares are owned by two or more business entities. Useful for sharing costs, risks and expertise | • Reporting of joint profits/losses difficult if partners are unwilling to share information or do not have an integrated system<br><br>• Quality, cost control and risk management difficult if partners have different opinions<br><br>• Security of confidential information a concern |
| **Strategic alliance** - similar to a joint venture but a separate business entity is not formed | • Independence is retained making it difficult to put common performance measures in place and to collect and analyse management information<br><br>• Security of confidential information a concern |
| **Multinationals** - have subsidiaries or operations in a number of countries _within – internal_ | • Open to greater levels of uncertainty, e.g. due to exchange rate movements, changes in government policy, recession |

_a – June 2012_

| Virtual organisations - operate with little physical presence and use IT to enable professionals to collaborate without ever meeting face to face | • Loss of control may result in a fall in quality<br>• Difficult to collect data from a large number of dispersed sources<br>• Refer also to test your understanding 4 |
|---|---|
| Supply chains - a network of organisations which relate to each other through the linkages between the different processes involved in producing the finished product | Collaboration between partners can assist in maximising customer satisfaction and hence profitability. Partners will have to work together and share information in order to measure and control performance. However, this process of collaboration may prove difficult |
| Divisionalised structures (see chapter 8) | See chapter 8 |

## 3.3 Lean management information systems

The need for new ideas in management accounting is particularly evident in lean manufacturing organisations. In order to appreciate lean accounting systems, it is helpful to understand the concepts of lean manufacturing.

**Lean manufacturing** is a philosophy of management based on cutting out waste and unecessary activities. Organisations can become 'lean and mean' if they get rid of their unecessary fat. Two elements in lean manufacturing are:

• just-in-time production and purchasing (JIT)

• total quality management (TQM).

These will be reviewed in detail in chapter 11.

**Illustration 1 - JIT and management accounting control systems**

Management accounting systems within a JIT environment must be capable of producing performance and control information consistent with a JIT philosophy. Information must therefore be produced that directs management attention to the following issues:

- elimination of waste
- reduction in set-up time
- continuous improvement.

## Lean accounting

Lean accounting is the application of the idea that accounting systems should be simplified, to remove waste. Management should be provided with statements that are:

- instantly accessible through an IT system, and
- simple to read.

## 4 Sources of management information

### 4.1 Internal and external sources

#### Internal sources

Internal sources of information may be taken from a variety of areas such as the sales ledger (e.g. volume of sales), payroll system (e.g. number of employees) or the fixed asset system (e.g. depreciation method and rate).

**Examples of internal sources of information**

Examples of internal data:

| Source | Information |
|---|---|
| Sales ledger system | Number and value of invoices<br>Volume of sales<br>Value of sales, analysed by customer<br>Value of sales, analysed by product |
| Purchase ledger system | Number and value of invoices<br>Value of purchases, analysed by supplier |

| Payroll system | Number of employees<br>Hours worked<br>Output achieved<br>Wages earned<br>Tax deducted |
|---|---|
| Fixed asset system | Date of purchase<br>Initial cost<br>Location<br>Depreciation method and rate<br>Service history<br>Production capacity |
| Production | Machine breakdown times<br>Number of rejected units |
| Sales and marketing | Types of customer<br>Market research results |

## External sources

In addition to internal information sources, there is much information to be obtained from external sources such as suppliers (e.g. product prices), customers (e.g. price sensitivity) and the government (e.g. inflation rate).

### Examples of external sources of information

| External source | Information |
|---|---|
| Suppliers | Product prices<br>Product specifications |
| Newspapers, journals | Share price<br>Information on competitors<br>Technological developments<br>National and market surveys |
| Government | Industry statistics<br>Taxation policy<br>Inflation rates<br>Demographic statistics<br>Forecasts for economic growth |
| Customers | Product requirements<br>Price sensitivity |

| Employees | Wage demands |
| | Working conditions |
| Banks | Information on potential customers |
| | Information on national markets |
| Business enquiry agents | Information on competitors |
| | Information on customers |
| Internet | Almost everything via databases (public and private), discussion groups and mailing lists |

## Test your understanding 5

**Required:**

What are the limitations of using externally generated information?

The internal and external information may be used in **planning** and **controlling** activities. For example:

- Newspapers, the Internet and business enquiry agents (such as Dun and Bradstreet) may be used to obtain external competitor information for benchmarking purposes.

- Internal sales volumes may be obtained for variance analysis purposes.

## Test your understanding 6

**Required:**

Briefly explain the use of customer data for control purposes.

### 4.2 The costs of information

The benefit of management information must exceed the cost (**benefit > cost**) of obtaining the information.

## Benefits and costs of information

The design of management information systems should involve a cost/benefit analysis. A very refined system offers many benefits, but at a cost. The advent of modern IT systems has reduced that cost significantly. However, skilled staff have to be involved in the operation of information systems, and they can be very expensive to hire.

Let us illustrate this with a simple example. Production costs in a factory can be reported with varying levels of frequency ranging from daily (365 times per year) to annually (once per year). Costs or benefits of reporting tend to move as follows in response to increasing frequency of reporting.

- Information has to be gathered, collated and reported in proportion to frequency and costs will move in line with this. Experience suggests that some element of diseconomy of scale may set in at high levels of frequency.

- Initially, benefits increase sharply, but this increase starts to tail off. A point may come where 'information overload' sets in and benefits actually start to decline and even become negative. If managers are overwhelmed with information, then this actually starts to get in the way of the job.

The position may be represented graphically as follows:

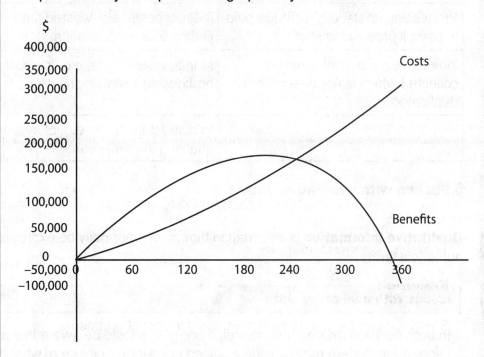

An information system is just like any part of a business operation. It incurs costs and it offers benefits. In designing an information system, the accountant has to find some means of comparing the two for different options and determining which option is optimal. In this sense, system design follows the same practices for investment appraisal and decision making which are explored later in this text.

In the above case it can be seen that net benefits (benefits less costs) are maximised at around 120 reports per year – suggesting an optimal information cycle of about 3 days. The system should be designed to gather, collate and report information at three-day intervals. This is an over-simplified example but it serves to illustrate a general logic which can be applied to all aspects of information system design.

**Test your understanding 7**

**Required:**

Discuss the factors that need to be considered when determining the capacity and development potential of a system.

The costs of information can be classified as follows:

| Costs of internal information | Costs of external information |
|---|---|
| Direct data capture costs, e.g. the cost of barcode scanners in a supermarket. | Direct costs, e.g. newspaper subscriptions. |
| Processing costs, e.g. salaries paid to payroll processing staff. | Indirect costs, e.g. wasted time finding useful information. |
| Indirect costs, e.g. information collected which is not needed or is duplicated. | Management costs, e.g. the cost of processing information. |
|  | Infrastructure costs, e.g. of systems enabling Internet searches. |

## 5 Dealing with qualitative data

**Qualitative information** is information that cannot normally be expressed in numerical terms.

**Issues with qualitative data**

In both decision making and control, managers should be aware that an information system may provide a limited or distorted picture of what is actually happening. In many situations, sensitivity has to be used in interpreting the output of an information system.

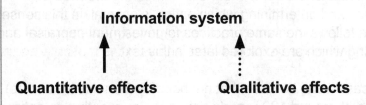

**Information system**

**Quantitative effects**          **Qualitative effects**

It is worth noting that as many economies move from being manufacturing based to service based there may be fewer opportunities to use quantitative measures and that qualitative measures become more important.

Qualitative information is often in the form of opinions, for example:

- **employees** – who will be affected by certain decisions which may threaten their continued employment, or cause them to need re-training

- **customers** – who will be interested to know about new products, but will want to be assured that service arrangements, etc. will continue for existing products

- **suppliers** – who will want to be aware of the entity's plans, e.g a move to a just-in-time (JIT) environment.

It is difficult to record and process data of a qualitative nature but qualitative factors still need to be considered when making a decision. These include:

- **The effects on the environment**: certain decisions may affect emissions and pollution of the environment. The green issue and the entity's responsibility towards the environment may seriously affect its public image.

- **Legal effects**: there may be legal implications of a course of action, or a change in law may have been the cause of the decision requirement.

- **Political effects**: government policies, in both taxation and other matters, may impinge on the decision.

- **Timing of decision**: the timing of a new product launch may be crucial to its success.

These factors must be considered before making a final decision. Each of these factors is likely to be measured by opinion. Such opinions must be collected and co-ordinated into meaningful information.

### Illustration 2 – Dealing with qualitative data

Here are some examples of qualitative effects.

- The impact of a decreased output requirement on staff morale is something that may be critical but it is not something that an information system would automatically report.

- The impact of a reduction in product range may have a subtle impact on the image that a business enjoys in the market – again something that an information system may not report.

### Test your understanding 8

**Information and Investment**

Moffat commenced trading on 01/12/X2, it supplies and fits tyres and exhaust pipes and service motor vehicles at thirty locations. The directors and middle management are based at the Head Office of Moffat.

Each location has a manager who is responsible for day-to-day operations and is supported by an administrative assistant. All other staff at each location are involved in the fitting and servicing operations.

The directors of Moffat are currently preparing a financial evaluation of an investment of $2 Million in a new IT system for submission to its bank. They are concerned that sub-optimal decisions are being made because the current system does not provide appropriate information throughout the organisation. They are also aware that not all of the benefits from the proposed investment will be qualitative in nature.

**Required:**

(a) Explain the characteristics of THREE types of information required to assist in decision-making at different levels of management and on differing timescales within Moffat, providing two examples of information that would be appropriate to each level.

(b) Identify and explain THREE approaches that the directors of Moffat might apply in assessing the QUALITATIVE benefits of the proposed investment in a new IT system.

(c) Identify TWO QUALITATIVE benefits that might arise as a consequence of the investment in a new IT system and explain how you would attempt to assess them.

## 6 Output reports

The output reports produced for management should contain good information.

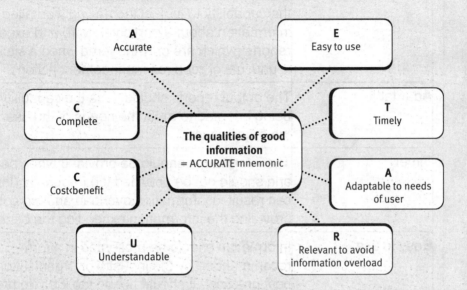

**Qualities of output reports**

The output reports from an information system should allow the organisation to run the business effectively both today and in the future. Output reports should have the following characteristics:

| Characteristic | Explanation |
|---|---|
| **A**ccurate | For example, figures should add up and there should be no typos. |
| **C**omplete | The reports should include all the information that is needed by the readers of the report and should be aligned to the overall objectives of the report or of the organisation. |
| **C**ost < benefit | The benefit of having the information must be greater than the cost of providing it. |
| **U**nderstandable | The readers of the report must be able to understand the contents and use the contents to fulfil their needs. Presentation should be clear and in line with best practice. |

| Relevant | Information that is not needed by the reader(s) of the report should be omitted.  Information overload can be a huge problem and can detract from the usefulness of the report.  The problem of information overload may be overcome using, for example, drill-down reports (provide users with the capability to look at increasingly detailed information about a particular item) and exception reports (which are only triggered when a situation is unusual or requires management action). |
|----------|-----|
| Adaptable | The output reports should have the capability of being adapted to meet the needs of the user or the organisation. |
| Timely | The information should be provided when needed and should not be provided too frequently (this can result in information overload and the cost of providing the information exceeding the benefit). |
| Easy to use | Information should be presented in a form recommended by the industry or organisation's best practice.  It should not be too long (to prevent information overload) and it should be sent using the most appropriate communication channel to ensure user needs are met. |

**Test your understanding 9**

**Required:**

Discuss the weaknesses in an information system that could result in poor output reports.

**Question focus**:  Now complete or review questions 9 and 10 from chapter 13.  These are not past exam questions but should help to give you a broader understanding of some of the areas covered above and in the previous chapter.

June 2012

# 7 Behavioural aspects of performance management

## 7.1 Introduction

The design of a management accounting system must take into account human behaviour.

```
┌─────────────────────┐
│   Human Behaviour   │
└─────────────────────┘
```

**Learning curves**
- as workers become more familiar with the production of a new product the average time per unit will decline

Take into account when:
- setting standards
- budgeting
- work scheduling
- considering price and product viability

**Learning styles**
- individuals learn in different ways. e.g theorists take an intellectual, non-practical approach where as activists take a practical approach

Need to take into account when considering how information:
- should be sent
- will be responded to

## 7.2 The relationship between people management and organisational success

```
┌──────────────────────────┐
│  People are fundamental  │
│    to an organisation    │
└──────────────────────────┘
```

**Strategic significance**
- the creation and fulfilment of the strategy relies on the skills, knowledge and creativity of the people

**Operational significance**
- successful completion of a task relies on having employees with appropriate skills and abilities to carry out their work

An organisation uses human resource management (HRM) to ensure that it has the correct people in place to fulfil its strategic and operational objectives.

**HRM** is the 'strategic and coherent approach to the management of an organisation's most valued assets: the people working there who individually and collectively contribute to the achievement of its objectives for sustainable competitive advantage' (Armstrong).

The following aspects of HRM are of particular importance:

- **Recruitment** - careful recruitment will be necessary to ensure that the organisation has in place the correct number of staff with the right skills base.

- **Performance management** - individual objectives should be set which support the organisation's overall targets and goals. These should be communicated to and understood by employees.

- **Retention and motivation** - motivated staff are more likely to achieve targets and organisational goals. Vroom's motivation theory is examinable:

  **Vroom** believed that people will be motivated to do things to reach a goal if they believe in the worth of that goal and if they can see that what they do will help them in achieving it. Vroom's expectancy model is stated as:

  **Force = valence × expectancy**
  where:
  Force = the strength of a person's motivation
  Valence = the strength of an individual's desire for an outcome
  Expectancy = the probability that they will achieve that outcome

| **Employee retention** |
| --- |
| Retention may be achieved using:<br><br>- induction<br>- training<br>- job design<br>- rewards. |

Some examples of the link between HRM and strategy are as follows:

If competitive advantage is sought through differentiation then HRM needs to ensure that high quality, skilled staff are recruited, that these staff are given the freedom to be creative and innovate, that a culture of service and quality is prevalent, and that rewards are geared towards long-term success and beyond short-term financial measures.

On the other hand, if a strategy of cost leadership was pursued, then HRM needs to focus on recruiting low skilled workers, providing repetitive, simple tasks, minimising staff numbers, providing strict controls, and focusing appraisals and rewards on short-term cost measures.

**Test your understanding 10**

**Required:**

If an organisation planned to grow through acquisition, how might HRM contribute to the achievement of this strategy?

## 7.3 Using appraisal to improve business performance

**Performance appraisal** is the process of evaluating employee performance against predetermined objectives and providing feedback to the employee so that any necessary adjustments to performance can be made.

**Test your understanding 11**

**Required:**

The most usual rationalisation and justification for appraisal is to improve individual performance. However, there are a number of other reasons. Identify four of these reasons.

The reasons for appraisal were discussed in the TYU above. These can be grouped into two broad categories:

*Control*

- The **judgement purpose** - the appraiser exercises their judgement to make decisions regarding factors such as pay, promotion and work responsibilities.

*Identify development needs*

- The **development purpose** - the appraiser strives to bring about employee performance improvements through the identification of training and development needs. An action plan should be implemented to meet these needs.

This can lead to a conflict in the process between on the one hand assessing value (judgement purpose), and on the other hand offering support (development purpose).

### Illustration 4 - Conflicts in the appraisal process

A judgmental analysis may lead to an assessment that the employee has failed to achieve goals or objectives that had been agreed upon in advance. This judgement might result in the employee not receiving a pay rise or promotion or a bonus. The employee will therefore feel that he/she has been criticised as this part of the assessment and build up resistance to the appraiser and the appraisal process.

But at the same time the appraiser will want to make a developmental appraisal. They will want to determine why the employee has failed and offer support in avoiding these failures in the future by developing the employee's skills (e.g. via training).

It is therefore important that the employee understands that the appraisal is as much for their benefit as for the employers. This is why feedback is important.

## Barriers to the appraisal process

Lockett suggests that appraisal barriers can be identified as follows:

| Barrier | Example |
| --- | --- |
| Appraisal is confrontation | Differing views regarding performance |
| | Feedback is biased |
| | Feedback is badly delivered |
| Appraisal is judgement | Appraisal is one-sided |
| | Appraisal is imposed |
| Appraisal is chat | An unproductive conversation |
| Appraisal is bureaucracy | Form filling and depersonalised |
| | No real purpose or worth |
| Appraisal is an event | A traditional ceremony |
| | No real purpose or worth |
| Appraisal is unfinished business | No belief that issues will be followed up |

*transparent, equitable, just, fair*

## Test your understanding 12

**Required:**

Critically evaluate the statement that appraisal will lead to improvements in business performance.

## The importance of target selection

Appraisal (performance management) will only be beneficial and achieve its aims if appropriate targets (performance measures) are set. Targets should be:

- **Relevant** to the organisation's overall objective, e.g. if the organisation has an objective of 100% quality then an individual production worker maybe set a target to produce products with zero defects. (It is worth noting that quality initiatives are often undermined by targets that focus on short term profits).

- **Achievable** - employees may be unmotivated if they consider targets are very difficult or impossible to achieve, e.g. zero defects may be seen as impossible. However, it is worth noting that the same may be true if targets are too easy to achieve.

- **Controllable** - the individual will be unmotivated if they feel they can't control the target set, e.g. a production worker may not be responsible for defects if poor quality materials are purchased.

- **Prioritised** - employees will be overwhelmed and hence unmotivated if they are set a large number of targets.

### 7.4 Performance measurement and reward systems

The **reward system** of an organisation comprises the monetary and non-monetary payments given to employees in return for work performed.

### The purpose of reward systems

- To provide a fair and consistent basis for rewarding employees.
- To motivate staff and maximise performance.
- To further company objectives through the achievement of employee's objectives.
- To reward performance through promotion or progression.
- To control salary costs.

### Methods of reward

Employee rewards fall into three categories:

- **Basic pay** - determined in a number of ways such as market rates or job evaluation.

- **Performance-related pay** - pay is based on the level of performance. Rewards may be based on individual, group or organisational performance, all of which will have a different impact on behaviour.

- **Benefits** - a wide range of non-monetary rewards such as company cars or health insurance.

- share option

### Test your understanding 13

**Required:**

Evaluate the three different reward methods.

## Benefits and problems of linking reward schemes to performance

The benefits and problems were touched on in the test your understanding but a more detailed list is included below:

| Benefits of linking reward schemes and performance | Potential problems of linking reward schemes and performance |
|---|---|
| • It gives individuals an incentive to achieve a good performance level since they know that this will be rewarded.<br><br>• Schemes based on shares can motivate employees/managers to act in the long-term interests of the organisation.<br><br>• Effective schemes also attract and keep the employees valuable to an organisation.<br><br>• By tying an organisation's key performance indicators to a scheme, it is clear to all employees that performance creates organisational success.<br><br>• By rewarding performance, an effective scheme creates an organisation focused on continuous improvement. | • Employees will prioritise the achievement of their reward which may impact their risk appetite. Employees may become too cautious and risk averse or conversely they may take bigger risks.<br><br>• Employees may be unmotivated if they feel that they were penalised financially for circumstances outside of their control, e.g. an employee may have hit their quality target but did not receive a reward because the company's annual performance was poor.<br><br>• Employees may become highly stressed if a significant proportion of their income is performance related.<br><br>• Employees will have an extra incentive towards the dysfunctional behaviour, i.e. making decisions that are not in the best interests of the business.<br><br>• Should targets be based on individual, team, division or group performance? |

**Illustration 5 – Reward schemes and risk appetite**

As mentioned above, one of the problems associated with linking reward schemes to performance is that employees will prioritise the achievement of their reward which may impact their risk appetite.

UK banking executive's pay has received widespread political and media coverage since the 2008 financial crisis. It is argued that performance related bonuses have incentivised excessive risk taking and short-termism and there are widespread concerns that remuneration policies may have been a contributory factor to the financial crisis.

### Reward management in the modern business environment

We have already discussed the need for individual staff targets and hence rewards to be aligned with strategic goals. There have been some common changes to strategic goals in the modern business environment:

- **Quality** - as mentioned previously, strategic quality objectives should be translated into individual quality objectives. Pay or rewards should then be linked to the achievement of these targets.

- **Process re-design** - a change to a process and hence job roles will result in changes to organisational and individual goals. Rewards should be based on the achievement of these new goals. Managers should be aware that employees may be resistant to changes in their job role and must therefore ensure that the reward scheme provides sufficient incentives for change.

- **E-business** - an organisation embarking on a strategy of e-business (i.e. using the Internet to connect with customers, partners and suppliers) will have to ensure that an individual's objectives and rewards reflect the new process and technological objectives of the organisation.

**Question focus**: Now attempt question 8 from chapter 13.

### 7.5 Other behavioural aspects of performance measurement

### Wrong signals and inappropriate action

A control system which is badly designed or which is applied in an insensitive manner may end up doing more harm than good.

**Illustration 6 – Behavioural aspects of performance measurement**

For example, the manager of a production line may get his costs within budget by cutting back on inspection costs – with adverse consequences for the business as a whole when customers report consequent higher numbers of defective units.

There are many ways in which poorly designed performance measurement can result in wrong signals and dysfunctional behaviour. Berry, Broadbent and Otley identified the following problem areas:

- **Misrepresentation** – 'creative' reporting to suggest that a result is acceptable.

- **Gaming** – deliberate distortion of a measure to secure some strategic advantage.

- **Misinterpretation** – failure to recognise the complexity of the environment in which the organisation operates.

- **Short-termism** – leading to the neglect of longer-term objectives.

- **Measure fixation** – measures and behaviour in order to achieve specific performance indicators which may not be effective.

- **Tunnel vision** – undue focus on stated performance measures to the detriment of other areas.

- **Sub-optimisation** – focus on some objectives so that others are not achieved.

- **Ossification** – an unwillingness to change the performance measurement scheme once it has been set up.

A number of actions might be taken in order to minimise the impact of imperfections that may exist within the performance measurement system. These methods will be explored in later chapters.

**Management Styles**

**Hopwood** identified three distinct management styles of performance appraisal. The style needs to be considered when designing an effective performance measurement system.

## Hopwood styles

### Budget constrained style

The manager's performance is primarily evaluated upon the basis of his ability to continually meet the budget on a short-term basis. The manager will receive unfavourable feedback from his superior if, for instance, his actual costs exceed the budgeted costs, regardless of other considerations.

### Profit-conscious style

The manager's performance is evaluated on the basis of his ability to increase the general effectiveness of his unit's operations in relation to the long-term purposes of the organisation.

### Non-accounting style

The budgetary information plays a relatively unimportant part in the superior's evaluation of the manager's performance.

|  | Budget constrained | Profit-conscious | Non-accounting |
|---|---|---|---|
| **Characteristics** | • Pressure to hit short-term financial targets. | • Focus on longer-term performance. | • Little emphasis on financial performance.<br>• Look at non-financial aspects instead. |
| **Advantages** | • Should ensure short-term targets are met. | • Give flexibility to go 'off plan' if justifiable. | • Focus on causes rather than effects.<br>• Targets may be more meaningful to staff. |

| Disadvantages | • Short-termism (e.g. cost cutting). | • Loss of short-term control. | • Financial implications of behaviour may be neglected. |
|---|---|---|---|
| | • Results may be 'distorted'. | | |
| | • Stress. | | |
| | • Lack of flexibility. | | |
| | • Stifles ingenuity. | | |

## Accountability and performance measurement

**Agency theory** considers the relationship between a principal and an agent.

### Illustration 7 – Agent and principal

In companies, the identification of the principal (shareholders) and agent (managers and employees) is relatively straightforward.

In the public sector and not-for-profit organisations the relationship is more complex and there may be several principals. For example, in a government funded hospital the principals may include the government (who provide the funds) and the patients (as recipients of the treatment). The agent will be the doctors, managers and other hospital staff.

The achievement of accountability, i.e. holding the agent to account is an important aspect of the relationship between the principal and the agent.

### Illustration 8 – Agency theory applied to a performance

In the case of performance measurement:

* the principal is the employer
* the agent is the employee.

The problem is how the agent can be motivated and monitored so that they do what the principal wants. In reality this may be achieved by aligning the principal's goals with the agent's goals and the reward system (as previously discussed).

## Chapter summary

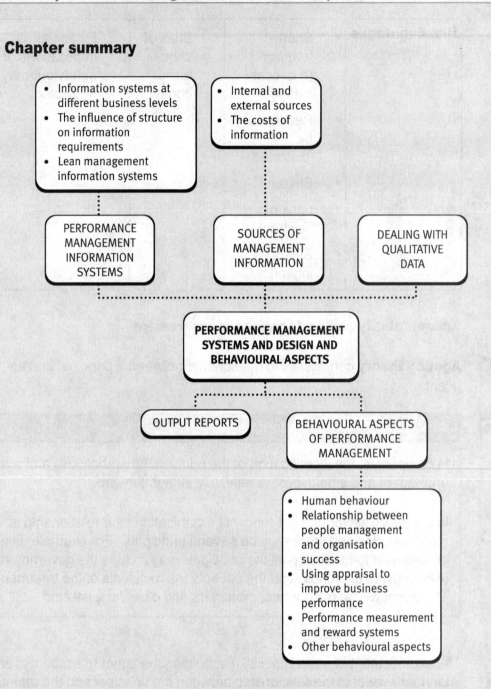

- Information systems at different business levels
- The influence of structure on information requirements
- Lean management information systems

- Internal and external sources
- The costs of information

PERFORMANCE MANAGEMENT INFORMATION SYSTEMS

SOURCES OF MANAGEMENT INFORMATION

DEALING WITH QUALITATIVE DATA

**PERFORMANCE MANAGEMENT SYSTEMS AND DESIGN AND BEHAVIOURAL ASPECTS**

OUTPUT REPORTS

BEHAVIOURAL ASPECTS OF PERFORMANCE MANAGEMENT

- Human behaviour
- Relationship between people management and organisation success
- Using appraisal to improve business performance
- Performance measurement and reward systems
- Other behavioural aspects

# Test your understanding answers

| Advantages | Disadvantages |
|---|---|
| • Benefit of real time data input and access. | • Cost of real time data input. |
| • Improved decision making, e.g. the EIS should allow drill-down access of data to operational level but presentation of data should be based on the KPIs of the company. | • Cost of linking the EIS to new, external data sources. |
| | • Cost of implementation and training. |
| | • Risk that the system does not work properly or that training is inadequate. |
| • The EIS will link to external data sources thus reducing the risk of ignoring issues from the wider environment. | • Increased security threat since the data is only held in one place. |
| • The database will reduce/eliminate the problem of data redundancy since data is only held in one place. | • Potential information overload, especially for senior managers. |
| • Improved data integrity. Data is only held in one place and therefore time and effort will be taken to ensure it is 'ACCURATE'. | |

**Test your understanding 2**

As businesses become larger and more diverse, it becomes more difficult for top management to control them in any way other than by strict financial targets. The diversity of information and complexity is simply too great. Targets on profitability, return on investment and residual income are easy to set and monitor without knowing much about the details of business activities.

If there is high diversity, then sub-units are largely independent of one another so that each can be judged fairly in isolation, i.e. poor performance in one division should have no effect on another.

## Test your understanding 3

With additional information the production manager may attempt to persuade the purchasing manager to try alternative sources of supply.

## Test your understanding 4

**Performance measurement problems**

- Key players in the business processes and supply chains are not on site.
- Collecting and monitoring data about employees working from home or about outsourcing partners is difficult.
- Outsourcing partners will have their own (potentially incompatible) systems.
- The organisation and the outsourcing partners may have differing objectives.

**Performance management problems**

- Difficulty monitoring the actions and performance of employees working at home.
- Difficulty managing outsourcing partners, for example:
  - potential loss of confidential information
  - partners providing a business critical role may prove unreliable
  - wasted time managing the relationship with outsourcing partners
  - difficulty negotiating a contract that is motivating and profitable for both parties.

## Test your understanding 5

- External information may not be accurate.
- External information may be out of date.
- The company publishing the data may not be reputable.
- External information may not meet the exact needs of the business.
- It may be difficult to gather external information, e.g. from customers or competitors.

### Test your understanding 6

Historical customer data will give information about:

- product purchases and preferences
- price sensitivity
- where customers shop
- who customers are (customer profiling).

For a business that prioritises customer satisfaction this will give important control information. Actual customer data can be compared with plans and control action can be taken as necessary, e.g. prices may be changed or the product mix may be changed.

### Test your understanding 7

An information system can be developed to varying levels of refinement. Specifically:

- **Reporting frequency** - information can be collected and reported with varying levels of frequency, e.g. for example, the management accounting system of a manufacturer can report actual production costs on a daily, weekly, monthly or even annual basis

- **Reporting quantity and level of detail** - information can be collected and reported at varying levels of detail e.g. in absorbing overheads into product costs one can use a single factory overhead absorption rate (OAR) or one can operate a complex ABC system. The information requirements of the latter are far more elaborate than those of the former

- **Reporting accuracy and back-up** - subtle qualitative factors can be incorporated into information systems at varying levels, e.g. information can be rigorously checked for accuracy or a more relaxed approach can be adopted.

Broadly, the more refined the system is, then the more expensive it is to establish and operate. The organisation has to decide if the increased benefits outweigh the increased costs.

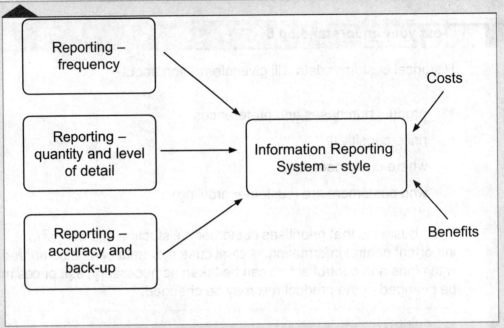

## Test your understanding 8

### Information and Investment – Moffat

(a) The management of an organisation need to exercise control at different levels within an organisation. These levels are often categorised as being strategic, tactical and operational. The information required by management at these levels varies in nature and content.

#### Strategic information

Strategic information is required by the management of an organisation in order to enable management to take a longer term view of the business and assess how the business may perform during the period. The length of this long term view will vary from one organisation to another, being very much dependent upon the nature of the business and the ability of those responsible for strategic decisions to be able to scan the planning horizon.

Strategic information tends to be holistic and summary in nature and would be used by management, when for example, undertaking SWOT analysis.

In Moffat strategic information might relate to the development of new services such as the provision of a home-based vehicle recovery service or the provision of 24hr servicing. Other examples would relate to the threats posed by Moffat's competitors or assessing the potential acquisition of a tyre manufacturer in order to enhance customer value via improved efficiency and lower costs.

### Tactical information

Tactical Information is required in order to facilitate management planning and control for shorter time periods than strategic information. Such information relates to the tactics that management adopt in order to achieve a specific course of action. In Moffat this might involve the consideration of whether to open an additional outlet in another part of the country or whether to employ additional supervisors at each outlet in order to improve the quality of service provision to its customers.

### Operational information

Operational information relates to a very short time scale and is often used to determine immediate actions by those responsible for day-to-day management.

In Moffat the manager at each location within Moffat would require information relating to the level of customer sales, the number of vehicles serviced and the number of complaints received during a week. Operational information might be used within Moffat in order to determine whether staff are required to work overtime due to an unanticipated increase in demand, or whether operatives require further training due to excessive time being spent on servicing certain types of vehicle.

(b)   One approach that the directors of Moffat could adopt would be to ignore the qualitative benefits that may arise on the basis that there is too much subjectivity involved in their assessment.

The problem that this causes is that the investment will probably look unattractive since all the costs will be included in the valuation whereas significant benefits and savings will have been ignored. This approach lacks substance and would not be recommended.

An alternative approach would involve attempting to attribute values to each of the identified benefits that are qualitative in nature. Such an approach will necessitate the use of management estimates in order to derive the cash flows to be incorporated in a cost benefit analysis. The problems inherent in this approach include gaining consensus amongst interested parties regarding the footing of the assumptions from which estimated cash flows have been derived. Furthermore, if the proposed investment does take place then it may well prove impossible to prove that the claimed benefits of the new system have actually been realised.

Perhaps the preferred approach is to acknowledge the existence of qualitative benefits and attempt to assess them in a reasonable manner acceptable to all parties including the company's bank. The financial evaluation would then not only incorporate 'hard' facts relating to costs and benefits that are qualitative in nature, but also would include details of qualitative benefits which management consider exist but have not attempted to assess in financial terms. Such benefits might include, for example, the average time saved by location managers in analysing information during each operating period.

Alternatively the management of Moffat could attempt to express qualitative benefits in specific terms linked to a hierarchy of organisational requirements.

For example, qualitative benefits could be catergorised as being:

(1)  Essential to the business

(2)  Very useful attributes

(3)  Desirable, but not essential

(4)  Possible, if funding is available

(5)  Doubtful and difficult to justify

(c)  One of the main qualitative benefits that may arise from an investment in a new IT system by Moffat is the improved level of service to its customers in the form of reduced waiting times which may arise as a consequence of better scheduling of appointments and inventory management. This could be assessed via the introduction of a questionnaire requiring customers to rate the service that they have received from their recent visit to a location within Moffat according to specific criteria such as adherence to appointed times, time taken to service a vehicle, cleanliness of the vehicle and attitude of staff.

Alternatively a follow-up telephone call from a centralised customer services department may be made by Moffat personnel in order to gather such information.

Another qualitative benefit may arise in the form of competitive advantage. Improvement in customer specific information and service levels may give Moffat a competitive advantage.

Likewise improved inventory management may enable costs to be reduced thereby enabling a 'win-win' relationship to be enjoyed with customers.

### Test your understanding 9

- **Unreliable information**: Information must be sufficiently reliable (e.g. accurate and complete) so that managers trust it to make judgements and decisions.

- **Presentation**: The information system may not be capable of presenting the information in a user-friendly format.

- **Appropriate information**: The information produced by the system should assist in meeting the organisation's objectives and should meet the needs of the users.

- **Timeliness**: Information must be available in time for managers to use it to make decisions.

- **Responsibility and controllability**: Information systems might fail to identify controllable costs, or indicate management responsibility properly. Information should be directed to the person who has the authority and the ability to act on it.

- **Information overload:** In some cases, managers might be provided with too much information, and the key information might be lost in the middle of large amounts of relatively unimportant figures.

- **Cost and value**: The cost of providing the information should not exceed the benefits obtained.

### Test your understanding 10

HRM may have to:

- plan potential redundancies when staff are measured

- facilitate and manage the changes in culture and performance that are necessary

- ensure that corporate goals and missions are understood and communicated

- unify reward systems

- redesign jobs

- plan training.

This is just one further example of the link between HRM and strategy, but it should illustrate how HRM plays a role in contributing to the achievement of an organisation's objectives.

### Test your understanding 11

The main purpose of appraisal is to improve individual performance. Other purposes include:

- to review past performance:
    - action should be taken to solve any problems identified
    - rewards should be determined
- to assess future potential/promotion prospects
- to set future performance objectives (these should be aligned to the overall objectives)
- to improve motivation and morale since employees can see a clear link between the achievement of their objectives and their rewards.

### Test your understanding 12

Appraisal may lead to business improvements because:

- employees will be more motivated (and hence more productive) since they feel that they are rewarded for achieving their objectives
- employees will be more motivated since they feel that their developmental needs are being addressed
- individual employee objectives should be aligned with business objectives. Therefore, if an employee achieves their objectives the performance of the business should also improve.

However, the judgemental purpose of appraisal has the ability to demotivate (and hence to reduce productivity) because:

- employees may feel that they are being criticised
- employees may not consider the assessment to be fair
- employees may not think that the appraisal has any purpose or worth.

KAPLAN PUBLISHING

**Test your understanding 13**

|  | Advantages | Disadvantages |
| --- | --- | --- |
| **Basic pay** | • Easy to administer<br>• Basic employee needs taken care of | • Does not motivate employees to achieve strategy<br>• Does not motivate employees to improve performance |
| **Performance-related pay** | • Motivates employees to achieve strategy<br>• Motivates employees to improve performance | • Can be subjective and inconsistent<br>• Can be viewed as unfair if based on team/ company performance<br>• Stressful for employee if they rely on this to pay for basic needs |
| **Benefits** | • Can be tailored to the individual employee | • Employees may not want<br>• Does not motivate employees to achieve strategy<br>• Big additional cost |

# Financial performance measures in the private sector

## Chapter learning objectives

Upon completion of this chapter you will be able to:

- demonstrate why the primary objective of financial performance should be primarily concerned with the benefits to shareholders

- justify, for a profit-seeking organisation, the crucial objectives of survival and business growth

- discuss the appropriateness of, and apply the following as measures of performance:
  - return on capital employed (ROCE)
  - earnings per share (EPS)
  - earnings before interest, tax and depreciation adjustment (EBITDA)
  - net present value (NPV)
  - internal rate of return and modified internal rate of return (IRR, MIRR)

- discuss why indicators of liquidity and gearing need to considered in conjunction with profitability

- compare and contrast short and long run financial performance and the resulting management issues

- explore the traditional relationship between profits and share value with the long-term profit expectations of the stock market and recent financial performance of new technology/communications companies

- assess the relative financial performance of the organisation compared to appropriate benchmarks.

```
          ┌──────────────────────────┐
          │  FINANCIAL PERFORMANCE   │
          │     MEASURES IN THE      │
          │      PRIVATE SECTOR      │
          └──────────────────────────┘
```

| OBJECTIVES OF PROFIT-SEEKING ORGANISATIONS | FINANCIAL PERFORMANCE MEASURES | LONG AND SHORT TERM FINANCIAL PERFORMANCE |
| --- | --- | --- |

## 1 Exam focus

| Exam sitting | Area examined | Question number | Number of marks |
| --- | --- | --- | --- |
| June 2012 | Performance measurement systems and design | 1 | 40 |
| December 2009 | Evaluation of financial performance | 4(a) | 6 |
| June 2009 | NPV calculation | 2(a) | 6 |
| December 2008 | Assessment of financial performance | 2(a) | 14 |
| June 2008 | NPV and sensitivity analysis | 4(b)(i)(ii) | 8 |
| Pilot paper | Assessment of financial performance and EBITDA | 4 | 20 |

## 2 The objectives of profit-seeking organisations

### 2.1 Maximising shareholder wealth

- The primary objective of a profit seeking organisation is to maximise shareholder wealth.

- This is based on the argument that shareholders are the legal owners of a company and so their interests should be prioritised.

- Shareholders are generally concerned with the following:
  - current earnings
  - future earnings
  - dividend policy
  - relative risk of their investment.

All of these are driven by financial performance.

## Test your understanding 1

**Required:**

What will be the primary objective of a commercial bank? What might be some of its subsidiary or secondary objectives?

## 2.2 Survival and growth

The objective of wealth maximisation is usually expanded into three sub-objectives:

- to make a **profit** (see above)

- to continue in existence (**survival**) - survival is the ultimate measure of success of a business. Without survival then obviously there will be no fulfilment of other objectives. In order to survive in the long-term a business must be financially successful

- to maintain **growth** and development - growth is generally seen as a sign of success, provided it results in improvements in financial performance.

## Illustration of survival and growth

Growth can be identified in a number of ways both financial and non-financial.

**Financial:**

- profitability
- revenue
- return on investment (ROI)
- cash flow.

**Non-financial:**

- market share
- number of employees
- number of products.

## Objectives according to Drucker

**Peter Drucker** has suggested that profit-seeking organisations typically have objectives relating to the following:

- market standing
- innovation
- productivity
- physical and financial resources
- profitability
- manager performance and development
- worker performance and attitude
- public responsibility.

### 2.3 The relationship between profits and shareholder value

Rather than focusing on achieving higher profit levels, companies are under increasing pressure to look at the long-term value of the business. This is due to the following factors.

- research has suggested a poor correlation between shareholder return and profits
- investors are increasingly looking at long-term value
- reported profits may not be comparable between companies.

While these issues have been known for some time, they have come into sharp focus due to the performance of new technology/communications companies.

### Illustration 1 – Profits and shareholder value

**Timescales**

In calculating shareholder value it is customary to make a distinction between the 'planning' period (usually less than 5 years), and the 'continuing period' beyond. Results for different industries show the following:

| Industry | % of value in the planning period | % of value in the continuing period |
|---|---|---|
| Tobacco | 40 | 60 |
| Sporting goods | 20 | 80 |
| Skin care | 5 | 95 |
| High tech | −20 | 120 |

### The correlation between shareholder return and profits

Total shareholder return (TSR) is the return shareholders receive both in dividends and capital growth.

Studies have found that there is little correlation between TSR and earnings per share (EPS) growth, and virtually no relationship at all with return on equity, yet many companies are still using profit as their only measure of performance.

Even where companies state that their objective is to maximise shareholder value, often directors' bonuses are still based on short-term profitability or EPS targets.

However strong evidence has been found between shareholder value and future cash flows.

## 3 Financial performance measures

This chapter is concerned with measuring:

- the financial performance of the organisation as a whole
- the performance of the key projects.

Chapter 8 will cover divisional performance.

KAPLAN PUBLISHING

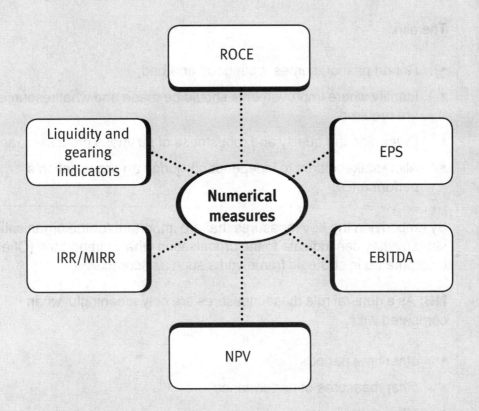

## Performance measures

A good performance measurement system should have the following
characteristics:

- Support corporate strategy, its communication and implementation.

- Measure performance from a financial, non-financial, quantitative
  and qualitative perspective.

- Attuned to the needs of decision makers and their activities.

- Reporting is produced at sufficient regularity to properly support
  decision-making.

- Attention to the accuracy of data and calculation of measures is
  important for trust in the information.

Any performance measurement system requires the identification of
indicators which can identify past, current or potential future outcomes.

The aim:

- Report past outcomes, both good and bad;

- Identify where improvements should be made and what resources are required;

- Determine the quality and robustness of business processes; and

- Allow stakeholders to independently judge an organisation's performance.

By embodying the key measures that are important for the organisation's strategy they can indicate to the organisation what is important. (Often incorporated in strategic frameworks such as scorecards).

**NB:** As a general rule these measures are only meaningful when compared with:

- other time periods

- other measures of performance

- other companies

- other industries

- budget.

## 3.1 Return of capital employed (ROCE)

**ROCE** is a key measure of profitability. It shows the net profit that is generated from every $1 of assets employed.

$$ROCE = \frac{\text{Net profit}}{\text{Capital employed}} \times 100$$

- ROCE is sometimes calculated using PBIT instead of net profit. Use whichever figure is given in the exam.

- Capital employed = total assets less current liabilities or total equity plus long-term debt.

- Capital employed may be based on net book value (NBV), gross book value or replacement cost. Use whichever figure is given in the exam.

| Advantages | Disadvantages |
|---|---|
| • Easy to calculate.<br>• Figures are readily available.<br>• Measures how well a business is utilising the funds invested in it.<br>• Often used by external analysts/investors. | • Research shows a poor correlation between ROCE and shareholder value.<br>• Care must be taken to ensure that like is compared with like, when comparing with different companies – e.g. inclusion of intangibles in capital employed.<br>• Can be distorted by accounting policies.<br>• ROCE can be improved by cutting back investment – this may not be in the company's long-term best interest. |

**Other profitability measures**

ROCE is usually calculated as part of a range of profitability measures. Most of these were covered in paper F5 and include:

| Measure | Calculation |
|---|---|
| Gross profit margin | (Gross profit ÷ Sales) × 100% |
| Net profit margin | (Net profit ÷ Sales) × 100% |
| Asset turnover | Sales ÷ Capital employed |
| Dividend cover | PAT ÷ Dividends paid during the year |
| Dividend yield | (Dividend per share ÷ Current share price) × 100% |
| P/E ratio | Share price ÷ EPS |
| Earnings yield | (EPS ÷ Share price) × 100% |
| EPS | Covered below |
| EBITDA | Covered below |

## Test your understanding 2

|  | Company A | Company B |
|---|---|---|
|  | $ | $ |
| PBIT | 20,000 | 1,000,000 |
| Sales | 200,000 | 2,000,000 |
| Capital employed | 100,000 | 10,000,000 |

**Required:**

For companies A and B, which of the following statements are true?

(1)  Company A has a higher ROCE than company B.

(2)  Company B has a higher ROCE than company A.

(3)  Company A is more profitable than company B.

(4)  Company A is better utilising the funds invested in it than company B.

Choose:

A    1, 3 and 4.

B    2 only.

C    1 and 4.

D    None of these.

### 3.2 EPS

**EPS** is a measure of the profit attributable to each ordinary share.

$$EPS = \frac{\text{Profit after tax less preference dividends}}{\text{Weighted average number of ordinary shares in issue}}$$

For EPS to be truly meaningful, it must be set in context.

*   Is EPS growing or declining over time?

*   Is there likely to be significant dilution of EPS?

*   Is it calculated consistently?

| Advantages | Disadvantages |
|---|---|
| <ul><li>Easily understood by shareholders.</li><li>Calculation is precisely defined accounting standards.</li><li>Figures are readily available.</li><li>Often used as a performance measure between companies, sectors, periods within the same organisation.</li></ul> | <ul><li>Research shows a poor correlation between EPS growth and shareholder value.</li><li>Accounting treatment may cause ratios to be distorted.</li></ul> |

### Test your understanding 3

A company's share capital is as follows:

| | |
|---|---|
| Ordinary shares ($1 each) | $6,000,000 |
| 9% Preference shares | $1,000,000 |

The company made profits before tax of $5,500,000. Corporation tax on this is calculated as $2,100,000

**Required:**

Calculate the company's EPS.

## 3.3 EBITDA

**EBITDA** is earnings before interest, tax and depreciation adjustment.

| Advantages | Disadvantages |
|---|---|
| <ul><li>It is a proxy for cash flow from operations and is therefore a measure of underlying performance.</li><li>Tax and interest are externally generated and therefore not relevant to the underlying success of the business.</li></ul> | <ul><li>It ignores changes in working capital and their impact on cash flow.</li><li>It fails to consider the amount of fixed asset replacement needed by the business.</li></ul> |

| | |
|---|---|
| • Depreciation and amortisation represent a write off of expenditure over a number of years and might therefore be excluded when examining the performance of a particular year.<br><br>• Easy to calculate.<br><br>• Easy to understand. | • It can easily be manipulated by aggressive accounting policies related to income recognition and capitalisation of expenses. |

### 3.4 Net present value (NPV)

The **NPV** is the present value (PV) of all cash inflows less the PV of all cash outflows of a project.

- NPV represents the increase or decrease in value of an organisation today as a result of accepting the project being reviewed.
- **Decision rule**: any project that generates a positive NPV is viable.

| Advantages | Disadvantages |
|---|---|
| • Strong correlation with shareholder value.<br><br>• It considers the time value of money.<br><br>• Risk can be allowed for by adjusting the cost of capital.<br><br>• Cash flows are less subject to manipulation and subjective decisions than accounting profits.<br><br>• Considers all cash flows of a project.<br><br>• Superior measure to IRR for mutually exclusive projects. | • Difficult to calculate/understand.<br><br>• It does not easily allow two projects of very different scales to be compared.<br><br>• It is based on assumptions about cash flows, the timing of those cash flows and the appropriate cost of capital.<br><br>• Many firms use NPV for investment appraisal and then switch to profit-based measures to motivate managers. |

KAPLAN PUBLISHING

## Test your understanding 4

Oracle invests in a new machine at the beginning of Year 1 which costs $15,000. It is hoped that the net cash flows over the next five years will correspond to those given in the table below.

| Year | 1 | 2 | 3 | 4 | 5 |
|---|---|---|---|---|---|
| Net cash flow ($) | 1,500 | 2,750 | 4,000 | 5,700 | 7,500 |

**Required:**

(i)   Calculate the NPV assuming a 15% cost of capital.

(ii)  Calculate the NPV assuming a 10% cost of capital

(iii) Draw a conclusion based on your findings.

## Sensitivity analysis

Sensitivity analysis calculates the percentage change in a variable, e.g. sales volume, that would have to occur before the original investment decision is reversed, i.e. the project NPV changes to $0.

$$\text{Sensitivity} = \frac{\text{NPV}}{\text{PV of flows under consideration}} \times 100$$

## Benchmarking

Benchmarking has already been covered in chapter 1. In the exam, you may be required to assess the relative financial performance of an organisation compared to appropriate benchmarks.

## Test you understanding 5

JDL manufactures a range of solar panel heating. They have recently developed the new EF solar panel. The directors of JDL recently spent $20,000 on market research, the findings of which led them to believe that a market exists for the EF panels

The finance director of JDL has gathered relevant information and prepared the following evaluation relating to the proposed manufacture and sale of the EF solar panels:

(1)   Sales are expected to be 2,700 units per annum at a selling price of $3,000 per unit.

(2) Variable material, labour, and overhead costs are estimated at $1,580 per unit.

(3) In addition, a royalty of $250 per unit would be payable to EF (Environmental Friends), for the use of their brand name.

(4) Fixed overheads are estimated at $900,000 per annum. These overheads cannot be avoided until the end of the year in which the EF solar panels is withdrawn from the market.

(5) An initial investment of $7 million would be required. A government grant equal to 50% of the initial investment would be received on the date the investment is made. No tax allowances would be available on this initial investment. The estimated life cycle of the EF solar panels is six years.

(6) Corporation tax at the rate of 30% per annum is payable in the year in which profit occurs.

(7) The cost of capital is 12%.

**Required:**

(a) Calculate the net present value (NPV) of the EF solar panels proposal and recommend whether it should be undertaken by the directors of JDL.

(b) Using sensitivity analysis, estimate by what percentage each of the under-mentioned items, taken separately, would need to change before the recommendation in (a) above is varied:
(i) Initial outlay of $7,500; $7M
(ii) Annual contribution.

(c) Comment on THREE factors other than NPV that the directors of JDL should consider when deciding whether to manufacture the EF solar panels.

(d) Explain the term 'benchmarking' and briefly discuss the potential benefits that JDL can obtain as a result of undertaking a successful programme of benchmarking.

### 3.5 Internal rate of return (IRR) max cost we can accept

The **IRR** is the discount rate when the NPV = 0.

$$IRR = L + \frac{NPVL}{NPVL - NPVH} \times (H - L)$$

where:

L = lower cost of capital

H = higher cost of capital

NPVL= the NPV at the lower cost of capital

NPVH= the NPV at the higher cost of capital

- When presented with uncertainty about the cost of capital, some managers prefer to assess projects by reference to the IRR.
- **Decision rule**: the project should be accepted if the IRR is greater than the firm's cost of capital.

### Test you understanding 6

A project's predicted cash flows give:

- a NPV of $50,000 at a cost of capital of 10%
- a NPV of ($10,000) at a cost of capital of 15%.

**Required:**

$$= 10\cdot1. + \left( \frac{50\,000}{50\,000 + 60\,000} \right) \times (5)$$

Calculate the IRR.

$$= 14.17\cdot1$$

**Question focus**: now attempt Q11 from chapter 13.

### 3.6 Modified internal rate of return (MIRR)

- One drawback of IRR is that it is possible to get multiple rates of return.
- MIRR eliminates this possibility.

The **MIRR** represents the actual return generated by a project.

**Method:**

**Step 1:** The cash inflows after the initial investment are converted to a single cash inflow at the end of the last year of the project by assuming that the cash inflows are reinvested. Use the reinvestment rate if given in the question or, if not, use the organisation's cost of capital.

**Step 2**: The MIRR is calculated as the return which equates to the present value of the outflows to this single inflow, using present value tables.

Illustration 2 - MIRR

The following information is available for a project:

| Year | 0 | 1 | 2 | 3 | 4 |
|---|---|---|---|---|---|
| **Cash flow ($)** | (5,000) | 2,000 | (1,000) | 3,500 | 3,800 |

The cost of capital is 10%.

**Required:**

Calculate the MIRR of the project.

**Solution:**

**Step 1** Find value of Inflows

| Year | Cash inflows ($) | Value at the end of year 4 ($) |
|---|---|---|
| 1 | 2,000 | $2.000 \times (1.10)^3 = 2.662$ |
| 3 | 3,500 | $3,500 \times 1.10 = 3,850$ |
| 4 | 3,800 | $= 3,800$ |
| | | **Total = 10,312** |

**Step 2** Find value of outflows

| Year | Cash outflows ($) | Value in year 0 ($) |
|---|---|---|
| 0 | 5,000 | 5,000 |
| 2 | 1,000 | $1000 \div (1.10)^2 = 826$ |
| | | **Total = 5,826** |

$10,312 \times \text{Cost of capital}_{\text{yr 4 @ MIRR}} = 5,826$

$\text{Cost of capital}_{\text{yr 4 @ MIRR}} = 5,826 \div 10,312$

$= 0.565$

From tables, MIRR is approximately **15%**

$$MIRR = \left( \sqrt[n]{\frac{PVR}{PVI}} \times (1 + \text{cost of capital}) \right) - 1$$

**Decision rule**: the project should be accepted if the MIRR is greater than the firm's cost of capital.

## 3.7 Liquidity and gearing indicators

### Liquidity ratios

These ratios measure the ability of the company to meet its short-term obligations:

| Measure | Calculation |
|---|---|
| Current ratio | Current assets ÷ Current liabilities |
| Acid test or quick ratio | (Current assets − inventories) ÷ Current liabilities |
| Raw material period | (Ave. value of raw materials ÷ Purchases)×365 |
| WIP period | (Ave. value of WIP ÷ Cost of sales) × 365 |
| Finished goods period | (Ave. value of finished goods ÷ Cost of sales) x365 |
| Receivables period | (Ave. receivables ÷ Sales)×365 |
| Payables period | (Ave. payables ÷ Purchases)×365 |

There is often a trade-off between liquidity and profitability. Companies can be highly profitable but get into trouble when they run out of cash (overtrading).

Therefore liquidity needs to be considered alongside profitability when appraising a company's financial situation.

### Gearing ratios

These ratios measure the ability of the company to meet its long-term liabilities:

- Gearing = (Long-term debt/Shareholder funds) × 100% **or**

- Gearing = (Long-term debt/(Long-term debt + Shareholders funds)) × 100%

- Interest cover = (PBIT/Interest charges)

## Test your understanding 7

AK is a privately owned manufacturing company and has been experiencing difficulties.

**Required:**

You have been asked to assess the current position of AK using appropriate performance measures:

|  | 20X6 $000 | 20X5 $000 |
|---|---|---|
| Receivables | 5,200 | 3,120 |
| Inventory | 2,150 | 2,580 |
| Cash | 350 | 1,350 |
| Total current assets | 7,700 | 7,050 |
| Non Current assets | 14,500 | 14,500 |
| Total payables | 4,500 | 3,150 |
| Sales | 17,500 | 16,625 |
| Operating costs | 14,000 | 12,950 |
| Operating profit | 3,500 | 3,675 |
| Earnings | 2,625 | 2,756 |

There are 2.5 million share in issue.

## Assessing financial performance

BPG is a Telecommunications company who commenced trading in 20X1 through the country of Brean. In 20X6 they established a similar division in the country of Porlet.

**Required:**

Assess the financial performance of BPG and its operations in Brean and Portlet during the years ended 20X8 and 20X9. Using the data provided below.

*Note:* you should highlight any information that would be required to make a more comprehensive assessment of financial performance.

## Summary Income Statements

| | Brean 20X9 $000 | Portlet 20X9 $000 | Company 20X9 $000 | Brean 20X8 $000 | Portlet 20X8 $000 | Company 20X8 $000 |
|---|---|---|---|---|---|---|
| Revenue | 14,400 | 2,900 | 17,300 | 14,040 | 1,980 | 16,020 |
| Salaries | 4,450 | 1,340 | 5,790 | 4,125 | 1,185 | 5,310 |
| Consumables | 2,095 | 502 | 2,597 | 1,950 | 380 | 2,330 |
| Other operating costs | 2,921 | 695 | 3,616 | 2,754 | 620 | 3,374 |
| | 9,466 | 2,537 | 12,003 | 8,829 | 2,185 | 11,014 |
| Marketing | 2,456 | 600 | 3,056 | 2,092 | 480 | 2,572 |
| Interest | | | 850 | | | 900 |
| Depreciation and amortisation | 400 | 160 | 560 | 400 | 100 | 500 |
| | 2,856 | 760 | 4,466 | 2,492 | 580 | 3,972 |
| Total costs | 12,322 | 3,297 | 16,469 | 11,321 | 2,765 | 14,986 |
| Profit/(loss) | 2,078 | (397) | 831 | 2,719 | (785) | 1,034 |

## Statement statements of profit or loss

| | Brean 20X9 $000 | Portlet 20X9 $000 | Company 20X9 $000 | Brean 20X8 $000 | Portlet 20X8 $000 | Company 20X8 $000 |
|---|---|---|---|---|---|---|
| Assets | | | | | | |
| Non current assets | 9,000 | 1,600 | 10,600 | 8,000 | 1,000 | 9,000 |
| Current assets | 4,550 | 1,000 | 5,550 | 5,000 | 800 | 5,800 |
| Total assets | 13,550 | 2,600 | 16,150 | 13,000 | 1,800 | 14,800 |
| Equity and liabilities | | | | | | |
| Share capital | | | 9,150 | | | 7,800 |
| Non-current liabilities | | | | | | |
| Long term borrowings | | | 4,000 | | | 4,500 |
| Current liabilities | 2,400 | 600 | 3,000 | 2,000 | 500 | 2,500 |
| | | | 16,150 | | | 14,800 |

## Solution:

| Company | | 20X9 | 20X8 |
|---|---|---|---|
| ROCE = | PBIT/D+E | 12.8% | 15.7% |
| EBITDA = | EBITDA | 2,241 | 2,434 |
| Gearing = | D/E | 43.7% | 57.7% |
| or gearing = | D/D+E | 30.4% | 36.6% |

| Each operation | | 20X9 Brean | 20X9 Portlet | 20X8 Brean | 20X8 Portlet |
|---|---|---|---|---|---|
| Sales Margin = | Profit/ Revenue (%) | 14.4 | (13.7) | 19.4 | (39.6) |
| Non Current asset turnover = | Revenue / non curr assets | 1.6 | 1.8 | 1.76 | 1.98 |

| | Brean | Portlet | Company |
|---|---|---|---|
| % Revenue growth | 2.6 | 46.5 | 8 |
| % Profit growth | (23.6) | 49.4 | |
| % Increase in costs: | | | |
| Salaries | 7.9 | 13.1 | |
| Marketing | 7.4 | 32.1 | |
| Operating costs | 6.1 | 12.1 | |

The turnover in Brean has increased by 2.6% whilst in Portlet turnover has increased by 46.5% which is excellent since the business only commenced trading in 20X6. The overall growth amounted to 8% which is an acceptable level.

The profits in Brean are down by nearly 24% whilst in Portlet the loss has fallen by 49%. Portlet will need to make further growth in sales and monitor costs in order to become more profitable.

The costs within Brean have risen by 8% for salaries, 7% for marketing and 6% for operating costs yet sales have only increased by 2.6%.

The costs within Portlet have risen substantially more than in Brean. Marketing for example has risen by 32%. This may be due to the fact that this is a necessary cost to develop the growth in revenue within the newly established operation.

Salaries and operating costs have risen by between 12 and 13%, yet sales have increased by 46%. These costs should be monitored as the business grows further.

The EBITDA has fallen by 8% from $2,434,000 to $2,241,000 and ROCE has also fallen from 13.1% to 10.4%. This is not a very good sign for the company.

The non current asset utilisation ratios of Brean shows a decrease from 20X8 to 20X9. Portlet also shows a decrease from 2 to 1.8, this is less surprising given that the operation has only recently been established. Portlet is clearly in a rapid growth phase hence the need for investment in non-current assets.

It would be useful to have previous years data for Brean to observe longer term trends for revenue and costs. Data for Portlet from its first year of operation in 20X6 would enable a complete picture to be taken.

Competitor information would allow us to establish the market share and establish how well the operations are performing in comparison to competitors.

It is clear that long term borrowings have decreased from 20X8 to 20X9 and that BPG has sufficient cash flow to repay some of the debt finance. However it would be useful to have a breakdown of working capital for each operation.

It would also be useful to have future market and financial projections for Brean and Porlet, which should reflect the actual results in 20X8 and 20X9.

Budgeted data would be useful to see if they have managed to meet the targets set.

**Note**: You may be tempted to review the cash flows. This is not required in the question and the examiner is unlikely to expect this from you in this type of question.

### Test your understanding 8

Water Supply Services (WSS) and Enterprise Activities (EA) are two wholly-owned subsidiaries of Aqua Holdings. You have recently qualified as an accountant and have joined the finance team of Aqua Holdings at headquarters. Your finance director is not satisfied with the performance of these two subsidiaries and has asked you to prepare a report covering the following issues:

(1) The profitability of the two subsidiaries.

(2) The competence of the EA manager to make financial decisions.

(3) The consequences of having a common management information system serving both companies.

The finance director has also provided you with the following background information on the two companies.

## WSS

The company holds a licence issued by the government to be the sole supplier of drinking water to a large town. The business necessitates a considerable investment in infrastructure assets and is therefore highly capital intensive. To comply with the licence the company has to demonstrate that it is maintaining guaranteed service standards to its customers. WSS is extensively regulated requiring very detailed annual returns concerning costs, prices, profits and service delivery standards. The government enforces a price-capping regime and therefore the company has limited freedom in tariff determination – the government will normally only sanction a price increase following a demonstrable rise in costs.

## EA

In contrast to WSS, EA operates in a very competitive market offering a plumbing service to domestic properties. The business has the following characteristics:

- rapidly changing market conditions
- a high rate of new entrants and business failures
- occasional shortages of skilled plumbers
- fluctuating profits.

In addition to this background information you also have summarised statements of profit or loss and balance sheets for the last two years for both companies.

**Water Supply Services**

**Summary statement of profit or loss**

| | Year | |
|---|---|---|
| | **20X9** | **20X8** |
| | $m | $m |
| Turnover | 31 | 30 |
| Less: Staff costs | 3 | 2 |
| General expenses | 2 | 2 |
| Depreciation | 12 | 9 |
| Interest | 5 | 5 |
| Profit | 9 | 12 |

### Summary balance sheet (statement of financial position)

| | Year | |
|---|---|---|
| | **20X9** | **20X8** |
| | $m | $m |
| Non-current assets | 165 | 134 |
| Current assets | 5 | 6 |
| Total assets | 170 | 140 |
| Current liabilities | (3) | (6) |
| Debentures | (47) | (47) |
| Net assets | 120 | 87 |
| Shareholders equity | 120 | 87 |

### Enterprise activities – summary statement of profit or loss

| | Year | |
|---|---|---|
| | **20X9** | **20X8** |
| | $m | $m |
| Turnover | 20 | 35 |
| Less: Staff costs | 5 | 6 |
| General expenses | 10 | 10 |
| Materials | 3 | 6 |
| Depreciation | 1 | 1 |
| Profit | 1 | 12 |

### Summary balance sheet

| | Year | |
|---|---|---|
| | **20X9** | **20X8** |
| | $m | $m |
| Non-current assets | 22 | 22 |
| Current assets | 13 | 12 |
| Total assets | 35 | 34 |
| Current liabilities | (4) | (4) |
| Net assets | 31 | 30 |
| Shareholders equity | 31 | 30 |

### Required:

Prepare a report on the comparative financial performance of Water Supply Services and Enterprise Activities from the above financial statements. Your report should incorporate an assessment of the potential limitations of undertaking such a comparison.

## 4 Short and long-term financial performance

- Short-term financial performance measures are used for:
  - control purposes *-variance analysis*
  - determining executive rewards
  - assessing the quality of past decisions and assessing the impact of decisions yet to be made.

- However, there is always a danger that longer-term performance can be compromised by pressure to achieve these short-term targets.

### Steps to reduce short termism

- **Use financial and non-financial measures**: these should focus manager's attention on long-term financial performance.  Methods such as the balanced scorecard can be used (these methods will be discussed in detail in chapter 10). *common ask*

- **Switch from a budget-constrained style**: a switch should be made to a profit-conscious or non-accounting style (Hopwood). *both have a more long term focus*

- **Share options**: if these are given to management they should focus their attention on improving share price and hence long-term performance.

- **Bonuses**: these should be linked to profits over timescales greater than one year.

- **NPV**: should be used to appraise investments.

- **Reduce decentralisation**: this should increase central control and reduce the problem of dysfunctional behaviour.

- **Value-based techniques**: these techniques can be incorporated and will be discussed in more detail in chapter 8.

**Question focus**: now attempt Q12 from chapter 13.

*i) Problems.*

*ii) survival mode → short term / LPs*

## Chapter summary

```
┌─────────────────────────────┐
│   FINANCIAL PERFORMANCE      │
│      MEASURES IN THE         │
│       PRIVATE SECTOR         │
└─────────────────────────────┘
```

| OBJECTIVES OF PROFIT-SEEKING ORGANISATIONS | FINANCIAL PERFORMANCE MEASURES | LONG AND SHORT TERM FINANCIAL PERFORMANCE |
|---|---|---|
| • Max shareholder wealth<br>• Survival and growth<br>• Profits and shareholder value | • ROCE<br>• Other profitability measures<br>• EPS<br>• EBITDA<br>• NPV<br>• IRR/MIRR<br>• Liquidity ratios<br>• Gearing ratios | Reduce short-termism using:<br>• Financial and non-financial measures<br>• A profit conscious or non-accounting style<br>• Share options<br>• Bonus linked to long-term<br>• NPV<br>• Centralisation<br>• Value-based techniques |

## Test your understanding answers

### Test your understanding 1

A bank's primary objective will be profit maximisation for the benefit of the shareholders.

Secondary objectives may include:

- market share
- customer satisfaction
- revenue growth
- employee satisfaction.

### Test your understanding 2

**Answer is C.**

Company A has a ROCE of 20% ($20k ÷ $100k) compared with only 10% for Company B ($1m ÷ $10m). A higher ROCE means that the company is better at utilising the funds invested in it.

### Test your understanding 3

| | |
|---|---:|
| Profits before tax | $5,500,000 |
| Less tax | $2,100,000 |
| Less preference dividends (9% x 1,000,000) | $90,000 |
| | |
| Earnings | $3,310,000 |
| | |
| Number of ordinary shares | 6,000,000 |

EPS = (Profit after tax, – preference dividends)/Weighted average number of ordinary shares in issue

= $3.31m/6m

**= 55.2 cents**

## Test your understanding 4

| Year | Cash flow $ | DF 15% | PV $ | DF 10% | PV $ |
|---|---|---|---|---|---|
| 0 | (15,000) | 1.00 | (15,000) | 1.00 | (15,000) |
| 1 | 1,500 | 0.870 | 1,305 | 0.909 | 1,364 |
| 2 | 2,750 | 0.756 | 2,079 | 0.826 | 2,272 |
| 3 | 4,000 | 0.658 | 2,632 | 0.751 | 3,004 |
| 4 | 5,700 | 0.572 | 3,260 | 0.683 | 3,893 |
| 5 | 7,500 | 0.497 | 3,727 | 0.621 | 4,657 |
| **NPV** | | | **(1,997)** | | **190** |

(i) NPV @ 15% = ($1,997)

(ii) NPV @ 10% = $190

(iii) If the company's cost of capital is 10% the project would be accepted, if it were 15% it wouldn't.

## Test you understanding 5

(a)

| All figures in $000 | 0 | 1 | 2 | 3 | 4 | 5 | 6 |
|---|---|---|---|---|---|---|---|
| Sales revenue | | 8,100 | 8,100 | 8,100 | 8,100 | 8,100 | 8,100 |
| Variable costs | | (4,266) | (4,266) | (4,266) | (4,266) | (4,266) | (4,266) |
| Royalties | | (675) | (675) | (675) | (675) | (675) | (675) |
| Fixed costs | | (900) | (900) | (900) | (900) | (900) | (900) |
| Cash inflow from operations | | 2,259 | 2,259 | 2,259 | 2,259 | 2,259 | 2,259 |
| Tax payable (30%) | | (678) | (678) | (678) | (678) | (678) | (678) |
| Initial investment | (7,000) | | | | | | |
| Government grant received | 3,500 | | | | | | |
| | (3,500) | 1,581 | 1,581 | 1,581 | 1,581 | 1,581 | 1,581 |
| Discount factor @ 12% | 1 | 0.893 | 0.797 | 0.712 | 0.636 | 0.567 | 0.507 |
| | (3,500) | 1,412 | 1,260 | 1,126 | 1,006 | 897 | 802 |
| **NPV** | **3,002** | | | | | | |

KAPLAN PUBLISHING

229

Alternatively, an annuity approach can be taken:

| Time | Narrative | CF | DF | PV |
|------|-----------|-----|------|-------|
| 0 | Investment | (7,000) | 1 | (7,000) |
| 0 | Grant | 3,500 | 1 | 3,500 |
| 1 - 6 | Net inflow (see above) | 2,259 | 4.111 | 9,287 |
| 1 - 6 | Tax 30% | (678) | 4.111 | (2,787) |
| **NPV** | | | | **3,000** |

(b)  (i)

$$\text{Sensitivity} = \frac{\text{NPV}}{\text{PV of initial outlay}} \times 100$$

$$= \frac{3,002}{7,000} \times 100$$

= 42.9% i.e. the initial outlay would have to increase by 42.9% before decision is reversed

(ii)

| Figures in $000 | 1 | 2 | 3 | 4 | 5 | 6 |
|-----------------|------|------|------|------|------|------|
| Sales revenue | 8,100 | 8,100 | 8,100 | 8,100 | 8,100 | 8,100 |
| Variable costs | (4,266) | (4,266) | (4,266) | (4,266) | (4,266) | (4,266) |
| Royalties | (675) | (675) | (675) | (675) | (675) | (675) |
| Contribution before tax | 3,159 | 3,159 | 3,159 | 3,159 | 3,159 | 3,159 |
| Tax payable (30%) | (948) | (948) | (948) | (948) | (948) | (948) |
| Contribution after tax | 2,211 | 2,211 | 2,211 | 2,211 | 2,211 | 2,211 |
| Discount factor @ 12% | 0.893 | 0.797 | 0.712 | 0.636 | 0.567 | 0.507 |
| | 1,975 | 1,762 | 1,574 | 1,406 | 1,254 | 1,121 |

NPV contribution = **9,089**

Or using annuities:

| Time | Narrative | CF | DF | PV |
|------|-----------|-----|------|------|
| 1 - 6 | Contribution | 3,159 | 4.111 | 12,987 |
| 1 - 6 | Tax @ 30% | (948) | 4.111 | 3,897 |
| PV contribution | | | | |
| | | | | 9,089 |

Sensitivity = NPV / PV of contribution = 3002/9089 = 33%

i.e the annual contribution would have to decrease by 33% before the project was rejected.

(c) Factors that should be considered by the directors of JDL include:

 - How the cash flows are estimated. How accurate they are requires detailed consideration.

 - The cost of capital used by the finance director might be inappropriate. For example if the EF solar panels proposal is less risky than other projects undertaken by JDL then a lower cost of capital should be used.

 - How strong is the EF brand name? The directors are proposing to pay royalties equivalent to 8% of sales revenue during the six years of the anticipated life of the project. Should they market the EF solar panels themselves?

 - Would competitors enter the market and what would be the likely effect on sales volumes and selling prices?

 **N.B:** Only three factors were required.

(d) Benchmarking is the use of a yardstick to compare performance. The yardstick for benchmarking is based on best in class.

A major problem facing the management of JDL lies in the accessing of information regarding the activities of a competitor firm that may be acknowledged to display best practice. Internal benchmarking i.e. using another function within the same firm as the standard can help in the avoidance of the problems of information access, but that clearly limits the scope of what can be achieved. The most common approach is process benchmarking, where the standard of comparison is a firm which is not a direct competitor but is best in practice for a particular process or activity.

The objective is to improve performance. This is best achieved by means of the sharing of information which should prove of mutual benefit to both parties to the benchmarking programme. As a result of receiving new information each party will be able to review their policies and procedures. The very process of comparing respective past successes and failures can serve as a stimulus for greater innovation within each organisation.

To evaluate the performance JDL they need to establish a basis for targets which reflects the performance of an organisation which displays 'Best Practice'. As a direct consequence of a comparison of existing standards with the 'Best Practice' organisation, managers can focus upon areas where improvements can be achieved and evaluate measures to help attain those improvements.

A principal benefit that will be derived by JDL as a result of undertaking a successful programme of benchmarking will be the identification of areas where cost savings are possible. Hence the levels of cost of sales and operating expenses can be reduced leading to increased profitability.

## Test you understanding 6

$$IRR = 10\% + \frac{50,000}{50,000 - 10,000} \times (15\% - 10\%)$$

$$= 14.17\%$$

## Test your understanding 7

|  | 20X6 | 20X7 |
|---|---|---|
| Current ratio | 7,700 ÷ 4,500 = 1.7 | 7,050 ÷ 3,150 = 2.2 |
| Acid test ratio | 5,550 ÷ 4,500 = 1.2 | 4,470 ÷ 3,150 = 1.4 |
| Receivable days | (5,200 ÷ 17,500) × 365 =108 days | (3,120 ÷ 16,625) × 365 = 68 days |
| Inventory days | (2,150 ÷ 14,000) × 365 = 56 days | (2,580 ÷ 12,950) × 365 = 73 days |
| Asset turnover | 17,500 ÷ 17,700 = 1.0 times | 16,625 ÷ 18,400 = 0.9 times |
| ROCE | (3,500 ÷ 17,700) × 100 = 19.8% | (3,675 ÷ 18,400) × 100 = 20.0% |
| EPS | 2,625 ÷ 2,500 = 1.05 | 2,756 ÷ 2,500 = 1.10 |

The company has high receivables, low inventories, a low cash balance and high trade payables.

The philosophy is to chase sales by offering lax trade credit to customers, while attempting to maintain adequate liquidity by taking extensive credit from suppliers.

This is a risky policy since it involves the risk of:

- long-standing receivables balances going bad
- discouraging potential customers since low inventory means an increased risk of goods being out of stock.

The low cash balance means that unexpected expenditures cannot be paid for out of cash. Specific funds would have to be organised.

The high trade payables will upset the suppliers; they may even stop supply until the balance outstanding is paid.

### Test your understanding 8

Report on the comparative financial performance of WSS and EA.

(i) **Summary of financial ratios**

|  | WSS | | EA | |
|  | 20X9 | 20X8 | 20X9 | 20X8 |
| --- | --- | --- | --- | --- |
| Profitability **(W1)** | | | | |
| ROCE | 8.4% | 12.7% | 3.2% | 40.0% |
| Profit margin | 45.2% | 56.7% | 5.0% | 34.3% |
| Asset utilisation | 18.6% | 22.4% | 64.5% | 116.7% |
| Liquidity | | | | |
| Current ratio | 1.7 | 1.0 | 3.25 | 3.0 |
| Risk | | | | |
| Gearing **(W2)** | 39.2 | 54.0 | 0 | 0 |
| Growth | | | | |
| Turnover | 3.3% | | (42.9%) | |
| Profit | (25%) | | (91.7%) | |
| Capital employed | 24.6% | | 3.3% | |

## (ii) Comments on ratios

Both companies have shown a significant fall in profits. The ratios show that this is due to both a reduction in margins and falling asset utilisation. Capital employed has grown (especially for WSS) and it may be that this extra investment needs more time to generate additional profit.

EA has witnessed a dramatic reduction in sales. Costs seem to be largely fixed as these have only fallen by 17%. Turnover for the regulated monopoly appears to be more stable.

Financial risk (gearing) is high in WSS (although no comparisons with similar companies are available), but the gearing ratio has fallen in the year. High gearing magnifies the effect of volatile turnover on profit. Although it would seem EA has high operating gearing (fixed to total costs), this is somewhat compensated by the fact that it has no financial gearing.

Liquidity for both companies has improved, although no benchmarks against respective industry averages are available.

## (iii) Limitations

**Accuracy of the figures** – are the two years under review representative?

**Short versus long term** – longer-term trends would be useful. Certain events in 20X9 (i.e. expenditure on fixed assets) will reduce short-term performance but fuel longer-term growth (and profit).

**The two companies cannot really be compared** – one is a regulated monopoly, the other has to compete in a competitive market based on the perception of its products, quality and value for money. As such, comparison may be better carried out using industry benchmarks.

**Profitability can only be fully appraised when compared against required returns of the shareholders.** This, in turn, reflects the perceived risks they take when investing in each company. This may be lower for a regulated monopoly, and thus ROCEs lower, although the monopoly does have a higher level of gearing.

**Workings**

**(1) Profitability ratios (20X9 shown)**

|  | WSS | EA |
|---|---|---|
| ROCE* | 14/167 × 100 = 8.4% | 1/31 × 100 = 3.2% |
| Profit margin | 14/31 × 100 = 45.2% | 1/20 × 100 = 5.0% |
| Asset utilisation | 31/167 × 100 = 18.6% | 20/31 × 100 = 64.5% |

*Note: profit before interest used as the objective is to measure internal efficiency rather than return to external shareholders.

**(2) Gearing ratios (20X9 shown)**

|  | WSS | EA |
|---|---|---|
| Debt / Equity | 47/120 = 39.2 | 0 |

# Divisional performance appraisal and transfer pricing

## Chapter learning objectives

Upon completion of this chapter you will be able to:

- Discuss the appropriateness of, and apply the following as measures of performance:
    - return on investment (ROI)
    - residual income (RI)
    - economic value added (EVA$^{TM}$)
- describe, compute and evaluate performance measures relevant in a divisionalised organisation structure including ROI, RI and economic value added (EVA)
- discuss the need for separate measures in respect of managerial and divisional performance
- discuss the circumstances in which a transfer pricing policy may be needed and discuss the necessary criteria for its design
- demonstrate and evaluate the use of alternative bases for transfer pricing
- explain and demonstrate issues that require consideration when setting transfer prices in multinational companies
- evaluate and apply the value-based management approaches to performance management
- evaluate the use and application of strategic models in assessing the business performance of an entity, such as Ansoff, Boston Consulting Group and Porter.

- discuss the problems encountered in planning, controlling and measuring performance levels, e.g. productivity, profitability, quality and service levels, in complex business structures.

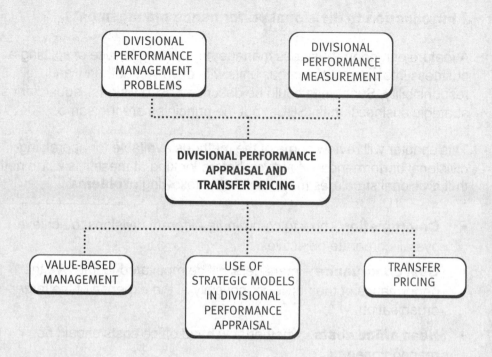

## 1 Exam focus

| Exam sitting | Area examined | Question number | Number of marks |
|---|---|---|---|
| June 2012 | EVA | 1(ii) | 3 |
| June 2011 | BCG analysis | 4 | 20 |
| June 2011 | RI, ROI, EVA, transfer pricing | 1(a)(b) | 24 |
| December 2010 | EVA | 3(b) | 12 |
| December 2010 | VBM | 3(a)(c) | 8 |
| December 2009 | Transfer pricing | 3 | 20 |
| December 2008 | Transfer pricing | 4(a) | 12 |
| June 2008 | ROI, RI and EVA | 1(a)(i)(ii) | 20 |
| December 2007 | Divisional performance measures, RI and EVA | 2 | 25 |
| Pilot paper | Transfer pricing | 3(a) | 10 |

**Student Accountant articles**: visit the ACCA website, www.accaglobal.com, to review the following articles on the topics in this chapter:

- Economic value added versus profit based measures of performance - July 2011

- Transfer pricing - October 2009

- Economic value added - October 2007

- Business strategy and performance models - April 2006

## 2 Introduction to divisional performance management

A feature of modern business management is the practice of splitting a business into semi-autonomous units with devolved authority and responsibility. Such units could be described as 'divisions', subsidiaries or strategic business units (SBUs) but the principles are the same.

This chapter will review some of the methods available for appraising divisional performance. However, before looking at these it is worth noting that divisional structures may result in the following **problems**:

- **Co-ordination** - how to co-ordinate different divisions to achieve overall corporate objectives.

- **Goal congruence** – managers will be motivated to improve the performance of their division, possibly at the expense of the larger organisation.

- **Head office costs** - whether/how head office costs should be reapportioned.

- **Transfer prices** - how transfer prices should be set as these effectively move profit from one division to another.

- **Controllability** - divisional managers should only be held accountable for those factors that they can control. The performance of a division's manager must be appraised separately to the performance of the division. It may be difficult to determine exactly what is and what is not controllable.

- **Inter-dependence of divisions** - the performance of one division may depend to some extent on others, making it difficult to measure performance levels.

### Illustration 1 - Inter-dependence of divisions

Suppose division A makes components that are subsequently used in division B to make the finished item that is then sold to customers. The following are examples of areas where the performance of B will be affected by problems in A.

- **Productivity** – suppose some staff in division A are ill, slowing down the supply of components to division B. This will slow down division B as well, unless adequate inventories are held.

- **Profitability** – suppose the transfer pricing system includes an element of actual cost. Cost overruns in A would be passed on to B.

- **Quality** – poor quality work in A will ultimately compromise the quality of the finished product.

- **Service levels** – customer queries to B could involve A's component in which case they need to be re-directed. Division A may not be as customer-focused as B, compromising customer goodwill.

## Management of a division

The management of a division are normally remunerated on a basis linked to the performance they achieve. Typically, they are given performance targets and only if they achieve those targets do they get a salary bonus.

The central idea is that the manager of a division is in the same position as an independent entrepreneur. If he experiences the risks and rewards of business ownership, then he/she will act in a manner calculated to maximise the value of the division – or that is the theory. The modern variation on this theme is to give management 'share options' – the right to buy shares at a given price. If the share price performs well, (and the stock market is a good judge of business performance), then the manager benefits. The theory is that this promotes goal congruence between managers and shareholders.

Having decentralised, it is essential that senior management monitor and control the performance of the divisions and of those people with direct responsibility for those divisions. An accounting information system (a management control system) must be in place to allow for divisional assessment. The system used must have a close bearing on divisional goals and must recognise that some costs of a division will be controllable by its managers and some will not.

# 3 Numerical measures of divisional performance

*Types of responsibility centres*

## Key considerations

When assessing divisional performance it is vital that the measures used match the type of division:

| Type of division | Description | Typical measures |
|---|---|---|
| Cost centre | • Division incurs costs but has no revenue stream. | • Total cost<br>• Cost variances<br>• Cost per unit and other cost ratios<br>• Non-financial performance indicators (NFPIs), for example related to quality, productivity, efficiency. |
| Profit Centre | • Division has both costs and revenue<br>• Manager **does not** have the authority to alter the level of investment in the division. | All of the above plus:<br><br>• sales<br>• profit<br>• sales variances<br>• margins<br>• market share<br>• working capital ratios (depending on the division concerned)<br>• NFPIs related to customer satisfaction. |
| Investment centre | • Division has both costs and revenue.<br>• Manager **does** have the authority to invest in new assets or dispose of existing ones. | All of the above plus:<br><br>• return on investment (ROI)<br>• residual income (RI)<br>• economic value added (EVA$^{TM}$).<br><br>These are discussed in more detail below. |

## 4 Return on Investment (ROI)

*operating profit generated for every $1 spent*

### 4.1 What is ROI?

$$ROI = \frac{\text{Controllable PBIT}}{\text{Capital employed}} \times 100$$

*use PBIT instead of profit on operations*

**Decision rule**: If ROI > cost of capital (required return), then accept the project.

### 4.2 Advantages and disadvantages of ROI

| Advantages | Disadvantages |
|---|---|
| • Widely used and accepted since it is in line with ROCE which is frequently used to assess overall business performance.<br><br>• As a relative measure it enables comparisons to be made with divisions or companies of different sizes.<br><br>• It can be broken down into secondary ratios for more detailed analysis, i.e. profit margin and asset turnover. | • May lead to dysfunctional decision making (see below).<br><br>• Increases with age of asset if net book values (NBVs) are used (see below).<br><br>• Different accounting policies can confuse comparisons.<br><br>• Exclusion from capital employed of intangible assets, such as brands and reputation.<br><br>• The corporate objective of maximising total shareholders' wealth is not achieved by making decisions on the basis of ROI.<br><br>• It may encourage the manipulation of profit and capital employed figures to improve results and, for example, to obtain a bonus payment. |

### Dysfunctional decision making

Where ROI is used as a performance measure – management may only take decisions which will increase divisional ROI, regardless of wider corporate benefits.

## Test your understanding 1

Managers within MV are appraised on the ROI of their division. The company's cost of capital is 15%.

Jon, a divisional manager, has the following results:

|  | $ |
|---|---|
| Annual profit | 30,000 |
| Investment | 100,000 |

Within his division, the purchase of a new piece of equipment has been proposed. This equipment would cost $20,000, would yield an extra $4,000 of profit per annum and would have many other non-financial and environmental benefits to the division and the company as a whole.

**Required:**

Will Jon invest in the new equipment? Is this the correct decision for the company?

## Age of assets

The ROI will increase with the age of the asset. This may encourage divisional managers to hold onto old, and potentially inefficient, assets rather than investing in new ones.

## Test your understanding 2

McKinnon Co sets up a new division in Blair Atholl investing $800,000 in fixed assets with an anticipated useful life of 10 years and no scrap value. Annual profits before depreciation are expected to be a steady $200,000.

**Required:**

You are required to calculate the division's ROI for its first three years based on the opening book value of assets. Comment on your results.

# 5 Residual income

## 5.1 What is residual income (RI)?

| | |
|---|---|
| Controllable PBIT | X |
| Less imputed interest (capital employed × cost of capital) | (X) |
| RI | X |

**Decision rule**: accept the project if the RI is positive.

## 5.2 Advantages and disadvantages of RI

*appraise the the division* (handwritten)

STFD (handwritten)

| Advantages | Disadvantages |
|---|---|
| *Improvement on ROI* (handwritten) <br> • It reduces the problems of ROI, i.e. dysfunctional behaviour and holding onto old assets. <br><br> • The cost of financing a division is brought home to divisional managers. <br><br> • Different cost of capitals can be applied to different divisions based on their risk profiles. | • It is difficult to decide upon an appropriate cost of capital. <br><br> • It does not facilitate comparisons between divisions since the RI is driven by the size of the divisions and their investment. <br><br> • It does not always result in decisions that are in the best interests of the company. <br><br> • Different accounting policies can confuse comparisons (as for ROI). <br><br> • It may encourage the manipulation of profit and capital employed figures to improve results and, for example, to obtain a bonus payment (as for ROI). |

### Illustration 2 – Residual Income (RI)

Black Dog has the following financial performance:

| | |
|---|---|
| Operating profit | $40,000 |
| Capital employed | $150,000 |
| Cost of capital | 10% |

Black Dog wishes to evaluate on the basis of residual income whether to accept a new possible investment costing $10,000 which would earn an annual operating profit of $2,000.

### Solution

Current RI = 40,000 – (10% × $150,000) = $25,000

Revised RI = 42,000 – (10% × $160,000) = $26,000

**Decision**: accept the project as RI after project > current RI.

### Test your understanding 3

Division Z has the following financial performance:

| | |
|---|---|
| Operating profit | $40,000 |
| Capital employed | $150,000 |
| Cost of capital | 10% |

**Required:**

Would the division wish to accept a new possible investment costing $10,000 which would earn an annual operating profit of $2,000 if the evaluation was on the basis of:

(a) ROI

(b) RI?

*handwritten annotations:* $\frac{operating\ M}{capital\ employed}$ = 26·7%.  $\frac{42}{160}$ · 26·25%. ROI reject: reducing

Is the division's decision in the best interests of the company?

### Test your understanding 4

KM is considering a new project and has gathered the following data:

The initial investment is $66 million which will be required at the beginning of the year. The project has a three year life with a nil residual value. Depreciation is calculated on a straight-line basis.

The project is expected to generate revenue of $85m in year 1, $90m in year 2 and $94m in year 3. These values may vary by 6%. +/–

The direct costs will be $50m in year 1, $60m in year 2 and $70m in year 3. These may vary by 8%. +/–

Cost of capital may also vary from 8% to 10% for the life of the project.

Use the written down value of the asset at the start of each year to represent the value of the asset for the year.

Ignore tax.

40

**Required:**

Prepare two tables for:

+ 6%  − 8%  8%.

(a)  the best outcome and

(b)  the worst outcome

− 6%  + 8%,  10%.

showing the annual operating profit, residual income and return on investment for each year of the project and the NPV.

**Question focus**: Question 13 in chapter 13 is a complex question on ROI, RI and NPV. Even if you do not have time to complete the entire question it is worth reviewing it since it will broaden your knowledge of the subject area and shows that exam questions in this paper will require an in depth application of knowledge.

## 6 Annuity depreciation

### Annuity depreciation

- As discussed, the use of ROI and RI does not always result in decisions that are in the best interests of the company.

- Specifically, a project with a positive net present value (NPV) at the company's cost of capital may show poor ROI or RI results in early years, leading to its rejection by the divisional manager.

- Annuity depreciation is one attempt to resolve this problem.

**Example:**

Division X is currently generating a ROI of 12%. It is considering a new project. This requires an investment of $1.4 million and is expected to yield net cash inflows of $460,000 per annum for the next four years. None of the initial investment will be recoverable at the end of the project.

The company has a cost of capital of 8%. Annual accounting profits are to be assumed to equal annual net cash inflows less depreciation, and tax is to be ignored.

**Required:**

(a)  Calculate and comment of the NPV of the project.

(b)  Calculate and comment on the ROI and RI of the project.

(c) Calculate and comment on the ROI and RI of the project using annuity depreciation.

(d) Calculate and comment on the ROI and RI of the project at the project IRR of 12%.

**Solution:**

(a) **NPV calculation**

| Time | CF ($) | DF 8% | PV ($) |
|------|--------|-------|--------|
| 0 | (1,400,000) | 1 | (1,400,000) |
| 1-4 | 460,000 | 3.312 | 1,523,520 |

**NPV =123,520**

**Conclusion:** the project has a positive NPV and is therefore worthwhile accepting from the company's point of view.

(b) **ROI and RI**

|  | Year 1 | Year 2 | Year 3 | Year 4 |
|--|--------|--------|--------|--------|
|  | $000 | $000 | $000 | $000 |
| NBV at start of year | 1,400 | 1,050 | 700 | 350 |
| Net cash inflow | 460 | 460 | 460 | 460 |
| Depreciation | (350) | (350) | (350) | (350) |
| Profit | 110 | 110 | 110 | 110 |
| Imputed interest @8% | (112) | (84) | (56) | (28) |
| RI | (2) | 26 | 54 | 82 |
| ROI | 7.9% | 10.5% | 15.7% | 31.4% |

**Conclusion**: If the manager's performance is measured (and rewarded) on the basis of RI or ROI, he is unlikely to accept the project. The first year's RI is negative, and the ROI does not exceed the company's cost of capital until year 2, or the ROI currently being earned until year 3. Divisional managers will tend to take a short-term view. More immediate returns are more certain, and by year 3 he may have moved jobs.

### (c) ROI and RI using annuity depreciation

Annuity depreciation is calculated as follows:

**Step 1**: Calculate the equivalent annual cost (EAC) of the initial investment

EAC = Initial investment ÷ cumulative discount factor at the company's cost of capital

   = $1.4m ÷ 3.312

   = $422,705

**Step 2**: Calculate annual depreciation

Annual depreciation = EAC – interest on opening NBV

   e.g for year 1 = 422,705 – (1,400,000 × 8%)

      = $310,705

The ROI and RI can now be calculated as follows:

|  | Year 1 | Year 2 | Year 3 | Year 4 |
|---|---|---|---|---|
|  | $000 | $000 | $000 | $000 |
| NBV at start of year | 1,400 | 1,089.3 | 753.7 | 391.3 |
|  | ——— | ——— | ——— | ——— |
| Net cash inflow | 460 | 460 | 460 | 460 |
| Depreciation | (310.7) | (335.6) | (362.4) | (391.4) |
|  | ——— | ——— | ——— | ——— |
| Profit | 149.3 | 124.4 | 97.6 | 68.6 |
| Imputed interest @8% | (112) | (87.1) | (60.3) | (31.3) |
|  | ——— | ——— | ——— | ——— |
| **RI** | **37.3** | **37.3** | **37.3** | **37.3** |
|  | ——— | ——— | ——— | ——— |
| **ROI** | **10.7%** | **11.4%** | **12.9%** | **17.5%** |

**Conclusion**: The project now has an equal, positive, RI over its life, which will encourage the manager to invest, a decision compatible with that using NPV.

However, there is still a problem if ROI is used as the performance measure, in that the short-term low rate of return may not encourage investment in what is, in fact, a worthwhile project. A way round this is to use annuity depreciation at a different rate that will ensure a level ROI over the project life. The rate to be used will be the IRR of the project.

### (d) ROI and RI using annuity depreciation at the project IRR

12% is now used instead of 8% in computing both the EAC of the investment and the interest on capital, yielding the following results:

|  | Year 1 | Year 2 | Year 3 | Year 4 |
|---|---|---|---|---|
|  | $000 | $000 | $000 | $000 |
| NBV at start of year | 1,400 | 1,108 | 781 | 414.7 |
| Net cash inflow | 460 | 460 | 460 | 460 |
| Depreciation | (292) | (327) | (366.3) | (410.2) |
| Profit | 168 | 133 | 93.7 | 49.8 |
| Imputed interest @12% | (168) | (133) | (93.7) | (49.8) |
| RI | 0 | 0 | 0 | 0 |
| ROI | 12% | 12% | 12% | 12% |

### Conclusion:

The ROI and the RI is now level over the project life, ensuring a consistent decision whether the short-term or long-term view is taken. Using 12% as an appraisal rate for the project yields consistent results under all three methods (NPV, ROI and RI) i.e. the project is at break-even.

This somewhat contrived approach is probably less useful than the one above when RI is used to assess performance.

In addition, the use of annuity depreciation does not produce helpful results when cash flows are uneven.

## 7 Economic Value Added (EVA)

### 7.1 What is EVA? *measure of performance that is directly linked to shareholders wealth*

- EVA$^{TM}$ is a measure of performance similar to residual income, except the profit figure used is ECONOMIC profit and the capital employed figure used is ECONOMIC capital employed. This is because it is argued that the profit and capital employed figures quoted in the financial statements do not give the true picture and that the accounting figures need to be adjusted to show the true underlying performance.

- The basic concept of EVA is that performance should be measured in terms of the value added during the period. It is a measure of performance that is directly linked to shareholder wealth.

### EVA calculation

| | |
|---|---|
| Net operating profit after tax (NOPAT) | X |
| Less economic value of capital employed × WACC | (X) |
| EVA | X |

**Decision rule:** accept the project if the EVA is positive.

### 7.2 What is NOPAT?

| | |
|---|---|
| Controllable PAT | X |
| **Add back non-cash items such as**: | |
| accounting depreciation | X |
| non-cash expenses | X |
| interest paid net of tax | X |
| **Add back items that add value such as**: | |
| goodwill amortisation | X |
| development and advertising costs | X |
| operating lease interest cost | X |
| **Deduct**: | |
| economic depreciation | (X) |
| impairment to the value of goodwill | (X) |
| amortisation of development and advertising costs | (X) |
| **= NOPAT** | X |

## Adjustments to PAT

| Add back: | Explanation |
|---|---|
| Accounting depreciation | We add this back to PAT, because EVA is calculated after profits have been charged with economic depreciation (not accounting depreciation). |
| Non-cash expenses | Add back any non-cash expenses discussed in the question since NOPAT is measured in cash flow terms. |
| Interest paid net of tax* <br><br> (*so if tax is at 35%, take interest payments x 0.65) | Interest payments are taken into account in the capital charge. |
| Goodwill amortisation | Payments in respect of goodwill may be viewed as adding value to the company. Therefore any amounts in respect of goodwill amortisation appearing in the income statement are added back to reported profit since they represent part of the intangible asset value of the business. |
| Development/advertising costs | Development and advertising costs are treated as expenses. However, these should be capitalised (i.e. add the entire expense back) and amortised (i.e. deduct amortisation for the period) since they are considered to be investments for the future. |
| Operating leases | These should be capitalised rather than expensed. The net effect with regards to NOPAT is to increase PAT by the implied interest cost of the operating lease. This adjustment can be ignored if sufficient information is not given in the question. |
| **Take off:** | |
| Economic depreciation | Considered to be a measure of the economic use of assets during a year and relates to the fall in value of an asset due to wear and tear or obsolescence. |
| Any impairment in the value of goodwill | We add back goodwill amortisation and should therefore deduct any impairment. Ignore this if it is not mentioned in the question. |

| Amortisation of development/ advertising costs | These should be capitalised and amortised (as discussed above). |
|---|---|
| **NOPAT** | |

## 7.3 What is the economic value of capital employed?

The main adjustments to the capital employed figure are as follows:

- an adjustment should be made to reflect the replacement cost of non-current assets rather than the book value.

- the net book value of any operating leases should be added back.

- the net book value of any development/advertising costs should be added back.

- the value of amortised goodwill should be added.

## 7.4 What is the WACC?

WACC = (proportion of equity × cost of equity) + (proportion of debt × post tax cost of debt)

For example, suppose that a company is 60% financed by equity which has a cost of 10% pa and 40% financed by debt which has an after tax cost of 6%

WACC = (0.60 x 0.10) + (0.40 x 0.06) = 0.084   therefore 8.4%

## 7.5 Advantages and disadvantages of EVA

| Advantages | Disadvantages |
|---|---|
| EVA is consistent with NPV. Maximisation of EVA will create real wealth for shareholders. | Requires numerous adjustments to profit and capital employed figures. |
| The adjustments made avoid the distortion of results by the accounting policies in place and should therefore result in goal congruent decisions. | Does not facilitate comparisons between divisions since EVA is an absolute measure (as is RI). |
| The cost of financing a division is bought home to the division's manager | There are many assumptions made when calculating the WACC. |
| Long-term value-adding expenditure can be capitalised, removing any incentive that managers may have to take a short-term view. | Based on historical data where as shareholders are interested in future performance. |

## Illustration 3 - Adjusting for operating leases

Division A is calculating EVA for the first time.  It has operating leases on equipment, for which it pays annual rental charges of $40,000.  The current value of the operating leases is estimated at $150,000.  The economic life of the leased asset is 5 years.

### Calculating NOPAT

- Add back the operating lease charge of $40,000.

- Deduct the annual 'economic' depreciation of $30,000 (assume equal annual depreciation of $150,000 ÷ 5 years).

- NET IMPACT - add back $10,000 (the implied interest charge on the lease).

### Calculating the economic value of capital employed

- The net book value of the operating leases should be added back, i.e. $150,000.

- The annual economic cost of these assets is $30,000 ($150,000 ÷ 5) and so the capital employed would be depreciated by this amount each year thereafter.

## Test your understanding 5

Division B has a reported profit after tax of $8.4 million, which includes a charge of $2million for the full cost of developing and launching a new product that is expected to generate profits for 4 years.

The company has an after tax weighted average cost of capital of 10%.

The operating book value of the division's assets is $60 million, and the replacement cost has been estimated at $75 million.

*assume tax = $0*

**Required:**

Calculate division B's EVA.

*article -2 new*

### Test your understanding 6

The Diva division of the Aria Group made a profit after tax in the year just ended of $100,000.

Annual depreciation was $80,000 and the operating net book value of the division's assets was $500,000.

Economic depreciation was $75,000.

It has been estimated that the net replacement cost of the division's non-current assets is 20% higher than their net book value.

The division obtains some assets under operating lease arrangements. It has been estimated that the net book value of the operating leases is $90,000 and that the notional interest expense of the operating lease payments was $8,000 for the year.

The company is 60% financed by equity, and 40% financed by debt. Equity capital has a cost of 10% p.a. and debt has an after tax cost of 6% p.a.

Interest expense in the year was $9,000.

Tax is 30% of net operating profits before tax.

**Required:**

Calculate the EVA.

**Question focus**: Now attempt question 14 from chapter 13.

## 8 Value-based management

This is a slight aside but it is worth covering here since it follows on from our discussion of EVA.

**Value-based management** (VBM) is an approach to management whereby the company's strategy, objectives and processes are aligned to help the company focus on the key drivers of shareholder wealth and hence the maximisation of this value.

### Measuring shareholder value

Traditionally, financial measures such as EPS and ROCE were used to quantify shareholder value. However, none of these measures directly correlates with the market value of the company (i.e. shareholder value).

Value-based performance management is an approach which takes the interests of the shareholders as its primary focus. Measures include:

- **EVA** - this is the primary measure used. A positive EVA indicates value creation while a negative one indicates destruction.
- **Market value added** (MVA) - this is the accumulated EVAs generated by an organisation since it was formed.
- **Shareholder value analysis** - this is the application of a discounted cash flow technique to valuing the whole business rather than a single potential investment.

## Other value-based measures

As well as EVA, consultants have produced a number of other value based measures, with each claiming its own merits.

### 1. Market value added (MVA)

MVA is the value added to the business by management since it was formed, over and above the money invested in the company by shareholders and long term debt holders. A positive MVA means value has been added and a negative MVA means value has been destroyed.

MVA can effectively be seen as the accumulated EVAs generated by an organisation over time. As such it should be highly correlated with EVA values. If year after year a company has a positive EVA then these will add up to give a high MVA.

### 2. Shareholder value analysis.

SVA is an application of discounted cash flow techniques to valuing the whole business rather than a potential investment.

One problem in the estimation of future values is that theoretically the cash flows go to infinity. A practical way to resolve this is to take free cash flows for a few years into the future (the 'competitive advantage period') and then estimate the residual value of the organisation using either some market multiple or book value. The valuation of the company and hence the individual shares can be directly derived from the SVA.

One criticism of the above is that the estimation of the terminal value is subjective. There is a problem in determining how many years' cash flows can be realistically projected into the future and therefore at which point the terminal value should be calculated. However, all valuation methods depend upon estimating either future dividends, earnings or cash flows and hence they all contain some element of subjectivity.

Companies using value-based management have implemented planning and control systems across the organisation to support it.

The techniques available for increasing and monitoring value will be/have been covered in other chapters and include:

- the balanced scorecard
- business process re-engineering *chp 4*
- TQM
- JIT
- ABC and ABM *chp 3*
- benchmarking. *chp 1*

*implement s VBM 4 steps*

*— strategy → develop to max value*

*EVA consistent with NPV*

## 9 The use of strategic models in divisional performance appraisal

- The matrices of Ansoff and the Boston Consulting Group (BCG) were met in paper P3 where they were used for strategic portfolio analysis.

- These frameworks can also be used for assessing performance management issues in divisionalised businesses.

### 9.1 Ansoff's matrix

- Ansoff's matrix is used to analyse the possible strategic directions that a division can follow.

- This in turn will highlight key areas, i.e CSFs, that need to be monitored and controlled.

|  | Existing products | New products |
|---|---|---|
| **Existing Markets** | **Protect/build**<br>• Consolidation (downsizing, withdrawal, holding market share).<br>• Market penetration (increasing market share in existing markets).<br>• Cost efficiences. | **Product development**<br>• New products for existing markets.<br>• Using existing capabilities or by developing new ones. |
| **New Markets** | **Market development**<br>• New markets for existing products.<br>• Options include new geographical areas and new segments of existing markets. | **Diversification**<br>• Related (similar industries).<br>• Unrelated. |

- These strategies may result in the development of new divisions, closure of existing divisions or changes within existing divisions.

## Ansoff's strategies

### Protect/build

Both short-term and long-term performance appraisal of products is required to determine which to divest and which to consolidate. The nature and strength of the firm's competitive advantage is likely to be central.

Market penetration is much easier if the market is growing as larger competitors may not invest sufficiently to meet extra demand. However, the extra investment required may depress reported performance, at least initially.

### Market development

Market development involves moving into new markets. Key areas of concern include:

- the attractiveness of the new market
- the risk of not fully understanding customer needs in the new market
- the effectiveness of barriers to entry
- the likely reaction of existing firms
- it may take time to achieve the required critical mass and the associated economies of scale. This is likely to depress performance in earlier years.
- a lack of an established reputation
- a lack of a supply chain infrastructure (e.g. distribution outlets).

### Product development

Product development involves new products. Key areas of concern are thus:

- Will customers want the new product? Has enough market research been carried out first?
- Development costs and learning effects may give poor ROI initially.
- Will new products be based on extending existing capabilities or will new capabilities have to be created / acquired first? The strength of such capabilities will have to be monitored carefully.
- Potential quality control problems.
- Production capacity.

> ## Diversification
>
> One would expect diversification to be the riskiest strategy on the matrix, involving the risks of both product development and market development.

## 9.2 The BCG Matrix

The BCG matrix shows whether the firm has a balanced portfolio in terms of products and market sectors.

Steps include:

(1) Divide the business into divisions. *(SBUs) or #products*

(2) Allocate to the matrix.

(3) Assess the prospects of each division.

(4) Develop strategies and targets for each division.

| | | |
|---|---|---|
| **High** | **Star**<br>• Large share of high-growth market.<br>• High reinvestment rate required to hold/build position.<br>• Moderate cash flow. | **Problem child**<br>• Small share of high-growth market.<br>• Large investment required to grow (so cash user).<br>• **Or** divest. |
| **Market growth**<br><br>**Low** | **Cash cow**<br>• Large share of low-growth market.<br>• Cash generator.<br>• Strategy is minimal investment to keep the product going. | **Dog**<br>• Small share of low-growth market.<br>• Moderate or negative cash flow.<br>• Divest.<br>*Product purposely kept for loss* |

**High**     **Relative market share**     **Low**

If the relevant information is available, market growth and relative market share should be calculated as follows:

*Historic growth model =* $g = \left( \sqrt[n]{\dfrac{\text{amount now}}{\text{amount years ago}}} \right) - 1$

*   **Market growth** = the % increase/decrease in annual market revenue

    Note: if market revenue is given for a number of successive years the average % increase/decrease in annual market revenue can be calculated as follows:

    $1 + g = \sqrt[n]{\text{most recent market revenue} \div \text{ealiest market revenue}}$

where g = the increase/decrease in annual market revenue as a decimal

**n = the number of periods of growth**

10% used as dividing between high and low growth.

- **Relative market share** = division's market share ÷ market leader's share

divisional market share = divisional revenue ÷ market revenue

## The BCG matrix

| Star | Problem Child |
|---|---|
| • Is the high investment being spent effectively? <br><br> • Is market share being gained, held or eroded? <br><br> • Is customer perception (eg. brand, quality) improving? <br><br> • Are customer CSFs changing as the market grows? <br><br> • What is the net cash flow? <br><br> • Is the star becoming a cash cow? | (1) **Assuming the strategy is to invest** <br><br> • Is market share being gained? <br><br> • Effectiveness of advertising spend. <br><br> (2) **Assuming the strategy is to divest** <br><br> • Monitor contribution to see whether to exit quickly or divest slowly. |
| **Cash Cow** | **Dog** |
| • What is the net cash flow? <br><br> • Is market share being eroded - could the cash cow be moving towards becoming a dog? | • Monitor contribution to see whether to exit quickly or divest slowly. <br><br> • Monitor market growth as an increase in the growth rate could justify retaining the product. |

## Test your understanding 7

Food For Thought (FFT) has been established for over 20 years and has a wide range of food products.

The organisation has four divisions:

(1) Premier

(2) Organic

(3) Baby

(4) Convenience

The Premier division manufactures a range of very high quality food products, which are sold to a leading supermarket, with stores in every major city in the country. Due to the specialist nature of the ingredients these products have a very short life cycle.

The Organic division manufactures a narrow range of food products for a well-established Organic brand label.

The Baby division manufactures specialist foods for infants, which are sold to the largest UK Baby retail store.

The Convenience division manufactures low fat ready-made meals for the local council.

The following revenue data has been gathered: 4 growths =7 n

### Year ending 31st March:

|  |  | $m | | | | |
|---|---|---|---|---|---|---|
|  |  | 20X3 | 20X4 | 20X5 | 20X6 | 20X7 |
| Premier | Market size | 180 | 210 | 260 | 275 | 310 |
|  | Sales revenue | 10 | 12 | 18 | 25 | 30 |
| Organic | Market size | 18.9 | 19.3 | 19.6 | 19.8 | 20.4 |
|  | Sales revenue | 13.5 | 14 | 14.5 | 15 | 16 |
| Baby | Market size | 65 | 69 | 78 | 92 | 96 |
|  | Sales revenue | 2.5 | 2.7 | 2.8 | 2.9 | 3 |
| Convenience | Market size | 26 | 27.2 | 27.6 | 28 | 29 |
|  | Sales revenue | 0.9 | 0.9 | 0.92 | 0.94 | 0.9 |

The management accountant has also collected the following information for 20X7 for comparison purposes.

| Market leader | % share |
|---|---|
| Premier | 17% |
| Organic | 78% |
| Baby | 25% |
| Convenience | 31% |

**Required:**

Using the BCG matrix assess the competitive position of Food For Thought.

### Where products stand within the BCG matrix

The logical thrust here is that, if you enjoy a high market share, then you will probably have a strong position because of low unit production cost and a high market profile. A product that has a high growth potential offers obvious advantages but it is typically associated with high development costs because of the need to develop the product itself and/or maintain the high market share.

The nature of the four classifications shown above is self-explanatory. An understanding of where given products stand in relation to this matrix can be another essential element in strategic planning. For example, if a product is a cash cow, then it may be very useful, but it should be appreciated that it may be at an advanced stage in its life cycle and the cash it generates should be invested in potential stars.

However, it is not always easy to distinguish between a star and a dog. Many businesses have poured money into the development of products that they believed were potential stars only to find that those products turned into dogs. The Sinclair C5 (a small, battery-powered car) is often quoted as an example of this phenomenon. The promoters of this product in the 1980s proceeded on the basis that there was a market for such a car as a means of urban transport and that the C5 would enjoy a high share of this market. In fact, the only niche it found was as a children's toy and it achieved only a low market share with little growth potential as such. The general point this model makes is that current period cash flow is not an unambiguous statement on the performance of a product or business sector. To appreciate fully the performance of a product, one has to appreciate where the product stands in terms of the above matrix. A poor current cash flow may be acceptable from a product or service considered to be a 'Star'.

## Use of BCG analysis as a performance management tool

| Benefits | Drawbacks |
|---|---|
| • Can view prospects of different divisions. | • Simplistic calculation. |
| • Can use to manage divisions in different ways, e.g. divisions in a mature market should focus on cost control and cash generation. | • Designed as a tool for product portfolio analysis rather than performance measurement. |
| • Metrics used by the division can be in line with the analysis, e.g. metrics for high growth prospects may be based on profit and ROI. | • Downgrades traditional measures such as profit and so may not be aligned with shareholder's objectives. |
| | • Starting point for performance management only. |
| | • Does not consider links between business units. |

## 10 Transfer pricing

### 10.1 Introduction

The **transfer price** is the price at which goods or services are transferred from one division to another within the same organisation.

### Characteristics of a good transfer price

- **Goal congruence** - the transfer price that is negotiated and agreed upon by the buying and selling divisions should be in the best interests of the company overall.

- **Fairness** - the divisions must perceive the transfer price to be fair since the transfer price set will impact divisional profit and hence performance evaluation. (+) qualitative - goods condition, timing etc

- **Autonomy** - the system used to set the transfer price should seek to maintain the autonomy of the divisional managers. This autonomy will improve managerial motivation.

- **Bookeeping** - the transfer price chosen should make it straightforward to record the movement of goods or services between divisions.

- **Minimise global tax liability** - multinational companies can use their transfer pricing policies to move profits around the world and thereby minimise their global tax liability.

### 10.2 The general rules for setting transfer prices

#### Scenario 1: There is a perfectly competitive market for the product/service transferred

Transfer price = market price

A perfect market means that there is only one price in the market, there are no buying and selling costs and the market is able to absorb the entire output of the primary division and meet all the requirements of the secondary division.

#### Scenario 2: the selling division has surplus capacity

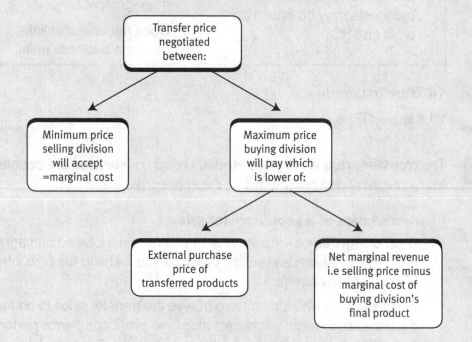

**Scenario 3: The selling division does not have any surplus capacity**

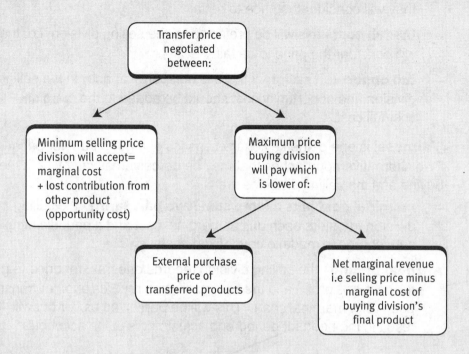

## 10.3 Practical methods of transfer pricing

### Method 1: Market based approach

- If a perfectly competitive market exists for the product, then the market price is the best transfer price.

- Care must be taken to ensure the division's product is the same as that offered by the market (e.g. quality, delivery terms, etc.).

- The market price should be adjusted for costs not incurred on an internal transfer, e.g. delivery costs.

### Method 2: Cost based approach

- Alternatively, if a perfectly competitive market does not exist for the product, the transfer price can be set at **cost + % profit.**

- Standard cost should be used rather than actual cost to avoid inefficiencies being transferred from one department to another and to aid planning and budgeting.

- The cost may be:
    - **the marginal cost** - this will be preferred by the buying division, i.e. they will consider the price to be fair.
    - **the full cost** - this will be preferred by the selling division, i.e. they will consider the price to be fair.
    - **the opportunity cost** - if there is no spare capacity in the selling division, the opportunity cost should be added to the marginal cost/full cost.

- **'Fairness'** is one of the key characteristics of a good transfer price. Two alternative approaches that may be perceived as fair by both the buying and the selling divisions are:
    - **marginal cost plus a lump sum (two part tariff)** - the selling division transfers each unit at marginal cost and a periodic lump sum charge is made to cover fixed costs.
    - **dual pricing** - the selling division records one transfer price (e.g. full cost + % profit) and the buying division records another transfer price (e.g. marginal cost). This will be perceived as fair but will result in the need for period-end adjustments in the accounts.

## Illustration 4 – Practical methods of transfer pricing

**Manuco**

Manuco has been offered supplies of special ingredient Z at a transfer price of $15 per kg by Helpco, which is part of the same group of companies. Helpco processes and sells special ingredient Z to customers external to the group at $15 per kg. Helpco bases its transfer price on total cost-plus 25% profit mark-up. Total cost has been estimated as 75% variable and 25% fixed.

**Required:**

Discuss the transfer prices at which Helpco should offer to transfer special ingredient Z to Manuco in order that group profit maximising decisions may be taken on financial grounds in each of the following situations.

(a) Helpco has an external market for all its production of special ingredient Z at a selling price of $15 per kg. Internal transfers to Manuco would enable $1.50 per kg of variable packing cost to be avoided.

(b) Conditions are as per (i) but Helpco has production capacity for 3,000kg of special ingredient Z for which no external market is available.

(c) Conditions are as per (ii) but Helpco has an alternative use for some of its spare production capacity. This alternative use is equivalent to 2,000kg of special ingredient Z and would earn a contribution of $6,000.

**Solution**

(a) Since Helpco has an external market, which is the opportunity foregone, the relevant transfer price would be the external selling price of $15 per kg. This will be adjusted to allow for the $1.50 per kg avoided on internal transfers due to packing costs not required, i.e. the transfer price is $13.50 per kg.

(b) In this situation Helpco has no alternative opportunity for 3,000kg of its special ingredient Z. It should, therefore, offer to transfer this quantity at marginal cost. This is variable cost less packing costs avoided = $9 – $1.50 = $7.50 per kg (note: total cost = $15 x 80% = $12; variable cost = $12 x 75% = $9). The remaining amount of special ingredient Z should be offered to Manuco at the adjusted selling price of $13.50 per kg (as above).

(c) Helpco has an alternative use for some of its production capacity, which will yield a contribution equivalent to $3 per kg of special ingredient Z ($6,000/2,000kg). The balance of its spare capacity (1,000kg) has no opportunity cost and should still be offered at marginal cost. Helpco should offer to transfer: 2,000kg at $7.50 + $3 = $10.50 per kg; 1,000kg at $7.50per kg (= marginal cost); and the balance of requirements at $13.50 per kg.

## Test your understanding 8

X, a manufacturing company, has two divisions: Division A and Division B. Division A produces one type of product, ProdX, which it transfers to Division B and also sells externally. Division B has been approached by another company which has offered to supply 2,500 units of ProdX for $35 each.

The following details for Division A are available:

| | $ |
|---|---|
| Sales revenue: | |
| Sales to division B @ $40 per unit  10,000 | 400,000 |
| External sales @ $45 per unit | 270,000 |
| less: | |
| Variable cost @$22 per unit | 352,000 |
| Fixed costs | 100,000 |
| | ——— |
| Profit | 218,000 |
| | ——— |

External sales of Prod X cannot be increased, and division B decides to buy from the other company.

**Required:**

(a)  Calculate the effect on the profit of division A.

(b)  Calculate the effect on the profit of company X.

### Test your understanding 9

A company operates two divisions, Able and Baker. Able manufactures two products, X and Y. Product X is sold to external customers for $42 per unit. The only outlet for product Y is Baker.

Baker supplies an external market and can obtain its semi-finished supplies (product Y) from either Able or an external source. Baker currently has the opportunity to purchase product Y from an external supplier for $38 per unit. The capacity of division Able is measured in units of output, irrespective of whether product X, Y or a combination of both are being manufactured.

The associated product costs are as follows:

|  | X | Y |
|---|---|---|
| Variable costs per unit | 32 | 35 |
| Fixed overheads per unit | 5 | 5 |
| Total unit costs | 37 | 40 |

**Required:**

(a)  Using the above information, provide advice on the determination of an appropriate transfer price for the sale of product Y from division Able to division Baker under the following conditions:

(i)  when division Able has spare capacity and limited external demand for  product X

(ii)  when division Able is operating at full capacity with unsatisfied external demand for product X.

(b)  The design of an information system to support transfer pricing decision making necessitates the inclusion of specific data.  Identify the data that needs to be collected and how you would expect it to be used.

**Question focus**: now attempt question 15 from chapter 13.

### 10.4 International transfer pricing

Almost two thirds of world trade takes place within multi-national companies. Transfer pricing in multi-national companies has the following complications:

**Taxation**

The selling and buying divisions will be based in different countries. Different taxation rates in these countries allows the manipulation of profit through the use of transfer pricing.

**e.g**

### Illustration 5 - Taxation and transfer pricing

Rosca Coffee is a multinational company. Division A is based in Northland, a country with a tax rate of 50%. This division transfers goods to division B at a cost of $50,000 per annum. Division B is based in Southland, a country with a tax rate of 20%. Based on the current transfer price of $50,000 the profit of the divisions and of the company is as follows:

|  | *Northland* Division A ($) | *Southland* Division B ($) | Company ($) |
| --- | --- | --- | --- |
| External sales | 100,000 | 120,000 | 220,000 |
| Internal transfers to div B | 50,000 | - | 50,000 |
| Fixed and variable costs | (70,000) | (40,000) | (110,000) |
| Transfer costs from div A | - | (50,000) | (50,000) |
|  | ——— | ——— | ——— |
| Profit before tax | 80,000 | 30,000 | 110,000 |
| Profit after tax | 40,000 | 24,000 | 64,000 |

Rosca Coffee want to take advantage of the different tax rates in Northland and Southland and have decided to reduce the transfer price from $50,000 to $20,000. This will result if the following revised profit figures:

|  | Division A ($) | Division B ($) | Company ($) |
| --- | --- | --- | --- |
| External sales | 100,000 | 120,000 | 220,000 |
| Internal transfers to div B | 20,000 | - | 20,000 |
| Fixed and variable costs | (70,000) | (40,000) | (110,000) |
| Transfer costs from div A | - | (20,000) | (20,000) |
|  | ——— | ——— | ——— |
| Profit before tax | 50,000 | 60,000 | 110,000 |
| Profit after tax | 25,000 | 48,000 | 73,000 |

**Conclusion**: the manipulation of the transfer price has increased the company's profits from $64,000 to $73,000.

### Remittance controls

- A country's government may impose restrictions on the transfer of profits from domestic subsidiaries to foreign multinationals.

- This is known as a 'block on the remittances of dividends' i.e. it limits the payment of dividends to the parent company's shareholders.

- It is often done through the imposition of strict exchange controls.

- Artificial attempts at reducing tax liabilities could, however, upset a country's tax authorities. Many tax authorities have the power to alter the transfer price and can treat the transactions as having taken place at a fair arms length price and revise profits accordingly.

### Test your understanding 10

**Required:**

Discuss how a multinational company could avoid the problem of blocked remittances.

### Additional example on international issues

A multinational organisation, C, has 2 divisions each in a different country – Divisions A and B. Suppose Division A produces a product X where the domestic income tax rate is 40% and transfers it to Division B, which operates in a country with a 50% rate of income tax. An import duty equal to 25% of the price of product X is also assessed. The full cost per unit is $190, the variable cost $60.

**Required:**
The tax authorities allow either variable or full cost transfer prices. Determine which should be chosen.

#### Solution

| | $ |
|---|---|
| Effect of transferring at $190 instead of $60: | |
| Income of A is $130 higher and so A pays $130 x 40% more income tax | (52) |
| Income of B is $130 lower and so C pays $130 x 50% less income tax | 65 |
| Import duty is paid by B on an additional $130, and so C pays $130 x 25% more duty | (32.5) |
| Net effect (cost) of transferring at $190 instead of $60 | (19.5) |

**Conclusion:** C should transfer at variable cost.

**Question focus**: Now attempt question 16 from chapter 13.

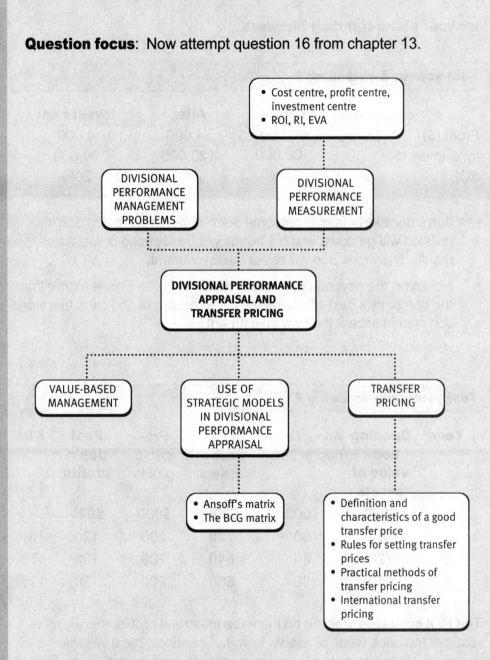

## Test your understanding answers

### Test your understanding 1

|  | Before | After | Investment |
|---|---|---|---|
| Profit ($) | 30,000 | 34,000 | 4,000 |
| Investment ($) | 100,000 | 120,000 | 20,000 |
| ROI | 30% | 28% | 20% |

- Jon's decision - from a personal point of view, the ROI of Jon's division will go down and his bonus will be reduced or lost as a result. Therefore, Jon will reject the investment.

- However, the new equipment has a ROI of 20%. This is higher than the company's cost of capital (required return) of 15% and therefore Jon should accept the new investment.

### Test your understanding 2

| Year | Opening book value of assets | Annual book depreciation | Closing value of assets | Pre-dep'n profits | Post dep'n profits | ROI |
|---|---|---|---|---|---|---|
|  | $000 | $000 | $000 | $000 | $000 |  |
| 1 | 800 | 80 | 720 | 200 | 120 | 15% |
| 2 | 720 | 80 | 640 | 200 | 120 | 17% |
| 3 | 640 | 80 | 560 | 200 | 120 | 19% |

The ROI increases, despite no increase in annual profits, merely as a result of the book value of assets falling. Therefore, the divisional manager will be rewarded for holding onto old, and potentially inefficient, assets.

## Test your understanding 3

(a) **ROI**

| | |
|---|---|
| Current ROI = ($40k/$150k) × 100 | 26.7% |
| ROI with new investment = ($42k/$160k) × 100 | 26.3% |
| ROI of the new investment = ($2k/$10k) × 100 | 20% |

**Decision**: The division would not accept the investment since it would reduce the division's ROI.

However, this is not in the best interests of the company since the ROI (20%) is greater than the company's cost of capital (10%).

(b) **RI**

| | |
|---|---|
| Current RI = $40k – (10% × $150k) | $25k |
| RI with new investment = $42k – (10% × $160k) | $26k |

**Decision**: The division would accept the investment since it generates an increase in RI of $1,000.

This decision is in the best interests of the company.

**Test your understanding 4**

(a)

| Best outcome | Year 1 | Year 2 | Year 3 |
|---|---|---|---|
| **RI and ROI** | **$m** | **$m** | **$m** |
| NBV @ start of year | (66.0) | (44.0) | (22.0) |
| | | | |
| Revenue (add 6%) | 90.1 | 95.4 | 99.6 |
| Less direct cost (minus 8%) | (46.0) | (55.2) | (64.4) |
| | | | |
| Net cash flow | 44.1 | 40.2 | 35.2 |
| Less depreciation | (22.0) | (22.0) | (22.0) |
| **Operating profit** | **22.1** | **18.2** | **13.2** |
| Less imputed interest @ 8% | (5.3) | (3.5) | (1.8) |
| **RI** | **16.8** | **14.7** | **11.4** |
| **ROI** | **33.5%** | **41.4%** | **60.0%** |

**NPV @ 8% discount factor**

| Timing | CF | DF | PV |
|---|---|---|---|
| $t_0$ | (66.0) | 1.000 | (66.0) |
| $t_1$ | 44.1 | 0.926 | 40.8 |
| $t_2$ | 40.2 | 0.857 | 34.5 |
| $t_3$ | 35.2 | 0.794 | 28.0 |
| | | | |
| **NPV** | | | **37.3** |

**(b) Worst outcome**

| RI and ROI | Year 1 | Year 2 | Year 3 |
|---|---|---|---|
| | $m | $m | $m |
| NBV @ start of year | (66.0) | (44.0) | (22.0) |
| | | | |
| Revenue (minus 6%) | 79.9 | 84.6 | 88.4 |
| Less direct cost (add 8%) | (54.0) | (64.8) | (75.6) |
| | | | |
| Net cash flow | 25.9 | 19.8 | 12.8 |
| Less depreciation | (22.0) | (22.0) | (22.0) |
| **Operating profit** | **3.9** | **(2.2)** | **(9.2)** |
| Less imputed interest @ 10% | (6.6) | (4.4) | (2.2) |
| **RI** | **(2.7)** | **(6.6)** | **(11.4)** |
| **ROI** | **5.9%** | **-5.0%** | **-41.8%** |

**NPV @ 10% discount factor**

| Timing | CF | DF | PV |
|---|---|---|---|
| $t_0$ | (66.0) | 1.000 | (66.0) |
| $t_1$ | 25.9 | 0.909 | 23.5 |
| $t_2$ | 19.8 | 0.826 | 16.4 |
| $t_3$ | 12.8 | 0.751 | 9.6 |
| | | | |
| **NPV** | | | **(16.5)** |

## NOPAT

| | $m |
|---|---|
| Controllable PAT | 8.4 |
| Add back items that add value: development costs | 2 |
| Deduct amortisation of development costs ($2m ÷ 4 years) | (0.5) |
| NOPAT | 9.9 |

## Economic value of capital employed

| | $m |
|---|---|
| Opening book value of assets | 60 |
| Adjustment to reflect the replacement cost of assets ($75m – $60m) | 15 |
| Net book value of development costs ($2m – $0.5m) | 1.5 |
| Economic value of capital employed | 76.5 |

## EVA

| | $m |
|---|---|
| NOPAT | 9.9 |
| Less: economic value of capital employed × WACC ($76.5m × 10%) | (7.65) |
| **EVA** | **2.25** |

## Test your understanding 6

**NOPAT**

|  | $'000 |
|---|---|
| Controllable PAT | 100 |
| Add back: accounting depreciation | 80 |
| Add back: interest paid net of tax ($9,000 × 70%) | 6.3 |
| Add back: operating lease interest cost | 8 |
| Deduct: economic depreciation | (75) |
| NOPAT | 119.3 |

**Economic value of capital employed**

|  | $'000 |
|---|---|
| Opening book value of assets | 500 |
| Adjustment to reflect the replacement cost of assets ($500,000 × 20%) | 100 |
| Net book value of operating leases | 90 |
| Economic value of capital employed | 690 |

**EVA**

|  | $'000 |
|---|---|
| NOPAT | 119.3 |
| Less: economic value of capital employed × WACC (w2) ($690k × 8.4%) | (57.96) |
| EVA | **61.34** |

**(W2):** WACC = (10% × 0.6) + (6% × 0.4) = 8.4%

### Test your understanding 7

| | Market growth (% change in annual market revenue) | Division's market share (most recent divisional revenue/market revenue) | Relative market share (division's market share/market leader's share) |
|---|---|---|---|
| **Premier** | 14.6% | 10% | 0.58 |
| **Organic** | 1.9% | 78% | 1.00 |
| **Baby** | 10.2% | 3% | 0.12 |
| **Convenience** | 2.8% | 3% | 0.10 |

The management could use the BCG matrix in order to classify its subsidiaries in terms of their rate of market growth and relative market share.

The model has four categories these are:

**Stars**

A star product has a relatively high market share in a growth market.

The **Premier** division is experiencing strong growth in a growing market.

It has a 10% market share and therefore it seems reasonable to categorise the Premier division as a star.

**Problem child**

They have a relatively low market share in a high growth market. The **Baby** division would appear to fall into this category. The market leader enjoys a 25% share whilst the Baby division appear to be struggling to achieve growth in turnover and hence profits.

**Cash cow**

A cash cow is characterised by a relatively high market share in a low growth market and should generate significant cash flows.

The **Organic** division appears to be a cash cow since it has a very high market share in what can be regarded as a low growth market.

### Dog

A dog is characterised by a relatively low market share in a low growth market and might well be loss making. The **Convenience** division would appear to fall into this category since its market share is very low and it has low growth.

Food for thought has a dog and a problem child that both require immediate attention.

Competitors within the sector will resist any attempts to reduce their share of a low growth or declining market. As far as the problem child is concerned, the management need to devise appropriate strategies to convert them into stars.

### Test your understanding 8

(a)  Division A will lose the contribution from internal transfers to Division B.  Contribution foregone = 2,500 × $(40-22) = $45,000 reduction.

(b)

|  | $ per unit |
|---|---|
| Cost per unit from external supplier | 35 |
| Variable cost of internal manufacture saved | 22 |
|  | --- |
| Incremental cost of external purchase | 13 |
|  | --- |

Reduction in profit of X    =  $13 x 2,500 units
                             =      $32,500

### Test your understanding 9

(a)

    (i)    The transfer price should be set between \$35 (minimum price Able will sell for) and \$38 (maximum price Baker will pay). Able has spare capacity, therefore the marginal costs to the group of Able making a unit is \$35. If the price is set above \$38, Baker will be encouraged to buy outside the group, decreasing group profit by \$3 per unit.

    (ii)    If Able supplies Baker with a unit of Y, it will cost \$35 and they (both Able and the group) will lose \$10 contribution from X. Therefore, the minimum price able will sell for is \$45. So long as the bought-in external price of Y to Baker is less than \$45, Baker should buy from that external source.

(b)    The following are required.

    –    Marginal costs (i.e. unit variable costs) and incremental fixed costs for various capacity levels for both divisions.

    –    External market prices if appropriate.

    –    External bought-in prices from suppliers outside the group.

    –    Opportunity costs from switching products.

    –    Data on capacity levels and resource requirements.

### Test your understanding 10

Blocked remittances might be avoided by means of:

- increasing transfer prices paid by the foreign subsidiary to the parent company (see below)

- lending the equivalent of the dividend to the parent company

- making payments to the parent company in the form of:
  - royalties
  - payments for patents
  - management fees and charges

- charging the subsidiary company additional head office overheads.

Note: The government of the foreign country might try to prevent many of these measures being used.

# Performance management in not-for-profit organisations

## Chapter learning objectives

Upon completion of this chapter you will be able to:

- highlight and discuss the potential for diversity in objectives depending on organisation type

- discuss the need to achieve objectives with limited funds that may not be controllable

- identify and discuss ways in which performance may be judged in not-for-profit organisations

- discuss the difficulties in measuring outputs when performance is not judged in terms of money or an easily quantifiable objective

- discuss how the combination of politics and the desire to measure public sector performance may result in undesirable service outcomes

- assess 'value for money' service provision as a measure of performance in not-for-profit organisations and the public sector.

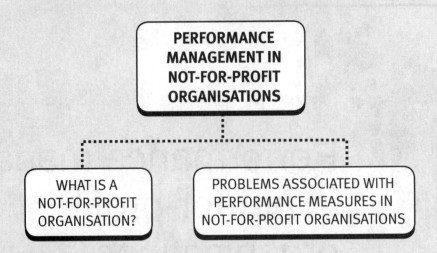

## 1 Exam focus

| Exam sitting | Area examined | Question number | Number of marks |
| --- | --- | --- | --- |
| June 2010 | VFM and economy, efficiency and effectiveness | 3(i)(ii) | 12 |
| December 2007 | Problems encountered when comparing public and private sector performance and VFM | 1(b)(c) | 12 |

**Student Accountant articles**: visit the ACCA website, www.accaglobal.com, to review the following articles on the topics in this chapter:

- Not-for-profit organisations part 1 - September 2009
- Not-for-profit organisations part 2 - October 2009

## 2 What is a not-for-profit (NFP) organisation?

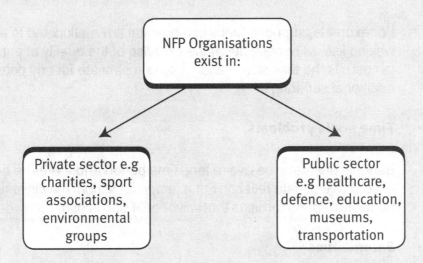

NFP organisations display the following characteristics:

- Most do not have external shareholders and hence the maximisation of shareholder wealth is not the primary objective.

- They do not distribute dividends.

- Their objectives normally include some social, cultural, philanthropic, welfare or environmental dimension which would not be readily provided in their absence.

When assessing the performance of NFP organisations it is important to include both financial and non-financial measures.

## 3 Problems associated with performance measurement in NFP organisations

### Problem 1: Non-quantifiable costs and benefits

### Introduction

Many of the benefits arising from expenditure by these bodies are non-quantifiable in monetary terms. The same can be true of costs. This is because:

- **No readily available scale exists.**

  For example, how to measure the impact of a charity providing a help line to people suffering from depression?

- **How to trade off cost and benefits measured in a different way.**

  For example, suppose funds in a hospital are reallocated to reduce waiting lists (a benefit) but at the expense of the quality of patient care (a cost). Is the time saved enough to compensate for any potential additional suffering?

- **Time scale problems.**

  Benefits often accrue over a long time period and therefore become difficult to estimate reliably. For example, a school may invest in additional sports facilities that will benefit pupils over many decades.

- **Externalities.**

  Suppose a council decides to grant planning permission for new houses to be built. The new residents will increase the number of cars on local roads, resulting in greater congestion and pollution, affecting other residents.

### Illustration 1 - Non-quantifiable costs and benefits

**Non-quantifiable benefits**

In 2001, the British government scrapped admission charges to some of the country's most famous museums and galleries. The policy has attracted approximately 50 million extra people to the nation's great artistic and cultural collections. Subjects such as history, art and geography have been enlivened by being able to go to a museum or gallery and see and touch the exhibitions. However, it is difficult to quantify the benefits.

**Non-quantifiable costs**

A hospital has decided to save money by using a cheaper cleaning firm. However, this decision may create problems in a number of areas:

- It may lead to the spread of infection.

- The general public may lose confidence in the quality of the cleaning.

- Medical staff may become demotivated because they are unable to carry out their work effectively.

However, it is difficult to measure these costs.

## Test your understanding 1

In an attempt to improve people's quality of life the UK government has introduced a range of performance measures to measure quality of life, including the following:

- the local bird population
- the stock of 'decent' housing
- traffic volumes.

### Required:

A town planning office is considering whether to approve a plan to build new houses on farmland. Assess the plan by reference to the three indicators given.

## Solution = cost benefit analysis (CBA)

Some NFP organisations, particularly in the public sector, attempt to resolve the above difficulties by quantifying **in financial terms** all of the costs and benefits associated with a decision.

## Illustration 2 – CBA

Suppose a local government department is considering whether to lower the speed limit for heavy goods vehicles (HGVs) travelling on a particular road through a residential area. The affected stakeholders may be identified as follows:

| Stakeholder | Cost | Benefit |
|---|---|---|
| HGV operators | • Extra journey time <br> • Potential speeding fines | • Fewer accidents |
| Other road uses | • Extra journey times | • Fewer accidents |
| Local residents | • Higher noise levels and pollution | • Fewer accidents |
| Local authority | • Cost of new signs, speed cameras <br> • Cost of enforcement | • Fines collected |

These costs and benefits then need to be quantified financially.

| Factor | How to measure |
|--------|----------------|
| Time | • For HGV operators this can be quantified as additional wages, overtime premiums, additional fuel costs, etc.<br><br>• For other road users we need to quantify how much people value their time. One way this can be done is by comparing the costs of different modes of transport (e.g. coach versus rail versus air) to see the premium travellers will pay to save time.<br><br>• Another approach is to compare property prices as they get further away from train stations as this will in part reflect longer journey times. |
| Noise | • Cost of installing double glazing to reduce noise levels.<br><br>• Difference in house prices between houses next to the busy road and those set further back. |
| Pollution | • Cost of cleaning off soot and other pollutants.<br><br>• Comparison of house prices near/away from main roads. |
| Accidents | • Impact on insurance premiums for drivers.<br><br>• For victims of accidents the value of not breaking a leg, say, or not being killed, is estimated in many ways, e.g. the present value of future earnings affected. |

Once these have been quantified, it is relatively straightforward to compare overall costs and benefits to see the net impact on society.

## Problem 2: Assessing the use of funds

### Introduction

Many NFP organisations, particularly public sector organisations, do not generate revenue but simply have a fixed budget for spending within which they have to keep. The funding in public sector organisations tends to come directly from the government.

There are a number of problems associated with this funding:

• The organisation may feel under pressure to hit government targets rather than focusing on what they would normally consider important.

- There is not necessarily a link between providing more service and obtaining more funds. Funding tends to be limited and may not be controllable.

- A failure to achieve objectives sometimes leads to higher levels of funding.

### Illustration 3 – Funding

An ineffective or inefficient police force will not be closed down, but is likely to justify and obtain additional funding.

### Solution = assess value for money

Value for money (VFM) is often quoted as an objective in NFP organisations, i.e. have they gained the best value from the limited funds available?

VFM can be assessed in a number of ways:

- through benchmarking an activity against similar activities in other organisations

- by using performance indicators/ measures (see TYU 2)

- through conducting VFM studies (possibly in conjunction with other institutions)

- by seeking out and then adopting recognised good practice where this can be adapted to the institution's circumstances

- through internal VFM audit work

- through retaining both documents that show how an activity has been planned to build in VFM, and evidence of the good practices adopted

- by examining the results or outcomes of an activity.

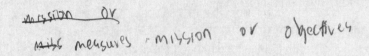

### Test your understanding 2

Maple Council is concerned about the performance of St George's School, one of the primary schools within its jurisdiction and, in order to substantiate this concern, the Council's Education Department has collected the following information regarding the last two years.

|  | 20X7 | | 20X8 |
|---|---|---|---|
| School Roll (no of pupils) | 502 | 4~ | 584 |
| Number of teaching staff | 22 | (1) | 21 |
| Number of support staff | 6 | - | 6 |
| Number of classes | 20 | - | 20 |
| Possible teaching days in a year | 290 | - | 290 |
| Actual teaching days in a year | 279 | 3 | 282 |
| Total pupil absences (in pupil teaching days) | 2,259 | 807 | 3,066 |
| Total teaching staff absences (in pupil teaching days) | 132 | 57 | 189 |
|  | $ | | $ |
| Budgeted expenditure | 2,400,000 | | 2,600,000 |
| Actual expenditure | 2,200,000 | | 2,900,000 |

The data has been sent to the council's finance department in which you work for analysis.

### Required:

Calculate performance measures for St George's School for each of the last two years.

Based on your calculations analyse the school's performance and explain any reservations you may have about their use as measures of performance.

## The 3Es

Value for money is interpreted as providing an economic, efficient and effective service.

**Economy** - an input measure.  Are the resources the cheapest possible for the quality desired?

**Efficiency** - here we link inputs and outputs.  Is the maximum output being achieved from the resources used?

**Effectiveness** - an output measure looking at whether objectives are being met.

Transparency

### Test your understanding 3

**Required:**

Explain the meaning of economy, efficiency and effectiveness for a university, incorporating specific examples for each of the 3Es.

### Other methods of evaluating performance

In addition to assessing value for money and the 3Es the following approaches can be used to assess the performance of NFP organisations:

- The '**goal approach**' looks at the ultimate objectives of the organisation, i.e. it looks at output measures.

  For example for a hospital: Have waiting lists been reduced? Have mortality rates gone down? How many patients have been treated?

- The '**systems resources approach**' looks at how well the organisation has obtained the inputs it needs to function.

  For example, did the hospital manage to recruit all the nurses it needed?

- The '**internal processes approach**' looks at how well inputs have been used to achieve outputs – it is a measure of efficiency.

  For example, what was the average cost per patient treated?

### Problem 3: Multiple and diverse objectives

### Diverse objectives

As mentioned, NFP organisations are unlikely to have an objective of maximisation of shareholder wealth. Instead they are seeking to satisfy the particular needs of their members or sections of society, which they have been set up to benefit.

#### Illustration 4 - Diverse objectives

Diverse objectives in NFP organisations include:

- A hospital's objective is to treat patients.
- A council's objective is care for the local community.
- A charity's objective may be to provide relief for victims of a disaster.

### Multiple objectives

Multiple stakeholders in NFP organisations give rise to multiple objectives. This can be problematic when assessing the performance of these organisations.

### Solution

The problem of multiple objectives can be overcome by prioritising objectives or making compromises between objectives.

#### Illustration 5 - The problem of multiple objectives

A hospital will have a number of different groups of stakeholders, each with their own objectives. For example:

- Employees will seek a high level of job satisfaction. They will also aim to achieve a good work-life balance and this may result in a desire to work more regular daytime hours.
- Patients will want to be seen quickly and will demand a high level of care.

There is potential conflict between the objectives of the two stakeholder groups. For example, if hospital staff only work regular daytime hours then patients may have to wait a long time if they come to the hospital outside of these hours and the standard of patient care will fall dramatically at certain times of the day.

The hospital must prioritise the needs of different stakeholder groups. In this case, the standard of patient care would be prioritised above giving staff the regular daytime working hours that they would prefer. However, in order to maintain staff morale an element of compromise should also be used. For example, staff may have to work shifts but will be given generous holiday allowances or rewards to compensate for this.

## Test your understanding 4

### Required:

Describe the different groups of stakeholders in an international famine relief charity. Explain how the charity might have conflicting objectives and the impact this conflict may have on the effective operation of the organisation.

## Problem 4: The impact of politics on performance measurement

The combination of politics and performance measurement in the public sector may result in undesirable outcomes.

- The public focus on some sectors, such as health and education, make them a prime target for political interference.

- Long-term organisational objectives are sacrificed for short-term political gains.

### Illustration 6 - Impact of politics

Politicians may promise 'increased funding' and 'improved performance' as that is what voters want to hear, but it may result in undesirable outcomes.

Increased funding:

- may be available only to the detriment of other public sector organisations

- may be provided to organisations in political hot-spots, not necessarily the places that need more money

- may not be used as efficiently or effectively as it could be

- may only be available in the short-term, as a public relations exercise.

Improved performance:

- may be to the detriment of workers and clients

- may come about as the result of data manipulation, rather than real results

- may be a short-term phenomenon

- may result in more funds being spent on performance measurement when it might better be used on improvements, e.g. hospitals under increasing pressure to compete on price and delivery in some areas may result in a shift of resources from other, less measurable areas, such as towards elective surgery and away from emergency services.

### Test your understanding 5 - Long practice question on NFPOs

**Public versus private sector**

The objective of a health authority (a public sector organisation) is stated in its most recent annual report as:

> 'To serve the people of the region by providing high-quality health care within expected waiting times'.

The 'mission statement' of a large company in a manufacturing industry is shown in its annual report as:

> 'In everything the company does, it is committed to creating wealth, always with integrity, for its shareholders, employees, customers and suppliers and the community in which it operates.'

**Required:**

(a) Discuss the main differences between the public and private sectors that have to be addressed when determining corporate objectives or missions.

(b) Describe three performance measures which could be used to assess whether or not the health authority is meeting its current objective.

(c) Explain the difficulties which public sector organisations face in using such measures to influence decision making.

**Question focus**: now attempt question 17 from chapter 13.

# Chapter summary

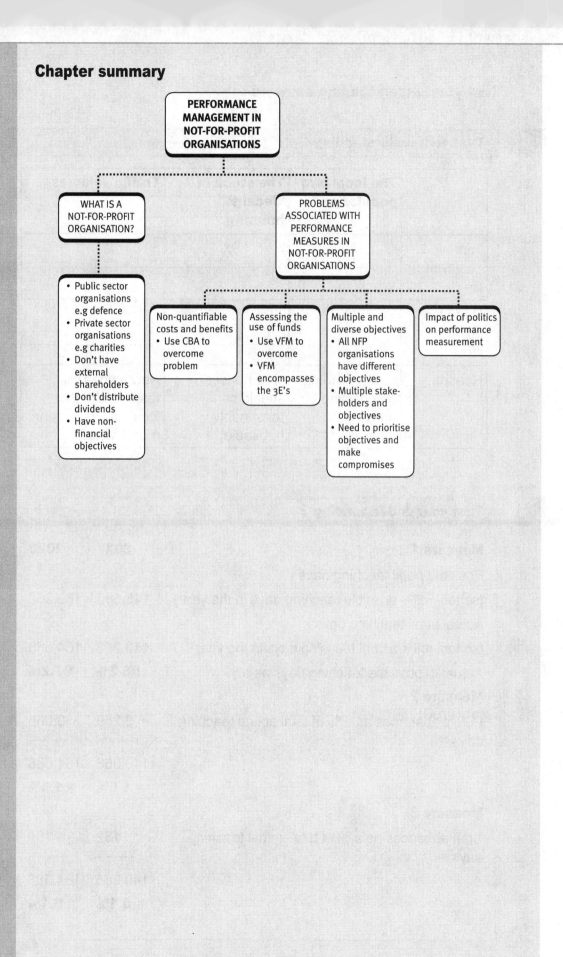

## Test your understanding answers

### Test your understanding 1

|  | The local bird population | The stock of 'decent' housing | Traffic volumes |
|---|---|---|---|
| Improved quality of life |  | X |  |
| Reduced quality of life | X |  | X |
| Reason | Fewer feeding and nesting areas | New houses should be reasonably habitable! | New homes will result in a higher local population and more traffic |

### Test your understanding 2

| **Measure 1** | **20X7** | **20X8** |
|---|---|---|
| Possible pupil teaching days = | | |
| (school roll × possible teaching days in the year) | 145,580 | 169,360 |
| Actual pupil teaching days = | | |
| (school roll × actual teaching days in the year) | 140,058 | 164,688 |
| Actual to possible teaching days as a % | **96.2%** | **97.2%** |

**Measure 2**

Pupils absences as a % of total actual teaching days =

$$\frac{2,259}{140,058} = \textbf{1.6\%} \qquad \frac{3,066}{164,688} = \textbf{1.9\%}$$

**Measure 3**

Staff absences as a % of total actual teaching days =

$$\frac{132}{140,058} = \textbf{0.1\%} \qquad \frac{189}{164,688} = \textbf{0.1\%}$$

**Measure 4**

| Pupil teacher ratio | 502:22 | 584:6 |
| --- | --- | --- |
| | **=22.8:1** | **=27.8:1** |

**Measure 5**

| Pupil to non teaching staff ratio | 502:6 | 584:6 |
| --- | --- | --- |
| | **= 83.7:1** | **= 97.3:1** |

**Measure 6**

Average class size

| | 502 | 584 |
| --- | --- | --- |
| (school / number of classes) | 20 | 20 |
| | **= 25.1** | **= 29.2** |

**Measure 7**

Budgeted expenditure per pupil

| | 2,400,000 | 2,600,000 |
| --- | --- | --- |
| | 502 | 584 |
| | **= $4780.88** | **= $4452.05** |

| Actual expenditure per pupil | 2,200,000 | 2,900,000 |
| --- | --- | --- |
| | 502 | 584 |
| | **= 4382.47** | **= 4965.75** |

**Comments**

In certain circumstances, the schools performance has been fairly consistent over the two years. Staff and pupil absences as a percentage of total actual pupil teaching days have deteriorated marginally, whilst actual to possible total teaching days has shown a slight improvement.

The major area of concern is the number of pupils on the school roll is roughly 16% higher than last year. This may have an impact on performance. Pupil to teaching staff, pupil to non teaching staff, and average class size has worsened. Whether this is enough to effect the quality of provision is impossible to say without further investigation.

Expenditure per pupil has fallen but this is a function of the increased pupil numbers.

Overall it is not really possible to arrive at a firm conclusion about the schools performance. This is partly due to a lack of data from the school, and partly because of a lack of data from other schools against which to compare it.

## Test your understanding 3

Value for money for a university would comprise three elements:

**Economy** - this is about balancing the cost with the quality of resources. Therefore, it will review areas such as the cost of books, computers and teaching compared with the quality of these resources. It recognises that the organisation must consider its expenditure but should not simply aim to minimise costs, e.g. low cost but poor quality teaching or books will hinder student performance and will damage the reputation of the university.

**Efficiency** - this focuses on the efficient use of any resources acquired, for example:

- How often are the library books that are bought by the university taken out by students?

- What is the utilisation of IT resources?

- What % of their working time do academic staff spend lecturing and researching?

**Effectiveness** - this measures the achievement of the organisation's objectives, for example:

- The % of students achieving a target grade.

- The % of graduates who find full time employment within 6 months of graduating.

## Test your understanding 4

The stakeholders will include donors, people needing aid, voluntary staff, paid staff, the governments of the countries granting and receiving aid.

There may be conflicting objectives. Donors and people needing aid will want all of the funds to be spent on famine relief. Management staff may require a percentage of the funds to be spent on administration and promotion in order to preserve the long-term future of the charity. Donors may have their own views about how donations should be spent which conflict with management staff.

The charity may wish to distribute aid according to perceived need. Governments in receiving countries may have political reasons for distorting information relating to need. These conflicts may make it difficult to set clear objectives on which all stakeholders agree.

## Test your understanding 5 - Long practice question on NFPOs

(a) The main differences between the public and private sector regarding corporate objectives are:

The objectives of a public sector body are usually set out in the Act of Parliament or legal document that brought the body into existence. They are therefore difficult to change, even as environmental conditions change around the body. The directors of a private sector body have more freedom in making up the objectives of the company as they go along, and can change the objectives rapidly in response to changing conditions.

The value of the output of a private sector body can be easily determined in an unbiased way, by looking at the sales revenue achieved. Such numbers can therefore be part of the objectives to be achieved. There is no easy way for determining the economic value of the output of a public sector body; placing a value on the achievements of a country's Navy last year is almost impossible.

The mission statement of the company in the question recognises the role of the company in having responsibilities to different groups of stakeholders: shareholders, customers, the community at large, etc. Some public sector bodies appear to ignore the interests of certain stakeholders; you might for example be able to think of bodies that appear to be run more for the employees of the body itself rather than the public it is supposed to be serving. Private sector bodies that ignore stakeholders go bust and leave the marketplace. Failing public sector bodies often are rewarded with greater slices of public money to finance their inadequacies.

Private sector companies can attract finance in a free marketplace if they wish to expand. Public sector bodies are constrained by short-term cash limits set by the government depending on the state of the public finances. This acts against the construction of long-term strategic plans in the public sector.

The public sector has historically had little understanding of capital as a scarce resource. In the objective quoted in the question for the health authority, there is no mention of giving value for money to the taxpayers who finance the services. Private sector companies have to give value for money to their shareholders; otherwise the shareholders will sell their shares and the share price will fall, making future capital issues more expensive.

(b)  In terms of the health authority's current objective, three performance measures that could be used are:

Number of patients who survive serious surgery: this would give a measure of the quality of emergency health care provided, and could be calculated as an absolute figure and a percentage, and compared with the figures for the previous year and nationally.

Length of time (on average) before an ambulance arrives after an emergency call is made: this could be compared with the figure for the previous year and for other similar regions of the country.

Length of waiting list for serious operations, i.e. the average time period between a patient being recommended for an operation by his doctor and the operation actually taking place: this figure could be compared with the figure for the previous year and with national figures.

(c)  Decisions have to be made at both a local level (the tactical and operational decisions in running the public sector organisation) and a national level (mainly in terms of the amount of money to be made available to the service).

If insufficient funds have been made available to a health authority, the only way it can maintain standards is to let the waiting list increase. This might reflect badly on the local managers, but the responsibility for the problem really lies with the politicians who have decided to inadequately finance the organisation.

Similar problems exist in other public sector areas. Consider the police, for example. If they arrest more criminals, is this good or bad? Some people would say it is a good thing in that they are detecting more crime; others would say it is a failure of their crime prevention measures. If the statistical percentage of successful prosecutions brought was to be used as a performance measure, this might pressure the police to release on caution all those suspects against whom the police felt they did not have a watertight case. This is surely not in the public interest.

The recommended solution is for public sector organisations to rephrase their statements of objectives to bring more stakeholders into view, and then to construct a range of performance measures, which takes into account the wishes of each of these stakeholders.

# 10

# Non-financial performance indicators and corporate failure

## Chapter learning objectives

Upon completion of this chapter you will be able to:

- discuss the interaction of non-financial performance indicators with financial performance indicators

- discuss the implications of the growing emphasis on non-financial performance indicators

- discuss the significance of non-financial performance indicators in relation to employees

- identify and discuss the significance of non-financial performance indicators in relation to product/service quality, e.g. customer satisfaction reports, repeat business ratings, access and availability

- discuss the difficulties in interpreting data on qualitative issues

- discuss the significance of brand awareness and company profile and their potential impact on business performance

- evaluate the 'balanced scorecard' approach as a way in which to improve the range and linkage between performance measures

- evaluate the 'performance pyramid' as a way in which to link strategy, operations and performance

- evaluate the work of Fiitzgerald and Moon that considers performance measurement in business services using building blocks for dimensions, standards and rewards

- discuss and apply the Performance Prism

- assess the potential likelihood of corporate failure, utilising quantitative and qualitative performance measures and models (such as Z-scores and Argenti)

- assess and critique quantitative and qualitative corporate failure prediction models

- identify and discuss performance improvement strategies that may be adopted in order to prevent corporate failure

- discuss how long-term survival necessitates consideration of life-cycle issues

- identify and discuss operational changes to performance management systems required to implement the performance improvement strategies.

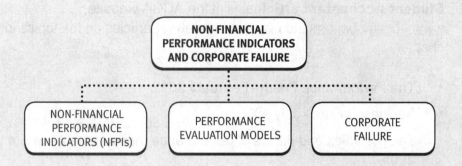

Corporate Failure
Performance prism
Xq 2012

# 1 Exam focus

| Exam sitting | Area examined | Question number | Number of marks |
|---|---|---|---|
| June 2012 | Performance prism | 2(b) | 14 |
| December 2011 | Performance pyramid | 2(b)(c) | 19 |
| June 2011 | Building block model | 3 | 20 |
| June 2011 | Balanced scorecard | 2(a)(b)(d) | 21 |
| December 2010 | Environmental performance | 4(b)(c) | 12 |
| December 2010 | Corporate failure | 5 | 20 |
| June 2010 | NFPIs and the balanced scorecard | 1(i) | 13 |
| June 2010 | Assessment of financial and non-financial performance | 5(b) | 12 |
| December 2009 | Assessment of financial and non-financial performance using Fitzgerald and Moon | 1(ii) | 10 |
| June 2009 | Balanced scorecard | 1 | 31 |
| June 2009 | Discussion of sole reliance on financial performance measures | 2(c) | 6 |
| December 2008 | Evaluation of performance including Fitzgerald and Moon | 1(a) | 29 |
| December 2007 | Indicators of corporate failure | 5(b) | 10 |
| Pilot paper | Assessment of financial and non-financial performance | 2(a)(ii)(iii)(iv) | 15 |
| Pilot paper | Performance pyramid | 2(b) | 5 |

**Student Accountant articles**: visit the ACCA website, www.accaglobal.com, to review the following articles on the topics in this chapter:

- The Performance Prism - February 2012
- Business failure - July 2008
- The pyramids and pitfalls of performance measurement - September 2005

## 2 Introduction

Chapters 7, 8 and 9 have concentrated on financial performance measures. This chapter discusses the use on non-financial performance indicators (NFPIs) and introduces some of the models that are available for evaluating financial and non-financial performance.

The final part of the chapter covers the separate topic of corporate failure.

**Question focus**: Many of the areas covered in this chapter have already been touched upon in Paper F5. You may want to test your assumed knowledge by completing Q18 from chapter 13.

## 3 Drawbacks of sole reliance on financial performance measures

As mentioned, so far we have concentrated on financial performance measures. However, there are a number of problems associated with the use of financial performance indicators to monitor performance:

### Short-termism

Linking rewards to financial performance may tempt managers to make decisions that will improve short-term financial performance but may have a negative impact on long-term profitability. For example, a manager may decide to delay investment in order to boost the short-term profits of their division.

### Internal focus

Financial performance measures tend to have an internal focus. In order to compete successfully it is important that external factors (such as customer satisfaction and competitors' actions) are also considered.

### Manipulation of results

In order to achieve target financial performance (and hence their reward), managers may be tempted to manipulate results, e.g. costs recorded in the current year may be wrongly recorded in the next year's accounts in order to improve current year performance.

### Do not convey the whole picture  *one snapshot*

The use of financial performance indicators has limited benefit to the company since they do not convey the full picture regarding the factors that drive long-term success and maximisation of shareholder wealth, e.g. customer satisfaction, ability to innovate, quality.

### Backward looking

Financial performance measures are traditionally backward looking.  This is not suitable in today's dynamic business environment.

## 4 Solution = use financial and non-financial performance indicators

In order to overcome the problems discussed in section 3, a broader range of measures should be used.

The optimum system for performance measurement and control will include:

- Financial performance indicators (FPIs) - it is still important to monitor financial performance, e.g. using ROCE, EBITDA, EVA.

- Non-financial performance indicators (NFPIs)  - these measures will reflect the long-term viability and health of the organisation.

The models used to evaluate financial and non-financial performance will be reviewed in section 7.

---

### FPIs and NFPIs

The following table gives examples of possible FPIs and NFPIs:

| Financial performance | <ul><li>cost</li><li>profitability</li><li>liquidity</li><li>budget variance analysis</li><li>market ratios</li><li>level of bad debts</li><li>return on capital employed (ROCE).</li></ul> |
|---|---|
| Competitiveness | <ul><li>sales growth by product or service</li><li>measures of customer base</li><li>relative market share and position.</li></ul> |

| Activity | • sales units |
| | • labour/machine hours |
| | • number of passengers carried |
| | • number of material requisitions serviced |
| | • number of accounts reconciled |
| | • whichever measurement is used it may be compared against a pre-set target. |
| Productivity | • efficiency measurements of resources planned against consumed |
| | • measurements of resources available against those used |
| | • productivity measurements such as production per person or per hour or per shift. |
| Quality of service | • quality measures in every unit |
| | • evaluate suppliers on the basis of quality |
| | • number of customer complaints received |
| | • number of new accounts lost or gained |
| | • rejections as a percentage of production or sales. |
| Customer satisfaction | • speed of response to customer needs |
| | • informal listening by calling a certain number of customers each week |
| | • number of customer visits to the factory or workplace |
| | • number of factory and non-factory manager visits to customers. |
| Quality of working life | • days' absence |
| | • labour turnover |
| | • overtime |
| | • measures of job satisfaction. |
| Innovation | • proportion of new products and services to old ones |
| | • new product or service sales levels. |

## 5 NFPIs and business performance

### 5.1 Introduction

There are a number of areas that are particularly important for ensuring the success of a business and where the use of NFPIs plays a key role. These include:

- the management of human resources
- product and service quality
- brand awareness and company profile.

Each of these will be reviewed in turn.

### 5.2 The management of human resources

- Traditionally the main performance measure for staff was cost (a FPI).
- However, businesses have started to view staff as a major asset and recognise that it is important to attract, motivate and retain highly qualified and experienced staff.
- As a result, NFPIs are now also used to monitor and control staff.

> **Test your understanding 1**
>
> **Required:**
>
> Discuss, with reasons, two non-financial performance indicators that can be used to monitor and control employees.

### 5.3 Product and service quality

Problems with product or service quality can have a long-term impact on the business and they can lead to customer dissatisfaction and loss of future sales.

## Product and service quality

- A product (or service) and its components should be critically and objectively compared both with competition and with customer expectation and needs, for example:

    - Is it good value?

    - Can it really deliver superior performance?

    - How does it compare with competitor offerings?

    - How will it compare with competitor offerings in the future given competitive innovations?

- Product and service quality are usually based on several critical dimensions that should be identified and measured over time. Performance on all these dimensions needs to be combined to give a complete picture. For example:

    - an automobile firm can have measures of defects, ability to perform to specifications, durability and ability to repair

    - a bank might be concerned with waiting time, accuracy of transactions, and making the customer experience friendly and positive

    - a computer manufacturer can examine relative performance specifications, and product reliability as reflected by repair data.

- The relative importance of different factors will vary from company to company and between customers, but achieving high quality means ensuring all the factors of the product or service package meet customer requirements.

- Measures should be tracked over time and compared with those of competitors. It is the relative comparisons and changes that are most important.

- One of the most important assets of many firms is the loyalty of the customer base. Measures of sales and market share are useful but are crude indicators of how customers really feel about a firm.

- Often the most sensitive and insightful information comes from those who have decided to leave a brand or firm. Thus, 'exit interviews' for dissatisfied customers who have 'left' a brand can be very productive.

- Another key area is access and availability of products and services, as failure in these areas can cause a loss of customers.

- Other possible sources of non-financial information related to product and service quality and customer satisfaction are:

  - repeat business ratings, which is useful as a complement to measurements of absolute sales.

  - general customer satisfaction surveys

  - monitoring of complaints both in terms of numbers and type of complaint.

## Illustration 1 - BAA plc's service quality

BAA (the former state owned British Airports Authority) uses regular customer surveys for measuring customer perceptions of a wide variety of service quality attributes, including, for example, the cleanliness of its facilities, the helpfulness of its staff and the ease of finding one's way around the airport. Public correspondence is also analysed in detail, and comment cards are available in the terminals so that passengers can comment voluntarily on service levels received. Duty terminal managers also sample the services and goods offered by outlets in the terminals, assessing them from a customer perspective.

They check the cleanliness and condition of service facilities and complete detailed checklists which are submitted daily to senior terminal managers. The company has also a wealth of internal monitoring systems that record equipment faults and failures, and report equipment and staff availability. These systems are supported by the terminal managers who circulate the terminals on a full-time basis, helping customers as necessary, reporting any equipment faults observed and making routine assessments of the level of service provided by BAA and its concessionaires.

**BAA plc**

| Quality characteristic | Measures | Mechanisms |
|---|---|---|
| Access | Walking distance/ease of finding way around | Surveys/operational data |
| Aesthetics | Staff appearance/airport appearance/quality of catering | Surveys/inspection |
| Availability | Equipment availability | Internal fault monitors |
| Cleanliness | Environment and equipment | Surveys/inspection |
| Comfort | Crowdedness | Surveys/inspection |
| Communication | Information clarity/clarity of labelling and pricing | Surveys/inspection |
| Competence | Staff efficiency | Management inspection |
| Courtesy | Courtesy of staff | Surveys/inspection |
| Friendliness | Staff attitude | Surveys/inspection |
| Reliability | Equipment faults | Surveys/inspection |
| Responsiveness | Staff responsiveness | Surveys/inspection |
| Security | Efficiency of security checks/ number of urgent safety reports | Surveys/internal data |

*indicator of strength of a product's/service's place in the customer's minds*

## 5.4 Brand awareness and company profile

Developing and maintaining a brand and/or a company profile can be expensive. However, it can also enhance performance. The value of a brand/company profile is based on the extent to which it has:

- high loyalty
- name awareness
- perceived quality
- other attributes such as patents or trademarks.

NFPIs may focus on areas such as customer awareness and consumer opinions.

*customers*

**Brand awareness and company profile**

- If potential customers do not know about a company, they will not purchase from it. Therefore, one of the main goals of any business should be to build brand awareness.

- Assessment of brand awareness means identifying the product or company's associations in the minds of customers, and its perceived quality. This is related to but can be very different from actual quality – but ultimately it is the consumer who decides what a brand is really worth.

- Associations can be monitored in an effective way by talking to groups of customers informally on a regular basis. The identification of changes in important associations is likely to emerge from such efforts. More structured tools are also available.

- A brand or firm can be scaled on its key dimensions using a representative sample of customers. Key dimensions can then be tracked over time.

- For companies with a high company profile it is particularly important that brand awareness is positive.

- Measures of brand awareness can either look at the direct link between the brand and overall results, e.g. by considering the price premiums which the company obtains, or monitor the more intangible aspects such as awareness and consumer opinion.

**Test your understanding 2**

**Required:**

How are the measures of product and service quality related to brand awareness and company profile?

## 6 Difficulties in using and interpreting qualitative data

Most NFPIs are in non-financial terms. In section 5 of chapter 6 we discussed the difficulties in recording and processing data of a qualitative nature and looked at how a business can deal with qualitative data.

## Qualitative data

### Difficulties in using and interpreting qualitative information

Particularly at higher levels of management, non-financial information is often not in numerical terms, but qualitative, or soft, rather than quantitative. Qualitative information often represents opinions of individuals and user groups. However there are issues related to its use:

- Decisions often appear to have been made on the basis of quantitative information; however qualitative considerations often influence the final choice, even if this is not explicit.

- Conventional information systems are usually designed to carry quantitative information and are sometimes less able to convey qualitative issues. However the impact of a decreased output requirement on staff morale is something that may be critical but it is not something that an information system would automatically report.

- In both decision making and control, managers should be aware that an information system may provide a limited or distorted picture of what is actually happening. In many situations, sensitivity has to be used in interpreting the output of an information system.

- Information in the form of opinions is difficult to measure and interpret. It also requires more analysis.

- Qualitative information may be incomplete.

- Qualitative aspects are often interdependent and it can be difficult to separate the impact of different factors.

- Evaluating qualitative information is subjective, as it is not in terms of numbers – there are no objective formulae as there are with financial measures.

- The cost of collecting and improving qualitative information may be very high.

- Difficulties in measurement and interpretation mean that qualitative factors are often ignored.

### Working with qualitative information

Despite the challenges it presents, there may be ways of improving the use of qualitative information.

- Where it is important to make use of qualitative information, it is essential to ensure that users are aware of any assumptions made in analysis and of the difficulties involved in measuring and counting it.

KAPLAN PUBLISHING

- It is sometimes possible to quantify issues which are initially qualitative, by looking at its impact, e.g. when looking at service quality, considering the cost of obtaining the same quality of service elsewhere.

- Even if it is not possible to quantify issues precisely, attempting to do so is likely to improve decision making as the issues are likely to have been thought through more thoroughly.

## Test your understanding 3

### Required:

Your company is considering replacing its current products with a new range which will use different production techniques. What qualitative issues will you need to consider?

## 7 Models for evaluating financial and non-financial performance

### 7.1 Introduction

As discussed, it is important that a business appraises both financial and non-financial performance. There are four key tools available:

- Kaplan and Norton's balanced scorecard ✓ & mock
- The performance pyramid
- Fitzgerald and Moon's building block model
- The performance prism

Each of these will be reviewed in turn.

The benefits of these models are as follows:

- financial and non-financial performance measures are included
- they are linked in to corporate strategy
- include external as well as internal measures
- include all important factors regardless of how easy they are to measure
- show clearly the tradeoffs between different dimensions of performance
- show how measures will motivate managers and employees.

### 7.2 Kaplan and Norton's balanced scorecard

### What is the balanced scorecard?

The balanced scorecard includes:

- financial measures (these reveal the results of actions already taken)

- non-financial measures (these are drivers of future financial performance)

- external as well as internal information.

The balanced scorecard allows managers to look at the business from four important perspectives:

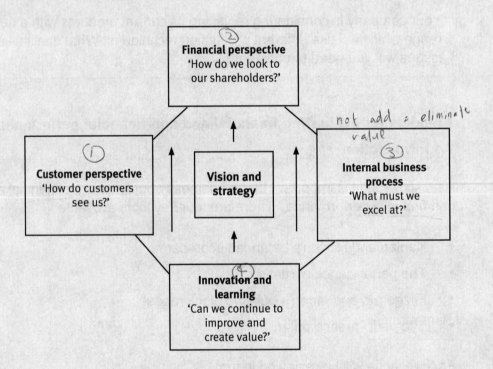

The balanced scorecard allows managers to look at the business from four important perspectives:

**② Financial perspective**
'How do we look to our shareholders?'

not add = eliminate value

**① Customer perspective**
'How do customers see us?'

**Vision and strategy**

**③ Internal business process**
'What must we excel at?'

**④ Innovation and learning**
'Can we continue to improve and create value?'

Within each of these perspectives a business should seek to identify a series of goals (CSFs) and measures (KPIs). These should be in line with the overall strategic objectives and vision of the organisation.

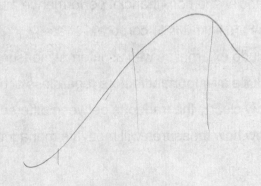

Illustration 2 – Examples of goals and measures

A balanced scorecard for an electronics company could include the following goals and measures:

| | Goals (CSFs) | Measures (KPIs) |
|---|---|---|
| **Customer perspective** | Low cost | Benchmark cost vs competitor's cost |
| | High quality | % defects |
| | Responsive service | % on-time deliveries |
| **Internal perspective** | Operational excellence *efficiency refine the buss* | Production cycle time, rectification time, % of production completed on time and within budget |
| | Employee satisfaction | Staff turnover |
| **Innovation and learning** | Innovation | % of income from new products |
| | Internal learning | Number of employee suggestions and % implemented, % of time spent on staff development |
| **Financial perspective** | Growth and development | Quarterly sales growth |
| | Survival | Cash flow |
| | Profitability | ROCE |

It would be beneficial to rank the goals and measures in order of importance.

*doesn't tell specific measures    – disadvantages*

## Test your understanding 4

**Required:**

Suggest some performance measures for a building company involved in house building and commercial property and operating in a number of different countries.

## Test your understanding 5

**Required:**

Discuss the disadvantages of the balanced scorecard.

### Implementing the balanced scorecard

There are four essential activities which have to be executed rigorously if the implementation of the balanced scorecard is to succeed:

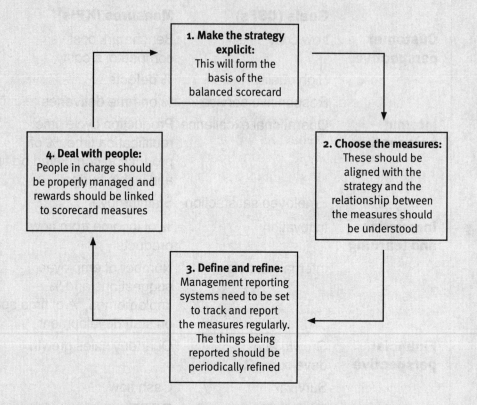

1. **Make the strategy explicit:** This will form the basis of the balanced scorecard

2. **Choose the measures:** These should be aligned with the strategy and the relationship between the measures should be understood

3. **Define and refine:** Management reporting systems need to be set to track and report the measures regularly. The things being reported should be periodically refined

4. **Deal with people:** People in charge should be properly managed and rewards should be linked to scorecard measures

 **Steps involved in implementing the scorecard**

**(1) Make the strategy explicit**

The starting point in producing a balanced scorecard is identifying the strategic requirements for success in the firm. Typically, those strategic requirements will relate to products, markets, growth and resources (human, intellectual and capital).

For example, businesses like Dell may want to be low-cost producers achieving competitive advantage from selling undifferentiated products at lower prices than those of competitors, or a business may have a product development strategy to become a leader in technology and command a premium like Apple. Their strategy may also be to develop and maintain market share, like Microsoft, or their strategy may be to occupy the number-one or number-two position in their lines of business.

## (2) Choose the measures

Performance measures have to be selected that clearly relate to the achievement of the strategies identified in the earlier process. As has been seen throughout the discussion of performance measures in this text, the selection of appropriate indicators and measures is critical. The selected measures form the goals that management communicates to staff as being important. Those goals are what staff will strive to achieve. If the wrong goals are selected then the firm may find itself doing the wrong things.

The general problem is that performance measures that relate to limited parts of the business can be very prone to inducing dysfunctional behaviour. For example, a firm might minimise its inventory holding in order to meet some inventory holding target – but at the expense of total operating costs.

## (3) Define and refine

Management reporting systems and procedures need to be set up to track and report the measures regularly. This involves all the issues relating to the processing of data and the reporting of information discussed earlier in this text.

The precise requirements of reporting associated with the use of the balanced scorecard will make demands on both the management accounting and IT systems in an organisation. Fully satisfying those demands has a cost and sometimes compromises may have to be made in order to contain that cost.

All sorts of practical problems may be encountered in reporting on an indicator. For example, when reporting on revenue:

- How is revenue calculated and when is it recorded?
- Should it include the non-core business activity?
- Should revenue be reported under product, region or customer headings?
- How should interdivisional transactions be reported?

Operating the management accounting system associated with the balanced scorecard requires that the things being reported should be defined and periodically refined.

### (4) Deal with people

The balanced scorecard is an exercise in modifying human behaviour. It is its interaction with people that determines whether or not it will work.

Balanced scorecards can easily become a confusing mass of measures, some of which even contradict each other. There may be too many measures and action to achieve some of them may contribute to failure to achieve others. The measures may not always be prioritised.

To be effective, the measures contained in the scorecard should be limited in number, reasonably consistent and ranked in some order of priority. Further, performance measures should be aligned with the management structure. Career progression and remuneration should be appropriately linked to scorecard measure linked performance. Organisations which adopt a balanced scorecard but continue to reward managers on the basis of a narrow range of traditional financial measures are likely to be disappointed by the results.

## Practical example of scorecard implementation

One example reported in management literature of how the balanced scorecard might be applied is the US case of Analog Devices (a semi-conductor manufacturer) in the preparation of its five-year strategic plan for 1998-2002.

Analog Devices had as its main corporate objective: 'Achieving our goals for growth, profits, market share and quality creates the environment and economic means to satisfy the needs of our employees, stockholders, customers and others associated with the firm. Our success depends on people who understand the interdependence and congruence of their personal goals with those of the company and who are thus motivated to contribute towards the achievement of those goals.'

Three basic strategic objectives identified by the company were market leadership, sales growth and profitability.

The company adopted targets as follows:

### Customer perspective

- Percentage of orders delivered on time: a target was set for the five-year period to increase the percentage of on-time deliveries from 85% to at least 99.8%.

- Outgoing defect levels: the target was to reduce the number of defects in product items delivered to customers, from 500 per month to fewer than 10 per month.

- Order lead time: a target was set to reduce the time between receiving a customer order to delivery from 10 weeks to less than three weeks.

## Internal perspective

- Manufacturing cycle time: to reduce this from 15 weeks to 4 to 5 weeks over the five-year planning period.

- Defective items in production: to reduce defects in production from 5,000 per month to fewer than 10 per month.

## Learning and innovation perspective

- Having products rated 'number one' by at least 50% of customers, based on their attitudes to whether the company was making the right products, performance, price, reliability, quality, delivery, lead time, customer support, responsiveness, willingness to co-operate and willingness to form partnerships.

- The number of new products introduced to the market.

- Sales revenue from new products.

- The new product sales ratio: this was the percentage of total sales achieved by products introduced to the market within the previous six quarters.

- Average annual revenues for new products in their third year.

- Reducing the average time to bring new product ideas to market.

**Financial targets** were set for revenue, revenue growth, profit and return on assets, but the idea was that the financial targets would flow from achieving the other targets stated above.

Analog Devices sought to adopt financial and non-financial performance measures within a single system, in which the various targets were consistent with each other and were in no way incompatible.

## Test your understanding 6

JMP is a privately owned IT company. They employ various IT specialists and technical engineers who specialise in (VOIP) Voice Over Internet Protocol.

JMP has established a good reputation for competitive prices, yet good quality and performance, but has less than 1% of the market in this sector and faces stiff competition especially in the internal markets, which has grown from $3 billion to $8 billion in the last seven years.

The Managing Director has become increasing concerned about one of its main customers who account for 40% of it's sales. Also JMP's inabilities to recruit high calibre staff, identify market trends, scan its competitive environments and create marketing strategies and plans.

Financial data:

|  | | Forecast | | |
|  | 20X3 | 20X4 | 20X5 | 20X6 |
| --- | --- | --- | --- | --- |
|  | $000 | $000 | $000 | $000 |
| Sales: | | | | |
| Domestic | 4,500 | 6,300 | 6,930 | 6,235 |
| Export | 300 | 500 | 650 | 520 |
| Total Sales | 4,800 | 6,800 | 7,580 | 6,755 |
| Cost of sales | 2,640 | 3,770 | 4,550 | 4,320 |
| **Gross margin** | **2,160** | **3,030** | **3,030** | **2,435** |
| Expenses: | | | | |
| Admin | 500 | 630 | 700 | 665 |
| Distribution | 715 | 940 | 945 | 885 |
| Marketing | 50 | 60 | 70 | 70 |
| R&D | 495 | 590 | 870 | 690 |
| Overheads | 200 | 280 | 320 | 325 |
| Total expenses | 1,960 | 2,500 | 2,905 | 2,635 |
| **Operating profit** | **200** | **530** | **125** | **(200)** |
| Sales interest paid | 25 | 120 | 150 | 165 |
| **Net profit** | **175** | **410** | **(25)** | **(365)** |
|  | 20X3 | 20X4 | 20X5 | 20X6 |
| Financing: | | | | |
| Long term liabilities | | 160 | 750 | 1,000 | 1,100 |
| Share capital and reserves | | 375 | 605 | 600 | 575 |

Other information:

| | | | | |
|---|---|---|---|---|
| Employees | 50 | 60 | 75 | 60 |
| % Late orders | 5 | 7 | 10 | 6 |
| Order book | 4,725 | 4,150 | 3,150 | 2,500 |

**Required:**

Using the above financial and qualitative data provide:

- a financial analysis of JMP, highlighting any problem areas and

- apply the balance scorecard.

## Strategy mapping

Strategy mapping was developed by Kaplan and Norton as an extension to the balanced scorecard and to make the implementation of the scorecard more successful.

The steps involved are:

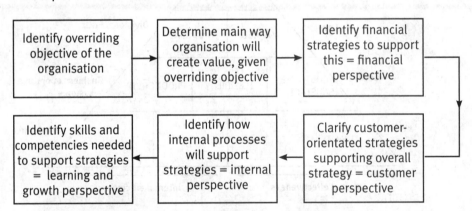

- At the head of the strategy map is the overriding objective of the organisation which describes how it creates value. This is then connected to the organisation's other objectives, categorised in terms of the four perspectives of the balanced scorecard, showing the cause-and-effect relationships between them.

- The strategy map helps organisations to clarify, describe and communicate the strategy and objectives, both within the organisation and to external stakeholders by presenting the key relationships between the overall objective and the supporting strategy and objectives in one diagram.

**Issues when implementing the strategy map:**

- Organisations have often found it difficult to translate the corporate vision into behaviour and actions which achieve the key corporate objectives.

- In practice, many employees do not understand the organisation's strategy, and systems such as performance management and budgeting are not linked to the strategy.

## 7.3 Performance pyramid

- The performance pyramid, developed by Lynch and Cross, includes a hierarchy of financial and non-financial performance measures.

- The diagram below shows actions to assist in the achievement of corporate vision may be cascaded down through a number of levels, i.e. it shows the link between strategy and day to day operations.

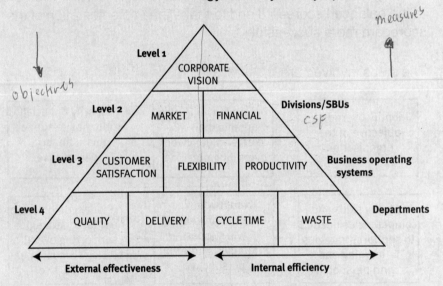

**Level 1**: At the top of the organisation is the corporate vision through which the organisation describes how it will achieve long-term success and competitive advantage.

**Level 2**: This focuses on the achievement of an organisation's CSFs in terms of market-related measures and financial measures. The marketing and financial success of a proposal is the initial focus for the achievement of corporate vision.

**Level 3**: The marketing and financial strategies set at level 2 must be linked to the achievement of customer satisfaction, increased flexibility and high productivity at the next level. These are the guiding forces that drive the strategic objectives of the organisation.

**Level 4**: The status of the level 3 driving forces can be monitored using the lower level departmental indicators of quality, delivery, cycle time and waste. *efficiency*

*how long cash is being cycled*

The left hand side of the pyramid contains measures which have an external focus and which are predominantly non-financial. Those on the right are focused on the internal efficiency of the organisation and are predominantly financial.

**Test your understanding 7**

**Required:**

Suggest two measures (KPIs) for each of the three categories at the business operating systems level, i.e. customer satisfaction, flexibility and productivity.

The main **drawback** of the performance pyramid is that it does tend to concentrate on two groups of stakeholders, i.e. shareholders and customers. It is necessary to ensure that measures are included which relate to other stakeholders as well.

## 7.4 Fitzgerald and Moon's building block model

Fitzgerald and Moon have developed an approach to performance measurement in business services that is based on the three building blocks of dimensions, standards and rewards.

```
┌──────────────────────────┐
│ Dimension                │
│ Competitiveness          │
│ Financial performance    │
│ Quality of service       │
│ Flexibility              │
│ Resource utilisation     │
│ Innovation               │
│         ┌────────────────┴──────────┐
┌─────────┴──────────┬────────────────┐
│ Standards          │ Rewards        │
│ Ownership          │ Clarity        │
│ Achievability      │ Motivation     │
│ Fairness           │ Controllability│
└────────────────────┴────────────────┘
```

## Dimensions

The dimensions are the goals, i.e. the CSFs for the business and suitable measures must be developed to measure each performance dimension. For example:

| Dimension | Type of measure |
|---|---|
| Competitiveness | Relative market share |
| Financial performance | Turnover growth |
| Quality of service | Product reliability |
| Flexibility | Delivery time |
| Resource utilisation | Productivity |
| Innovation | New product numbers |

### Dimensions of performance

The table above identifies the dimensions of performance. The first two of these relate to downstream results, the other four to upstream determinants. For example, a new product innovation will not impact on profit, cash flow and market share achieved in the past – but a high level of innovation provides an indicator of how profit, cash flow and market share will move in the future. If innovation is the driver or determinant of future performance, it is a key success factor.

## Standards

The standards set, i.e. the KPIs, should have the following characteristics:

- **Ownership**: Managers who participate in the setting of standards are more likely to accept and be motivated by the standards than managers on whom standards are imposed.

- **Achievability**: An achievable, but challenging, standard is a better motivator than an unachievable one.

- **Fairness**: When setting standards across an organisation, care should be undertaken to ensure that all managers have equally challenging standards.

*whats get measured gets done*

## Rewards

To ensure that employees are **motivated** to meet standards, the standards need to be **clear** (e.g. the target is to 'achieve four product innovations per year' rather than to simply 'innovate') and linked to **controllable** factors. The actual means of motivation may involve performance related pay, a bonus or a promotion.

### Fitzgerald and moon example

Fitzgerald and Moon applied to a Washing Machine Manufacturer:

| Dimension = CSF | Flexibility – On time delivery | Quality of service | Financial performance |
|---|---|---|---|
| Standard = KPI | Delivery speed | Reliability | Profitability |
| Reward | Points for each on time delivery – leading to a bonus | % commission for repair engineers from fee or warranty paid | Management profit related bonuses |

### Test your understanding 8

FL provides training on financial subjects to staff of small and medium-sized businesses. Training is at one of two levels – for clerical staff, instructing them on how to use simple financial accounting computer packages, and for management, on management accounting and financial management issues.

Training consists of tutorial assistance, in the form of workshops or lectures, and the provision of related material – software, texts and printed notes.

Tuition days may be of standard format and content, or designed to meet the client's particular specifications. All courses are run on client premises and, in the case of clerical training courses, are limited to 8 participants per course.

FL has recently introduced a 'helpline' service, which allows course participants to phone in with any problems or queries arising after course attendance. This is offered free of charge.

FL employs administrative and management staff. Course lecturers are hired as required, although a small core of technical staff is employed on a part-time basis by FL to prepare customer-specific course material and to man the helpline.

Material for standard courses is bought in from a group company, who also print up the customer-specific course material.

**Required:**

Suggest a measure for each of the six dimensions of the building block model.

## Advantages of the building block model

- All key determinants of success in performance will be measured.

- Targets are set in such a way to engage and motivate staff, i.e. through ownership, achievability and fairness.

## 7.5 The Performance Prism

### What is the Performance Prism?

- The Performance Prism is an approach to performance management which aims to effectively meet the needs and requirements of **all stakeholders**. This is in contrast with the performance pyramid which tends to concentrate on customers and shareholders and is also in contrast with value based management (covered in chapter 8) which prioritises the needs of shareholders.

- Managers can actually measure too many things, thus losing sight of the strategic side of management and incurring costs (in providing the information) which outweigh the benefits.

- It recognises that most performance measurement frameworks ignore the changes that must be made to the organisation's strategies, processes and capabilities in order to meet the needs of stakeholders.

- It recognises the need to work with stakeholders to ensure that their needs are met.

## The framework

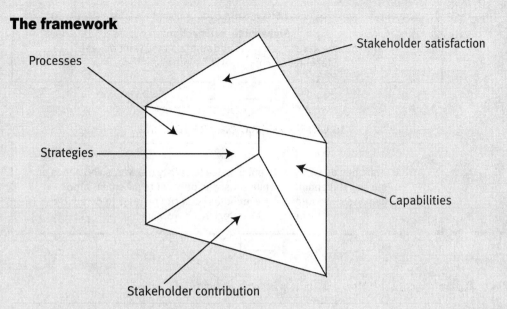

The Performance Prism poses five questions. The answers to these questions from the starting point for defining performance measures.

> **Stakeholder satisfaction**
> Who are the key stakeholders and what do they want or need?
> Stakeholder mapping will be important here.

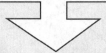

*What it takes to achieve the goal*

> **Strategies**
> What strategies do we need to put in place to satisfy the wants and needs of
> our key stakeholders, while satisfying our own requirements too?
> Performance measures will be identified that can be used to determine
> whether the strategies are working.

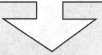

> **Processes**
> What processes do we need to put in place to enable us to achieve our strategies?
> Business process re-engineering and value chain analysis may be used.
> Measures will be developed to see how well the processes are working.

*all models*

> **Capabilities**
> What capabilities do we need to put in place to allow us to operate, maintain
> and enhance our processes?
> Benchmarking is likely to be used to measure the organisation's capabilities.
> The Mckinsey 7s model may be used to ensure capabilities are co-ordinated.
> Measures will be developed to see how well the capabilities are being performed.

*BPR — rarely work*

> **Stakeholder contribution**
> What contribution do we want or need from our stakeholders if we are to
> maintain and develop these capabilities?

## Illustration 3 - The Performance Prism at DHL

In 2000, the board of DHL (UK) decided to replace monthly performance meetings (which focused too much on operational data) with quarterly meetings which took a more strategic approach. The Performance Prism was used as a framework at these meetings.

| | |
|---|---|
| What do DHL's regular customers want and need? | • Delivery speed<br>• Confidence in DHL<br>• Relationship<br>• Information accessibility |
| What strategies has/will DHL adopt(ed) to ensure that these wants and needs are satisfied? | • Local contact<br>• Proactive availability of information<br>• Promote superiority of core service |
| What processes has/will DHL put in place to ensure that these strategies are delivered? | • Customer service strategy<br>• Proactive traces<br>• Local sales & courier network<br>• Customer access tools |
| What capabilities does DHL require to ensure that these processes can be operated? | • Teamwork<br>• Technology<br>• Robust network<br>• Skills |
| What does DHL want from its stakeholders to allow the above to happen? | • Confidence in data<br>• Empowerment<br>• People-based culture |

> ### Test your understanding 9
>
> Phoenix Fund Management (PFM) has been responsible for the investment of pension and life insurance funds for the past twenty years. It claims to be a 'fund manager with a difference' by seeking to gain active involvement in under-performing or poorly managed businesses. PFM requires that companies it has invested in be run in the long-term interests of the shareholders. PFM assesses such companies in terms of communication, financial, strategic and ethical performance against certain principles it has developed. (For instance, one financial principle is that 'companies should have performance evaluation and incentive systems to provide managers with an incentive to deliver long term shareholder value').
>
> PFM's belief is that there is a lack of 'real' accountability between boards of directors and shareholders and that too often shareholders concentrate on short-term financial gains. PFM argues that if other investors believe that a company is poorly run they merely sell their shares and invest elsewhere. Thus boards of directors are not held properly to account over poor performance. Where it believes companies it invests in are under-performing, PFM enters into dialogue with the board and seeks changes in practice. PFM is increasingly being recognised as a major driver of change in corporate life.
>
> ### Required:
>
> Explain how the Performance Prism can assist companies in developing performance management indicators which take account of the needs of stakeholders such as PFM.

## 8 Corporate failure

### 8.1 Introduction

Corporate failure occurs when a company cannot achieve a satisfactory return on capital over the longer-term.

If unchecked, the situation is likely to lead to an inability of the company to pay its obligations as they become due.

The company may still have an excess of assets over liabilities, but if it is unable to convert those assets into cash it will be insolvent.

*Corporate failure*

*Per. Prism*

> ### Test your understanding 10
>
> ### Required:
>
> Identify some of the reasons for corporate failure.

## Why do companies fail?

Reasons include:

### (1) Failing to adapt to changes in the environment

Reasons for failing to adapt include:

- complacency
- risk-averse decision making
- economies of production and administration
- limited opportunities for innovation and diversification
- limited mental models.

Complacency is a charge frequently levelled at managers, and there are, no doubt, occasions when senior managers convince themselves that everything is fine, when it is not. However, the charge is frequently made with the benefit of hindsight, rather than observation of the efforts made by those managers at the time. There are several entirely sensible reasons why managers are reluctant to make large strategic changes.

First, it is not possible to quantify the risks of making a major change. Several studies have shown that predicting changes in the environment and devising appropriate counter-measures is among the most difficult things a manager is required to do. Only in hindsight are the dynamics clear. It is worth remembering that case studies are written backwards, where a known outcome is traced back to its origins.

Faced with such difficulties, managers are reluctant to make large-scale changes that might risk increasing the problems, and might be very difficult to implement adequately. Rather, they select options of relatively limited impact – a process referred to as logical incrementalism.

Secondly, changes to production can reduce the opportunities for economies of scale, and raise the firm's cost base. There is always a temptation to try to retain share, by reducing price, rather than make fundamental changes to a product of its method of production and risk escalating costs.

Thirdly, it may be that management is entirely aware that the strategic situation is worsening, but be unable to see opportunities to innovate or diversify out of trouble. It must be accepted that there are situations where there are no feasible solutions, and there might be better uses of the shareholders' funds than attempts to turn the business round.

Finally, a large part of the problem is caused by the mental models of those who have control of the strategy within an organisation. A mental model is the way that individuals think about problems and issues. We look (below) at Johnson's notion of strategic drift, where the firm's mental models stop the company from changing quickly enough to keep up with environmental change.

## (2) Strategic drift

Strategic drift is a term devised by **Johnson** (1988) to describe as a warning to those who champion the idea of strategy emerging as a series of logical, incremental steps. Johnson argues that this limits the rate of change to the speed at which management might feel comfortable, which has many advantages (particularly in implementation), but might be inappropriate in periods when the environment moves very quickly.

As outlined above, the organisation takes a series of logical, incremental steps that enables it to change ahead of the market, developing a competitive advantage. However, the rate of change in the market place speeds up, and the firm's incrementalist approach is not enough to maintain its advantage, and it is left behind. At this point, the firm must abandon the approach, and adopt radical, discontinuous change in order to stay with the market leaders.

Johnson's main argument is that the reasons for failing to increase the tempo of change are largely cultural, rather than technical. He argues that the corporate paradigm, as revealed by its cultural web and described in an earlier chapter, is the biggest constraint on strategic thinking and action. It is important to see that management cannot change a corporate paradigm, partly because they are themselves caught up in it, and partly because some elements of it are not amenable to management techniques. Logical incrementalism is successful because it does not challenge the underlying paradigm, allowing change to take place relatively smoothly. More revolutionary change must damage the paradigm before it can begin.

## 8.2 Assessing the likelihood of failure

The following information can be used when assessing the likelihood of corporate failure:

| Quantitative information | Qualitative information |
|---|---|
| • Analysis of the company accounts to identify problems relating to key ratios such as liquidity, gearing and profitability. | • Information in the chairman's report and the director's report (including warnings, evasions and changes in the composition of the board since last year). |
| • Other information in the published accounts such as: | • Information in the press (about the industry and the company or its competitors). |
|   – very large increases in intangible fixed assets | • Information about environmental or external matters such as changes in the market for the company's products or services. |
|   – a worsening cash position shown by the cash flow statement | |
|   – very large contingent liabilities | |
|   – important post balance sheet events. | |

### Test your understanding 11

**Required:**

You have been asked to investigate a chain of convenience stores and assess the likelihood of corporate failure. What would you include in your analysis?

### Additional example

Insureme was the market leader in home and motor vehicle insurance with a 28% market share. The company has lost its market share over the last two years and this may lead to the demise of the company.

**Required:**

Discuss five performance indicators, other than decreasing market share, which might indicate Insureme might fail as a corporate entity.

**Solution:**

**Poor cash flow**

Poor cash flow might render an organisation unable to pay its debts as and when they fall due for payment. This might mean, for example, that providers of finance might be able to invoke the terms of a loan covenant and commence legal action against an organisation which might eventually lead to its winding-up.

**Lack of new production/service introduction**

Innovation can often be seen to be the difference between 'life and death' as new products and services provide continuity of income streams in an ever-changing business environment. A lack of new product/service introduction may arise from a shortage of funds available for re-investment. This can lead to organisations attempting to compete with their competitors with an out of date range of products and services, the consequences of which will invariably turn out to be disastrous.

**General economic conditions**

Falling demand and increasing interest rates can precipitate the demise of organisations. Highly geared organisations will suffer as demand falls and the weight of the interest burden increases. Organisations can find themselves in a vicious circle as increasing amounts of interest payable are paid from diminishing gross margins leading to falling profits/increasing losses and negative cash flows. This leads to the need for further loan finance and even higher interest burden, further diminution in margins and so on.

**Lack of financial controls**

The absence of sound financial controls has proven costly to many organisations. In extreme circumstances it can lead to outright fraud (e.g. Enron and WorldCom).

**Internal rivalry**

The extent of internal rivalry that exists within an organisation can prove to be of critical significance to an organisation as managerial effort is effectively channeled into increasing the amount of internal conflict that exists to the detriment of the organisation as a whole. Unfortunately the adverse consequences of internal rivalry remain latent until it is too late to redress them.

**Loss of key personnel**

In certain types of organisation the loss of key personnel can 'spell the beginning of the end' for an organisation. This is particularly the case when individuals possess knowledge which can be exploited by direct competitors, e.g. sales contacts, product specifications, product recipes, etc.

## 8.3 Corporate failure prediction models

```
                    Two types of
                       model
```

**Quantitative models**
Indentify financial ratios with values which differ markedly between surviving and failing companies

**Qualitative models**
Assign scores to particular qualitative risk factors

### Quantitative models

| Model | Explanation |
|---|---|
| Beaver's univariate model (1966) | A simple, but flawed, model that assesses the financial status of a company by reviewing one ratio at a time. |
| The Z score (1968) | A more sophisticated model that combines key ratios into a single discriminate score. This is a key model and will be discussed in more detail below. |
| Taffler and Tishaw's model (1977) | Developed their own version of the Z score model based on a combination of four ratios. |
| The ZETA model (1977) | This model addressed some of the problems associated with the Z score model. |
| Performance analysis score | Ranks all company Z scores in percentile terms, measuring relative performance from 0 to 100. Any downward trend over time should be investigated. |

| H score model | Similar to the previous model in that it is a ranked percentile score of between 0 and 100. The threshold is 25, below which companies are described as being in the 'Warning Area'. This score means that only 25% of companies have characteristics even more indicative of failed companies and therefore corporate failure is a real concern. |
|---|---|

## Calculating a Z score

The Z score is generated by calculating five ratios, which are then multiplied by a pre-determined weighting factor and added together to produce the Z score. The formula is:

Z score = 1.2X1+ 1.4X2 + 3.3X3 + 0.6X4 + 1.0X5

Where:

X1 = working capital/total assets

X2 = retained earnings/total assets

X3 = earnings before interest and tax/total assets

X4 = market value of equity/total liabilities

X5 = sales/total assets

The score indicates the likelihood of failure:

- **Less that 1.81** - companies with a Z score of below 1.81 are in danger and possibly heading towards bankruptcy

- **Between 1.81 and 2.99** - companies with scores between 1.81 and 2.99 need further investigation.

- **3 or above** - companies with a score of 3 or above are financially sound.

## Test your understanding 12

### Required:

Using the data below calculate the Z score for each of the four companies and comment on your findings.

| | Company B | Company C | Company D | Company E |
|---|---|---|---|---|
| X1 = Working Capital / Total Assets | 0.717 | 0.06 | 1.3 | 0.25 |
| X2 = Retained earnings/ Total Assets | 0.847 | 0.03 | 0.8 | 0.21 |
| X3 = EBIT / Total Assets | 3.107 | 0.09 | 1.1 | 0.5 |
| X4 = Market value of Equity / Total Liabilities | 0.42 | 0.541 | - | - |
| X5 = Sales / Total Assets | 0.998 | - | 0.5 | 0.16 |

**Limitations** of quantitative models include:

- The score estimated is a snapshot.
- Further analysis is needed to fully understand the situation, e.g. cash flow projections, detailed cost information, environmental review.
- Scores are only good predictors in the short-term.
- Figures are open to manipulation.
- The Z score model only gives guidance below the danger level of 1.81. Further investigation is needed for those organisations with scores between 1.81 and 2.99.

### Qualitative models - Argenti's A score

Fin. measures are limited in describing circumstances.
The most notable qualitative model is Argenti's A score model.

Argenti suggested that the failure process follows a predictable sequence:

(1) **Defects** - include management weaknesses (such as an autocratic chief executive) and accounting deficiencies (such as no budgetary control). Each defect is given a score. A mark of 10 or more out of a possible 45 is considered unsatisfactory.

(2) **Mistakes** - will occur over time as a result of the defects above. Mistakes include high gearing, overtrading or failure of a big project. A score of more than 15 out of a possible 45 is considered unsatisfactory.

(3) **Symptoms of failure** - mistakes will eventually lead to visible symptoms of failure, e.g. deteriorating ratios or creative accounting.

If the overall score is more than 25, the company has many of the signs preceding failure and is therefore a cause for concern.

**Limitations** of qualitative models include:

- Based on the subjective judgement of experts (also a strength).

- Requires a large amount of financial and non-financial information (also a strength).

- Results are only as good as inputs into them.

## 8.4 Performance improvement strategies

The key to preventing corporate failure is to spot the warning signs early, and take corrective action quickly.

- The actions needed will depend on the particular situation. Once the signs of impending failure are seen, it is important to investigate and identify the causes.

- These may be related to a range of different functions within the business, such as financial management, marketing or production.

- It may sometimes be necessary to seek external advice to help to identify the problem.

- It is important that the managers of the business accept that there is a problem and that mistakes have been made and to move on to a solution, rather than apportioning blame.

- Actions may involve major strategic change, such as getting out of a loss-making business, or making changes to the way operations are managed, such as changes to production management.

- The action needed may include putting in controls to prevent further loss.

- The best strategy to prevent failure is to have effective management systems in place to begin with.

The performance management system will need to reflect the performance improvement strategies:

- a link should be established between the new strategic goals and CSFs

- performance targets should be set at all levels and these should relate to the achievement of strategic objectives

- continuous review of actual performance against targets will be required

- additional training and development needs must be met.

### Test your understanding 13

You have been asked to recommend actions which need to be taken to prevent failure of an electronics manufacturer which is in financial difficulties. On investigation, you ascertain that the company has been making losses for the last two years. Although the product is well thought of in the market, sales are decreasing slightly. Returns and customer complaints are high. The manufacturing time for the products is 30 days and raw materials inventories are generally held for two weeks. There are also high levels of finished goods inventories. Receivables days are 100.

**Required:**

What actions do you suggest should be taken?

**Question focus**: now attempt question 19 from chapter 13

### 8.5 Long-term survival and the product life cycle

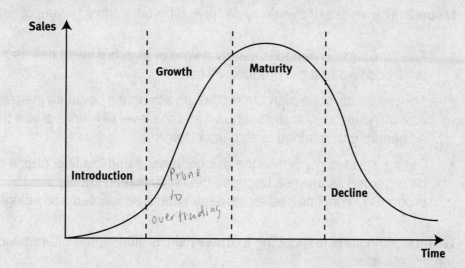

### Classic life cycle

The 'classic' life cycle for a product has four phases, with different CSFs.

*   An **introduction phase**, when the product or service is first developed and introduced to the market. Sales demand is low whilst potential customers learn about the item. There is a learning process for both customers and the producer, and the producer might have to vary the features of the product or service, in order to meet customer requirements more successfully.

- A **growth phase**, when the product or service becomes established and there is a large growth in sales demand. The number of competitors in the market also increases, but customers are willing to pay reasonably high prices. The product becomes profitable. Variety in the product or service increases, and customers are much more conscious of quality issues.

- A **maturity phase**, which might be the longest stage in the product life cycle. Demand stabilises, and producers compete on price.

- A **decline phase**, during which sales demand falls. Prices are reduced to sustain demand and to slow the decline in sales volume. Eventually the product becomes unprofitable, and producers stop making it.

Long-term survival necessitates consideration of life-cycle issues:

**Issue 1**: There will be different CSFs at different stages of the life cycle. In order to ensure that performance is managed effectively KPIs will need to vary over different stages of the life cycle.

**Issue 2**: The stages of the life cycle have different intrinsic levels of risk:

- The introduction period is clearly a time of high business risk as it is quite possible that the product will fail.

- The risk is still quite high during the growth phase because the ultimate size of the industry is still unknown and the level of market share that can be gained and retained is also uncertain.

- During the maturity phase the risk decreases and the final phase should be regarded as low risk because the organisation knows that the product is in decline and its strategy should be tailored accordingly.

Understanding and responding to these risks is vital for the future success of the organisation.

If there is an analysis of the developing risk profile it should be compared with the financial risk profiles of various strategic options, making it much easier to select appropriate combinations and to highlight unacceptably high or low total risk combinations. Thus for an organisation to decide to finance itself with debt during the development stage would represent a high total risk combination.

# Chapter summary

```
                    ┌─────────────────────────┐
                    │      NON-FINANCIAL      │
                    │  PERFORMANCE INDICATORS │
                    │   AND CORPORATE FAILURE │
                    └─────────────────────────┘
```

| NON-FINANCIAL PERFORMANCE INDICATORS (NFPIs) | PERFORMANCE EVALUATION MODELS | CORPORATE FAILURE |
|---|---|---|
| • Drawbacks of sole reliance on financial performance measures<br>• Use of financial and non-financial performance indicators<br>• NFPIs and business performance<br>• Difficulties in using and interpreting qualitative data | • Balanced scorecard<br>• Performance pyramid<br>• Building block model<br>• Performance prism | • Assessing the likelihood of failure<br>• Quantitative models, e.g the Z score<br>• Qualitative models, e g Argenti's A score<br>• Performance improvement strategies<br>• Long-term survival and the product life cycle |

## Test your understanding answers

### Test your understanding 1

The following NFPIs could be used:

- Absenteeism
- Productivity
- Turnover rate (analyse further to identify reasons for leaving)

These give an indication of the morale of employees.

### Test your understanding 2

The experience of existing customers and their perception of the quality of the products or services will help to determine whether the company profile is positive or negative. This is particularly important for a high profile company, about which everyone will have an opinion whether or not they have any experience as a customer. This will be based on the opinions of customers with whom they have contact, and on press reports which discuss the quality of the company's offering.

### Test your understanding 3

- The impact on and the views of employees. Any decision which affects working practices will have a morale effect on employees. Some decisions, such as to close a department, will have a greater effect than others, for example an increase in production, but both will affect employees.

- The impact on and opinion of customers who will be affected by any decision which changes the finished product or its availability. For example, the deletion of a product will force customers to choose an alternative item.

- Suppliers will be affected by changes to production which require different raw materials or delivery schedules. For example, an increase in production may cause the supplier to increase production of the raw material.

- The response of competitors. Any decision to changes in product specification or pricing will affect competitors who will then choose whether or not to respond.

- The impact on demand for scarce resources. A change in production as a result of the decision may alter the demand for individual resources and the result of the decision may alter availability.

- Any social and environmental effects.

## Test your understanding 4

### Financial perspective

- ROCE and RI – overall and by SBU.
- Margins – overall and by product/customer/country.
- Different costs as a percentage of sales – e.g. labour costs/sales, sub-contractor costs/sales.
- Sales growth.
- Cash flow targets.
- Market share.

### Customer perspective

- Percentage of scheduled targets met – especially whether contracts are finished on time.
- Percentage of repeated business.
- Number of complaints received.
- Targets for new customers won.
- Percentage of apartments sold off-plan.

### Internal business perspective

- Percentage of tenders won.
- Percentage of utilisation of fixed assets – vehicles, plant and machinery.
- Percentage of contracts with cost overruns.
- Cost overrun as percentage of budgeted cost.
- Targets for employee productivity.
- For staffing, environmental and health and safety measures.

### Innovation and learning perspective

- Number of patents established for new methods/technologies.
- Percentage of new materials used compared with total materials.
- Percentage of total revenue coming from new buildings using new structural innovations in their design.

### Test your understanding 5

The disadvantages are as follows:

- It is difficult to record and process data of a non-financial, i.e. qualitative, nature.
- Information overload due to the large number of measures that may be chosen. However, Kaplan and Norton recommended that only a handful of measures are used.
- Potential conflict between measures, e.g. profitability may increase in the short-term through a reduction in product development.
- The measures chosen may not align with the strategy and/or vision of the organisation.
- Poor communication to employees/managers - organisations which adopt the balanced scorecard but continue to reward managers on the basis of a narrow range of traditional financial measures are likely to be disappointed with the results.

KAPLAN PUBLISHING

## Test your understanding 6

### Financial Analysis

The significant slowdown in sales growth is predicted to decline in 20X6 is a major cause for concern. It would be useful to compare the performance of JMP with its competitors and the market place as a whole.

Export sales continue to form less than 10% of total sales and this is worrying as the company is operating in a global industry. In 20X6 JMP predicts a more significant decline in export sales this must be addressed.

Between 20X3 and 20X5 there is an upward drift in cost of sales, which may be due to supplier issues or production scheduling problems. The inevitable result of falling sales and increased costs of sales is falling gross margin.

Expenses do not seem to have been controlled, increasing at a faster rate than turnover. The impact of this on net profit is all too obvious. Failure to control expenses in a period of reduced growth suggests poor management control systems and inadequate management response. This is forecast to continue in 20X6.

Commitment to research and development in a high tech business is crucial to continued product innovation. JMP has maintained an R & D : Total sales ratio of 10% or more a year.

However, R & D is difficult to predict in terms of its success and timing of breakthroughs.

The commitment of JMP is good but if this is from increased borrowing, then banks and other financial intermediaries will be getting worried about JMP's ability to repay.

Gearing has increased from 42% in 20X3 to 160% in 20X5 and forecast to be 190% in 20X6.

There has been little spending on marketing, which is not untypical in a high tech business; perhaps the company is under the impression that the products sell themselves.

JMP has had some success when marketing spend was relatively low.

Perhaps one of the most worrying performance features is the slowing down in new business generated. In 20X3 unfulfilled orders virtually matched total sales but the forecast for 20X6 sees that the key ratio falls to barely one-third of total sales. This clearly needs to be addressed.

### Balance Scorecard

The balanced scorecard could be used to good effect.

Financially, the current position does not look good. The growth in turnover is slowing down, profitability is falling and the debt ratio is high.

Customer measures are mixed – the company's products are well regarded but there is an increase in the waiting time for customers. JMP's market share is small and measuring the market share in VOIP is very difficult because of the bespoke nature of the product.

There is a mixture of signals in terms of progress being made with internal processes. Products are innovative, but operational and management control procedures appear weak.

Finally, from the perspective of learning / innovation, JMP has recognised the need for good people to grow the business, but seems to be unable to recruit and retain the right calibre of people. Evidence suggests that a few key personnel have left the company.

### Test your understanding 7

### Possible measures (KPIs)

Customer satisfaction

- Repeat purchases.
- Numbers of complaints.
- Value of refunds.
- Sales growth by market segment.

Flexibility

- Product/service introduction time.
- Product/service mix flexibility.
- Internal setup times – the time taken to switch production from one product to another.
- Delivery response time – the time taken to meet customer delivery requests.

Productivity

- Revenue per employee.
- Sales and administration costs as a percentage of sales revenue.
- Units of output per unit of resource.
- Capital asset utilisation.

**Note**: only two measures were required for each category.

## Test your understanding 8

Possible measures include:

### Financial performance

- Fee levels.
- Material sales.
- Costs.
- Net profit.
- Outside lecturer costs.

### Competitiveness

- Market share.
- Sales growth.
- Success rate on proposals.

### Quality of service

- Repeat business levels.
- Number of customer complaints.
- Help-line use may be related to tuition quality.

### Flexibility

- Availability and use of freelance staff.
- Breadth of skills and experience of lecturers.

### Resource utilisation

- Use of freelance lecturers.
- Levels of non-chargeable staff time.

### Innovation

- Number of new in-company courses.
- Time to develop new courses.
- New course formats.

**Note**: only one measure was required for each dimension.

## Test your understanding 9

The Performance Prism is an approach to performance measurement which is designed to take account of the interests of all stakeholders, such as suppliers, employees, legislators, and local communities. In doing this it takes a broader approach to stakeholder interests than many other performance management models which pay limited attention to stakeholders other than customers and shareholders. The Performance Prism is based on the principle that the performance of an organisation depends on how effectively it meets the needs and requirements of all its stakeholders takes stakeholder requirements as the start point for the development of performance measures rather than the strategy of the organisation. It also recognises the need to work with stakeholders to ensure that their needs are met. The framework can be used to identify measures at all levels within the organisation.

The Performance Prism has five facets which are different perspectives on performance which prompt specific questions. The answers to these questions form the starting point for defining performance measures.

These facets are as follows:

**Stakeholder satisfaction** – Who are our key stakeholders and what do they want and need? PFM is a key stakeholder of the investee companies, and invested in, with a clear requirement for long term shareholder value. It also has other wants and needs relating to communication, financial, strategic and ethical performance.

**Strategies** – What strategies do we need to put in place to satisfy the wants and needs of our key stakeholders, while satisfying our own requirements too? For example, strategies to deliver long term shareholder value are likely to meet the requirements of an investee company as well as PFM's.

**Processes** – What processes do we need to put in place to enable us to execute our strategies? Depending on the strategy chosen, companies will identify changes which need to be made to the company and its operations to meet the strategic objectives. These should be reflected in the performance indicators for the company.

**Capabilities** – What capabilities do we need to put in place to allow us to operate, maintain and enhance our processes? An example of this has already been identified by PFM in the performance evaluation and incentive scheme for managers.

**Stakeholder contribution** – What contributions do we want and need from our stakeholders if we are to maintain and develop these capabilities? PFM appears to be a company which wants to make a significant contribution to the companies it invests in and presumably has experience which investee businesses can benefit from.

**Test your understanding 10**

Reasons include:

- Poor leadership leading to poor business planning, financial planning, marketing and management.
- Failure to focus on a specific market because of poor research.
- Failure to control cash by carrying too much stock, paying suppliers too promptly, and allowing customers too long to pay.
- Failure to control costs ruthlessly.
- Failure to adapt your product to meet customer needs.
- Failure to carry out decent market research.
- Failure to build a team that is compatible and has the skills to finance, produce, sell and market.
- Failure to pay taxes.

- Failure of businesses' need to grow, merely attempting stability or having less ambitious objectives.

- Failure to gain new markets.

- Under-capitalisation.

- Cash flow problems.

- Tougher market conditions.

- Poor management.

- Companies diversifying into new, unknown areas without a clue about the costs.

- Company directors spending too much money on frivolous purposes thus using all available capital.

### Test your understanding 11

Examples of issues to include:

- an analysis of key ratios, such as liquidity, gearing, cash flow and activity ratios, including trends

- changes in the cash flow of the business

- any history of significant losses

- liability position

- ability to pay creditors on time

- human resources, for example level of dependence on key staff, labour difficulties

- skills and abilities of senior management and an assessment of the strengths and weaknesses of the company

- developments in the market, such as the likelihood of new supermarkets being built near stores

- any regulatory changes which are likely to affect the company

- an analysis of the company report to identify any significant changes over the year.

**Test your understanding 12**

|  | Company B | Company C | Company D | Company E |
|---|---|---|---|---|
| 1.2X1 | 0.86 | 0.07 | 1.56 | 0.3 |
| 1.4X2 | 1.19 | 0.04 | 1.12 | 0.29 |
| 3.3X3 | 10.25 | 0.3 | 3.63 | 1.65 |
| 0.6X4 | 0.25 | 0 .32 | 0 | 0 |
| 1.0X5 | 1 | 0 | 0.5 | 0.16 |
| **Z score** | **13.55** | **0.74** | **6.81** | **2.4** |

Companies with a Z score of below 1.81 are in danger and possibly heading towards bankruptcy, i.e. company C.

A score between 1.81 and 2.99 means that they need further investigation, i.e. company E.

A score of 3 or above companies are financially sound, i.e. companies B and D.

**Test your understanding 13**

The evidence suggests that the company has problems in financial management, production, purchasing and marketing.

Actions required:

- Improve credit control to reduce the debtor days.
- Address the production process to:
  - reduce manufacturing time and stock levels to reduce the requirement for working capital and save costs. This should also improve the ability to respond to customer demands and reduce the need to hold stocks of finished goods
  - improve final product quality to reduce returns and improve customer satisfaction.
- Improve marketing activity to address customer satisfaction issues and increase sales.

# 11

# The role of quality in performance management

## Chapter learning objectives

Upon completion of this chapter you will be able to:

- discuss and evaluate the application of Japanese business practices and management accounting techniques, including:
  - Kaizen costing
  - Target costing
  - Just-in-time, and
  - Total Quality Management

- discriminate between quality, quality assurance, quality control and quality management

- assess the relationship of quality management to the performance management strategy of an organisation

- advise on the structure and benefits of quality management systems and quality certification

- justify the need and assess the characteristics of quality in management information systems

- discuss and apply Six Sigma as a quality improvement method using tools such as DMAIC for implementation.

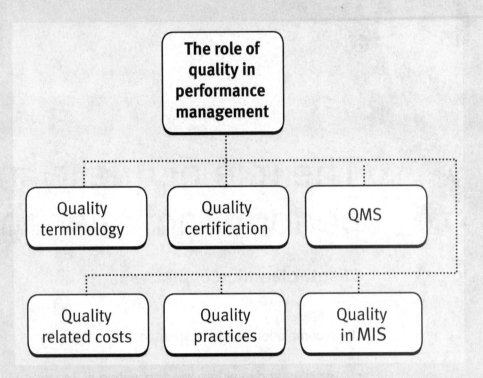

## 1 Exam focus

| Exam sitting | Area examined | Question number | Number of marks |
|---|---|---|---|
| June 2012 | Six Sigma | 3 | 17 |
| December 2011 | Quality costs, Kaizen and JIT | 5 | 20 |
| June 2010 | Cost targets and quality costs | 5(a) | 8 |
| June 2009 | Six Sigma | 5 | 20 |
| December 2008 | Quality costs | 4(b) | 8 |
| June 2008 | Quality costs and elimination of quality problems | 5 | 20 |

## 2 Introduction

In today's competitive global business environment, quality is one of the key ways in which a business can differentiate its product or service and gain competitive advantage.

**Quality** can be defined in a number of ways:

- Is the product/service free from errors and does it adhere to design specifications?

- Is the product/service fit for use?

- Does the product/service meet customers' needs?

**Test your understanding 1**

**Required:**

Explain the reasons why quality may be important to an organisation?

Some other important definitions include:

**Quality management** involves planning and controlling activities to ensure the product or service is fit for purpose, meets design specifications and meets the needs of customers. Quality management should lead to improvements in performance.

**Quality control** involves a number of routine steps which measure and control the quality of the product/service as it is developed.

**Quality assurance** involves a review of the quality control procedures, usually by an independent third party, such as ISO (see section 3). It aims to verify that the desired level of quality has been met.

## 3 Quality certification  *able to write couple of sentence.*

The International Organisation for Standardisation (**ISO**) is one of the major bodies responsible for producing quality standards that can be applied to a variety of organisations.

The ISO 9000 quality standards have been adopted by many organisations. An ISO 9000 registered company must:

- submit its quality procedures for external inspection
- keep adequate records
- check outputs for differences
- facilitate continuous improvement.

A certified company will be subject to continuous audit.

**Test your understanding 2**

**Required:**

Explain the advantages and disadvantages to a fast growing UK based mobile phone company of becoming ISO certified.

### 4 Quality management systems

A **quality management system** (QMS) is a set of co-ordinated activities to direct and control an organisation in order to continually improve its performance.

A QMS should pervade the whole organisation. There are a number of ways of implementing a QMS.

For example, ISO 9001:2005 recommends that the design should be based on 8 principles:

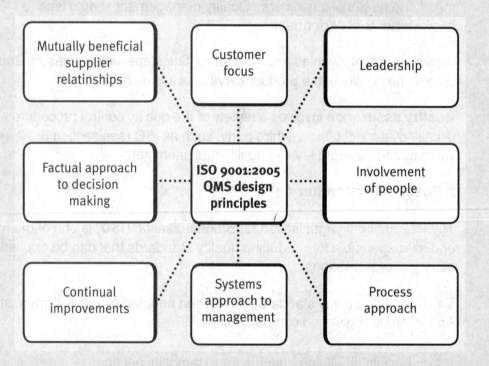

| | | |
|---|---|---|
| Mutually beneficial supplier relatinships | Customer focus | Leadership |
| Factual approach to decision making | **ISO 9001:2005 QMS design principles** | Involvement of people |
| Continual improvements | Systems approach to management | Process approach |

---

### Test your understanding 3

**Required:**

Explain how the 8 principles of ISO 9001:2005 should result in quality improvements.

---

The adoption of a QMS should complement an organisation's strategy.

### 5 Quality-related costs

- Monitoring the costs of quality is central to the operation of any quality improvement programme.
- KPIs should be developed based on the costs of quality and these can be used as a basis for staff rewards.

increase in costs

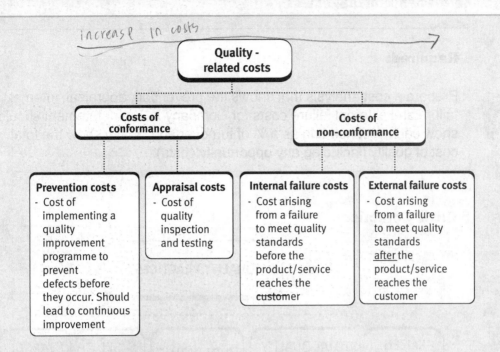

**Quality - related costs**

**Costs of conformance**

**Costs of non-conformance**

**Prevention costs**
- Cost of implementing a quality improvement programme to prevent defects before they occur. Should lead to continuous improvement

**Appraisal costs**
- Cost of quality inspection and testing

**Internal failure costs**
- Cost arising from a failure to meet quality standards before the product/service reaches the customer

**External failure costs**
- Cost arising from a failure to meet quality standards after the product/service reaches the customer

## Test your understanding 4

**Required:**

Provide and example for each of the four sub-categories of quality cost.

A quality management programme is a relatively **modern** approach to quality. It will require a significant investment in prevention costs but should minimise or eliminate appraisal, internal failure and external failure costs.

## Test your understanding 5

The following information has been supplied for Company X.

|  | $000 |
|---|---|
| Revenue | 320,000 |
| **Costs:** | |
| Design engineering | 5,000 P |
| Warranty | 8,950 E |
| Estimated lost contribution from public knowledge of poor quality | 9,561 E |
| Training | 560 P |
| Process engineering | 3,450 P |
| Rework | 7,545 I |
| Customer support per repaired unit | 645 |
| Product testing | 65 A |
| Transportation costs per repaired unit | 546 |
| Inspection | 13,800 A |

**Required:**

Prepare a cost analysis that shows the prevention, appraisal, internal failure and external failure costs for Company X. Your statement should show each cost heading as a % of turnover and clearly show the total cost of quality (including any opportunity costs).

## 6 Quality practices

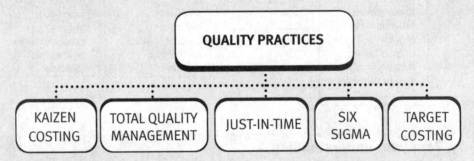

## 6.1 Kaizen Costing

**Kaizen** is a Japanese term for the philosophy of continuous improvement in performance via small, incremental steps.

Characteristics:

* Kaizen involves setting standards and then continually improving these standards to achieve long-term sustainable improvements.

* The focus is on eliminating waste, improving processes and systems and improving productivity.

* Involves all areas of the business.

* Employees often work in teams and are empowered to make changes.

* Allows the organisation to respond quickly to changes in the competitive environment.

**Illustration 1 - Kaizen**

Many Japanese companies have introduced a Kaizen approach:

* In companies such as Toyota and Canon, a total of 60-70 suggestions per employee are written down and shared every year.

* It is not unusual for over 90% of those suggestions to be implemented.

* In 1999, in one US plant, 7,000 Toyota employees submitted over 75,000 suggestions, of which 99% were implemented.

## Continuous improvement explained

Continuous improvement is the continual examination and improvement of existing processes and is very different from approaches such as business process re-engineering (BPR), which seeks to make radical one-off changes to improve an organisation's operations and processes. The concepts underlying continuous improvement are:

- The organisation should always seek perfection. Since perfection is never achieved, there must always be scope for improving on the current methods.

- The search for perfection should be ingrained into the culture and mindset of all employees. Improvements should be sought all the time.

- Individual improvements identified by the work force will be small rather than far-reaching.

**Kaizen costing** focuses on producing small, incremental cost reductions throughout the production process through the product's life.

One of the main ways to reduce costs is through the elimination of the seven main types of waste:

- **Over-production** - produce more than customers have ordered.

- **Inventory** - holding or purchasing unnecessary inventory.

- **Waiting** - production delays/idle time when value is not added to the product.

- **Defective units** - production of a part that is scrapped or requires rework.

- **Motion** - actions of people/equipment that do not add value.

- **Transportation** - poor planning or factory layout results in unnecessary transportation of materials/work-in-progress.

- **Over-processing** - unnecessary steps that do not add value.

### Test your understanding 6

Although the kaizen costing approach was developed in the manufacturing industry it could also be applied in the service sector.

**Required:**

Identify some possible sources of waste in a restaurant business and categorise them according to the seven main types of waste described above.

### Steps in kaizen costing

During the design phase, a target cost is set for each production function.

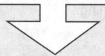

The target costs are totalled to give a total target cost for the product. This becomes the baseline for the first year of production.

As the production process improves, cost reductions reduce the baseline cost.

Cost reduction targets are set on a regular (e.g. monthly) basis and variance analysis is carried out at the end of each period to compare the target cost reduction with the actual cost.

## 6.2 Total Quality Management

Total Quality Management (TQM) is a philosophy of quality management that originated in Japan in the 1950s.

Fundamental features of TQM:

- **Prevention of errors before they occur**: The aim of TQM is to get things right first time. This contrasts with the traditional approach that less than 100% quality is acceptable. TQM will result in an increase in prevention costs, e.g. quality design of systems and products, but internal and external failure costs will fall to a greater extent.

- **Continual improvement**: Quality management is not a one-off process, but is the continuous examination and improvement of processes.

- **Real participation by all**: The 'total' in TQM means that everyone in the value chain is involved in the process, including:
  - Employees - they are expected to seek out, identify and correct quality problems. Teamwork will be vital.
  - Suppliers - quality and reliability of suppliers will play a vital role.
  - Customers - the goal is to identify and meet the needs of customers.

- **Management commitment**: Managers must be committed and encourage everyone else to be quality conscious.

### Illustration 2 - TQM success/failure

#### A TQM success story

Corning Inc is the world leader in speciality glass and ceramics. This is partly due to the implementation of a TQM approach. In 1983 the CEO announced a $1.6 billion investment in TQM. After several years of intensive training and a decade of applying the TQM approach, all of Corning's employees had bought into the quality concept. They knew the lingo - continuous improvement, empowerment, customer focus, management by prevention and they witnessed the impact of the firm's techniques as profits soared.

#### An example of TQM failure

British Telecom launched a total quality program in the late 1980s. This resulted in the company getting bogged down by quality processes and bureaucracy. The company failed to focus on its customers and later decided to dismantle its TQM programme. This was at great cost to the company and they have failed to make a full recovery.

Examples of **performance measures** in a TQM environment include:

- monetary measure - cost of rectification

- non-monetary measures - percentage of wastage

- variance analysis - care must be taken with regard to traditional performance reports such as favourable price variances, these can arise because of using poorer quality resources

- targets or benchmarks must be set against which the performance of suppliers can be measured

- outputs too must be measured for quality against pre-determined targets.

### 6.3 Just-in-time  *Mock*

**Just-in-time (JIT)** is a system whose objective is to produce or procure products or components as they are required rather than for inventory. This means that inventory levels of raw materials, work-in-progress and finished goods can be kept to a minimum.

JIT applies to both production within an organisation and to purchasing from external suppliers.

**JIT purchasing** is a method of purchasing that involves ordering materials only when customers place an order. When the goods are received they go straight into production.

**JIT production** is a production system that is driven by demand for the finished products (a 'pull' system), whereby each component on a production line is produced only when needed for the next stage.

| Illustration 3 - Toyota |
| --- |

Toyota pioneered the JIT manufacturing system, in which suppliers send parts daily - or several times a day - and are notified electronically when the production line is running out.

More than 400 trucks a day come in and out of Toyota's Georgetown plant in the USA, with a separate logistics company organising shipment from Toyota's 300 suppliers - most located in neighbouring state within half a day's drive of the plant.

Toyota aims to build long-term relationships with suppliers, many of whom it has a stake in, and says it now produces 80% of its parts within North America.

**Requirements** for successful operation of a JIT system:

- **High quality and reliability** - disruptions cause hold ups in the entire system and must be avoided. The emphasis is on getting the work right first time:
    - Highly skilled and well trained staff should be used.
    - Machinery must be fully maintained.
    - Long-term links should be established with suppliers in order to ensure a reliable and high quality service.

- **Elimination of non-value added activities** - for example, value is not added whilst storing the products and therefore inventory levels should be minimised.

- **Speed of throughput** - the speed of production should match the rate at which customers demand the product. Production runs should be shorter with smaller stocks of finished goods.

- **Flexibility** - a flexible production system and workforce is needed in order to be able to respond immediately to customers' orders.

- **Lower costs** - another objective of JIT is to reduce costs by:
    - Raising quality and eliminating waste.
    - Achieving faster throughput.
    - Minimising inventory levels.

### Test your understanding 7

**Required:**

Explain the advantages and disadvantages to an organisation of operating a JIT system.

## JIT and service operations

Although it originated with manufacturing systems, the JIT philosophy can also be applied to some service operations.

- Whereas JIT in manufacturing seeks to eliminate inventories, JIT in service operations will seek to eliminate internal or external queues of customers.

- Other concepts of JIT, such as eliminating wasteful motion and seeking ways of achieving continuous improvement are also applicable to services as much as to manufacturing activities.

**The impact on management accounting**

The introduction of a JIT system will have a number of effects on the costing system and performance management.

- Allowances for waste, scrap and rework are moved to the ideal standard, rather than an achievable standard.

- Costs are only allowed to accumulate when the product is finished.

- The inevitable reduction in inventory levels will reduce the time taken to count inventory and the clerical cost.

- Minimal inventory makes it easier for a firm to switch to backflush accounting (a simplified method of cost bookeeping covered in paper F5).

- Traditional performance measures such as inventory turnover and individual incentives are replaced by more appropriate performance measures, such as:
  - total head count productivity
  - inventory days
  - ideas generated and implemented
  - customer complaints.

## JIT and supplier relationships

A company is a long way towards JIT if its suppliers will guarantee the quality of the material they deliver and will give it shorter lead-times, deliver smaller quantities more often, guarantee a low reject rate and perform quality-assurance inspection at source. Frequent deliveries of small quantities of material to the company can ensure that each delivery is just enough to meet its immediate production schedule. This will keep its inventory as low as possible. Materials handling time will be saved because as there is no need to move the stock into a store, the goods can be delivered directly to a workstation on the shop floor. Inspection time and costs can be eliminated and the labour required for reworking defective material or returning goods to the supplier can be saved.

The successful JIT manufacturer deliberately sets out to cultivate good relationships with a small number of suppliers and these suppliers will often be situated close to the manufacturing plant. It is usual for a large manufacturer that does not use the JIT approach to have multiple suppliers. When a new part is to be produced, various suppliers will bid for the contract and the business will be given to the two or three most attractive bids.

A JIT manufacturer is looking for a single supplier that can provide high quality and reliable deliveries, rather than the lowest price. This supplier will often be located in close proximity to the manufacturing plant.

There is much to be gained by both the company and its suppliers from this mutual dependence. The supplier is guaranteed a demand for the products as the sole supplier and is able to plan to meet the customer's production schedules. If an organisation has confidence that suppliers will deliver material of 100% quality, on time, so that there will be no rejects, returns and hence no consequent production delays, usage of materials can be matched with delivery of materials and stocks can be kept at near zero levels.

Jaguar, when it analysed the causes of customer complaints, compiled a list of 150 areas of faults. Some 60% of them turned out to be faulty components from suppliers. One month the company returned 22,000 components to different suppliers. Suppliers were brought on to the multi-disciplinary task forces the company established to tackle each of the common faults. The task force had the simple objective of finding the fault, establishing and testing a cure, and implementing it as fast as possible. Jaguar directors chaired the task forces of the 12 most serious faults, but in one case the task force was chaired by the supplier's representative.

## 6.4 Six Sigma

- Six Sigma is a quality management programme that was pioneered by Motorola in the 1980s.

- The aim of the approach is to achieve a reduction in the number of faults that go beyond an accepted tolerance level. It tends to be used for individual processes.

- The sigma stands for the standard deviation. For reasons that need not be explained here, it can be demonstrated that, if the error rate lies beyond the sixth sigma of probability there will be fewer than 3.4 defects in every one million units produced.

- This is the tolerance level set. It is almost perfection since customers will have room to complain fewer than four times in a million.

### Illustration 4 – The Six Sigma approach

A hospital is using the Six Sigma process to improve patient waiting times. An investigation of the views of patients has revealed that:

- patients do not want to be called before their appointment time as they do not want to feel that they have to be at the hospital early to avoid missing an appointment

- the maximum length of time they are prepared to wait after the appointment time is 30 minutes.

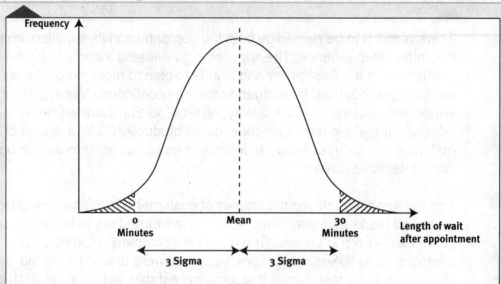

The aim of the Six Sigma programme will be to ensure that no more than 3.4 waits in every million occurrences exceed 30 minutes or are less than 0 minutes.

## Key requirements and criticisms

There are a number of **key requirements** for the implementation of Six Sigma.

- Six Sigma should be focused on the customer and based on the level of performance acceptable to the customer.

- Six Sigma targets for a process should be related to the main drivers of performance.

- To maximise savings Six Sigma needs to be part of a wider performance management programme which is linked to the strategy of the organisation. It should not be just about doing things better but about doing things differently.

- Senior managers within the organisation have a key role in driving the process.

- Training and education about the process throughout the organisation are essential for success.

- Six Sigma sets a tight target, but accepts some failure – the target is not zero defects.

Literature on Six Sigma contains some **criticisms** of the process and identifies a number of limitations as follows.

- Six Sigma has been criticised for its focus on current processes and reliance on data. It is suggested that this could become too rigid and limit process innovation.

- Six Sigma is based on the use of models which are by their nature simplifications of real life. Judgement needs to be used in applying the models in the context of business objectives.

- The approach can be very time consuming and expensive. Organisations need to be prepared to put time and effort into its implementation.

- The culture of the organisation must be supportive – not all organisations are ready for such a scientific process.

- The process is heavily data-driven. This can be a strength, but can become over-bureaucratic.

- Six Sigma can give all parts of the organisation a common language for process improvement, but it is important to ensure that this does not become jargon but is expressed in terms specific to the organisation and its business.

- There is an underlying assumption in Six Sigma that the existing business processes meet customers' expectations. It does not ask whether it is the right process.

## The five steps of the Six Sigma process (DMAIC)

**Step 1: Define an opportunity**
- quality problem defined in specific, quantifiable terms.
- a mission statement is prepared explaining what will be done about the problem. This should also be in specific, quantifiable terms
- a project team is set up from across the organisation and is given the resources to address the problem.

**Step 2: Measure performance**
The project team does some preliminary work to measure how the current process is working and identifies what is causing the quality problem

**Step 3: Analyse the opportunity**
The project team investigates their preliminary concerns and test different theories to get to the root cause of the problem

**Step 4: Improve performance**
Potential solutions are developed for process re-design. The most appropriate solution will be the one that achieves the mission statement

**Step 5: Control performance**
New controls are designed to compare actual performance with targeted performance to make sure the improvements to the process are being sustained

**Test your understanding 8**

**Required:**

How can management accountants contribute to the Six Sigma process?

**Question focus**: now attempt question 20 from chapter 13.

## 6.5 Target costing

**Steps:**

(1) Estimate a selling price for the product - consider how much customers will pay and how much competitors charge for similar products.

(2) Deduct the required profit.

(3) Produce a target cost figure.

(4) Reduce cost gap, i.e the difference between the current cost and the target cost.

**Techniques** to reduce the cost gap include:

- JIT
- TQM
- Kaizen
- ABC
- Value analysis: a systematic examination of the product which asks questions such as:
  - can another dependable supplier be found for less cost?
  - does it need all of its features?

Many of the techniques above have a **'quality'** focus

## Key features of target costing

- **Target costing forces a focus on the customer:** Product decisions and cost analysis have to take account of customer requirements such as quality, features and price. This is not always the case with other cost management methods.

- **Successful target costing considers all costs** related to production and distribution of the products and involves the whole supply chain. This may even include joint working between suppliers and manufacturers to share information and enable cost reductions, particularly for products for which raw materials contribute a high proportion of the manufactured cost.

- **Target costing considers the entire life-cycle** of the product, so that total costs to the manufacturer are minimised.

- **Target costing begins very early in the development** phase of new products, so that changes are made before production begins. Decisions made at this stage generally determine a high proportion of the costs of any product.

- **Target costing is a multi-disciplinary approach** which involves staff from all functions in the analysis and decision making.

- **Target costing is an iterative process** in which teams are making judgements and trade-offs between product features, price, sales volumes, costs and investment requirements.

- **Target costing provides cost targets** for individual inputs and processes which can be used for performance monitoring.

## Test your understanding 9

Edward Electronics assembles and sells many types of radio. It is considering extending its product range to include digital radios. These radios produce a better sound quality than traditional radios and have a large number of potential additional features not possible with the previous technologies (station scanning, more choice, one touch tuning, station identification text and song identification text etc).

A radio is produced by assembly workers assembling a variety of components. Production overheads are currently absorbed into product costs on an assembly labour hour basis.

Edward Electronics is considering a target costing approach for its new digital radio product.

**Required:**

(a) Briefly describe the target costing process that Edward Electronics should undertake.

**(3 marks)**

(b) Explain the benefits to Edward Electronics of adopting a target costing approach at such an early stage in the product development process.

**(4 marks)**

A selling price of $44 has been set in order to compete with a similar radio on the market that has comparable features to Edward Electronics' intended product. The board have agreed that the acceptable margin (after allowing for all production costs) should be 20%.

Cost information for the new radio is as follows:

**Component 1** (Circuit board) – these are bought in and cost $4.10 each. They are bought in batches of 4,000 and additional delivery costs are $2,400 per batch.

**Component 2** (Wiring) – in an ideal situation 25 cm of wiring is needed for each completed radio. However, there is some waste involved in the process as wire is occasionally cut to the wrong length or is damaged in the assembly process. Edward Electronics estimates that 2% of the purchased wire is lost in the assembly process. Wire costs $0.50 per metre to buy.

**Other material** – other materials cost $8.10 per radio.

**Assembly labour** – these are skilled people who are difficult to recruit and retain. Edward Electronics has more staff of this type than needed but is prepared to carry this extra cost in return for the security it gives the business. It takes 30 minutes to assemble a radio and the assembly workers are paid $12.60 per hour. It is estimated that 10% of hours paid to the assembly workers is for idle time.

**Production Overheads** – recent historic cost analysis has revealed the following production overhead data:

| | Total production overhead ($) | Total assembly labour hours |
|---|---|---|
| Month 1 | 620,000 | 19,000 |
| Month 2 | 700,000 | 23,000 |

Fixed production overheads are absorbed on an assembly hour basis based on normal annual activity levels. In a typical year 240,000 assembly hours will be worked by Edward Electronics.

**Required:**

(c)  Calculate the expected cost per unit for the radio and identify any cost gap that might exist.

**(13 marks)**
**(Total: 20 marks)**

## Additional question on quality

**Required:**

Explain how management accounting/management techniques such as total quality management, just in time, value analysis, activity based costing and the balanced scorecard could contribute towards the analysis of the relationship between costs and quality.

**Answer:**

### Total Quality Management (TQM)

TQM is an approach that seeks to ensure that all aspects of providing goods and services are delivered at the highest possible standard, and that standards keep improving. The underlying principle is that the cost of preventing deficient quality is less than the costs of correcting poor quality. This denies the idea that improved quality can only be secured with greater expenditure, but adopts the approach that improved quality will reduce costs.

Quality related costs are concerned with both achieving quality and failure to achieve quality.

Quality costs can categorised as:

*   **Prevention costs** – communicating the concept, training, establishing systems to deliver quality services

*   **Appraisal costs** – e.g. inspection and testing

*   **Internal failure costs** – wasted materials used in rejects, down time resulting from internal service quality failures, resources devoted to dealing with complaints

- **External failure costs** – loss of goodwill and future business, compensation paid to customers and rectification costs

The TQM view is that by getting it right first time and every time, the prevention and appraisal costs will be outweighed by the savings in failure costs, hence lower costs and improved quality are congruent goals. TQM requires everyone in the organisation to have identified customers, whether external or internal, so that a continuous service quality chain is maintained all the way through the organisation to the final customer.

## Just In Time (JIT)

JIT is a manufacturing and supply chain process that is intended to reduce inventory levels and improve customer service by ensuring that customers receive their orders at the right time and in the right quantity. The system should facilitate a smooth workflow throughout the business and reduce waste. Goods are produced to meet customer needs directly, not for inventory.

Cost reductions should arise from:

- Lower raw material and finished goods inventory levels, therefore reduced holding costs

- Reduced material handling

- Often a reduction in the number of suppliers and lower administration and communication costs

- Guaranteed quality of supplies reduces inspection and rectification costs

Quality improvements should arise from:

- Fewer or even single sourcing of supplies strengthens the buyer–supplier relationship and is likely to improve the quality.

- The absence of customer stockholding compels the supplier (if they want continued business) to guarantee the quality of the material that they deliver.

- The necessity to work regularly and closer with hauliers strengthens the relationship with them. The deliveries become high priority and more reliable.

- Customers are not faced with the traditional problems of having to wait until their suppliers inventories are replenished. The system is designed to respond to customers' needs rapidly.

- Direct focus on meeting an identified customer's need, production is merely to add to an anonymous pile of inventory.

## Value Analysis

Value analysis is concerned with concentrating on activities that add value to the product/service as perceived by the customer. It examines business activities and questions why they are being undertaken and what contribution do they make to customer satisfaction. Value added activities include designing products, producing output and developing customer relationships. Non-value added activities include returning goods, inventory holding, and checking on the quality of supplies received. Wherever possible eliminate the non-value added activities.

Value analysis commences with a focus on customers. What do they want? What do they regard as significant in the buying decision: function, appearance, longevity or disposal value? This is concerned with identifying what customers regard as quality and then providing it: do not expend effort on what they regard as unimportant. It is about clarifying what the constituents of quality are on the Costs and Quality diagram. Having decided this there is a need to develop alternative designs, estimate costs and evaluate alternatives.

## Activity Based Costing (ABC)

ABC is concerned with attributing/assigning costs to cost units on the basis of the service received from indirect activities e.g. public relations, recruitment, quality assurance general meetings. The organisation needs to identify cost drivers – the specific activities that cause costs to arise e.g. number of orders taken, telephone calls made, number of breakdowns or the number of visitors to an attraction.

ABC intends to avoid the arbitrary allocation of overheads to products/services by identifying a causal link between costs, activities and outputs. Because of higher degrees of automation, the increasing significance of overheads in the cost make up of output intensifies the need to improve the apportionment of them. Accountants can contribute towards providing better cost information to the value analysis referred to above. Product managers need to know what they are getting for their money – what is the real cost of quality? What are the cost driving activities that do not impact on quality? What activities that generate minimal costs have a significantly favourable impact on quality?

**The Balanced Scorecard (Kaplan and Norton)**

The Balanced Scorecard provides a framework for a business to achieve its strategic objectives include both financial and non-financial objectives. The approach claims that performance has four dimensions: financial, customer, internal business, and innovation and learning. The customer perspective asks: How does the business appear to the customers? The internal business perspective asks :What do we need to do to satisfy shareholders and customers, including the monitoring of unit costs? The innovation and learning perspective looks at how products and processes should be changed and improved.

The scorecard is concerned with monitoring and measuring the critical variables that comprise the customer and internal perspective. The choice of variables for inclusion in the scorecard is significant because the scorecard report is a design for action. Inappropriate indicators will trigger damaging responses. For example, the organisation needs to monitor what factors customers regard as contributing to improved quality, not what the business thinks it should provide. Therefore the scorecards would be suitable for inclusion as quantifiable indicators on the axis on the Costs and Quality diagram. The Balanced Scorecard attempts to improve the range and relationship between alternative performance measures, in the case under discussion, costs and quality.

# 7 Section - Quality in management information systems

## 7.1 Features of a quality system

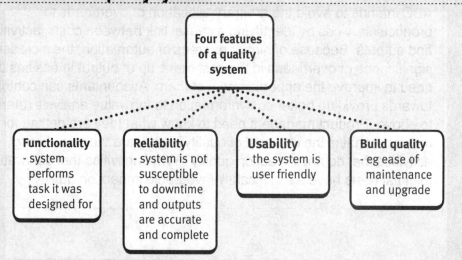

page 372

## Test your understanding 10

### Required:

Explain the consequences of failing to include these four features in a management information system.

## 7.2 Designing a quality system

### Designing a quality system

In order to ensure that the system fulfils the quality criteria of functionality, reliability, usability and build quality a structured approach to development should be used. One such approach is the systems development life cycle (SDLC):

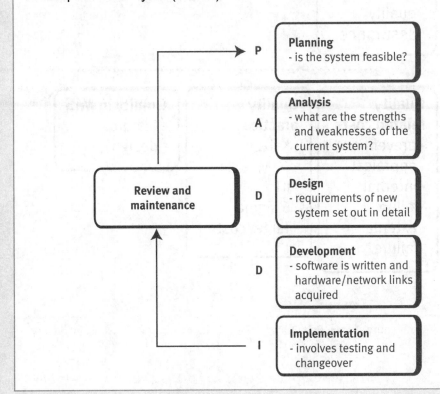

## 8 Chapter summary

```
                    ┌─────────────────┐
                    │  The role of    │
                    │  quality in     │
                    │  performance    │
                    │  management     │
                    └─────────────────┘
```

**Quality terminology**
- quality
- quality management
- quality control
- quality assurance

**Quality certification**
- ISO certification
- pros/cons

**QMS**
- definition
- design

**Quality related costs**
- prevention
- appraisal .
- internal failure
- external failure

**Quality practices**
- Kaizen
- TQM
- JIT
- 6 sigma
- Target costing

**Quality in MIS**
- features
- design

## Test your understanding answers

### Test your understanding 1

Higher quality can help to increase revenue and reduce costs:

- Higher quality improves the perceived image of a product or service. As a result, more customers will be willing to purchase the product/service and may also be willing to pay a higher price.

- A higher volume of sales may result in lower unit costs due to economies of scale.

- Higher quality in manufacturing should result in lower waste and defective rates, which will reduce production costs.

- The need for inspection and testing should be reduced, also reducing costs.

- The level of customer complaints should fall and warranty claims should be lower. This will reduce costs.

- Better quality in production should lead to shorter processing times. This will reduce costs.

## Test your understanding 2

### Advantages

- Recognised standard - the company's reputation for quality will be enhanced since ISO is a recognised international standard of quality.

- Marketing - ISO certification will act as an excellent marketing tool. It will help to differentiate the company, on the grounds of quality, in the customers' eyes.

- Improved profitability - fulfilment of the ISO criteria should help the company to improve quality. This, in turn, should reduce costs and improve quality.

- International competitiveness - ISO certification is becoming increasingly useful in international markets and may help the company to compete on a world stage.

### Disadvantages

- Cost - fees are upward of $1,500 depending on the size of the company.

- Time - documentation can be time consuming to produce.

- Bureaucracy - the scheme encourages bureaucracy with lots of form filling and filing rather than positive actions.

- Rigid policies - these might discourage initiative and innovation and may therefore hinder the quality process.

- Not all embracing - ISO certification will form a small part of a quality practice such as TQM.

KAPLAN PUBLISHING

### Test your understanding 3

The 8 principles of ISO 9001:2005 should result in quality improvements as follows:

- **Customer focus** - quality may be defined as 'the product/service meeting the customer's needs' and therefore a customer focus should improve quality.

- **Leadership** - leaders should communicate the importance of quality and drive a culture of quality.

- **Involvement of people** - everyone in the organisation should have a quality focus.

- **Process approach** - related activities and resources should be managed in an integrated quality process.

- **Systems approach to management** - groups of related processes should be managed in an integrated quality system.

- **Continual improvement** - quality management is not a one off process, but is the continuous examination and improvement of processes.

- **Factual approach to decision making** - quality procedures should be documented and applied consistently.

- **Mutually beneficial supplier relationships** - long-term links should be established with suppliers in order to ensure a reliable and high quality service.

## Test your understanding 4

### Prevention costs

- Cost of designing products and services with built in quality.
- Cost of training employees in the best way to do their job.
- Cost of equipment testing to ensure it conforms with quality standards required.

### Appraisal costs

- Inspection and testing, for example of a purchased material or service.

### Internal failure costs

- Cost of scrapped material due to poor quality.
- Cost of re-working parts.
- Reinspection costs.
- Lower selling prices for sub-quality products.

### External failure costs

- Cost of recalling and correcting products.
- Cost of lost goodwill.

## Test your understanding 5

| | $000 | % of revenue |
|---|---|---|
| **Prevention costs:** | | |
| Design engineering | 5,000 | 1.56 |
| Process engineering | 3,450 | 1.08 |
| Training | 560 | 0.18 |
| **Total** | **9,010** | **2.82** |
| **Appraisal costs:** | | |
| Inspection | 13,800 | 4.31 |
| Product testing | 65 | 0.02 |
| **Total** | **13,865** | **4.33** |
| **Internal failure costs** | 7,545 | 2.36 |
| **Total** | **7,545** | **2.36** |
| **External failure costs:** | | |
| Warranty | 8,950 | 2.80 |
| Customer support | 645 | 0.20 |
| Transportation | 546 | 0.17 |
| **Total** | **10,141** | **3.17** |
| | | |
| **Sub-total** | **40,561** | **12.68** |
| Opportunity costs | 9,561 | 2.99 |
| **Total quality costs** | **50,112** | **15.66** |

## Test your understanding 6

**Suggestions could include**

- Pre-preparing plated servings of perishable desserts which are not ordered and need to be thrown away – over-production.

- Poor kitchen layout which could lead to unnecessary movement of staff and result in waste from motion and from transportation of material or lead to accidents and spillages and waste in processes and methods.

- Poorly trained cooking staff who produce sub-standard meals which cannot be served – product defects.

- Producing too many pre-prepared components such as sauces to be incorporated in dishes which are then not needed – waste from inventory.

- Poor scheduling in the kitchen leading to serving staff waiting for meals to be ready – waste from waiting time.

## Test your understanding 7

### Advantages of JIT

- Lower stock holding costs means a reduction in storage space which saves rent and insurance costs.

- As stock is only obtained when needed, less working capital is tied up in stock.

- There is less likelihood of stock perishing, becoming obsolete or out of date.

- Avoids the build up of unsold finished products that occurs with sudden changes in demand.

- Less time is spent checking and re-working the products as the emphasis is on getting the work right first time.

The result is that costs should fall and quality should increase. This should improve the company's competitive advantage.

### Disadvantages of JIT

- There is little room for mistakes as little stock is kept for re-working a faulty product.

- Production is very reliant on suppliers and if stock is not delivered on time or is not of a high enough quality, the whole production schedule can be delayed.

- There is no spare finished product available to meet unexpected orders, because all products are made to meet actual orders.

- It may be difficult for managers to empower employees to embrace the concept and culture.

- It won't be suitable for all companies. For example, supermarkets must have a supply of inventory.

- It can be difficult to apply to the service industry. However, in the service industry a JIT approach may focus on eliminating queues, which are wasteful of customers' time.

**Test your understanding 8**

- The provision of data at all stages in the process.

- Providing expertise in the identification of appropriate output, input and process measures (financial and non-financial) and ways to collect the data.

- Analysis of data.

- Evaluation of possible solutions.

- Identification of performance measures for the control process and monitoring after changes have been implemented.

- Taking part in multi-disciplinary Six Sigma teams.

**Test your understanding 9**

(a) The target costing process should be undertaken as follows:

**Step 1**: Establish the selling price by considering how much customers will be willing to pay and how much competitors charge for similar products.

**Step 2**: Deduct the required profit from the selling price.

**Step 3**: Calculate the target cost, i.e. selling price minus profit.

**Step 4**: Find ways to reduce the cost gap, e.g. cheaper materials, cheaper labour, increased productivity, reduced waste.

(b) The benefits are as follows:

- Target costing has an external focus, i.e. it considers how much customers will pay/competitors will charge.

- Cost control can occur earlier in the design process and the required steps can be taken to reduce the cost gap.

- The performance of the business should be enhanced due to better management of costs.

- The focus will be on getting things right first time which should reduce the development time.

(c) **W1 Production overhead** (using high low method)

| | Production overhead ($) | Labour hours |
|---|---|---|
| High | 700,000 | 23,000 |
| Low | 620,000 | 19,000 |
| Difference | 80,000 | 4,000 |

– Variable overhead = $80,000 ÷ 4,000 = $20 per hour

– Total cost $700,000 = fixed cost + variable cost ($20/hour × 23,000). This gives a monthly fixed cost of $240,000. (Note: the total cost at the low level of production could also be used to find the fixed cost).

– Annual fixed cost = $240,000 × 12 = $2,880,000

– Overhead absorption rate (OAR) = $2,880,000 ÷ 240,000hours = $12 per hour

### Cost card and cost gap calculation

| | $ per radio |
|---|---|
| Component 1 | 4.10 |
| Component 1 delivery = $2,400 ÷ 4,000 | 0.60 |
| Component 2 wiring = $0.50 × 0.25metres × 100/98 | 0.128 |
| Other material | 8.10 |
| Assembly labour = $12.60 × 0.5hours × 100/90 | 7.00 |
| Variable production overhead = $20/hour (W1) × 0.5hours | 10.00 |
| Fixed production overhead = $12/hour (W1) × 0.5hours | 6.00 |
| **Total cost** | **35.928** |
| Desired cost | 35.20 |
| **Cost gap** | **0.728** |

## Test your understanding 10

- **Poor functionality and reliability** may result in:
  - user dissatisfaction, e.g. because the system does not perform the desired task
  - additional costs, e.g. to correct inaccurate reports.

- **Poor usability** may result in:
  - staff dissatisfaction
  - excessive staff training
  - excessive time spent by staff trying to operate the system.

- **Poor build quality** will result in difficulties maintaining and upgrading the system which will impact long-term profit.

# 12

# Current developments in performance management

## Chapter learning objectives

Upon completion of this chapter you will be able to:

- discuss, evaluate and apply environmental management accounting using for example lifecycle costing, input/output analysis and activity-based costing

- discuss the use of benchmarking in public sector performance (league tables) in public sector performance and its effects on operational and strategic management and behaviour

- discuss the issues surrounding the use of targets in public sector organisations

- discuss contemporary issues in performance management

- discuss how changing organisation's structure, culture and strategy will influence the adoption of new performance measurement methods and techniques.

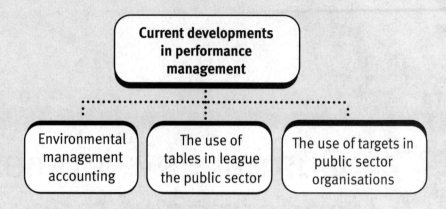

## 1 Exam focus

| Exam sitting | Area examined | Question number | Number of marks |
|---|---|---|---|
| June 2011 | EMA | 5 | 20 |
| December 2008 | League tables | 1(b) | 6 |

**Student Accountant articles**: visit the ACCA website, www.accaglobal.com, to review the following articles on the topics in this chapter:

- Environmental management accounting - July 2010

- Environmental management accounting - June 2004

## 2 Introduction

The area of performance management is constantly evolving. The techniques and systems used today are very different from those of 50 years ago and there are current issues and pressures which are likely to lead to further developments:

- changes in technology may have significant impact on measuring performance

- a recognition that there is a broader picture than just financial performance

- issues relating to governance.

New performance measurement methods and techniques have been developed as a result of a change in an organisation's structure, culture and strategy.

## Contemporary issues in performance management

### Changes in technology

Improvements in technology have a significant impact on performance management.

- It is possible to measure more and more different indicators of performance – the challenge now is to ensure that the aspects being measured and managed are the right ones.

- Improved technology also means that it is possible to produce information much more quickly and in real time.

- Information is now made directly available to managers on their desks at the touch of a button. The production of performance reports is no longer the responsibility of a small number of specialists – rather their role is to design the overall system to ensure that it provides the information required by managers.

- The availability of more data does not automatically mean that there is more useful information – it is still important to ensure that the data is interpreted to ensure that it is useful.

- Performance management is about more than the information produced – however much information is provided, what is important is how it is used and how the organisation acts in response to it.

### Broadening performance management

There is a growing recognition that the performance of organisations depends on more than purely financial performance.

- There has been significant growth in the use of non-financial measures of performance.

- Techniques have been developed to enable measurement of performance in a number of different dimensions, and this trend looks set to continue. Examples are the balanced scorecard and the performance prism.

- Historically the focus of performance management has been on outputs of the organisation's activities. Organisations are now beginning to focus on outcomes, or achievements, and then using output measures to achieve those outcomes.

- There is a recognition that everyone in the organisation needs to be involved in performance management.

- There is also a need to extend involvement outside the organisation to the entire supply chain, as organisations recognise that others have an influence on their performance.

## Governance

Over recent years, the issue of corporate governance has become a major area for concern in many countries. Organisations are now under increased pressure to demonstrate that they are effectively managed. This has led to:

- pressure to demonstrate improvements in performance
- more demands for accountability from external agencies
- legislation and regulation relating to performance reporting
- companies looking for ways to measure and report on improvements in governance.

## 3 Environmental management accounting

### 3.1 Introduction

Organisations are becoming increasingly aware of the environmental implications of their actions.

## Test your understanding 1

**Required:**

Discuss the potential benefits to a company of reducing the negative environmental impact of its operations, products or services.

## Illustration 1 - Environmental management at BP

BP plc's previous Annual Review describes a number of activities aimed at reducing the environmental impact of the company's operations:

- improving the integrity of its equipment and pipelines to reduce the spillage of oil
- reducing the emissions of greenhouse gases, which is measured and reported within the Annual Review
- introducing environmental requirements for new projects
- supporting the use of market mechanisms to bring about emission reductions across industry
- launching a new business providing energy from alternative sources

- investing in research into biofuels

- developing and marketing fuel which produces lower emissions compared with standard fuels.

### 3.2 Drawbacks of traditional management accounting

Management accounts provide us with an analysis of the performance of the business. However, traditional accounting systems are unable to deal adequately with environmental costs. As a result, managers are unaware of these costs and have no information with which to manage or reduce them.

| Environmental cost category | Description | Problem |
|---|---|---|
| Conventional costs | Costs such as raw material and energy costs | Will not be prioritised by management since often hidden within overheads |
| Contingent costs | Costs such as future compliance costs or remediation costs when a site is decommissioned | Often incurred towards the end of a project so are ignored by managers who focus on short-term performance |
| Relationship costs | Image costs such as the cost of producing environmental information for public reporting | Ignored by managers who are unaware of their existence |
| Reputational costs | Costs associated with failing to address environmental issues, e.g. lost sales | Ignored by managers who are unaware of the risk of incurring them |

### Illustration 2 - Reputational costs

In April 2010 a blast at the Deepwater Horizon rig in the Gulf of Mexico killed eleven people and caused one of the worst oil spills in history. The US presidential commission concluded that the oil spill was an avoidable disaster caused by a series of failures and blunders made by BP, its partners and the government departments assigned to regulate them. It also warned that such a disaster was likely to recur because of complacency in the industry.

> For BP, the company at the heart of the disaster, the effects have had a deep and widespread impact. The company has become synonymous with everything that is dangerous about oil exploration causing massive reputational damage.

## 3.3 Using environmental management accounting to address these problems

To ensure that environmental costs are fully considered and to improve the environmental performance of an organisation, a new technique called environmental management accounting (EMA) has been introduced. EMA:

- identifies and estimates the costs of environment-related activities and seeks to control these costs

- identifies and separately monitors the usage and cost of resources such as water, electricity and fuel and enables these costs to be reduced

- ensures environmental considerations form a part of capital investment decisions

- assesses the likelihood and impact of environmental risks

- includes environment-related indicators as part of routine performance monitoring

- benchmarks activities against environmental best practice.

In summary, the focus of EMA is not all on financial costs but it also considers the environmental cost or benefit of any decisions made.

## 3.4 EMA techniques

Four key techniques exist. The techniques can assist an organisation in improving its performance. They are not mutually exclusive.

### Activity-based costing (ABC)

ABC distinguishes between:

- environment-related costs which can be attributed directly to a cost centre, e.g. a waste filtration plant, and

- environment-driven costs which are generally hidden in overheads.

The environment-driven costs are removed from general overheads and traced to products or services. This means that cost drivers are determined for these costs and products are charged for the use of these environmental costs based on the amount of cost drivers that they contribute to the activity. This should give a good attribution of environmental costs to individual products and should result in better control of costs.

| **Advantages and disadvantages of ABC** | |
| --- | --- |
| **Advantages** | **Disadvantages** |
| • Better/fairer product costs | • Time consuming |
| • Improved pricing - so that the products which have the biggest environmental impact reflect this by having higher selling prices | • Expensive to implement |
| | • Determining accurate costs and appropriate cost drivers is difficult |
| • Better environmental control | • External costs, i.e not experienced by the company (e.g. carbon footprint) may still be ignored/unmeasured |
| • Facilitates the quantification of cost savings from 'environmentally-friendly' measures | |
| | • A company that integrates external costs voluntarily may be at a competitive disadvantage to rivals who do not do this |
| • Should integrate environmental costing into the strategic management process | |
| | • Some internal environmental costs are intangible (e.g. impact on employee health) and these are still ignored |

## Input/output analysis

This technique compares the physical quantities input into a process and compares this with the output quantities. The physical quantities can be translated into monetary terms.

## Illustration 3 - Input/output analysis

|  | Physical units (kgs) | Revenue/(cost) ($) |
|---|---|---|
| **Input** | 100 | (700,000) |
| **Output** Product | 60 | 900,000 |
| Scrap for recycling | 20 | 45,000 |
| Disposed of as waste | 20 | (300,000) |
| Total | | **(55,000)** |

A reduction in waste could help to eliminate the loss.

## Flow cost accounting

This is associated with input/output analysis since it looks at the physical quantities of material involved in different processes. The aim is to reduce the quantities of material and hence the cost.

## Lifecycle costing

Lifecycle costing considers the costs and revenues of a product over its whole life rather than one accounting period. Therefore, the full environmental cost of producing a product will be taken into account. In order to reduce lifecycle costs an organisation may adopt a TQM approach.

It is arguable that TQM and environmental management are inextricably linked insofar as good environmental management is increasingly recognised as an essential component of TQM. Such organisations pursue objectives that may include zero complaints, zero spills, zero pollution, zero waste and zero accidents. Information systems need to be able to support such environmental objectives via the provision of feedback – on the success or otherwise – of the organisational efforts in achieving such objectives.

**Note**: The benefit of each of the techniques must be weighed against the cost of providing the additional information.

KAPLAN PUBLISHING

### Illustration 4 - Cost reduction at McCain Foods

One example of energy saving is McCain Foods, which buys an eighth of the UK's potatoes to make chips. It has cut its Peterborough plant's $CO_2$ footprint by two-thirds, says corporate affairs director Bill Bartlett. It invested £10m (approximately $15m) in three 3MW turbines to meet 60 per cent of its annual electricity demand. McCain spent another £4.5m (approximately $6.75m) on a lagoon to catch the methane from fermenting waste water and particulates, which generates another 10 per cent of the site's electricity usage. It also wants to refine its used cooking oil, either for its own vehicles fleet or for selling on.

McCain want to become more competitive and more efficient.

## 4 The use of league tables (benchmarking) in the public sector

A **league table** is a chart or list which compares one organisation with another by ranking them in order of ability or achievement.

Benchmarking will be used to rank the organisations in the league table.

League tables have become a popular performance management tool in the public sector in recent years, for example in hospitals and schools.

### Illustration 5 - The use of league tables in schools

In January 2010 the secondary schools league tables showed that London is the highest performing region in England at GCSE level (exams sat by students at the age of 16) with 54% of pupils achieving the benchmark at GCSE of five A* to C grades including English and mathematics. This is a striking turnaround in just over a decade. In 1997 only 29.9% of London pupils reached this level.

### Advantages of league tables

- Implementation stimulates competition and the adoption of best practice. As a result, the quality of the service should improve.

- Monitors and ensures accountability of the providers.

- Performance is transparent.

- League tables should be readily available and can be used by consumers to make choices.

**Test your understanding 2**

**Required:**

Discuss the disadvantages of using league tables in the public sector.

**Test your understanding 3**

A government has decided to improve school performance by the use of league tables with schools assessed on the following:

- percentage pass rates in examinations
- absenteeism.

It has been proposed that funding be linked to these measures.

**Required:**

Suggest some potentially negative outcomes of this system.

## 5 The use of targets in public sector organisations

'A **performance target** represents the level of performance that the organisation aims to achieve for a particular activity.  Such targets should be consistent with the SMART criteria' (Government and Audit Commission).

The results from the benchmarking process (discussed above) can be used to set attainment targets for public sector organisations such as schools, hospitals and the police force.

These should act as an invaluable tool for improvement.  However, there are a number of issues associated with the use of targets.

## Issues

- **Central control** - most targets are set centrally by government. It may be more appropriate for targets to be drawn up locally by professionals who are aware of the challenges faced in different parts of the country.

- **Difficulty level** - targets that are too difficult tend to debilitate rather than motivate and those that are too easy lead to complacency.

- **All or nothing** - not meeting the target can be seen as a sign of failure. However, if an aspirational target is set it may not be met but may still result in improvements and act as a motivator.

- **Too many targets** - there is a tendency to set too many targets to try to measure every aspect of service delivery. However, a manager responsible for service delivery will be unable to concentrate on more than a handful of targets at any one time.

- **Targets not always appropriate** - it is not always appropriate to set targets, e.g. if the activity is not within the control of the person responsible for meeting the target.

- **Cost** - the cost of setting the target may outweigh the benefit.

- **Lack of ownership of targets** - each target should have a named person who is accountable for the performance and achievement of the objective.

- **Gaming** - there may be a tendency for people to 'play the system' rather than using the targets as a tool for improvement, i.e. people want to look good rather than be good.

- **Conflict** - conflict between targets may occur, e.g. a reduction in the number of children on the Child Protection Register may coincide with an increase in child abuse cases.

## Chapter summary

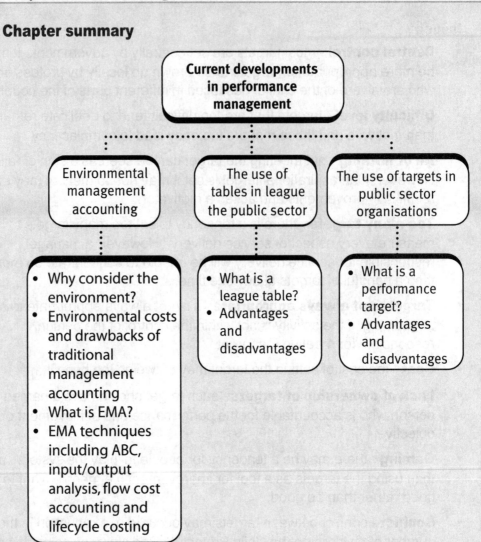

**Current developments in performance management**

- Environmental management accounting
- The use of tables in league the public sector
- The use of targets in public sector organisations

Environmental management accounting:
- Why consider the environment?
- Environmental costs and drawbacks of traditional management accounting
- What is EMA?
- EMA techniques including ABC, input/output analysis, flow cost accounting and lifecycle costing

The use of tables in league the public sector:
- What is a league table?
- Advantages and disadvantages

The use of targets in public sector organisations:
- What is a performance target?
- Advantages and disadvantages

# Test your understanding answers

## Test your understanding 1

The benefits are as follows:

- An environmental approach ensures the organisation meets with legal and regulatory standards.

- Increased sales as a result of meeting with customers' needs.

- Helps to maintain a positive public image.

- Manages risk, e.g. of an environmental disaster.

- Can reduce costs, e.g. through improved use of fuel and water.

## Test your understanding 2

- Encourages providers to focus on performance measures rather than the quality of the service.

- Costly and time consuming.

- May encourage creative reporting.

- The value of any performance indicator depends on the quality of any data in the calculation. The data management systems in the public sector do not always provide quality data.

- Many of the outcomes valued by society are not measurable but many of the performance indicators have been selected on the basis of what is practical rather than what is meaningful.

- Differences between public sector organisations may make comparisons meaningless, e.g. a school in a deprived area will be at a natural disadvantage. This may result in employees being held responsible for things over which they have no control.

- A poor ranking may have a negative impact on public trust and employee morale.

- A poor ranking may lead to a worsening of future performance, e.g. gifted children are no longer sent to a poorly performing school and this results in an even lower ranking in future years.

### Test your understanding 3

- Children with special needs/disabilities will find it harder to gain school places as they may be perceived as having less chance of passing examinations reducing school performance and funding. (The irony here is that schools which are willing to accept children with disabilities often need more funding, not less.)

- Truants are likely to be expelled at the school's first realistic opportunity. This may result in the school performing better but only transfers the 'problem' somewhere else.

- Schools may focus on examination performance to the detriment of other educational goals, e.g. art, sports.

- Schools facing difficulties will receive less funding to help overcome those problems.

- There will be increased competitiveness and decreased collaboration between schools.

# 13

# Questions & Answers

## Question 1 - KPIs and beyond budgeting

### Question

The RRR Group (RRR) provides roof repair, refurbishment and renewal services to individual customers on a nationwide basis. RRR operates a large number of regional divisions, each of which offers a similar range of services.

RRR expects divisional management to prepare its own annual budget by focusing on the achievement of a net profit figure set at group level. This budget is currently used for planning and reporting.

Table A shows actual results for Alpha division for the years ending 30 November 20X7 and 30 November 20X8, together with data representing an average of a number of similar competitor company divisions.

RRR has given Alpha division a budgeted profit requirement of $20m for the year to 30 November 20X9. The management of Alpha division has prepared the strategy shown in Table B as the framework for the achievement of the budget profit requirement for the year to 30 November 20X9.

RRR plc has, however, decided that in line with current 'beyond budgeting' philosophy, each division should follow a number of adaptive processes including the following:

(1) Setting 'stretch goals' aimed at relative improvement and avoiding dysfunctional decision-making.

(2) Evaluation and rewards at each division based on relative improvement contracts (with hindsight).

(3) Action planning that focuses on a strategy to achieve continuous value creation for the group.

As an incentive to the overall achievement of goals and the creation of 'value', a set of KPI's (key performance indicators) will be introduced in 20X9 and used on the basis of the data in Table C.

Divisional staff will be paid a bonus as a percentage of salary based on the overall weighted percentage score deduced from the analysis as per table C.

**Required:**

(a) Evaluate the extent to which the budget of Alpha division for the year ending 30 November 20X9 is achievable and consistent with the 'beyond budgeting' philosophy detailed above.

Note: Your answer should include specific examples from the data contained in the question to illustrate your discussion.

**(14 marks)**

(b) Apply the KPI performance appraisal process shown and explained in Table C, using actual data for 20X7 and 20X8 in order to show the bonus (as a % of salary) that would have been achieved by Alpha division for the year ending 30 November 20X8.

**(12 marks)**

(c) Discuss potential benefits that may be derived from the application of the KPI appraisal and bonus approach, both for Alpha division and throughout the RRR Group.

**(4 marks)**
**(Total: 30 marks)**

**Table A - Summary of financial and other operating information**

|  | Alpha division 20X8 ($m) | Alpha division 20X7 ($m) | Competitor divisions 20X8 ($m) |
|---|---|---|---|
| Sales revenue | 90.0 | 80.0 | 85.0 |
| Less costs: |  |  |  |
| Cost of sales (note 1) | 60.0 | 50.0 |  |
| Marketing | 8.5 | 8.0 |  |
| Staff training | 4.0 | 4.0 |  |
| Remedial work on orders (note 2) | 0.8 | 0.5 |  |
| Customer enquiry costs (note 3) | 1.5 | 1.4 |  |
| Customer complaint related costs (note 4) | 0.2 | 0.1 |  |
| Total costs | 75.0 | 64.0 | 69.5 |
| Net profit | 15.0 | 16.0 | 15.5 |

Number of:

| | | |
|---|---|---|
| Customer enquiries | 15,000 | 16,000 |
| Customer orders placed | 10,000 | 8,00 |
| Orders placed requiring remedial work | 300 | 440 |
| Customer complaints | 100 | 132 |

Note 1: includes materials, wages/salaries, vehicle and machine costs, etc

Note 2: following inspection by surveyors after work implemented

Note 3: initial survey and site analysis

Note 4: investigation & action on complaints.

### Table B
### Proposed strategy for Alpha division for year to 30 November 20X9

It is estimated that the budgeted profit requirement of $20m will be achieved as a consequence of the following:

- The number of orders received and processed will be 11,000 (with average price levels remaining as per 20X8 actual price levels) from an initial total of 15,500 customer enquiries

- The marketing cost allowance would be reduced to $7.2m

- The training cost allowance would be reduced to $3m

- Cost of sales ($) will rise by 10% from the 20X8 actual total to allow for the combined effect of volume and price changes

- Remedial work on orders will total $1m for material, labour and overhead costs

- Initial survey and analysis costs on customer enquiries will remain at the 20X8 average cost per enquiry

- Customer complaint related costs are expected to rise to $0.25m.

**Table C**
**Staff bonus calculation for the year ended 30 November 20X8 using Key Performance Indicators (KPI's) based on relative contract factors**

| KPI | Weighting Factor (A) | KPI Total Score % (B)* (see below) | Weighted score % (A) × (B) |
|---|---|---|---|
| Revenue 20X8 versus previous year | 0.15 | | |
| Revenue 20X8 versus competitor | 0.20 | | |
| Profit 20X8 versus previous year | 0.15 | | |
| Profit 20X8 versus competitor | 0.20 | | |
| Quality items 20X8 versus previous year: | | | |
| No. of orders requiring remedial work | 0.075 | | |
| No. of complaints investigated | 0.075 | | |
| % of enquiries converted into orders | 0.15 | | |
| | ⎯⎯⎯ | | ⎯⎯⎯ |
| Total | 1.000 | Bonus (%) = | ? |
| | ⎯⎯⎯ | | ⎯⎯⎯ |

(B)* – each KPI score value is positive (+) where the 20X8 value shows an improvement over the previous year OR negative (–) where the 20X8 value shows poorer performance than in the previous year.

Each KPI score value is the % increase (+) or decrease (–) in 20X8 as appropriate.

## Question 2 - Environmental influences

### Question

Hawk Leathers ("Hawk") is a company based in the UK that employs around 60 people in the manufacture and sale of leather jackets, jeans, one and two piece suits, and gloves. These are aimed primarily at motorcyclists, although a few items are sold as fashion garments.

Hawk sells 65% of its output to large retail chains such as Motorcycle City and Carnells, exports 25% to the USA and Japan, and sells the remaining 10% to individuals who contact the company directly. The latter group of customers specify their requirements for a made to measure suit (they are often professional racers whose suits must be approved by the authorities such as the Auto Cycle Union). The large retailers insist on low margins and are very slow to settle their debts.

There are around a dozen companies in the UK who make similar products to Hawk, plus very many other companies who compete with much lower prices and inferior quality. Hawk's typical selling price for a onepiece suit is £1,000 (approximately $1,500), whereas the low quality rivals' suits retail at around £400 (approximately $600). As Hawk say in their literature "if you hit the tarmac,there's no substitute for a second skin from Hawk". Synthetic materials are waterproof, unlike leather, but do not currently offer sufficient protection in an accident.

Sales of leathers in the UK are growing rapidly, mainly due to a resurgence of biking from more mature riders of large, powerful machines. Such riders are often wealthy and have family and financial commitments. Currently Hawk, and its rivals for quality leathers are finding it hard to keep up with demand. However, Government policy and EU emissions controls are likely to limit motorcycle performance, and some experts predict that these regulations will cause sales of large motorcycles to level off.

Whilst supplies of leather from Asia, Scandinavia and the UK are plentiful, a key problem is recruiting and training machinists to stitch and line the garments. Hawk has been able to invest in modern machinery to help production but the process is still labour intensive. Hawk has found that the expertise, reputation and skilled labour needed to succeed in the industry takes years to build up.

Although the industry is fairly traditional, there are some new developments such as a website for individual customers to browse and specify requirements, and new colours such as metallics for leathers, and a small but growing demand from non bikers who are interested in 'recreational' and 'club wear' items.

KAPLAN PUBLISHING

**Required:**

(a) Analyse the issues facing Hawk's industry using PEST analysis.

**(10 marks)**

(b) Using Porter's 5 forces, evaluate the strength of each competitive pressure facing Hawk.

**(10 marks)**
**(Total: 20 marks)**

## Question 3 - Budgetary information

### Question

You have been asked to provide budgetary information to the board of Directors for a meeting where they will decide the pricing of an important product for the next period.

The following information is available from the records:

| | **Last year**<br>$000 | | **This year**<br>$000 |
|---|---|---|---|
| Sales (100,000 @ $13) | 1,300 | Sales (106,000 @ $13) | 1,378 |
| Costs | 1,000 | Costs | 1,077.4 |
| Profit | 300 | Profit | 300.6 |

You find that between the previous and current periods there was a 4% general inflation rate and it is forecast that costs will further increase by 6% in the next period.

The firm did not increase the selling price in the current period although competitors raised their prices by 4% to allow for the increased costs.

A survey by economic consultants was commissioned and has found that the demand for the product is elastic with an estimated price elasticity of demand of 1.5. This means that volume will fall by one and a half times the rate of real price increase.

**Required:**

(a) Show the budgeted position if the firm maintains a $13 selling price for the next period (when it is expected that competitors will increase their prices by 6%)

**(10 marks)**

(b) Show the budgeted position if the firm increases its prices by 6%

**(6 marks)**

(c) Write a short report to the Board, with appropriate figures, recommending whether the firm should maintain the $13 selling price or raise it by 6%

**(4 marks)**

**(Total: 20 marks)**

## Question 4 - ZBB

### Question

NN manufactures and markets a range of electronic office equipment. The company currently has a turnover of $40 million per annum. The company has a functional structure and currently operates an incremental budgeting system. The company has a budget committee that is comprised entirely of members of the senior management team.

No other personnel are involved in the budget-setting process.

Each member of the senior management team has enjoyed an annual bonus of between 10% and 20% of their annual salary for each of the past five years. The annual bonuses are calculated by comparing the actual costs attributed to a particular function with budgeted costs for that function during the twelve month period ended 31 December in each year.

A new Finance Director, who previously held a senior management position in a 'not for profit' health organisation, has recently been appointed. Whilst employed by the health service organisation, the new Finance Director had been the manager responsible for the implementation of a zero-based budgeting system which proved highly successful.

**Required:**

(a) As the new Finance Director, prepare a memorandum to the senior management team of NN which identifies and discusses:

(i) factors to be considered when implementing a system of zero-based budgeting within NN;

**(10 marks)**

(ii) the behavioural problems that the management of NN might encounter in implementing a system of zero-based budgeting, recommending

**(6 marks)**

(b) Explain how the implementation of a zero-based budgeting system in NN may differ from the implementation of such a system in a 'not for profit' health organisation.

**(4 marks)**

**(Total: 20 marks)**

## Question 5 - ABB and benchmarking

### Question

The activity matrix below shows the budget for the sales order department of Cognet. Relevant information with regard to the operation of the sales order department is as follows:

I    A team of staff deals with existing customers in respect of problems with orders or with prospective customers enquiring about potential orders.

II   The processing of orders requires communication with the production and despatch functions of the company.

III  The nature of the business is such that there is some despatching of part-orders to customers which helps reduce stock holding costs and helps customers in their work flow management.

IV   Sales literature is sent out to existing and prospective customers by means of a monthly mail shot.

Cognet has decided to acquire additional computer software with internet links in order to improve the effectiveness of the sales order department. The cost to the company of this initiative is estimated at $230,000 pa.

It is estimated that there will be the following cost and volume changes to activities in the sales order department:

(1) Reduction in overall salaries by 10% per annum, applied to the existing salary apportionments.

(2) Reduction of 60% in the stores/supplies cost in the sales literature activity only.

(3) $20,000 of the computer software cost will be allocated to the sales literature activity. The balance will be shared by the other activities in proportion to their existing share of IT costs.

(4) Sundry costs for customer negotiation, processing of orders and implementing despatches will vary in proportion to the number of units of each activity. Sundry costs for sales literature and general administration will be unchanged.

(5) Amended volume of activity will be: total customers 2,600; customer negotiations 6,000; home orders 5,500; export orders 2,000; despatches to customers 18,750.

Recent industry average statistics for sales order department activities in businesses of similar size, customer mix and product mix are as follows:

| | |
|---|---:|
| Cost per customer per year | $300 |
| Cost per home order processed | $50 |
| Cost per export order processed | $60 |
| Cost per despatch | $8 |
| Sales literature cost per customer | $35 |
| Average number of orders per customer per year | 4.1 |
| Average number of despatches per order | 3.3 |

**Activity cost matrix – Sales order department**

| Cost pool | Total cost | Customer negoti-ations | Processing of orders | | Implementing despatches | Sales liter-ature | General admin. |
|---|---|---|---|---|---|---|---|
| | | | Home | Export | | | |
| | $000 | $000 | $000 | $000 | $000 | $000 | $000 |
| Salaries | 500 | 80 | 160 | 100 | 90 | 20 | 50 |
| Stores/ Supplies | 90 | | 16 | 6 | 8 | 60 | |
| IT | 70 | 10 | 30 | 20 | 10 | | |

| Sundry costs | 80 | 8 | 10 | 6 | 20 | 10 | 26 |
|---|---|---|---|---|---|---|---|
| Total | 740 | 98 | 216 | 132 | 128 | 90 | 76 |
| Volume of activity | 2,000 customers | 3,000 negoti-ations | 5,000 orders | 1,200 orders | 11,500 despatches | | |

**Required:**

(a) Prepare a summary of the amended activity cost matrix (per matrix above) for the sales order department after implementing the proposed changes.

**(8 marks)**

(b) Prepare an analysis (both discursive and quantitative/monetary as appropriate) which examines the implications of the IT initiative. The analysis should include the following:

A benchmarking exercise on the effectiveness of the sales order department against both its current position and the industry standards provided.

You should incorporate comment on additional information likely to improve the relevance of the exercise.

**(12 marks)**

**(Total: 20 marks)**

## Question 6 - Value chain

### Question

Woodsy is a garden furniture manufacturing company, which employs 30 people. It buys its timber in uncut form from a local timber merchant, and stores the timber in a covered area to dry out and season before use. Often this takes up to two years, and the wood yard takes up so much space that the production area is restricted.

The product range offered by the company is limited to the manufacture of garden seats and tables because the owner-manager, Bill Thompson, has expanded the business by concentrating on the sale of these items and has given little thought to alternative products.

Bill is more of a craftsman than a manager, and the manufacturing area is anything but streamlined. Employees work on individual units at their own pace, using little more than a circular saw and a mallet and wooden pegs to assemble the finished product. The quality of the finished items is generally good but relatively expensive because of the production methods employed.

Marketing has, to date, been felt to be unnecessary because the premises stand on a busy road intersection and the company's products are on permanent display to passing traffic. Also, satisfied customers have passed on their recommendations to new customers. But things have changed. New competitors have entered the marketplace and Bill has found that orders are falling off. Competitors offer a much wider range of garden furniture and Bill is aware that he may need to increase his product range, in order to compete.  As the owner-manager, Bill is always very busy and, despite working long hours, finds that there is never enough time in the day to attend to everything. His foreman is a worthy individual but, like Bill, is a craftsman and not very good at man-management. The overall effect is that the workmen are left very much to their own devices. As they are paid by the hour rather than by the piece, they have little incentive to drive themselves very hard.

### Required:

(a)  Explain what is meant by the terms 'value chain' and 'value chain analysis'?

**(5 marks)**

(b)  Use a diagram to give a brief explanation of the two different categories of activities that Porter describes.

**(5 marks)**

(c)  Analyse the activities in the value chain to identify the key problems facing Woodsy.

**(5 marks)**

(d)  Based on your analysis, prepare a set of recommendations for Bill Thompson to assist in a more efficient and effective operation of his business.

**(5 marks)**

**(Total: 20 marks)**

## Question 7 - BPR

### Question

Explain the term 'Business process re-engineering' and how its application might enable overall business performance to be improved. Briefly discuss potential problems which may be encountered in the implementation of a business re-engineering programme.

**(15 marks)**

## Question 8 - Reward schemes

### Question

You are the Senior Management Accountant of Better Gardens and Lawns (BGL), a well-established manufacturer of a range of conservatories, summerhouses and large garden ornaments. The company's revenue and after-tax profits for the year ending 31 May 20X7 are forecast to be $100 million and $20 million respectively. The company has 350 employees in total who are comprised as follows:

| Function level: | Number of employees |
|---|---|
| Directors/ Senior managers | 20 |
| Sales staff | 40 |
| Assembly staff | 250 |
| Administrative and support staff | 40 |

BGL's products are sold to specialist 'Garden Centres' by its sales staff, each of whom is home-based. The forty sales staff work from home and are supported by administrative and support staff who also undertake telephone-based selling activities.

The manufacture of conservatories and summer-houses is undertaken by 210 assembly staff, some of whom work in teams and others who work on an individual basis.

The large garden ornaments, each of which is hand-finished, are produced by 40 assembly staff who are responsible for their individual output.

The directors of BGL are considering whether to implement a reward scheme for all employees within the organisation. They have approached you for advice with regard to this matter. The production director recently stated 'if we implement a reward scheme then it is bound to be beneficial for BGL'.

**Required:**

(a) Explain the potential benefits to be gained from the implementation of a reward scheme.

(6 marks)

(b) Explain the factors that should be considered in the design of a reward scheme for BGL.

(7 marks)

(c) Explain whether you agree or not with the statement made by the production director.

(3 marks)

(d) Briefly discuss how stakeholder groups (other than management and employees) may be rewarded for 'good' performance.

(4 marks)

(Total: 20 marks)

## Question 9 - Operational and strategic issues

## Question

You have recently been appointed the finance manager for a small/medium engineering company that makes components for the shipping industry. The company experienced rapid growth in turnover and profits from 1990 – 1998, but since then its profits and turnover have slumped. It has relied on a loyal but slowly contracting client base and has never concerned itself with exploring new markets of products. The company's management spends most of its time on day to day operational issues with limited consideration given to the analysis of strategic issues.

**Required:**

Prepare a memo to the Managing Director covering the following issues:

(a) A discussion of the concentration on operational matters to the exclusion of strategic planning and management.

**(7 marks)**

(b) The changes in attitude and approach that will be required if strategic management is to be implemented.

**(6 marks)**

**(Total: 13 marks)**

## Question 10 - Management information system

### Question

During 1990 a printing company designed and installed a Management Information System that met the business needs of a commercial environment which was characterised at that time by:

- a unitary structure with one profit centre
- central direction from senior managers
- 100% internal resourcing of ancillary services
- the employment exclusively of permanent full-time employees
- customers holding large inventories who accepted long delivery times
- most of the work concerned with long print runs for established large publishing houses.

A radical change in the business environment has resulted in the following outcomes:

- the development of a divisionalised structure with four profit centres that utilise each others services
- empowerment of team leaders and devolved decision making
- considerable outsourcing of activities
- a significant proportion of the employees work part-time and/or on temporary contracts

- customers now commonly operate JIT systems requiring immediate replenishment of inventories

- the typical customer requires specialist low volume but complex high value printing.

## Required:

Recommend the significant changes in the Management Information Systems that would probably be required to meet the needs of this new situation. Explain the reasons for your recommendations.

**(20 marks)**

**Note:** your answer does not require a consideration of technical matters.

## Question 11 - NPV/IRR

### Question

SC Co is evaluating the purchase of a new machine to produce product P, which has a short product life-cycle due to rapidly changing technology. The machine is expected to cost $1 million. Production and sales of product P are forecast to be as follows:

| Year | 1 | 2 | 3 | 4 |
|---|---|---|---|---|
| **Production and sales (units/year)** | 35,000 | 53,000 | 75,000 | 36,000 |

The selling price of product P (in current price terms) will be $20 per unit, while the variable cost of the product (in current price terms) will be $12 per unit. Selling price inflation is expected to be 4% per year and variable cost inflation is expected to be 5% per year. No increase in existing fixed costs is expected since SC Co has spare capacity in both space and labour terms.

Producing and selling product P will call for increased investment in working capital. Analysis of historical levels of working capital within SC Co indicates that at the start of each year, investment in working capital for product P will need to be 7% of sales revenue for that year.

SC Co pays tax of 30% per year in the year in which the taxable profit occurs. Liability to tax is reduced by capital allowances on machinery (tax-allowable depreciation), which SC Co can claim on a straight-line basis over the four-year life of the proposed investment. The new machine is expected to have no scrap value at the end of the four-year period.

SC Co uses a nominal (money terms) after-tax cost of capital of 12% for investment appraisal purposes.

**Required:**

(a) Calculate the net present value of the proposed investment in product P.

**(12 marks)**

(b) Calculate the internal rate of return of the proposed investment in product P.

**(3 marks)**

(c) Advise on the acceptability of the proposed investment in product P and discuss the limitations of the evaluations you have carried out.

**(5 marks)**

(d) Discuss how the net present value method of investment appraisal contributes towards the objective of maximising the wealth of shareholders.

**(5 marks)**

**(Total: 25 marks)**

## Question 12 - Financial performance

### Question

UKCOM is a large US owned company that was formed in 20X0 and operates only within the UK. The company has grown rapidly via acquisition and concentrates its activities in the rapidly growing and highly competitive mobile phone market. The acquired companies have substantial infrastructure assets with only 10% of the available network capacity being utilised in the provision of services to customers. 35% of the assets are categorised as intangible and are composed of goodwill and license acquisition expenditures. The Board has announced that it will not acquire any further companies and will maintain the same level of debt for the next decade. The Board of Directors based in the US take all the strategic decisions concerned with financing and acquisition policy but leave the operating activities to the UK based Chief Executive Officer (CEO).

## Financial highlights ($millions)

| | 20X1 | 20X2 | 20X3 | 20X4 |
|---|---|---|---|---|
| Turnover | 173 | 491 | 747 | 1,591 |
| Operating costs | 76 | 301 | 376 | 813 |
| Selling costs | 87 | 169 | 293 | 566 |
| Depreciation | 40 | 153 | 273 | 791 |
| Interest | - | 203 | 336 | 689 |
| Profit /(loss) | (30) | (335) | (531) | (1,268) |
| Average Net Assets (NBV) | 463 | 2,347 | 6,318 | 12,261 |
| Average Long Term debt | - | 1,529 | 4,214 | 8,997 |
| Year End Share Price | $5 | $34 | $76 | $110 |

## Further information:

Management have provided the following estimates of projected cash flows*:

| Year | 20X5 | 20X6 | 20X7 | 20X8 | 20X9 |
|---|---|---|---|---|---|
| Cash outflows | 2,500 | 2,600 | 2,700 | 2,800 | 2,900 |
| Cash inflows | 4,100 | 4,700 | 6,100 | 7,500 | 9,000 |

These cash flows are based on the current level of competition and the current state of governmental legislation.

* Received and paid at the end of each year.

The cash outflows can be estimated with a high degree of certainty owing to the fixed nature of the costs. On the other hand, the cash inflow estimates are subject to considerable uncertainty because of the alternative outcomes that may arise. There are three possible market scenarios that are likely to impact on the inflows:

(1) Intensified competition – there is a 40% probability of this occurring and the consequences will be a reduction of 10% on the estimate of cash inflows.

(2) Government price regulation – there is a 20% probability of this occurring and it will reduce the estimated inflows by 20%.

(3) Less competition – this would result in cash inflows increasing by 5%. There is a 40% probability of this scenario developing.

The company's cost of capital is set at 4% above the average weighted cost of debt interest in the year prior to the first year of the forecast period (rounded up to the nearest percentage point).

**Required:**

(a) Provide a report on the financial performance of UKCOM from 20X1 to 20X4 from the perspective of the parent company.

**(8 marks)**

(b) The UK based CEO maintains that his/her team's financial performance has continued to improve throughout the period. Explain how this claim might be substantiated. Your answer should include a relevant indicator of each of the year 20X1-20X4 which the COE could use.

**(6 marks)**

(c) (i) Calculate the NPV of the future cash flows for the period 20X5–20X9.

**(4 marks)**

(ii) Comment on the relevance of your answer in the evaluation of future performance.

**(2 marks)**

**(Total: 20 marks)**

## Question 13 - Divisional performance 1

### Question

Tannadens Division is considering an investment in a quality improvement programme for a specific product group which has an estimated life of four years. It is estimated that the quality improvement programme will increase saleable output capacity and provide an improved level of customer demand due to the enhanced reliability of the product group.

Forecast information about the programme in order that it may be evaluated at each of best, most likely and worst scenario levels is as follows:

- There will be an initial investment of $4,000,000 on 1 January, year 1, with a programme life of four years and nil residual value. Depreciation will be calculated on a straight line basis.

- Additional costs of staff training, consultancy fees and the salary of the programme manager are estimated at a most likely level of $100,000 per annum for each year of the proposal. This may vary by ±2.5%. This is the only relevant fixed cost of the proposal.

- The most likely additional output capacity which will be sold is 1,000 standard hours in year 1 with further increases in years 2, 3 and 4 of 300, 400 and 300 standard hours respectively. These values may vary by 5%.

- The most likely contribution per standard hour of extra capacity is $1,200. This may vary by ±10%.

- The most likely cost of capital is 10%. This may vary from 8% to 12%.

Assume that all cash flows other than the initial investment take place at the end of each year. Ignore taxation.

**Required:**

(a) Present a table (including details of relevant workings) showing the net profit, residual income and return on investment for each of years 1 to 4 and also the net present value (NPV) for the **best outcome** situation of the programme.

**(10 marks)**

Using the information provided above, the net profit, residual income (RI), and return on investment (ROI) for each year of the programme have been calculated for the most likely outcome and the worst outcome as follows:

| Most likely outcome: | Year 1 | Year 2 | Year 3 | Year 4 |
|---|---|---|---|---|
| Net profit ($) | 100,000 | 460,000 | 940,000 | 1,300,000 |
| Residual income ($) | −300,000 | 160,000 | 740,000 | 1,200,000 |
| Return on investment | 2.5% | 15.3% | 47.0% | 130.0% |
| **Worst outcome:** | Year 1 | Year 2 | Year 3 | Year 4 |
| Net profit ($) | −76,500 | 231,300 | 641,700 | 949,500 |
| Residual income ($) | −556,500 | −128,700 | 401,700 | 829,500 |
| Return on investment | −1.9% | 7.7% | 32.1% | 95.0% |

In addition, the net present value (NPV) of the programme has been calculated as most likely outcome: $1,233,700 and worst outcome: $214,804.

It has been decided that the programme manager will be paid a bonus in addition to the annual salary of $40,000 (assume that this salary applies to the best, most likely and worst scenarios). The bonus will be paid on ONE of the following bases:

A   Calculated and paid each year at 1.5% of any profit in excess of $250,000 for the year.

B   Calculated and paid each year at 5% of annual salary for each $100,000 of residual income in excess of $250,000.

C   Calculated and paid at 15% of annual salary in each year in which a positive ROI(%) is reported.

D   Calculated and paid at the end of year 4 as 2.5% of the NPV of the programme.

**Required:**

(b)  Prepare a table showing the bonus to be paid in each of years 1 to 4 and in total for each of methods (A) to (D) above, where the **most likely** outcome situation applies.

**(9 marks)**

(c)  Discuss which of the bonus methods is likely to be favoured by the programme manager at Tannadens Division. You should refer to your calculations in (b) above as appropriate. You should also consider the total bonus figures for the best outcome and worst outcome situations which are as follows:

|                        | Best outcome | Worst outcome |
|------------------------|-------------:|--------------:|
|                        | $            | $             |
| Net profit basis       | 43,890       | 16,368        |
| Residual income basis  | 48,150       | 14,624        |
| ROI basis              | 24,000       | 18,000        |
| NPV basis              | 60,323       | 5,370         |

**(11 marks)**

(d)  'The achievement of the quality improvement programme will be influenced by the programme manager's:

–   level of effort

–   attitude to risk, and

–   personal expectations from the programme'.

Discuss this statement.

**(5 marks)**

**(Total: 35 marks)**

## Question 14 - Divisional performance 2

### Question

E&F use a range of metrics to assess the performance of the company.

The following information has been extracted from the accounts for the last two years

### Statement of Profit or Loss ($000)

|                                | 20X8  | 20X9  |
|--------------------------------|-------|-------|
| Profit Before Interest and Tax | 360   | 380   |
| Interest                       | (40)  | (40)  |
| Profit Before Tax              | 320   | 340   |
| Tax @25%                       | (80)  | (85)  |
| Profit After Tax               | 240   | 255   |
| Dividends                      | (120) | (155) |
| Retained Earnings              | 120   | 100   |

### Balance Sheet ($000)

|                    | 20X8  | 20X9  |
|--------------------|-------|-------|
| Non-Current Assets | 2,050 | 2,000 |
| Net Current Assets | 470   | 530   |
|                    | 2,520 | 2,530 |
| Total Equity       | 1,770 | 1,780 |
| Long Term Debt     | 750   | 750   |
|                    | 2,520 | 2,530 |

Additional information is as follows :

(i)   Capital employed at the end of 20X7 was $2,480k. This included $2,100k of Non-Current Assets.

(ii)  The pre-tax cost of debt for 20X8 and 20X9 was 5%.

(iii) E&F had operating leases of $100k in both years. The leases were not subject to amortisation.

(iv) Amortised goodwill was $120k in 20X8 and $130k on 20X9. The annual amortisation charge was $10k.

(v) The cost of equity was estimated at 8% for both years.

(vi) The economic depreciation for both years was the same as the depreciation used for accounting and tax purposes. However, the replacement cost of Non-Current Assets is 10% higher than stated in the accounts.

(vii) The target capital structure was 40% debt and 60% equity for both years.

(viii) The company uses a cost of capital of 8% to assess the viability of any new projects being considered.

**Required:**

(a) Calculate the following performance metrics for both years:

- Return on Investment
- Residual Income
- Economic Value Added.

All calculations should use a capital employed figure at the beginning of the year.

**(8 marks)**

(b) Discuss the similarities and differences between the three metrics used in part (a)

**(4 marks)**

**(Total: 12 marks)**

## Question 15 - Transfer pricing

### Question

FP sells and repairs photocopiers. The company has operated for many years with two departments, the Sales Department and the Service Department, but the departments had no autonomy. The company is now thinking of restructuring so that the two departments will become profit centres.

### The Sales Department

This department sells new photocopiers. The department sells 2,000 copiers per year. Included in the selling price is $60 for a one year guarantee. All customers pay this fee. This means that during the first year of ownership if the photocopier needs to be repaired then the repair costs are not charged to the customer. On average 500 photocopiers per year need to be repaired under the guarantee. The repair work is carried out by the Service Department who, under the proposed changes, would charge the Sales Department for doing the repairs. It is estimated that on average the repairs will take 3 hours each and that the charge by the Service Department will be $136,500 for the 500 repairs.

### The Service Department

This department has two sources of work: the work needed to satisfy the guarantees for the Sales Department and repair work for external customers. Customers are charged at full cost plus 40%. The details of the budget for the next year for the Service Department revealed standard costs of:

Parts - at cost
Labour - $15 per hour
Variable overheads - $10 per labour hour
Fixed overheads - $22 per labour hour

The calculation of these standards is based on the estimated maximum market demand and includes the expected 500 repairs for the Sales Department. The average cost of the parts needed for a repair is $54. This means that the charge to the Sales Department for the repair work, including the 40% mark-up, will be $136,500.

### Proposed Change

It has now been suggested that FP should be structured so that the two departments become profit centres and that the managers of the Departments are given autonomy. The individual salaries of the managers would be linked to the profits of their respective departments.

Budgets have been produced for each department on the assumption that the Service Department will repair 500 photocopiers for the Sales Department and that the transfer price for this work will be calculated in the same way as the price charged to external customers.

However the manager of the Sales Department has now stated that he intends to have the repairs done by another company, RS, because they have offered to carry out the work for a fixed fee of $180 per repair and this is less than the price that the Sales Department would charge.

**Required:**

(a) Calculate the individual profits of the Sales Department and the Service Department, and of FP as a whole from the guarantee scheme if:

   (i) the repairs are carried out by the Service Department and are charged at full cost plus 40%

   (ii) the repairs are carried out by the Service department and are charged at marginal cost

   (iii) the repairs are carried out by RS.

   **(8 marks)**

(b) Explain, with reasons, why a 'full cost plus' transfer pricing model may not be appropriate for FP and comment on other issues that the managers of FP should consider if they decide to allow RS to carry out the repairs.

   **(7 marks)**

(c) Briefly explain how the problems encountered above can be overcome using

   – negotiation

   – profit Maximisation Rules

   – dual Pricing

   – two part tariff

   **(5 marks)**
   **(Total: 20 marks)**

## Question 16 - International transfer pricing

### Question

A multinational computer manufacturer has a number of autonomous subsidiaries throughout the world. Two of the group's subsidiaries are in America and Europe.

The American subsidiary assembles computers using chips that it purchases from local companies. The European subsidiary manufactures exactly the same chips that are used by the American subsidiary but currently only sells them to numerous external companies throughout Europe. Details of the two subsidiaries are given on the next page.

### America

The American subsidiary buys the chips that it needs from a local supplier. It has negotiated a price of $90 per chip. The production budget shows that 300,000 chips will be needed next year.

### Europe

The chip production subsidiary in Europe has a capacity of 800,000 chips per year. Details of the budget for the forthcoming year are as follows:

Sales  600,000 chip
Selling price  $105 per chip
Variable costs  $60 per chip

The fixed costs of the subsidiary at the budgeted output of 600,000 chips are $20 million per year but they would rise to $26 million if output exceeds 625,000 chips.

**Note:** The maximum external demand is 600,000 chips per year and the subsidiary has no other uses for the current spare capacity.

### Group Directive

The Managing Director of the group has reviewed the budgets of the subsidiaries and has decided that in order to improve the profitability of the group the European subsidiary should supply chips to the American subsidiary.

She is also thinking of linking the salaries of the subsidiary managers to the performance of their subsidiaries but is unsure which performance measure to use.

The Manager of the European subsidiary has offered to supply the chips at a price of $95 each. He has offered this price because it would earn the same contribution per chip that would be earned on external sales (this is after adjusting for increased distribution costs and reduced customer servicing costs).

**Required:**

(a) Assume that the 300,000 chips are supplied by the European subsidiary at a transfer price of $95 per chip. Calculate the impact of the profits on each of the subsidiaries and the group.

**(5 marks)**

(b) Demonstrate how application of the profit maximisation rules would enable the Group to increase the profit declared in part (a). You should explain the price that should be charged by the European Division, and the likely sourcing decisions taken by the American Division.

**(6 marks)**

(c) Using the Two Part Tariff approach demonstrate how any arising conflict from the application of profit maximisation rules, can be resolved.

**(3 marks)**

(d) Briefly explain and illustrate how multi-national companies can use transfer pricing to reduce their overall tax charge and the steps that national tax authorities have taken to discourage the manipulation of transfer prices.

**(6 marks)**

**(Total: 20 marks)**

## Question 17 - Not for profit organisations

### Question

AV is a charitable organisation, the primary objective of which is to meet the accommodation needs of persons within its locality.

BW is a profit-seeking organisation which provides rented accommodation to the public. Income and Expenditure accounts for the year ended 31 May 20X4 were as follows:

| | AV $ | BW $ |
|---|---|---|
| Rents received | 2,386,852 | 2,500,000 |
| Less: | | |
| Staff and management costs | 450,000 | 620,000 |
| Major repairs and planned maintenance | 682,400 | 202,200 |
| Day-to-day repairs | 478,320 | 127,600 |
| Sundry operating costs | 305,500 | 235,000 |
| Net interest payable and other similar charges | 526,222 | 750,000 |
| | | |
| Total costs | 2,442,442 | 1,934,800 |
| Operating (deficit)/surplus | (55,590) | 565,200 |

Operating information in respect of the year ended 31 May 20X4 was as follows:

**(1) Property and rental information:**

| | AV | | BW | |
|---|---|---|---|---|
| Size of Property | Number of properties | Rent payable per week ($'s) | Number of properties | Rent payable per week ($'s) |
| 1 bedroom | 80 | 40 | 40 | 90 |
| 2 bedrooms | 160 | 45 | 80 | 101 |
| 3 bedrooms | 500 | 50 | 280 | 130 |
| 4 bedrooms | 160 | 70 | nil | 170 |

**(2) Staff salaries were payable as follows:**

| | AV | | BW | |
|---|---|---|---|---|
| Number of staff | Salary ($'s) per staff member per annum | | Number of staff | Salary ($'s) per staff member per annum |
| 2 | 35,000 | | 3 | 50,000 |
| 2 | 25,000 | | 2 | 35,000 |
| 3 | 20,000 | | 20 | 20,000 |
| 18 | 15,000 | | – | – |

(3) **Planned maintenance and major repairs undertaken:**

| Nature of work | AV | | BW | |
|---|---|---|---|---|
| | Number of properties | Cost per property $ | Number of properties | Cost per property $ |
| Miscellaneous construction work | 20 | 1,250 | – | – |
| Fitted kitchen replacements (all are the same size) | 90 | 2,610 | 10 | 5,220 |
| Heating upgrades/replacements | 15 | 1,500 | – | – |
| Replacement sets of windows and doors for 3-bedroomed properties | 100 | 4,000 | 25 | 6,000 |

All expenditure on planned maintenance and major repairs may be regarded as revenue expenditure.

(4) **Day-to-day repairs information:**

| Classification | AV | | BW |
|---|---|---|---|
| | Number of repairs undertaken | Total cost of repair | Number of repairs undertaken |
| Emergency | 960 | $134,400 | 320 |
| Urgent | 1,880 | $225,600 | 752 |
| Non-urgent | 1,020 | $118,320 | 204 |

Each repair undertaken by BW costs the same irrespective of the classification of repair.

**Required:**

(a) Critically evaluate how the management of AV could measure the 'value for money' of its service provision during the year ended 31 May 20X4.

**(7 marks)**

(b)

    (i)   Identify TWO performance measures in relation to EACH of the following dimensions of performance measurement that could be used by the management of AV when comparing its operating performance for the year ended 31 May 20X4 with that of the previous year:

         –   flexibility

         –   service quality.

**(2 marks)**

    (i)   Calculate and comment on THREE performance measures relating to 'cost and efficiency' that could be utilised by the management of AV when comparing its operating performance against that achieved by BW.

**(6 marks)**

(c)   Explain why differing objectives make it difficult for the management of AV to compare its operating and financial performance with that of BW, and comment briefly on additional information that would assist in the appraisal of the operating and financial performance of BW for the year ended 31 May 20X4.

**(5 marks)**

**(Total: 20 marks)**

## Question 18 - Financial/non-financial performance

### Question

The following information relates to Preston Financial Services, an accounting practice. The business specialises in providing accounting and taxation work for dentists and doctors. In the main the clients are wealthy, self-employed and have an average age of 52.

The business was founded by and is wholly owned by Richard Preston, a dominant and aggressive sole practitioner. He feels that promotion of new products to his clients would be likely to upset the conservative nature of his dentists and doctors and, as a result, the business has been managed with similar products year on year.

You have been provided with financial information relating to the practice in appendix 1. In appendix 2, you have been provided with non-financial information which is based on the balanced scorecard format.

## Appendix 1: Financial information

|  | Current year | Previous year |
|---|---|---|
| Turnover ($000) | 945 | 900 |
| Net profit ($000) | 187 | 180 |
| Average cash balances ($000) | 21 | 20 |
| Average trade receivables days (industry average 30 days) | 18 days | 22 days |
| Inflation rate (%) | 3 | 3 |

## Appendix 2: Balanced scorecard (extract)

|  | Current year | Previous year |
|---|---|---|
| **Internal business processes** | | |
| Error rates in jobs done | 16% | 10% |
| Average job completion time | 7 weeks | 10 weeks |
| **Customer knowledge** | | |
| Number of customers | 1,220 | 1,500 |
| Average fee levels ($) | 775 | 600 |
| Market share | 14% | 20% |
| **Learning and growth** | | |
| Percentage of revenue from non-core work | 4% | 5% |
| Industry average of the proportion of revenue from non-core work in accounting practices | 30% | 25% |
| Employee retention rate | 60% | 80% |

### Notes

(1) Error rates measure the number of jobs with mistakes made by staff as a proportion of the number of clients serviced.

(2) Core work is defined as being accountancy and taxation. Non-core work is defined primarily as pension advice and business consultancy. Non core work is traditionally high margin work.

### Required:

(a) Using the information in appendix 1 only, comment on the financial performance of the business (briefly consider growth, profitability, liquidity and credit management).

**(8 marks)**

(b) Using the data given in appendix 2 comment on the performance of the business. Include comments on internal business processes, customer knowledge and learning/ growth, separately, and provide a concluding comment on the overall performance of the business.

**(12 marks)**

(c) Explain why non financial information, such as the type shown in appendix 2, is likely to give a better indication of the likely future success of the business than the financial information given in appendix 1.

**(5 marks)**

**(Total: 25 marks)**

## Question 19 - Corporate failure

### Question

Assume that 'now' is June 20X6.

Ears'n'eyes is a well-known and respected chain of stores selling books, CDs and DVDs.

Following a number of very successful years, the company decided to embark on a programme of expansion by opening new stores in different geographical markets. This has been ongoing for the last few years. Current plans are to continue this expansion. There are now 50 superstores across the world, 40 in Ears'n'eyes' home country, 10 overseas and a number of smaller stores at stations and airports. There are plans to open five more superstores in the next year.

The company's revenue comes from the sales of books, CDs, and DVDs through its stores, with a small proportion from internet sales via a third party internet-based retailer.

The company has recently developed a card-based loyalty programme based on rewards collected through an EPoS (electronic point of sale) system in the stores. Managers have been pleased with the number of customers signing up for the card.

The board of the company are now concerned as poor profits are forecast for the current financial year to date. In addition the company is receiving increasingly negative reports from analysts and the share price has dropped more than the market as a whole.

The latest summarised accounts of are shown below:

**Balance sheets as at**

|  | 31 March 20X6 | | 31 March 20X5 | |
|---|---|---|---|---|
| Non-current assets | $ million | $ million | $ million | $ million |
| Land and buildings (net) | | 252 | | 225 |
| Other non-current assets (net) | | 233 | | 207 |
| | | 485 | | 432 |
| Current assets | | | | |
| Inventory | 733 | | 660 | |
| Receivables | 75 | | 69 | |
| Cash | 65 | | 100 | |
| | | 873 | | 829 |
| Current liabilities | | | | |
| Trade payables | 610 | | 551 | |
| Dividend | 20 | | 20 | |
| Taxation | 20 | | 27 | |
| | | (650) | | (598) |

| Non-current liabilities | | |
|---|---|---|
| 11% loan stock | (160) | (160) |
| Floating rate bank term loans | (27) | (11) |
| | 521 | 492 |
| Shareholders funds | | |
| Ordinary shares (50 cents par) | 150 | 150 |
| Reserves | 371 | 342 |
| | 521 | 492 |

**Statement of profit or loss for the years ending**

| | 31 March 20X6 | 31 March 20X5 |
|---|---|---|
| | $ million | $ million |
| Turnover | 2050 | 1966 |
| Earnings before interest and tax | 87 | 108 |
| Interest | 18 | 17 |
| Profit before tax | 69 | 91 |
| Taxation | 20 | 27 |
| Available to shareholders | 49 | 64 |
| Dividend | 20 | 20 |
| Retained earnings | 29 | 44 |

**Additional information:**

The share price of Ears'n'eyes on 1 April 20X6 was 108 cents. The price on 1 April 20X5 was 133 cents.

The modified version of Altman's Z score model for corporate failure prediction for non-manufacturing companies is given by:

$$Z = 6.56X_1 + 3.26X_2 + 6.72X_3 + 1.05X_4 \text{ where:}$$

$X_1$ = working capital / total assets.

$X_2$ = accumulated retained earnings / total assets.

$X_3$ = earnings before interest and tax / total assets.

$X_4$ = market value of equity / book value of total liabilities.

It has been found that that:

- Companies with a Z' score of below 1.81 are in danger and possibly heading towards bankruptcy.

- Companies with a score of 3 or above are financially sound.

- Companies with scores between 1.81 and 2.99 need further investigation.

**Required:**

You have been requested by the managing director of Ears'n'eyes to prepare a briefing document that includes:

(a) An assessment of the financial health of Ears'n'eyes based on the accounts above.

**(10 marks)**

(b) A brief discussion of any further investigations required to ascertain whether or not Ears'n'eyes is likely to experience financial distress and/or corporate failure.

**(3 marks)**

(c) Recommendations for any actions which the company should take to improve its future prospects, based on your findings in (a) and (b) above and any other considerations.

**(7 marks)**

(d) Suggested performance indicators to be used to monitor the future performance of the business and the impact of actions suggested in (c) above.

**(5 marks)**

**(Total: 25 marks)**

## Question 20 - Six sigma

### Question

The There 4 U Company (T4UC) commenced trading on 1 January 20X6. It was founded by Ken Matthews, who is the managing director of T4UC.

The initial aim of T4UC was to provide 'good quality' repairs and servicing to customers with domestic central heating systems and domestic 'white goods' (white goods are items such as washing machines, tumble dryers, dishwashers, refrigerators and freezers).

T4UC provides contract services on an annual basis to individual customers who require insurance covering the repair and servicing of their central heating systems and domestic white goods. T4UC charge an annual contract fee and undertake all client repair and servicing requirements without further charge.

Ken, who has a very strong background in sales and marketing, recruited engineers who came from a variety of engineering backgrounds.

Initial growth was prolific with Ken being very successful in establishing a good sized customer base within the first two years of the business. Ken believes that staff utilisation is the key driver of profitability within T4UC.

T4UC set up a website where clients could access product manuals and other diagnostic data as well as being able to book an appointment with a service engineer.

The following data is available:

|  | 20X6 | 20X7 | 20X8 |
| --- | --- | --- | --- |
| Number of contracted clients | 13,000 | 15,000 | 14,800 |
| Number of visits to contracted clients | 23,400 | 30,000 | 32,000 |
| Number of clients gained via recommendation | 200 | 100 | 5 |
| Number of telephone calls for product support received | 52,500 | 62,000 | 59,500 |
| Number of telephone calls for product support answered | 52,000 | 60,000 | 58,000 |
| Number of product support issues resolved by telephone | 46,800 | 51,000 | 46,400 |

At the end of 20X8 Ken became anxious regarding the fact that the growth in the customer base had stopped and that a number of clients had chosen not to renew their contracts with T4UC. In view of these facts, Ken undertook an extensive survey of the customers who had entered into contracts with T4UC since it commenced trading.

Ken received the following comments which were representative of all other comments that he received. 'T4UC ought to adopt a 'right first time' mentality.'

'I booked an engineer for last Monday who never arrived but two engineers turned up on Tuesday!'

'You send me a different engineer each time to inspect my central heating system. Some are here for an hour and yet others are here for the whole day and some of those even have to come back the next day.'

'Your people never seem to have the required parts with them and have to come back the next day!'

'An engineer arrived at my home to repair my washing machine but the required parts which were shipped to my home direct from the manufacturer arrived three days later! I've heard that 'Appliances R Us' is the best organisation in your service sector and that they provide a much more efficient service than T4UC and unlike T4UC is always contactable on a twenty-four hours basis during every day of the year! When I have tried to contact you on Saturdays and Sundays I have often given up out of sheer frustration!'

Ken also obtained the following data from the 'Centre for Inter-Firm Comparison'.

|  | T4UC | Appliances R Us | Industry average |
|---|---|---|---|
| Customer satisfaction rating (%) | 65 | 92 | 75 |
| Remedial visits (%) of client visits | 8 | 1 | 4 |
| Cost per client per visit ($) | 150 | 75 | 100 |
| Client to staff ratio | 250:1 | 200:1 | 225:1 |

Ken undertook further investigations which revealed remedial visits were frequently due to staff servicing appliances with which they were not completely familiar.

**Required:**

(a) Describe the Six-Sigma methodology for the improvement of an existing process.

**(8 marks)**

(b) Explain how the above-mentioned problems at T4UC could be analysed and addressed using the Six Sigma methodology. Your answer should include suggestions regarding additional activities that should be undertaken in order to improve the performance of T4UC.

**(12 marks)**

**(Total: 20 marks)**

# Test your understanding answers

## Question 1 - KPIs and beyond budgeting

### Answer

(a) Significant items in the budget prepared for the year ending 30 November 20X9 are as follows:

- Sales revenue is budgeted to increase by 10% from the 20X8 actual level. It is questionable whether this is likely to be achievable given cost changes that are planned as discussed below.

- Cost of sales has the same percentage relationship to sales (66.7%) as in 20X8. Note that the corresponding figure for 20X7 was 62.5%. The percentage differences may be influenced by the change in mix of work – repairs, refurbishment, renewals that are planned for 20X9.

- Marketing expenditure has been reduced by $1.3m which is a 15% reduction from the 20X8 actual figure. It must be asked whether demand is sufficiently buoyant to achieve the planned 10% sales increase with this marketing reduction.

- Staff training has been reduced to $1.0m which is a 25% reduction from 20X8. Will the quality of work be reduced through this reduction and lead to increased costs, remedial work and customer complaints in 20X9 and future years?

- Uptake of orders from customer enquiries is planned at 71% compared with 66.7% in 20X8 and 55% in 20X7. Is this forecast improvement realistic or achievable? This requires very careful consideration especially given the planned decrease in marketing expenditure in the 20X9 budget.

Problems relating to the likely achievement of the 20X9 budget and its inconsistency with the 'beyond budgeting' points 1 to 3 raised in the question may be viewed as follows:

- 'Stretch goals' are intended as moving away from fixed targets (as in the budget) that may lead to 'gaming' and irrational behaviour. Relative improvements should be the outcome of strategic changes agreed, whereas the budget focus seems to be a continuation of the 'status quo' linked to arbitrary value changes. The budgeting system is also seen to be meeting the planned target through arbitrary costs, particularly in discretionary areas such as training and marketing (see Table A in the question).

– Evaluation and rewards should be based on relative improvement contracts (with hindsight). Until 20X8, no such evaluation and reward processes seem to have been in place. The question indicates that a bonus system will be implemented in 20X9 using a set of Key Performance Indicators as an incentive to the overall achievement of goals and the creation of value.

– The existing budget process does not focus on a strategy to achieve continuous value creation for RRR. The budget planned for 20X9 has a target profit of $20m which is a 33% increase on the actual profit achieved in 20X8, linked to a 10% increase in sales volume. It would appear that (as discussed in answer (a) (ii) above) this expresses an arbitrary set of data that is NOT the outcome of a new charge strategy.

(b) Staff bonus calculation: Year ended 30 November 20X8 using Key Performance Indicators (KPI's) based on relative improvement contract factors

| KPI | Weighting Factor (A) | KPI Total Score % (B)* (see below) | Weighted score % (A) × (B) |
|---|---|---|---|
| Revenue 20X8 versus previous year (90/80) | 0.15 | 12.50 | 1.875 |
| Revenue 20X8 versus competitor (90/85) | 0.20 | 5.88 | 1.176 |
| Profit 20X8 versus previous year | 0.15 | –6.25 | –0.938 |
| Profit 20X8 versus competitor (15/15.5) | 0.20 | –3.23 | –0.646 |
| Quality items 20X8 versus previous year: | | | |
| No. of orders requiring remedial work (W1) | 0.075 | 31.80 | 2.385 |
| No. of complaints investigated (W2) | 0.075 | 24.20 | 1.815 |
| % of enquiries converted into orders (W3) | 0.15 | 21.30 | 3.195 |
| (improvements are positive) | ‾‾‾ | | ‾‾‾ |
| Total | 1.000 | Bonus (%) = | 8.863 |

KAPLAN PUBLISHING

(B)* – each KPI score value is positive (+) where 20X8 value is greater than the previous year or negative (–) where 20X8 value is less than previous year. Each KPI score value is the % increase (+) or decrease (–) in 20X8 as appropriate

**W1** $(1 - (300/440)) \times 100 = 31.8$

**W2** $(1 - (100/132)) \times 100 = 24.2$

**W3** 20X8 = (10,000/15,000) = 66.7%; 20X7 = (8,800/16,000) = 55%

improvement in 20X8 = (66.7 – 55)/55 = 21.3%

(c) The KPI appraisal and bonus process provides a broad range of indicators that may be monitored, both individually and collectively over time in respect of the relative improvement in Alpha Division. The analysis may also be used in order to give a spectrum of measures against which to compare the Alpha division relative improvement against that of other divisions in RRR plc.

In addition, the factors which improve or detract from the size of the bonus earned are clearly shown. This should act as an additional incentive for staff, particularly where an improvement in the weighted score for any particular element is required. For example, in profit versus that of competitor, which shows a negative score in the 20X8 comparison in (b) above.

### Question 2 - Environmental influences

## Answer

### (a) PEST analysis

#### Political factors

Approval from the ACU is vital for Hawk's racing suits. Whilst this will require regular inspections, it is important for credibility amongst customers. It may be seen as an endorsement of quality for the entire range (the socalled "halo effect").

Government/EU regulation that could damage motorcycle sales is an issue for the whole industry. If there is a clamp down it might seriously threaten sales. Hawk might consider setting up a lobby group with other manufacturers.

#### Economic factors

The recession in the UK economy (and foreign markets) is likely to result in lower disposable incomes for what is often a luxury purchase. Hawk may well find a major dip in sales as the recession continues.

The weakening £ is making exports to the USA and Europe easier, but increases the import costs of leather. There is little Hawk can do about that, so it is likely to seek new global markets such as the BRICS economies [Brazil, Russia, India, China and South Africa].

#### Social factors

There has been a growth in demand from mature riders ("born--again bikers"). Have companies such as Hawk done any research to assess the life of this trend? How effective is Hawk's marketing at reaching this potentially important market segment?

More emphasis on safety of riders who often have family; this is a boost for the industry and Hawk's customers are likely to be responsible bikers.

#### Technological factors

Relevant issues include website ordering and metallic paints but neither of these is especially important. However, Hawk and others should be aware of new ideas that could help with their processes.

KAPLAN PUBLISHING

## (b) **Porter's 5 forces**

### *Threat of new entrants*

The threat of new entrants is reasonably high from overseas rivals but is limited by existing entry barriers. These include recruiting skilled staff, close associations with racing teams, established relationships with major retailers and brand reputation.

### *Bargaining power of customers*

The power of customers depends on which customers are being considered. For those individual customers it is low because they will be loyal to the brand and are not buying in bulk.

However for the large retailers there is higher power that arises from the volumes purchased. Retail chains will exercise this power in terms of designs, lead times, prices paid and credit period taken. Hawk need to meet these needs or risk losing major customers to existing/new competition.

It will also be high for the professional racing teams. Having Hawk's products associated with top class racing teams is imperative to maintain the quality of its brand in the market place. Suits must be made to a high quality and exactly to customer specification/ compliance with the Auto Cycle Union's requirements.

### *Bargaining power of suppliers*

The power of suppliers is generally low, because leather and machinery are readily available (note: it may be that supply of leather of the required quality for professional suits is limited, in which case the power would be higher).

However, supplies of skilled labour are limited and Hawk may find it has to pay high wages.

### *Threat of substitutes*

Hawk believes that the threat from substitutes is low and states that only leather can offer the required degree of abrasion resistance. Clearly this must be kept under review as newer fabrics and technologies may change this perception.

The threat of substitute products/fabrics may be higher in the fashion lines, although this does not yet constitute a major proportion of Hawk's turnover.

## Question 3 - Budgetary information

### Answer

(a)  In the next period the firm's prices will become 6% cheaper in real terms, so demand will increase by 1.5 * 6% = 9%.

Sales will therefore be 106,000 * 1.09 = 115,540 units.

To determine the next period's costs we can use the high low method to identify fixed and variable elements from the data in the question.

| | |
|---|---|
| 100,000 units cost | $1,000,000 |
| 106,000 units cost 1,077.4 / 1.04 | $1,036,000 |

So the variable cost per unit is $36,000 / 6000 = $6.

The fixed costs in the previous period are ($1,000 – (100 * $6)) = $400,000.

We are now in a position to restate the numbers into the next period and show the budgeted position if the firm maintains the $13 selling price.

| | Next year |
|---|---|
| | $000 |
| Sales (115,540@ $13) | 1,502.02 |
| Variable costs (115,540 * $6 * 1.04 * 1.06) | 764.23 |
| Contribution | 737.79 |
| Fixed Costs ($400,000 * 1.04* 1.06) | 440.96 |
| Profit | 296.83 |

(b)  If the firm raises its prices by 6% it will be selling goods to the market in the next period at a price unchanged in real terms, so it will continue to sell 106,000 units. The budgeted position will be as follows:

|  | Next year |
| --- | ---: |
|  | $000 |
| Sales (106,000@ $13 * 1.06) | 1,460.68 |
| Variable costs (106,000@ $6 * 1.04 * 1.06 ) | 701.13 |
| | |
| Contribution | 759.55 |
| Fixed Costs ($400,000 * 1.04* 1.06) | 440.96 |
| | |
| Profit | 318.59 |

(c)                              **REPORT**

| | |
| --- | --- |
| To: | The Board of Directors |
| From: | Accountant |
| Date: | Today |
| Subject: | Product pricing next year |

You have asked me to provide you with advice on pricing our product for the next period.

A survey has been commissioned from economic consultants to determine the effects on sales volumes of varying the sales price.

Following the receipt of this survey's results I have now calculated the budgeted effects of:

(1)  Maintaining the sales price at $13; or

(2)  Raising the sales price by 6%.

Maintaining the sales price means that our product becomes relatively more attractive in the market, and sales volumes will increase. A budgeted profit of $296,832 is expected for the period.

Raising the sales price by 6% in line with our competitors means that sales volume are unchanged, but sales revenues rise due to the increased price charged per item. A budgeted profit of $318,594 is expected for the period.

I therefore recommend that the selling price should be raised by 6% in order to obtain the larger budgeted profit figure.

### Question 4 - ZBB

## Answer

(a) (i) **Memorandum**

**To:** Board of Directors

**From:** Finance Director

**Date:** 11 June 20x4

### Re: The adoption of Zero-based budgeting within NN.

During recent years the management of NN has used the traditional approach of incremental budgeting. This approach entails the use of the previous year's budget as a baseline and adds or subtracts amounts to/ from that budget in order to reflect assumptions for the forthcoming budget year. The typical justification for increased expenditures, other than those related to volume changes, has been due to the increased cost of inputs to our business. This approach can lead to inefficiencies in the previous year's budget being rolled forward into the next year's budget purely by virtue of the fact that last year's budget is the base starting point for the construction of the new budget.

The implementation of a system of zero-based budgeting will require a consideration of the following:

– The need for major input by management;
– The fact that it will prove extremely time consuming;
– The need for a very high level of data capture and processing;
– The subjective judgement inherent in its application;
– The fact that it might be perceived as a threat by staff;
– Whether its adoption may encourage a greater focus upon the short-term to the detriment of longer-term planning.

Zero-based budgeting was developed to overcome the shortcomings of the technique of incremental budgeting. The implementation of a zero-based budgeting would require each manager within NN to effectively start with a blank sheet of paper and a budget allowance of zero. The managers would be required to defend their budget levels at the beginning of each and every year. Thus, past budget decisions would as part of the process of zero-based budgeting need to be re-evaluated each year.

The comprehensive resource cost-analysis process is a strong internal planning characteristic of zero-based budgeting. It follows that resource requirements are more likely to be adjusted to changing business conditions.

The development and implementation of the zero-based budgeting model will require managers and others in the organisation to engage in several major planning, analytical and decision-making processes. Our company has already established mission and goal statements. However, we as a management team ought to give consideration as to whether it is necessary to redefine the statements that are already in existence and/or create new ones. This redefinition of mission and goal statements will be of much value if we as a management team consider that major changes have occurred in the internal and external environment of our business.

A zero-based budgeting decision unit is an operating division for which decision packages are to be developed and analysed. It can also be described as a cost or a budget centre. Thus the manager responsible for each cost centre within NN would be responsible for developing a description of each program to be operated in the next budget year. In the context of zero-based budgeting such programs are referred to as decision packages, and each decision package usually will have three or more alternative ways of achieving the decision package's objectives. Briefly, each decision package alternative must contain, as a minimum, goals and/or objectives, activities, resources and their associated costs.

Each decision package should contain a description of how it will contribute to the attainment of the mission and goals of the organisation.

Each manager within NN will be required to review each decision package and its alternatives in order to be able to assess and justify its operation and in doing so, several questions must be answered. In particular, each manager will need to answer the following questions:

– Does this decision package support and contribute to the goals of the organisation?

– What would be the result to the organisation if the decision package were to be eliminated?

– Can this decision package's objectives be accomplished more effectively and/or efficiently?

The ranking process, based upon cost/benefit analysis is used to establish a prioritised ranking of decision packages within the organisation. During the ranking process managers and their staff will analyse each of the several decision package alternatives. The analysis allows the manager to select the one alternative that has the greatest potential for achieving the objective(s) of the decision package. Ranking is a way of evaluating all decision packages in relation to each other. Since, there are any number of ways to rank decision packages managers will no doubt employ various methods of ranking. The ranking process could prove to be problematic insofar as it will require our managers to make value judgements and thus subjectivity is an inherent factor in the application of zero-based budgeting. Although difficult, the ranking of decision packages is fundamental to the process of zero-based budgeting.

Following a review and analysis of all decision packages, managers will determine the level of resources to be allocated to each decision package. Managers at different levels of responsibility in the organisation usually perform the review and analysis. Sometimes, the executive levels of management may require the managers of the decision packages to revise and resubmit their decision packages for additional review and analysis.

Our budget will be prepared following the acceptance and approval of the decision packages. Once the company's budget has been approved, managers of the decision units will put into operation all approved decision packages during the budget year.

The last major process of zero-based budgeting is monitoring and evaluation. The processes of planning, analysis, selection and budgeting of decision packages will prepare our company for operation during the next year. However, what managers plan to happen during the next year may or may not occur. Adjustments may be essential during the year in order to achieve the decision package objectives. Also, there is a need to know whether or not the organisation did accomplish what it set out to achieve and what level of achievement was obtained. The monitoring and evaluation process of zero-based budgeting requires a number of features are incorporated in the overall design and implementation of decision packages.

–   It is essential that all decision packages include measurable performance objectives and identifies the appropriate activities as means for achieving the performance objectives.

- The required resources for conducting the activities, together with the planned methods for carrying out the activities should also be included.

- The decision package should also include a mechanism to evaluate whether an objective is being achieved both during and after the conclusion of the program of activities for subsequent reporting to management.

(ii) Implementation of zero-based budgeting will require a major planning effort by our personnel. It is through the planning process that important guidelines and directions are provided for the development and ranking of the decision packages. Also, the planning process will enable managers to prepare for the uncertainty of the future. Long-range planning allows managers to consider the potential consequences of current decisions over an extended timeframe.

Zero-based budgeting addresses and supports comprehensive planning, shared decision-making, the development and application of strategies and allocation of resources as a way of achieving established goals and objectives. In addition, zero-based budgeting supports the added processes of monitoring and evaluation.

Zero-based budgeting, when properly implemented, has the potential to assist the personnel of an organisation to plan and make decisions about the most efficient and effective ways to use their available resources to achieve their defined mission, goals and objectives.

There is no doubt that the process of zero-based budgeting will consume a great deal more management time than the current system of budgeting does. This will certainly be the case in implementation of the system because managers will need to learn what is required of them. Managers may object that it is too time-consuming to introduce zero-based budgeting, however, it could be introduced on a piece-meal basis. As regards the imposition upon management time, managers may object that they simply do not have the necessary time in order to undertake an in-depth examination of every activity each year. However, if this proves to be the case then we could consider the establishment of a review cycle aimed at ensuring that each activity is reviewed on at least one occasion during every two or three years.

I propose that we hold a series of training seminars for our management to help in the transition to a system of zero-based budgeting. We must also ensure that we 'sell the benefits' that would arise from a successful implementation.

A zero-based budgeting system would assist our managers to:

- Develop and/or modify the organisation's mission and goals.

- Establish broad policies based on the mission and goals.

- Efficiently identify the most desirable programs to be placed in operation.

- Allocate the appropriate level of resources to each program.

- Monitor and evaluate each program during and at the end of its operation and report the effectiveness of each program.

Thus, as a consequence of the adoption of zero-based budgeting our managers should be able to make decisions on the basis of an improved reporting system.

It is quite possible that zero-based budgeting would help identify and eliminate any budget bias or 'budget slack' that may be present. Budgetary slack is 'a universal behavioural problem' which involves deliberately overstating cost budgets and/or understating revenue budgets to allow some leeway in actual performance. We must acknowledge that in organisations such as ours where reward structures are based on comparisons of actual with budget results, bias can help to influence the amount paid to managers under incentive schemes. However, we should emphasise that if managers are to earn incentives as a consequence of incentive schemes that are based upon a comparison of actual outcomes with budgeted outcomes, then a zero-based budget would provide a fair yardstick for comparison.

It is important to provide reassurance to our managers that we do not intend to operate a system of zero-based budgeting against the backdrop of a blame-culture. This will help to gain their most positive acceptance of the change from a long established work practice that they may perceive afforded them a degree of 'insurance'.

Signed: **Finance Director**

(b) The finance director is probably aware that the application of zero-based budgeting within NN might prove most fruitful in the management of discretionary costs where it is difficult to establish standards of efficiency and where such costs can increase rapidly due to the absence of such standards.

A large proportion of the total costs incurred by NN will comprise direct production and service costs where the existence of input: output relationships that can be measured render them more appropriate to traditional budgeting methods utilising standard costs.

Since the predominant costs incurred by a not for profit health organisation will be of a discretionary nature, one might conclude that the application of zero-based budgeting techniques is more appropriate for service organisations such as the not for profit health organisation than for a profit-seeking manufacturer of electronic office equipment.

A further difference lies in the fact that the ranking of decision packages is likely to prove less problematic within an organisation such as NN which is only involved in the manufacture and marketing of electronic office equipment. By way of contrast, there is likely to be a much greater number of decision packages of a disparate nature, competing for an allocation of available resources within a not for profit health organisation.

## Question 5 - ABB and benchmarking

### Answer

(a)  Revised activity cost matrix – sales order department

| Cost | Total cost | Customer negoti-ations | Order processing | | Imple-menting despatches | Sales liter-ature | General admin. |
|---|---|---|---|---|---|---|---|
| | | | UK | Export | | | |
| Salaries | 450 | 72 | 144 | 90 | 81 | 18 | 45 |
| Stores/ supplies | 54 | | 16 | 6 | 8 | 24 | |
| IT | 300 | 40 | 120 | 80 | 40 | 20 | |
| Sunday costs | 106 | 16 | 11 | 10 | 33 | 10 | 26 |
| | — | — | — | — | — | — | — |
| Total | 910 | 128 | 291 | 186 | 162 | 72 | 71 |
| | — | — | — | — | — | — | — |
| Volume of activity | 2,600 customers | 6,000 negoti-ations | 5,500 orders | 2,000 orders | 18,750 despatches | | |

b

| | Industry average | Cognet | |
|---|---|---|---|
| | | Pre IT | Post IT |
| Cost per customer per year ($) | 300.0 | 370.00 (W1) | 350.00 |
| Cost per UK order ($) | 50.0 | 43.20 | 52.91 |
| Cost per export order ($) | 60.0 | 110.00 | 93.00 |
| Cost per despatch ($) | 8.0 | 11.13 | 8.64 |
| Sales literature per customer ($) | 35.0 | 45.00 | 27.69 |
| Average orders per customer – units | 4.1 | 3.10 (W2) | 2.88 |
| Average despatches per order | 3.3 | 1.85 (W3) | 2.50 |

(W1) Total cost/Customers = $740,000/2,000 = $370

(W2) Orders/Customers = 5,000 + 1,200/2,000 = 3.1 units

(W3) Number of despatches/Number of orders = 11,500/5,000 + 1,200
= 1.85

The IT initiative will reduce the average cost per customer by $20, i.e. by 5.4%, bringing it closer to the industry average of 300, although still 16.7% above this figure (at 350).

Customer numbers will increase by 600, i.e. 30%.

Orders will increase overall by 1,300, i.e. 21%, with UK orders increasing by 500, i.e. 10% and export orders by 800, i.e. 67%.

Cognet's cost per UK order increases under the post IT scheme to a level above the industry average, a rise of 22.5%. Costs per export order reduce post IT by 15.5% but remain significantly above the average (by 55%).

Cost per despatch falls post IT to a level close to the industry average (reducing from 11.13 to 8.64). The sales literature per customer falls by 38% to a new level below the industry average. When linked to the 30% customer increase this could be viewed as part of the effectiveness of the new system.

## Question 6 - Value chain

### Answer

(a) **'Value chain'** describes the full range of activities which are required to bring a product or service from conception, through the intermediary of production, delivery to final consumers, and final disposal after use. It is a way of looking at a business as a chain of activities that transform inputs into outputs that customers value. Customer value derives from three basic sources:

- activities that differentiate the product
- activities that lower its cost
- activities that meet the customer's need quickly.

The value chain includes a profit margin since a markup above the cost of providing a firm's value-adding activities is normally part of the price paid by the buyer – creating value that exceeds cost so as to generate a return for the effort.

'**Value chain analysis**' views the organisation as a sequential process of value-creating activities, and attempts to understand how a business creates customer value by examining the contributions of different activities within the business to that value. Value activities are the physically and technologically distinct activities that an organisation performs. Value analysis recognises that an organisation is much more than a random collection of machinery, money and people. These resources are of no value unless they are organised into structures, routines and systems, which ensure that the products or services that are valued by the final consumer are the ones that are produced.

(b) Porter describes two different categories of activities.

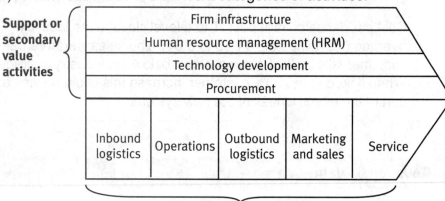

The primary activities, in the lower half of the value chain are grouped into five main areas:

- **Inbound logistics** are the activities concerned with receiving, storing and handling raw material inputs.

- **Operations** are concerned with the transformation of the raw material inputs into finished goods or services. The activities include assembly, testing, packing and equipment maintenance.

- **Outbound logistics** are concerned with the storing, distributing and delivering the finished goods to the customers.

- **Marketing** and sales are responsible for communication with the customers e.g. advertising, pricing and promotion.

- **Service** covers all of the activities that occur after the point of sale e.g. installation, repair and maintenance.

Alongside all of these primary activities are the secondary, or support, activities of procurement, technology development, human resource management and firm infrastructure. Each of these cuts across all of the primary activities, as in the case of procurement where at each stage items are acquired to aid the primary functions.

(c)  The key problem areas are as follows:

- **Inbound logistics** – Woodsy has problems with the procurement of the raw materials, labour and machinery. The company is buying its raw materials two years in advance of using it. This must be tying up capital that could be used to purchase new machinery and tools. Storing the timber entails large amounts of money being tied up in stocks, which are prone to damage, restrict the production area and is very slow moving. The workmen are being paid by the hour rather than by the piece and this means that they have little incentive to work harder.

- **Operations** are concerned with the transformation of the raw material inputs into finished goods or services. At Woodsy, employees work at their own pace on the assembly of the garden seats and tables, using very basic tools. The production methods used make the finished product relatively expensive. The linkages between the support activities are also causing some problems. Both the owner and the foreman have no man-management skills. Technological development is non-existent and the company needs re-structuring.

- **Outbound logistics** are concerned with storing, distributing and delivering the finished goods to the customers. Woodsy does not seem to have a system for distributing and delivering its goods.

- **Marketing and sales** are responsible for communication with the customers e.g. advertising, pricing and promotion. This seems to be non-existent at Woodsy as, in the past, satisfied customers have passed on their recommendations to new customers. The company relies on its position on a busy road intersection to displays its products, for customers to carry away themselves.

(d)  For Bill Thompson, the main task is to decide how individual activities might be changed to reduce costs of operation or to improve the value of the organisation's offerings. The recommendations would include the following:

- The business needs managing full-time. A new manager, or assistant manager, could encourage Bill to streamline the manufacturing process, introduce new technologies and new production and administrative systems. He or she could also negotiate new payment methods to give the workforce an incentive to work harder.

- To increase the production area the alternative strategies that the company could explore include storing the timber elsewhere, or purchasing it after it has dried out and seasoned.

- Holding high levels of finished goods might give a faster customer response time but will probably add to the total cost of operations.

- The purchase of more expensive power tools and equipment may lead to cost savings and quality improvements in the manufacturing process.

- The company needs a marketing and sales department to research the market, inform the customers about the product, persuade them to buy it and enable them to do so. The product range may need to be extended and alternative outlets for the products sought.

## Question 7 - BPR

### Answer

Business process re-engineering (BPR) involves examining business processes and making substantial changes to the way in which an organisation operates. It requires the redesign of how work is done through activities. A business process is a series of activities that are linked together in order to achieve the desired objective. For example material handling might be viewed as a business process which involves the separate activities of production scheduling, storing materials, processing purchase orders, inspecting materials and paying suppliers.

The aim of BPR is to enhance organisational performance by achieving improvements in the key business processes by focusing on simplification, improved quality, enhanced customer satisfaction and cost reduction. BPR can be applied not only to manufacturing processes but also to an extensive range of administrative activities. In the case of material handling an organisation might re-engineer the activity of processing purchase orders by collaboration with suppliers of components for their products by integration of their production planning system with that of their suppliers. This would enable purchase orders to be sent directly to their suppliers thereby obviating the need for any intermediate administrative activity. By the same token scheduled orders might be agreed with the supplier which would reduce the need to hold stocks of components. In circumstances where suppliers are working in close collaboration with an organisation, it may be possible to roll the quality back down the supply chain and agree quality control procedures with the supplier which would reduce the need to inspect incoming deliveries of components.

Thus savings in material handling costs could be achieved via reduced storage, processing and inspection costs. Such costs do not add value to the final product and thus are of no benefit to the customer. The focus of elimination of non-value added costs and cost reduction links BPR to Total quality management and Just-in-time philosophies.

BPR is sometimes regarded as a 'one-off' cost-cutting exercise even though its primary focus is not the reduction of costs. The above example shows that cost reductions can result from such activities. However it should not be regarded as 'one-off' but as a continuous activity. If the aims of BPR are not clearly understood across the entire organisation then staff may be suspicious of managerial motives for undertaking a programme of BPR. This may be partly attributable to the fact that BPR was seen as being connected with the downsizing and shedding of large numbers of jobs during the early part of the last decade.

A distinguishing feature of BPR is that it involves the radical overhaul and dramatic changes in processes entailing the abandonment of existing practices and the re-design of new ones.

However, BPR is still sometimes viewed as a way of making small improvements by 'tinkering' with existing practices.

In much the same way as a Total quality programme with its focus on continuous improvement, BPR requires the long-term commitment of management and staff within an organisation which is not always easily achievable.

## Question 8 - Reward schemes

### Answer

(a) **The potential benefits to be gained from the implementation of a reward scheme**

**Assists in achieving strategy** - rewards and incentives can make a positive contribution to strategy implementation by shaping the behaviour of individuals and groups. A well designed reward scheme will be consistent with organisational objectives and structure.

**Improves performance** - there is evidence which suggests that the existence of a reward scheme provides an incentive to achieve a good level of performance. Moreover, the existence of effective schemes also helps not only to attract but to retain employees who make positive contributions to the running of an organisation.

**Improves understanding of factors required for success** - key values can be emphasised by incorporating key performance indicators in the performance-rewards mechanisms which underpin the scheme. This helps to create an 'understood environment' in which it is clear to all employees what performance aspects precipitate organisational success.

**Continuous improvement** - an effective reward scheme will create an environment in which all employees are focused upon 'continuous improvement'.

**Long-term benefit** - schemes which incorporate equity share ownership for managers and employees alike can encourage behaviour which is in the longer-term interests of the organisation by focusing on actions aimed at increasing the market value of the organisation.

(b) **Factors that should be considered in the design of a reward scheme for BGL**

**Choice of performance target** - should performance targets should be set with regard to results or effort? It is more difficult to set targets for administrative and support staff since in many instances the results of their efforts are not easily quantifiable. For example, sales administrators will improve levels of customer satisfaction but quantifying this is extremely difficult.

**Type of reward** - should rewards should be monetary or non-monetary? Money means different things to different people. In many instances people will prefer increased job security which results from improved organisational performance and adopt a longer term-perspective. Thus the attractiveness of employee share option schemes will appeal to such individuals. Well designed schemes will correlate the prosperity of the organisation with that of the individuals it employs.

**Implicit or explicit reward** - should the reward promise should be implicit or explicit? Explicit reward promises are easy to understand but in many respects management will have their hands tied. Implicit reward promises such as the 'promise' of promotion for good performance is also problematic since not all organisations are large enough to offer a structured career progression. Thus in situations where not everyone can be promoted there needs to be a range of alternative reward systems in place to acknowledge good performance and encourage commitment from the workforce.

**The size and time span of the reward** - this can be difficult to determine especially in businesses such as BGL which are subject to seasonal variations. i.e. summerhouses will invariably be purchased prior to the summer season! Hence activity levels may vary and there remains the potential problem of assessing performance when an organisation operates with surplus capacity.

**Whether the reward should be individual or group based** - this is potentially problematic for BGL since the assembly operatives comprise some individuals who are responsible for their own output and others who work in groups. Similarly with regard to the sales force then the setting of individual performance targets is problematic since sales territories will vary in terms of geographical spread and customer concentration.

**Whether the reward scheme should involve equity participation** - such schemes invariable appeal to directors and senior managers but should arguably be open to all individuals if 'perceptions of inequity' are to be avoided.

**Tax** - tax considerations need to be taken into account when designing a reward scheme.

(c) **'If we implement a reward scheme then it is bound to be beneficial for BGL'.**

The statement of the manufacturing director is not necessarily correct. Indeed there is much evidence to support the proposition that the existence of performance-related reward schemes can encourage dysfunctional behaviour. This often manifests itself in the form of 'budgetary slack' which is incorporated into budgets in anticipation of subsequent cuts by higher levels of management or to make subsequent performance look better.

There is also a risk that employees may prioritise the achievement of their reward which could impact their risk appetite.

Employee morale (and hence productivity) may fall if employees feel that they are being penalised for circumstances outside of their control.

(d) Good performance should result in improved profitability and therefore other stakeholder groups may be rewarded for 'good performance' as follows:

- Shareholders may receive increased returns on equity in the form of increased dividends and /or capital growth

- Customers may benefit from improved quality of products and/service and possibly lower prices.

- Suppliers may benefit from increased volumes of purchases

- Government will benefit from increased amounts of taxation.

### Question 9 - Operational and strategic issues

**Answer**

**Memo**

**To: MD**

**From: Finance Manager**

**Subject:** The role and contribution of strategic planning within the company

(a) The management of our company have historically concentrated on operational issues that are characterised by:

- a predominantly internal focus
- short-term concerns
- frequently of a routine nature
- limiting decision-making and utilising the use of existing resources
- plans and control systems are precise and detailed
- control and feedback can be immediate.

In contrast, strategic planning and management tends to be:

- concerned with external considerations, the role of the organisation in the wider environment, anticipating environmental shifts and responding appropriately
- concerned with long-term issues, perhaps up to 20/30 years, and not merely with this month's or this year's budget
- the management have extensive freedom in their planning and decision-making, less variables are taken as given
- looking at broad issues, with detailed plans and activities deferred until nearer the time, when greater precision is required
- concerned with the acquisition of new/additional resources e.g. capex, and not merely the use of current resources
- concerned with achieving a vision, where the organisation is going.

(b) The successful implementation of strategic management will require the following conditions to prevail:

- Communicate and explain the need for the change in approach.

- Emphasise that strategic management is not displacing operational management, but is an additional activity to complement the current activities.

- Resources will have to be found to incorporate this new activity

- The MIS will have to be modified and developed to cope with the additional demands made upon it.

- Training and job changes may be required.

- New and broader performance indicators will need to be introduced e.g. market penetration in new business areas. This may provide the opportunity and incentive to introduce a new approach to performance assessment e.g. The Balanced Scorecard.

- The need to explore new products and new markets will inevitably create uncertainties and therefore a new approach towards risk will have to be adopted.

- The achievement of the new strategic plans will require operational decision makers to ensure that their activities are congruent with long term objectives. This new constraint upon their 'freedom of action' may cause discontent and needs to be handled with sensitivity.

## Question 10 - Management information system

### Answer

### Key answer tips

Although this question is framed from the viewpoint of a management information system, it is really an examination of your knowledge of the requirements of a divisionalised company.

### Unitary to divisionalised structure

- Each division will now require its own accounts.

- There is now a need to assess the financial and non-financial performance of every division.

- Internal and external income will have to be identified – a cross charging/transfer pricing system will have to be devised that ensures corporate goal congruence.

- Information concerning the various external markets is required to permit the performance of a manager to be distinguished from the performance of the business unit managed.

### Central direction to empowerment

- There may be a need to separate the transmission of strategic and operational information. The empowered team leaders will not require strategic information, but principally, data concerned with the day-to-day management of the business. Whereas the senior management may now be able to dispense with information concerned with operational details.

- This may also require the development of new reporting formats that are understandable to the team leaders. They may need even more detailed information at more frequent intervals than was available previously.

- New control systems will be required to meet the needs of the newly empowered team leaders and the senior management. The shift from a few too many decision makers will necessitate control systems to ensure standardisation and consistency throughout the company.

### The shift to outsourcing

- New information systems will be needed to facilitate access to the external providers of services e.g. approved contractor lists

- Authorisation/approval systems need to be developed to ensure procedures are being adhered to.

- Systems to monitor the price and quality of work undertaken by contractors will be needed.

- Financial appraisal systems may be installed to compare the 'life' costs of alternative suppliers in comparison with internal resourcing. If internal suppliers are permitted to bid for work and compete against contractors, then there is a need for the costing systems to clearly identify the activities driving costs.

## Expansion in part-time and temporary employees

- The traditional personnel systems will need to adapt to the new situation.

- The employment of part-time staff to replace full timers will result in greater numbers of employees, perhaps by a factor of two or three times. Can the existing system cope? Is there sufficient storage and memory capacity?

- Part-timers and temporary staff tend to stay in jobs for shorter periods and hence creating more activity within the personnel department. Once again can the system cope with the additional workload?

- Long serving full-time employees will have more opportunity, and perhaps more incentive to understand and use effectively a complex MIS. On the other hand, part-timers and temporary staff will have less opportunity to 'come to grips' with a complex system, therefore it may be necessary to modify simplify the systems to suit the new staffing situation.

## Customers adopting JIT systems

- The company could previously operate with low or zero stocks, and therefore a small/simple stock holding system might suffice. The advent of JIT for customers puts the onus on the company to replenish stocks immediately. This will necessitate the installation of a larger, accurate and responsive inventory system. The system adopted will need to provide information concerning minimum stock levels, re-order cycles and Economic Order Quantities. None of this information may have been required previously because stock levels were not so business critical.

## Long print runs to high value low volume

- The new customers will have more complex, individualistic and diverse requirements. The established ordering and printing systems will need to be modified to manage the heterogeneous business activity.

- High value business normally permits lower margins of error and deficiencies in quality standards. This may entail close monitoring and low tolerance control systems being installed.

**Note:** Marks would be awarded for other relevant points.

## Question 11 - NPV/IRR

### Answer

(a) **Calculation of NPV**

| Year | 0 | 1 | 2 | 3 | 4 |
|---|---|---|---|---|---|
| | $ | $ | $ | $ | $ |
| Sales revenue (working) | - | 728,000 | 1,146,390 | 1,687,500 | 842,400 |
| Variable costs (working) | - | (441,000) | (701,190) | (1,041,750) | (524,880) |
| Contribution | - | 287,000 | 445,200 | 645,750 | 317,520 |
| Tax at 30% | - | (86,100) | (133,560) | (193,725) | (95,256) |
| After-tax profit | - | 200,900 | 311,640 | 452,025 | 222,264 |
| Tax saved on CA ($250K at 30%) | - | 75,000 | 75,000 | 75,000 | 75,000 |
| After-tax cash flow | | 275,900 | 386,640 | 527,025 | 297,264 |
| Initial investment | (1,000,000) | - | - | - | - |
| Working capital (working) | (50,960) | (29,287) | (37,878) | 59,157 | 58,968 |
| Net cash flows | (1,050,960) | 246,613 | 348,762 | 586,182 | 356,232 |
| Discount at 12% | 1.000 | 0.893 | 0.797 | 0.712 | 0.636 |
| Present values | (1,050,960) | 220,225 | 277,963 | 417,362 | 226,564 |

**NPV: $91.154**

## Workings:

### Sales revenue

| Year | 1 | 2 | 3 | 4 |
|---|---|---|---|---|
| Selling price ($/unit) | 20.80 | 21.63 | 22.50 | 23.40 |
| Sales volumes (units) | 35,000 | 53,000 | 75,000 | 36,000 |
| Sales revenue ($) | 728,000 | 1,146,390 | 1,687,500 | 842,400 |

### Variable costs

| Year | 1 | 2 | 3 | 4 |
|---|---|---|---|---|
| Variable costs ($/unit) | 12.60 | 13.23 | 13.89 | 14.58 |
| Sales volume (units) | 35,000 | 53,000 | 75,000 | 36,000 |
| Variable costs ($) | 441,000 | 701,190 | 1,041,750 | 524,880 |

### Total investment in working capital

Year 0 investment = 728,000 × 0·07 = $50,960
Year 1 investment = 1,146,390 × 0·07 = $80,247
Year 2 investment = 1,687,500 × 0·07 = $118,125
Year 3 investment = 842,400 × 0·07 = $58,968

Incremental investment in working capital
Year 0 investment = 728,000 × 0·07 = $50,960
Year 1 investment = 80,247 – 50,960 = $29,287
Year 2 investment = 118,125 – 80,247 = $37,878
Year 3 recovery = 58,968 – 118,125 = $59,157
Year 4 recovery = $58,968

### (b) Calculation of internal rate of return

| Year | 0 | 1 | 2 | 3 | 4 |
|---|---|---|---|---|---|
| Net cash flows | (1,050,960) | 246,613 | 348,762 | 586,182 | 356,232 |
| Discount at 20% | 1.000 | 0.833 | 0.694 | 0.579 | 0.482 |
| Present values | (1,050,960) | 205,429 | 242,041 | 339,399 | 171,704 |

NPV at 20% = ($92,387)

NPV at 12% was calculated in part (a) and = $91,154

IRR = 12 + [(20 – 12) × 91,154/(91,154 + 92,387)] = 12 + 4 = **16%**

(c) **Acceptability of the proposed investment in Product P**

The NPV is positive and so the proposed investment can be recommended on financial grounds. The IRR is greater than the discount rate used by SC Co for investment appraisal purposes and so the proposed investment is financially acceptable. The cash flows of the proposed investment are conventional and so there is only one internal rate of return. Furthermore, only one proposed investment is being considered and so there is no conflict between the advice offered by the IRR and NPV investment appraisal methods.

**Limitations of the investment evaluations**

Both the NPV and IRR evaluations are heavily dependent on the production and sales volumes that have been forecast and so SC Co should investigate the key assumptions underlying these forecast volumes. It is difficult to forecast the length and features of a product's life cycle so there is likely to be a degree of uncertainty associated with the forecast sales volumes. Scenario analysis may be of assistance here in providing information on other possible outcomes to the proposed investment.

The inflation rates for selling price per unit and variable cost per unit have been assumed to be constant in future periods. In reality, interaction between a range of economic and other forces influencing selling price per unit and variable cost per unit will lead to unanticipated changes in both of these project variables. The assumption of constant inflation rates limits the accuracy of the investment evaluations and could be an important consideration if the investment were only marginally acceptable.

Since no increase in fixed costs is expected because SC Co has spare capacity in both space and labour terms, fixed costs are not relevant to the evaluation and have been omitted. No information has been offered on whether the spare capacity exists in future periods as well as in the current period. Since production of Product P is expected to more than double over three years, future capacity needs should be assessed before a decision is made to proceed, in order to determine whether any future incremental fixed costs may arise.

(d)  The primary financial management objective of private sector companies is often stated to be the maximisation of the wealth of its shareholders. While other corporate objectives are also important, for example due to the existence of other corporate stakeholders than shareholders, financial management theory emphasises the importance of the objective of shareholder wealth maximisation.

Shareholder wealth increases through receiving dividends and through share prices increasing over time. Changes in share prices can therefore be used to assess whether a financial management decision is of benefit to shareholders. In fact, the objective of maximising the wealth of shareholders is usually substituted by the objective of maximising the share price of a company.

The net present value (NPV) investment appraisal method advises that an investment should be accepted if it has a positive NPV. If a company accepts an investment with a positive NPV, the market value of the company, theoretically at least, increases by the amount of the NPV. A company with a market value of $10 million investing in a project with an NPV of $1 million will have a market value of $11 million once the investment is made. Shareholder wealth is therefore increased if positive NPV projects are accepted and, again theoretically, shareholder wealth will be maximised if a company invests in all projects with a positive NPV. This is sometimes referred to as the optimum investment schedule for a company.

The NPV investment appraisal method also contributes towards the objective of maximising the wealth of shareholders by using the cost of capital of a company as a discount rate when calculating the present values of future cash flows. A positive NPV represents an investment return that is greater than that required by a company's providers of finance, offering the possibility of increased dividends being paid to shareholders from future cash flows.

## Question 12 - Financial performance

### Answer

(a) The rapid growth in turnover has been exceeded by an even faster growth in costs and hence the growth in the annual loss sustained. The company's growth has been facilitated by extensive borrowing which has resulted in a substantial interest burden. In terms of key financial indicators we have:

|                  | 20X1   | 20X2    | 20X3   | 20X4    |
|------------------|--------|---------|--------|---------|
| net loss         | (17%)  | (68%)   | (71%)  | (79%)   |
| return on assets | (6.4%) | (14.2%) | (8.4%) | (10.4%) |
| debt/assets      | -      | 65%     | 67%    | 73%     |

The increasing loss and rising gearing would represent serious cause for concern in a traditional/conventional assessment of financial performance. In contrast, the increasing share price suggests that the shareholders are not taking a pessimistic view. They are aware of the financial results but still have confidence in the company – we need to investigate this apparent dichotomy in viewpoints. Share price is a measure of financial performance alongside sales and profit margins. Suggestions for the paradox:

- The company's financial performance is judged according to how it is performing in relation to a known business plan. The loss was predicted and revenues and costs are on target. The share price may begin to fall if the results do not adhere to the plan. Shareholder confidence and perceived performance is about the management delivering on their promises.

- The shareholders and the market are taking a long term view with the first four year results being regarded as only short to medium term. The long term financial performance is yet to be disclosed.

- The company owns substantial tangible assets in addition to intangibles that will provide the basis of future market growth. The licences and goodwill represent the purchase of future cash inflows and may be regarded as market entry costs.

(b) This is concerned with the issue of being able to differentiate the performance of the organisation from the performance of the manager. The CEO may argue that they do not determine either the amount of the assets under their control or the interest on the debt - acquisition and financing policy is determined by the board and therefore beyond their control. Instead of using the standard measure of profit as an indicator of performance, the CEO may be judged on Earnings Before Interest, Tax, Depreciation and Amortisation (EBITDA).

This represents the surplus after excluding two significant costs associated with the acquisition of the company's capital assets – depreciation (of tangible and intangible assets) and interest charges.

| | 20X1 | 20X2 | 20X3 | 20X4 |
|---|---|---|---|---|
| Loss (as per accounts) | (30) | (335) | (531) | (1,268) |
| Interest adjustment | - | 203 | 336 | 689 |
| Depreciation adjustment | 40 | 153 | 273 | 791 |
| **EBITDA** | 10 | 21 | 78 | 212 |

This shows a significant improvement in performance and therefore could be used to justify the assertion that the team's performance has improved.

(c) The uncertain cashflows require to be adjusted for the alternative potential scenarios.

Calculate the expected values by multiplying the cashflows by the probabilities:

| | |
|---|---|
| 0.4 x 0.9 = | 0.36 |
| 0.2 x 0.8 = | 0.16 |
| 0.4 x 1.05 = | 0.42 |
| | 0.94 |

| 20X5 | 20X6 | 20X7 |
|---|---|---|
| 4,100 x 0.94 = 3,854 | 4,700 x 0.94 = 4,418 | 6,100 x 0.94 = 5,734 |
| **20X8** | **20X9** | |
| 7,500 x 0.94 = 7,050 | 9,000 x 0.94 = 8,460 | |

| Year | 20X5 | 20X6 | 20X7 | 20X8 | 20X9 |
|---|---|---|---|---|---|
| Cash outflows | (2,500) | (2,600) | (2,700) | (2,800) | (2,900) |
| EV cash inflows | 3,854 | 4,418 | 5,734 | 7,050 | 8,460 |
| Net cash flow | 1,354 | 1,818 | 3,034 | 4,250 | 5,560 |
| 12% PV factor | 0.893 | 0.797 | 0.712 | 0.636 | 0.567 |
| PV | 1,209 | 1,449 | 2,160 | 2,703 | 3,153 |

Total NPV = $10.674 billion.

Cost of capital = 689/8,997 – 7.65% +4% = 11.65 or rounded up to 12%.

The cash inflow projections are likely to arise from the company entering into a period of stable capital costs and increasing revenues as the spare capacity in the network becomes utilised (mentioned in question brief).

The $10.7 billion is far in excess of the historic cumulative loss. The rising share price would have probably been influenced by these anticipated cashflows.

## Question 13 - Divisional performance 1

### Answer

(a) **Best outcome** situation for the quality improvement programme

|  | Year 1 | Year 2 | Year 3 | Year 4 |
|---|---|---|---|---|
| Additional output capacity (Std. hours)(W1) | 1,050 | 1,365 | 1,785 | 2,100 |
| Contribution ($)(W2) | 1,386,000 | 1,801,800 | 2,356,200 | 2,772,000 |
| Less: training, consultancy, salary costs ($)(W3) | 97,500 | 97,500 | 97,500 | 97,500 |
| Net margin ($) | 1,288,500 | 1,704,300 | 2,258,700 | 2,674,500 |
| Less: depreciation provision ($)(W4) | 1,000,000 | 1,000,000 | 1,000,000 | 1,000,000 |
| Net profit ($) | 288,500 | 704,300 | 1,258,700 | 1,674,500 |
| Less: imputed interest ($) (W5) | 320,000 | 240,000 | 160,000 | 80,000 |
| Residual income ($) | –31,500 | 464,300 | 1,098,700 | 1,594,500 |
| Return on investment (%) (W6) | 7.2% | 23.5% | 62.9% | 167.5% |

Net present value (NPV)(W7) = $2,412,901

**Workings**

(1) Using year 3 as an example: extra std. hours = (1,000 + 300 + 400) × 1.05 = 1,785.

(2) Contribution (e.g. for year 1 = 1,050 hours × ($1,200 × 1.10) = $1,386,000.

(3) Training, consultancy & salary cost for each year = $100,000 × 0.975 = $97,500.

(4) Depreciation provision per year = $4,000,000/4 = $1,000,000.

(5) Imputed interest charge (e.g. for year 2) = wdv. × cost of capital (%) = (4,000,000 −1,000,000) × 8% = $240,000.

(6) Return on investment (e.g. for year 4) = net profit/wdv. = $1,674,500/ $1,000,000 = 167.5%.

(7) NPV = (Net margin × discount factor at 8%) for each year – initial investment = $1,288,500 * 0.926 + $1,704,300 * 0.857 + $2,258,700 * 0.794 + $2,674,500 * 0.735 -$4,000,000 = $2,412,901.

(8) Bonus calculations – Most Likely Outcome situation

|  | Year 1 | Year 2 | Year 3 | Year 4 | Total |
|---|---|---|---|---|---|
|  | $ | $ | $ | $ | $ |
| Net profit basis (note 1) | 0 | 3,150 | 10,350 | 15,750 | 29,250 |
| Residual Income basis (note 2) | 0 | 0 | 9,800 | 19,000 | 28,800 |
| ROI basis (note 3) | 6,000 | 6,000 | 6,000 | 6,000 | 24,000 |
| NPV basis (note 4) | 0 | 0 | 0 | 30,843 | 30,843 |

**Working notes: (giving an example for one year in each case):**

(1) Year 2: Bonus = ($460,000 - $250,000) × 1.5% = $3,150.

(2) Year 3: Bonus = ($740,000 - $250,000) × (0.05 × $40,000)/100,000 = $9,800.

(3) Year 1: ROI is positive (2.5%). Bonus = $40,000 × 15% = $6,000.

(4) Year 4: Bonus = $1,233,700 × 2.5% = $30,843.

(c) The programme manager's choice of bonus method will be influenced by factors such as the timing of the bonus, its size, the relative ease with which it is earned and his attitude to risk.

The most likely outcome figures calculated in (b) show that the largest total bonus is $30,843 where 2.5% of NPV is used as the basis. The programme manager may, however, be influenced by the timing of the bonus payments. The NPV basis delays any payment until the end of year 4. The other bonus methods – ROI, net profit and RI – have initial bonus payments in years 1, 2 and 3 respectively. The programme manager may have a strong preference for early cash inflows from his bonus and choose the ROI basis which will yield $6,000 in year 1.

His choice may also be influenced by the relative ease with which the bonus is earned and the degree of control over the factors incorporated into its calculation. The RI and NPV bases are affected by the cost of capital percentage which is used. The programme manager may view this as unacceptable because of lack of control by him over the cost of capital percentage used in the calculation. The higher the cost of capital percentage, the lower the bonus paid even if the efficiency of implementation of the programme has been improved.

The ROI basis ensures a bonus of $6,000 per year so long as net profit is greater than $250,000. On the other hand, the net profit basis at a net profit of $250,001 per year will effectively yield a nil bonus.

The attitude to risk of the programme manager is also relevant. A risk-seeking manager may view the $60,323 bonus from the NPV basis where the best outcome occurs as very attractive. On the other hand, a risk averse manager may view as unacceptable the possibility of a bonus of only $5,370 from the NPV basis if the worst outcome occurs. He may then prefer the bonus of $18,000 from the ROI basis which is payable even if the worst outcome occurs.

(d) The outcome of the implementation of the programme will be influenced by the effort of the programme manager, his attitude to risk and the rationality of his decision-making. In the case of the programme manager, his level of effort and motivation may be affected by the bonus system or by promotion prospects. His attitude to risk may be related to the extent to which he feels he has control over the implementation of the programme and how it is monitored. It is also important that the manager is selected on the basis that he is suited to the job in hand and is capable of making relevant decisions about its effective implementation.

It may be argued that it is the individual who chooses actions and implements them. The strength of motivation to achieve the programme will be affected by the expectation that its achievement will result in some benefit and in the strength of preference of the programme manager for that benefit. His actions will be based on intrinsic and extrinsic factors. His motivation to achieve the implementation of the quality programme will be affected by both intrinsic and extrinsic factors and his preference for them. How highly motivated is he to receive a high bonus payment or possible recognition for promotion within the organisation? (extrinsic factors). How highly motivated is he by factors such as the 'feeling of achievement' or the driving force of 'professional pride'? (intrinsic factors).

## Question 14 - Divisional performance 2

### Answer

(a) **Return on Investment (ROI)**

ROI (20X8) = $360k ÷ $2,480k = 14.5%
ROI (20X9) = $380k ÷ $2,520k = 15.1%

**Residual Income (RI)**
RI (20X8) = $360k − ($2,480k × 0.08) = $161.6k
RI (20X9) = $380k − ($2,520k × 0.08) = $178.4k

**Economic value added (EVA)**
EVA (20X8) = $280k − ($2,910k × 0.063) = $96.7k (see workings)
EVA (20X9) = $340k − ($2,955k × 0.063) = $153.8k (see workings)
**W1 NOPAT ($000)**

|                                       | 20X8 | 20X9 |
|---------------------------------------|------|------|
| PAT                                   | 240  | 300  |
| Interest paid net of tax ($40k × 0.75) | 30   | 30   |
| Goodwill                              | 10   | 10   |
| NOPAT                                 | 280  | 340  |

### W2 Economic value of capital employed

|  | 20X8 | 20X9 |
|---|---|---|
| Capital employed at beginning of period | 2,480 | 2,520 |
| Leases | 100 | 100 |
| Goodwill | 120 | 130 |
| Historical cost adjustment | 210 | 205 |
| Adjusted capital employed | 2,910 | 2,955 |

### W3 WACC

WACC = $(0.4 \times 0.05 \times 0.75) + (0.6 \times 0.08) = 6.3\%$

(b) **Similarities and Differences**

All three measures consider the profitability of the organisation, and all three do take into account the level if investment that has been made in the organisation, because all three measures include a consideration of capital employed.

EVA and RI are both absolute measures where as ROI is a relative measure. If the company is pursuing a strategy of growth then ROI will allow a comparison to be made regarding the year on year on the efficiency in terms of profit generation of the company, where as RI and EVA will be able to show what the growth in profits are year on year.

EVA and RI are calculated differently though, and EVA will give a result that can be compared to other divisions in this international organisation, as it can be free from local differences in accounting standards.

## Question 15 - Transfer pricing

### Answer

(a)

**Full cost plus 40%**

|  | Sales Division ($) | Service Division ($) | FP Group ($) |
|---|---|---|---|
| Revenue | 120,000 | 136,500 | 120,000 |
| Cost | (136,500) | (97,500) | (97,500) |
| Profit/ (Loss) | (16,500) | 39,000 | 22,500 |

**Marginal cost**

|  | Sales Division ($) | Service Division ($) | FP Group ($) |
|---|---|---|---|
| Revenue | 120,000 | 64,500 | 120,000 |
| Cost | (64,500) | (97,500) | (97,500) |
| Profit/ (Loss) | 55,500 | (33,000) | 22,500 |

**Outsource to RS**

|  | Sales Division ($) | Service Division ($) | FP Group ($) |
|---|---|---|---|
| Revenue | 120,000 | 0 | 120,000 |
| Cost | (90,000) | (33,000) | (123,000) |
| Profit/ (Loss) | 30,000 | (33,000) | (3,000) |

*Note: Internal recharges are removed upon consolidation*

**Workings ($)**

| | |
|---|---|
| Materials (54 × 500) | 27,000 |
| Labour (15 × 3 × 500) | 22,500 |
| Variable overheads (10 × 3 × 500) | 15,000 |
| Marginal cost | 64,500 |
| Fixed overheads (22 × 3 × 500) | 33,000 |
| Full cost | 97,500 |
| Mark up (97,500 × 40%) | 39,000 |
| Full cost + 40% | 136,500 |

(b) The 'full cost plus' transfer pricing model is not appropriate for FP, as it will result in the Sales Division making a dysfunctional decision. To maximise their divisional profits and earn a larger bonus, the manager of the sales division will outsource to RS. This will ensure that a profit is generated, however it will leave Service Division with surplus capacity, generating insufficient contribution to cover their fixed costs. This will ultimately reduce group profit.

If RS are allowed to carry out the repairs then other factors should be considered, which could include:

- quality of the service undertaken
- impact upon customer satisfaction
- prioritisation by RS of FP customer requests
- future pricing strategy
- how to utilize the surplus capacity within the Service Division.

(c) How to overcome the issues encountered:

**Negotiation**
The respective Divisional managers could enter into negotiation to settle their disputed transfer price and arrive at a compromise. However it is difficult to ever reach a solution which appeals to both parties, and time may be wasted in lengthy discussions.

In the scenario, the Sales division hold the balance of power as they have the freedom to outsource to RS, there are unlikely therefore to want to pay more than the $180 per service as quoted by RS. This is likely to be unacceptable to the Service division as it will not cover their costs.

**Two Part Tariff**
Sales Division could pay the Marginal Cost ($64,500) for the services, and pay an annual lump sum ($33,000) to cover the fixed costs of the Service Division. However this would result in Sales reporting all the profit from the Guarantee scheme.

**Two part tariff**
**($)**

|  | Sales Division | Service Division | FP Group |
|---|---|---|---|
| Revenue | 120,000 | 97,500 | 120,000 |
| Cost | (97,500) | (97,500) | (97,500) |
| | | | |
| Profit/(loss) | 22,500 | 0 | 22,500 |

An additional element of $11,250 could be paid to ensure profit is shared.

## Dual Pricing

This would allow each division to record the transaction as they saw fit, with any discrepancy picked up by head office. This would appease both managers and ensure the work was completed within the group, however it may lead to manipulation of profit and larger than deserving bonuses.

Sales would perhaps be willing to pay $500 per service, $90,000 in total, whilst Service would be seeking $136,500. The balance of $46,500 would be absorbed at head office. All of these amounts remain internal recharges, which are removed upon consolidation of group accounts.

**Dual pricing**
**($)**

|  | Sales Division | Service Division | Head Office | FP Group |
|---|---|---|---|---|
| Revenue | 120,000 | 136,500 | 0 | 120,000 |
| Cost | (90,000) | (97,500) | (46,500) | (97,500) |
| Profit/(loss) | 30,000 | 39,000 | (46,500) | 22,500 |

## Profit Maximisation Rules
In order to ensure profit is maximised, the opportunity cost rules could be applied as follows:

| | |
|---|---|
| **Perfect market** | Transfer Price = Market Price + / - any incremental costs / savings |
| **Surplus capacity** | Transfer Price = Marginal cost |
| **Production constraint** | Transfer Price = Marginal cost + Lost contribution from external sales |

KAPLAN PUBLISHING

## Question 16 - International transfer pricing

### Answer

(a)  If Europe supplied all 300,000 chips to America the impact would be:

| | $000 |
|---|---|
| **Europe** | |
| Additional contribution from America (300,000 × $45) | 13,500 |
| Lost contribution from European sales foregone (100,000 x $45) | (4,500) |
| Net increase in contribution | 9,000 |
| Additional fixed costs | (6,000) |
| Net impact upon profit | 3,000 |
| **America** | |
| Profit reduced due to additional cost incurred (300,000 x ($95 - $90)) | (1,500) |
| **Group** | |
| Profit will increase by | **1,500** |

(b)  Europe has surplus capacity of 200,000 units, which should thus be transferred at the Internal Marginal Cost of $50 per chip.  This was established as the European Manager was willing to charge $95 which would earn the same contribution as external sales.  ($95 - $45 = $50)  America would accept these units which would save $40 per chip (current cost – marginal Cost).  The final 100,000 would be transferred at marginal cost plus lost contribution ($50 + $45 = $95).  America would reject these and source locally at $90 per chip.

| | $000 |
|---|---|
| **Europe** | |
| No additional contribution from American sales (200,000 × $0) | 0 |
| Additional fixed costs | (6,000) |
| Net impact on profit | (6,000) |
| **America** | |
| Savings made by sourcing from Europe (200,000 x $40) will boost profit | (8,000) |
| **Group** | |
| Profit will increase by | **2,000** |

(c) Conflict will arise as Europe will suffer a decline in profit, whilst America gains an additional $8m. This could be resolved by America contributing $6m to cover the additional fixed costs incurred in Europe

|  | $000 |
|---|---|
| **Europe** | |
| Net impact upon profit prior to annual lump sum from America | (6,000) |
| American contribution towards fixed costs | 6,000 |
| Net impact on profit | 0 |
| **America** | |
| Net impact upon profit prior to annual lump payment | 8,000 |
| Contribution towards Europe's fixed costs | (6,000) |
| Net impact on profit | 2,000 |
| **Group** | |
| Profit will remain at | **2,000** |

This could be taken a step further, with an additional $1m paid ($7m in total) to ensure the additional group profit is equally shared between divisions.

|  | $000 |
|---|---|
| **Europe** | |
| Net impact upon profit prior to annual lump sum from America | (6,000) |
| American contribution towards fixed costs | 7,000 |
| Net impact on profit | 1,000 |
| **America** | |
| Net impact upon profit prior to annual lump payment | 8,000 |
| Contribution towards Europe's fixed costs | (7,000) |
| Net impact on profit | 1,000 |
| **Group** | |
| Profit will remain at | **2,000** |

(d) When a company has operations in different countries with separate taxation systems, they may seek to minimise their total tax liability by declaring low profits in the nations with high corporation tax rates, and high profits in nations with low corporation tax rates. Using the example above, if we assume that America pays tax at 20% whilst Europe pays 40%, then the total tax liability will be $600,000.

| $000 | Europe | America | Group |
|---|---|---|---|
| Annual profit Before tax | 1,000 | 1,000 | 2,000 |
| Tax payable at 40%/20% | 400 | (200) | (600) |
| Profit after tax | 600 | 800 | 1,400 |

However the annual lump sum payment could be adjusted to reduce the profit declared in Europe. Let's assume that it will revert to $6m. This will result in the total tax liability being reduced to $400,000.

| $000 | Europe | America | Group |
|---|---|---|---|
| Adjusted profit before tax | 0 | 2,000 | 2,000 |
| Tax payable at 40%/20% | 0 | (400) | (400) |
| Profit after tax | 0 | 1,600 | 1,600 |

National governments are wising up to this manipulation, and are seeking greater transparency to ensure that the transfer prices have not been manipulated. They insist that the transaction is treated at as if the two subsidiaries are independent. Thus the charge should be based upon market price.

## Answer

(a) The term 'value for money' is often used to refer to economy, efficiency and effectiveness. Value for money audits can be undertaken in order to assess whether value for money has in fact been achieved. In order for such an audit to be effective the objectives of AV would need to be clearly understood by those undertaking the audit.

The management of AV could attempt to measure the value for money of its operating activities in terms of economy, efficiency and effectiveness. Economy is only concerned with inputs acquired by AV, and is achieved by obtaining those inputs at the lowest acceptable cost. For example, the prices at which with the replacement fitted kitchens are purchased ($2,610) could be compared with those obtainable from other vendors in order to assess whether the lowest acceptable cost is being achieved for the required level of quality. It is important that the management of AV realise that economy is measured by reference to quality of resource inputs. They need to recognise that the purchase of poor quality materials and inferior services represents 'false economy'.

Efficiency is focussed upon output, for example, maximising output for a given level of input. For example with regard to the replacement fitted kitchens, AV could use the tendering process in an attempt to maximise the number of fitted kitchens that would be installed for a given amount of money by the contractor awarded the tender. Efficiency is measured by the ratio of output to input. The ratio is not used in an absolute sense but in a relative sense and can be improved in four ways:

– By increasing output for the same input.

– By increasing output by a greater proportion than the proportionate increase in input.

– By decreasing input for the same output; and

– By decreasing input by a greater proportion than the decrease in output.

The denominator (input) is often measured in monetary terms whilst the numerator (output) can be measured in either monetary amounts or physical units, e.g. per property.

Effectiveness is focussed upon the achievement of objectives. A not for profit organisation will invariably have a number of objectives. For example AV may have the following objectives:

- To meet housing needs.
- To provide quality well-managed homes.
- To provide the services that clients want.
- To provide an effective care and repair service.
- To support the communities within which it operates.

The management of AV should be mindful that the three performance measures require individual consideration since for example, the degree to which effectiveness is achieved gives no indication about how much was spent to achieve it.

The management of AV should also recognise that these performance measures may conflict with one another. For example, during the year AV incurred expenditure amounting to $234,900 in respect of 90 replacement fitted kitchens. If AV had purchased the same replacement kitchen units as BW, then AV would only have been able to refit 45 properties ($234,900/$5,220). Hence, the efficiency ratio of inputs to outputs would have been halved. However, the purchase of replacement kitchen units at a cost of $5,220 might have resulted in a higher level of effectiveness being achieved through factors such as the longer life of the replacement kitchen units, higher quality fixtures and fittings, and enhanced aesthetic 'appeal' to residents.

The management of AV should also give consideration to benchmarking against other similar charities whose primary objective is the provision of accommodation to the communities in which they operate. Benchmarking is probably the most significant recent development in measuring the performance of not-for-profit organisations. The management of charities such as AV would be far more willing to share information about performance with similar organisations for their mutual benefit, than the management of many profit-seeking organisations who often view the sharing of information as a commercial threat. For example, the management of AV could attempt to establish whether $2,610 is the 'norm' in respect of the cost of a replacement fitted kitchen incurred by similar non profit-seeking organisations.

(b)

(i) **Service quality**

The time required in order to undertake repairs of an emergency nature, after notification of the requirement by a tenant.

The friendliness of staff employed by AV which could be measured via the completion of questionnaires by tenants.

**Flexibility**

Mean waiting time for a house to become available to a tenant.

Mean waiting time to re-house a tenant in a different sized house after receipt of a request from a tenant.

(i) The management of AV could use the following performance measures:

**Cost and efficiency**

|  | AV | BW |
|---|---|---|
| (1) The mean cost, per week per house on management. | $9.61 | $29.81 |
| (2) The mean cost per week, per house on general repairs. | $10.22 | $6.13 |
| (3) Percentage of rent available that was collected. | 98.5% | 100% |

**Notes/ comments:**

(1) The mean cost per week per house is calculated by dividing the amount of staff and management costs by the number of properties held by each of the respective organisations. Although the same number of staff, (25), are employed by each organisation, staff costs incurred by BW are 37.7% higher than those of AV. This could result from different pay structures and management policies regarding remuneration that are likely to be employed within a profit seeking organisation such as BW.

(2) AV currently pays, on average, $140 for each emergency repair, $120 for each urgent repair and $116 for each non-urgent repair. BW has benefited from the fact that each repair undertaken by BW costs the same (i.e. $100), irrespective of the classification of repair. This might be a result of a contractual arrangement with a subcontractor that each repair undertaken is charged at the same fee in return for guaranteed business volumes for the subcontractor. If this were the case, then AV would benefit from entering into such an arrangement for the supply of repair services.

(3) BW did not have any unoccupied properties at any time during the year. This would seemingly indicate a high level of demand for its properties. AV had potential gross rents receivable during the year of $2,423,200. Unoccupied properties resulted in lost revenues of $36,348 which amounted to 1.5% of gross rents receivable. Further information is required to in order to assess whether the lost revenue is attributable to 'void periods', i.e. properties becoming vacant or perhaps due to tenants who have defaulted.

**Note:** other ratios and relevant comments would have been acceptable.

(c) The primary objective of any commercial organisation such as BW is to maximise profit. Management may take a short or long-term view regarding the ways in which they seek to achieve this objective. Management may have to choose between available options, each of which might help them to achieve this objective. However, whilst many decisions may have to be made, the objective remains clear and identifiable.

The management of BW will most probably be concerned with the provision of high quality accommodation in order to generate higher revenues and profits. The management of BW are probably trying to appeal to those who are willing to pay high rents for high quality accommodation. The fact that replacement fitted kitchens and replacement windows and doors purchased by BW cost 100% and 50% respectively, more than those purchased by AV may be an indication of this.

The objectives of not-for-profit organisations such as AV can vary significantly. AV's primary objective is 'to meet the accommodation needs of persons within its locality'. This might distil down to ensuring that any person, who is in need of accommodation, is in fact provided for.

The absence of a profit measure makes it more difficult to measure whether objectives are in fact being achieved. It is difficult to judge whether non-quantitative objectives such as meeting accommodation needs of people have been met. This does not mean however, that such an assessment should be placed on the 'too difficult pile' and left unattended. A number of suitable measures need to be devised by the management accountant in order to assess the extent to which non-quantitative objectives have been met.

The management of AV would probably be better served in comparing the performance of their organisation with a similar non-profit seeking organisation that provides accommodation to meet the needs of society.

Additional information that would assist in appraising the performance of BW during the year ended 31 May 20X4 includes the following:

– Estimates of the financial effects of changes in demand for different levels of rents charged.

– Estimates of the financial effects of changes in demand for different costs/quality levels of accommodation provision.

– A detailed analysis of net interest payable – $750,000.

– A detailed analysis of sundry operating costs – $235,000.

– Management accounts for the current and prior years.

– Budget information for 20X4, 20X5 and, if available, 20X6.

It would also be useful to have details regarding the location of the properties held by BW. It is quite conceivable that the houses held by BW are situated in a sought after area. Benchmarking with a 'best practice' organisation from within the private sector would be of much assistance in the appraisal of the operating and financial performance of BW.

## Question 18 - Financial/non-financial performance

### Answer

### (a) Financial analysis

There are various financial observations that can be made from the data:

– Turnover is up 5%. This is not very high but is at least higher than the rate of inflation indicating real growth. This is encouraging and a sign of a growing business.

– The main weakness identified in the financial results is that the net profit margin has fallen from 20% to 19.8% suggesting that cost control may be getting worse or fee levels are being competed away.

– Profit is up 3.9%. In absolute terms profits are impressive given that Richard Preston is the sole partner owning 100% of the business.

– Average cash balances are up 5% indicating improved liquidity. Positive cash balances are always welcome in a business.

– Average debtors days are down by 3 days indicating improved efficiency in chasing up outstanding debts. It is noticeable that Preston's days are lower than the industry average indicating strong working capital management. The only possible concern may be that Richard is being particularly aggressive in chasing up outstanding debts.

Overall, with a possible concern about margins and low growth, the business looks in good shape and would appear to have a healthy future.

(b) The extra non-financial information gives much greater insight into key operational issues within the business and paints a bleaker picture for the future.

**Internal business processes**

– Error rates - Error rates for jobs done are up from 10% to 16%, probably a result of reducing turnaround times to improve delivery on time percentages. This is critical as users expect the accounts to be correct.

– Errors could lead to problems for clients with the Inland Revenue, bankers, etc. What is worse, Richard could be sued if clients lose out because of such errors. One could say that errors are unlikely to be revealed to clients. Businesses rarely advertise mistakes that have been made. They should of course put mistakes right immediately.

– Average job completion time - this has fallen by 30% from an average of 10 weeks to an average of 7 weeks. On the face of it this would look like a positive change since clients will appreciate the fast turnaround of their accounts/tax work. However, the quicker turnaround time could be linked to the increase in errors and should therefore be investigated further.

**Customer knowledge**

– Client retention - The number of clients has fallen dramatically – this is alarming and indicates a high level of customer dissatisfaction. In an accountancy practice one would normally expect a high level of repeat work – for example, tax computations will need to be done every year. Clearly existing clients are not happy with the service provided.

– Average fees - It would appear that the increase in revenue is thus due to a large increase in average fees rather than extra clients – average fee is up from $600 to $775, an increase of 29%! This could explain the loss of clients in itself, however there could be other reasons.

– Market share - The result of the above two factors is a fall in market share from 20% to 14%. Looking at revenue figures one can estimate the size of the market as having grown from $4.5m to $6.75m, an increase of 50%. Compared to this, Preston's figures are particularly worrying. The firm should be doing much better and looks to being left behind by competitors.

### Learning and growth

- Non-core services - The main weakness of the firm seems to be is its lack of non-core services offered. The industry average revenue from non-core work has increased from 25% to 30% but Richard's figures have dropped from 5% to 4%. It would appear that most clients are looking for their accountants to provide a wider range of products but Richard is ignoring this trend.

- Employee retention - Employee turnover is up indicating that the staff are dissatisfied. Continuity of staff at a client is important to ensure a quality product. Conservative clients may resent revealing personal financial details to a variety of different people each year.

Staff turnover is possibly a result of extra pressure to complete jobs more quickly without the satisfaction of a job well done. Also staff may realise that the lack of range of services offered by the firm will limit their own experience and career paths.

### Conclusion

In conclusion, the financial results do not show the full picture. The firm has fundamental weaknesses that need to be addressed if it is to grow into the future. At present it is being left behind by a changing industry and changing competition. It is vital that Richard reassesses his attitude and ensures that the firm has a better fit with its business environment. In particular he should seek to develop complementary services and reduce errors on existing work.

(c)

- Financial performance indicators will generally only give a measure of the past success of a business. There is no guarantee that a good past financial performance will lead to a good future financial performance. Clients may leave and costs may escalate turning past profits to losses in what can be a very short time period.

- Non financial measures are often termed 'indicators of future performance'. Good results in these measures can lead to a good financial performance. For example if a business delivers good quality to its customers then this could lead to more custom at higher prices in the future.

- Specifically the information is appendix 2 relates to the non financial measures within the balanced scorecard.

- Internal business processes are a measure of internal efficiency. Interestingly these measures can indicate current cost efficiency as much as any future result.

- Customer knowledge measure how well the business is dealing with its external customers. A good performance here is very likely to lead to more custom in the future.

- Innovation and learning measures that way the business develops. New products would be reflected here along with indicators of staff retention. Again this is much more focused on the future than the present.

- Measuring performance by way of non-financial means is much more likely to give an indication of the future success of a business.

## Question 19 - Corporate failure

### Answer

**Briefing document for Ears'n'eyes:**

(a) The **Z scores** may be estimated as follows.

**At 1 April 20X6:**

| | | Weighted score | See working |
|---|---|---|---|
| $6.56X_1$ | 6.56*223/1358 = | 1.08 | W1, W2 |
| $3.26X_2$ | 3.26*371/1358 = | 0.89 | W1 |
| $6.72X_3$ | 6.72*87/1358 = | 0.43 | W1 |
| $1.05X_4$ | 1.05*324/837 = | 0.41 | W3, W4 |
| Total Z score | | **2.81** | |

**At 1 April 20X5:**

| | | Weighted score | See working |
|---|---|---|---|
| $6.56X_1$ | 6.56*231/1261 = | 1.20 | W1, W2 |
| $3.26X_2$ | 3.26*342/1261 = | 0.88 | W1 |
| $6.72X_3$ | 6.72*108/1261 = | 0.58 | W1 |
| $1.05X_4$ | 1.05*399/769 = | 0.54 | W3, W4 |
| Total Z score | | **3.20** | |

In addition, it is useful to consider some ratios and trends over the two years:

**Selected trends:**

|  | % growth |
|---|---|
| Turnover | 4.2 |
| Non-current assets | 12.2 |
| Inventories | 11.1 |
| Trade payables | 10.7 |
| EBIT | (19.4) |

**Selected ratios:**

|  | 1 April 20X6 | 1 April 20X5 |
|---|---|---|
| Current ratio | 1.34 | 1.38 |
| Quick ratio | 0.21 | 0.28 |
| Gearing | 36% | 35% |
| Profitability – EBIT/ total assets | 6.4% | 8.6% |
| Inventory to turnover ratio – sales/inventory | 2.80 | 2.98 |

**Workings**

**W1 Total assets**

| $m | 1 April 20X6: | 1 April 20X5: |
|---|---|---|
| Non-current assets | 485 | 432 |
| Current assets | 873 | 829 |
| Total assets | 1358 | 1261 |

**W2 Working capital**

| $m | 1 April 20X6: | 1 April 20X5: |
|---|---|---|
| Current assets | 873 | 829 |
| Current liabilities | (650) | (598) |
| Working capital | 223 | 231 |

**W3 Market value of equity**

Number of 50c shares = 150/0.5 = 300m.

Market value of equity at 1 April 20X6 is 108c * 300m shares = $324m.

Market value of equity at 1 April 20X5 is 133c * 300m shares = $399m.

### W4 Book value of total liabilities

| $m | 1 April 20X6: | 1 April 20X5: |
| --- | --- | --- |
| Current liabilities | 650 | 598 |
| Loan stock | 160 | 160 |
| Long term loan | 27 | 11 |
| Total Liabilities | 837 | 769 |

### Comments:

### The Z scores

The Z score for year to 31 March 20X6 is below 3 and therefore under the cut-off point for companies which need further investigation. The score is also worsening. Although the score for the previous year was above 3, it was still low and should have been a signal to begin monitoring the situation carefully.

### Trends and ratios

There has been a considerable investment in non-current assets over the year as now stores have been opened. However the low growth in turnover suggests that the increase in store space has not led to a proportionate increase in turnover – in fact if the number opened over the last year is similar to the plan for the coming year (an increase of 10%), a growth in turnover of 4% suggests that sales could have actually dropped in the existing stores.

There has been a decrease in profitability which is likely to be a result of an increase in expenses through opening new stores which has not been matched by an increase in sales of a similar level.

There has also been an increase in inventory levels over the last year. The inventory turnover is also low and indicates that on average inventory remains on shelves for several months, which seems a poor performance for a retailer.

There has also been a worsening in other ratios.

All the above suggests that there is cause for concern over the future of this business.

(b) The financial analysis above indicates that there is a problem. However in order to come to a complete understanding there is further work which needs to be done:

Suggested areas for further investigation:

– A more in-depth analysis of the accounting information looking at areas such as levels of debt, liquidity, payment periods, contingent liabilities, and post balance sheet events.

– An analysis of sales trends by sector (both geographical and comparing internet sales with store-based purchases), with comparisons for individual stores and types of store.

– Market information, especially an assessment of the current purchasing methods of consumers such as the use of the internet.

– Benchmarking against other companies in the same of similar markets.

– Actions and strategies of competitors.

– Any macro events which have affected the company, including inflation and foreign exchange rates.

(c) **Other issues to consider.**

At this stage, without having carried out the further investigation above it is difficult to comment on the non-financial issues. However one point which can be made at this stage is that the market for books, CDs and DVDs has changed significantly over the last few years, in part due to changes in computer technology. There has been a move towards purchasing such goods over the internet, with on-line retailers (such as Amazon) gaining a substantial share of the market. There is no reason to suppose that this will not continue. In addition, more and more customers are downloading music from the internet instead of purchasing CDs. This is likely to be followed by downloading of films from the internet replacing DVD purchases. There is also a competitive market for DVD rental for which prices are decreasing. These changes in the market are particularly significant when looking at the poor performance of Ears'n'eyes in the context of its current strategy of opening new stores.

**Recommended actions:**

The company should stop its store expansion programme. This is expensive and is not resulting in increased sales, as customers are moving away from store-based purchasing.

Consideration should also be given to closing stores which are not profitable. Further analysis may also show whether there are particular types of store which are more profitable than others and which should form the focus for the future strategy (for example airport and station stores may be more successful than the superstores due to the high level of impulse purchases).

The two actions above should release resources to focus on increasing sales from the existing stores. This will probably only be achieved by enhancing the stores to improve the experience of visiting a store. With internet shopping becoming so easy customers need another reason to purchase there. Store prices will also need to be competitive.

Ears'n'eyes should also examine the possibility of establishing its own internet shopping service alongside the stores rather than using a third party. As the company has a good reputation and an existing customer base it will be important to ensure that those customers who want to buy online purchase from Ears'n'eyes rather than a competitor.

Inventory management must be improved. The current level is much too high. Again, reducing inventory carried will release resources.

The loyalty programme which seems to be popular with customers should be continued and could be used for internet purchases as well as in store. However as well as being used to encourage repeat purchases it should also be used to provide data for analysis of sales and to improve the company's understanding of its customers, their interests and buying habits.

(d) **Possible performance indicators**

The performance indicators chosen should relate to the actions described in (c) above. They will need to include both financial and non-financial indicators and include areas related to marketing and internal processes. However it is important to focus on a small number of key areas.

Suggested indicators:

– Profitability, overall and for individual stores.

- Sales growth at least on a quarterly basis, again overall and for individual stores and internet.

- Operating income.

- Inventory levels in stores and warehouses.

- Market share and pricing, including comparisons with internet based retailers.

- Numbers of new and repeat customers.

- Customer feedback, particularly concerning their experience of visiting stores.

## Question 20 - Six sigma

### Answer

(a) The Six Sigma approach to making improvements in existing processes involves a five stage process represented by the acronym DMAIC. The five stages are as follows:

#### Define an opportunity

A problem with quality is identified and then a problem statement is prepared. This statement will describe the nature of the problem, which must be defined in specific, quantifiable terms.

A 'mission statement' is then prepared. This is a statement of what will be done in order to address the problem. Like the problem statement the mission statement should also be expressed in specific quantifiable terms using the same units of measurement that are used in the problem statement.

A project team is set up and given the required resources in order to address the problem and make an improvement. The team should comprise personnel from each of the areas within the organisation that will be affected by the Six Sigma project.

#### Measure performance

At this stage in the project, the project team should undertake a preliminary analysis in order to measure how the process is working and obtain data that can be analysed in order to identify what seems to be causing the problem. Where there are a number of factors causing the problem the project team should focus their attention on what appear to be the main causes of the quality problem.

### Analyse the opportunity

At this stage the project team will investigate the preliminary concerns about what might be causing the quality problem in greater detail. The project team will test different theories in an attempt to discover the main cause (or causes) of the problem. Each theory is then tested in order to establish whether it might be correct. Theories are rejected when it is decided that they cannot be correct.

The 'root' cause (or causes) of the problem is identified when all of the theories has been completed.

### Improve performance

The cause (or causes) of the problem will be removed as a consequence of re-designing the process that is causing the problem. Alternative methods of improving the process should be evaluated in order to determine which will be the most effective method to achieve the 'mission statement' for the project. The chosen improvement is then designed in detail and implemented after being tested to prove its effectiveness.

### Control performance

New controls are designed and implemented to prevent the re-occurrence of the problem and to make sure that the improvements to the process are sustained. Controls will include regular measurements of output from the process, and a comparison of actual performance with targeted performance. The controls should be audited periodically in order to confirm their effectiveness.

The DMAIC framework can be applied to T4UC as follows:

(1) **Define**

The apparent problems are:

i   A decrease in the number of contracted clients
ii  An increase in the number of visits per clients
iii Very few clients being gained via recommendation
iv  An increasing number of unanswered telephone calls for product support
v   A lower percentage of issues resolved by telephone
vi  A lower customer satisfaction rating than the industry average and much lower than that of Appliances R Us.

**(2) Measure**

The primary source of information available to measure the issues is the customer survey undertaken by Ken which could then be added to by other information. Other measures which could be undertaken include:

- Measuring the response times of T4UC staff to telephone calls made by clients
- Measuring the reliability of the website, e.g. Downtime, establishment of appointments
- Identification of the reasons why service engineers failed to arrive at customers' premises
- Identification of the reasons why service engineers don't have appropriate spare parts available.

Other measures which could be undertaken include:

- Measuring the rate of problem resolution via telephone
- Measuring the incidence of remedial visits to clients

**(3) Analyse**

Analysis should assist in providing an explanation for the following problems:

- Why is it difficult to contact T4UC at weekends?
- Why are remedial visits necessary?
- Why are there significant variations in the time taken by different service engineers to service central heating systems?

**(4) Improve**

Suggesting solutions to the problems identified measured and analysed

| Issues | Remedy |
|--------|--------|
| Remedial visits | Staff training |
|  | Specialisation of staff in certain products i.e. central heating systems |
| Problem resolution by telephone | Staff training to increase the knowledge levels of those staff who receive telephone calls on behalf of T4UC |
| Weekend access | Staff contactability at weekends |
| Availability of parts | Stock management of delivery vehicles |

The project team within T4UC should analyse each possible solution paying particular attention to the costs and benefits that would result from their selection.

**(5) Control**

The Final phase would involve further monitoring of the relevant problem variables, in particular the number of clients, client recommendations, weekend accessibility, staff training, stock availability, and finally overall customer satisfaction with a view to exceeding the industry average as soon as possible and aspiring to similar results achieved by Appliances R Us.

# Index

# Index

KAPLAN PUBLISHING

# Index

# Index